The Challenge of Direct Democracy
The 1992 Canadian Referendum

In October 1992 Canada's political leaders asked voters to accept the Charlottetown Accord, a comprehensive package of constitutional amendments that was the product of years of negotiation, consultation, and compromise. Canadians rejected it outright, effectively halting the country's formal constitutional evolution. But what did the No vote mean? Were voters making a considered judgment after thorough consideration of the package or were they expressing their anger with politicians, particularly Prime Minister Brian Mulroney? *The Challenge of Direct Democracy* provides the definitive account of the 1992 referendum on the Charlottetown Accord.

Based on extensive surveys conducted during and after the campaign, *The Challenge of Direct Democracy* is a comprehensive investigation of voter opinion, intention, perception, and behaviour in a referendum. The authors investigate voters' responses to arguments for and against the Accord, examine how well informed voters were, and explore a variety of explanations to account for the negative result.

RICHARD JOHNSTON is professor of political science, University of British Columbia.
ANDRÉ BLAIS is professor of political science, Université de Montréal.
ELISABETH GIDENGIL is associate professor of political science, McGill University.
NEIL NEVITTE is professor of political science, University of Toronto.

The Challenge of Direct Democracy

The 1992 Canadian Referendum

RICHARD JOHNSTON

ANDRÉ BLAIS

ELISABETH GIDENGIL

NEIL NEVITTE

McGill-Queen's University Press
Montreal & Kingston • London • Buffalo

© McGill-Queen's University Press 1996
ISBN 0-7735-1504-6 (cloth)
ISBN 0-7735-1505-4 (paper)

Legal deposit fourth quarter 1996
Bibliothèque nationale du Québec

Printed in Canada on acid-free paper

This book has been published with the help of a grant from the Humanities and Social Sciences Federation of Canada, using funds provided by the Social Sciences and Humanities Research Council of Canada.

McGill-Queen's University Press is grateful to the Canada Council for support of its publishing program.

Canadian Cataloguing in Publication Data

The challenge of direct democracy: the 1992 Canadian referendum
   Includes bibliographical references and index.
   ISBN 0-7735-1504-6 (bound).–
   ISBN 0-7735-1505-4 (pbk.)
   1. Consensus Report on the Constitution (1992) 2. Referendum – Canada.
   3. Canada – Politics and government – 1984–1993. 4. Canada –
   Constitutional law – Amendments. I. Johnston, Richard, 1948–
   JL65.1992C43 1996   971.064'7   C96-900524-5

This book was typeset by Typo Litho Composition Inc.
in 10/12 Palatino.

Contents

Acknowledgments

When we embarked on this project we expected to study a 1992 election. Instead we got the 1992 referendum. Nothing in our experience with survey research, nor in the research experience of colleagues outside our group, prepared us for an event quite like the referendum on the Charlottetown Accord. But one of our first conclusions was that, with financial means in hand, we could not let the referendum just pass us by.

Our first and greatest debt, then, is to the Social Sciences and Humanities Research Council of Canada (SSHRCC). The debt is threefold. First, SSHRCC considered our application for an election-study grant with its usual professionalism and thoroughness. Second, the council responded with speed and flexibility in assenting to our request to modify the original design. And third, the council supplemented the original grant with a modest sum from the President's Discretionary Fund, in recognition of the fact that adding the referendum waves to what was still an election study would inevitably displace our original budget.

Also helping out financially were our respective universities, British Columbia, Montreal, McGill, and Calgary (where Nevitte then taught), each of which contributed cash toward referendum fieldwork. Money also came from the University of Toronto, home of Joe Fletcher. Joe was in on this study's ground floor, and played a key role in designing the referendum questionnaire and in acting as liasion with the fieldwork staff. Unfortunately, Joe felt compelled to stand down from the project in early 1993. Quebec's Fonds pour la formation des chercheurs et aide à la recherche (FCAR) was also a critical source of support.

All these universities supplied assistance in kind, especially in data processing. But two other universities must be singled out for special mention. In 1992–3 Johnston was in residence at Queen's University, as a Skelton-Clark Fellow. The fellowship itself was a critical piece of the material puzzle, as physical proximity to Toronto, where fieldwork was conducted, and Montreal, where Blais and Gidengil reside, was an enormous benefit, especially in the study's hectic early days. Also at Queen's, the School of Policy Studies covered duplicating and secretarial services and the Department of Political Studies funded mainframe computing. Beyond material things were intellectual and social ones, as Queen's was at that point something of an epicentre of constitutional tremors. Among Queen's staff, special mention must be made of Sharon Alton, who put up with an endless chain of unreasonable requests. In 1994–5 Johnston again deserted his home university, this time for Harvard, where he was Mackenzie King Professor of Canadian Studies. This university too covered all computing and related support needs, as well as providing an extraordinarily rich intellectual setting. Special mention at Harvard belongs to Beth Hastie.

The linchpin of data collection was the Institute for Social Research, York University. The institute also contributed financially, by absorbing some of the additional costs of fieldwork. Work began under extremely difficult circumstances, as what we hoped would be a leisurely walk into an election turned into a sprint into the referendum. Sample was drawn before we even had a questionnaire. The latter was constructed in a bizarre collection of places and at ridiculous hours of day and night. Mounting and pretesting the instrument took place over too short a period and our demands on the institute at this stage were little short of unreasonable. It was a small miracle that fieldwork began in earnest only four days after the official start of the campaign outside Quebec. David Northrup, the project manager, remains the straw that stirs the drink. We are thankful that John Tibert is as obsessive as ever. Rick Myles, assistant project manager, was endlessly patient, as were Tammy Chi and John Pollard, who oversaw data collection, and Anne Oram, who ultimately built the data set.

Research assistants on this project constitute a legion. They were: Christopher Fleury, Miriam Lapp, and Claude Blanchette at the Université de Montréal; Randy Connolly and Aleem Lakhani at McGill; Mebs Kanji and Shainoor Virani at the University of Calgary; Jon Wand at the University of British Columbia; and Bob Burge, who performed above and beyond the call of duty at Queen's.

We have benefited from the advice of colleagues in many places. Especially notable were Stéphane Dion, Richard Nadeau, Pierre Martin, Alain Noël, Maurice Pinard, Keith Banting, George Perlin, Phil Woods, Ned Franks, Ron Watts, Doug Brown, John Meisel, Hugh Segal, Peter Russell, Jon Pammett, Allan Frizzell, Sharon Sutherland, Tom Flanagan, Roger Gibbins, Chris Achen, Steve Rosenstone, Roy Pierce, Byron Shafer, David Butler, Michael MacKuen, and Gary King. Parts of the book were tested in seminars at Queen's University, the University of Toronto, the University of Calgary, Carleton University, the University of Michigan, Oxford University, and annual meetings of the Canadian and American Political Science Associations.

Four colleagues merit special mention. Joe Fletcher was a coinvestigator for parts of 1992 and 1993 and was committed heart and soul to design of the fieldwork. Henry Brady has been a coinvestigator all along, but played a smaller role on the 1992 referendum stages than with the 1993 election components of the larger study, even if his 1992 role was large in absolute terms. We had to accept, though, that his comparative advantage lay with elections. Then there are Arthur "Skip" Lupia and Elisabeth Gerber, who have swiftly carved out a special place for themselves in the us-based study of referendums and initiatives. Their work on direct democracy was just surfacing as we were girding ourselves to go into the field. I doubt that we would have had the wit to focus on information and interventions had we not encountered their work at the critical moment. The two of them lent considerable time to questions of design in September 1992, and have been friends of the project ever since. Skip was as critical at the end as at the beginning, for some of this book's key arguments did not fall into place until May 1995, when he came to Harvard for a special three-day seminar on his and Mathew McCubbins's manuscript on democracy.

McGill-Queen's University Press has once again been an enthusiastic supporter of the project, in its many imagined shapes. It started life as a "quick and dirty" book, and the first draft delivered on that ambiguous promise. The Press, specifically Philip Cercone, put up with us as we decided that we needed to reflect much further on the questions and produce a book with some polish, a book made to last. After Philip came the intrepid Diane Mew and Joan McGilvray, who laboured mightily to make our prose less lugubrious.

For all their best efforts, none of these persons and organizations bears any responsibilities for errors of fact or interpretation, nor for any lapses of style or taste. All such blame lies solely with the four of us.

This brings us to the outfits that have given us the greatest support, or at least paid the highest cost: our families. The 1992 event was described as a "Referendum on the Future of Canada." Whatever one thinks of that description, the event did force us to consider the future. It seems especially fitting, then, that we dedicate this book to our own contribution to Canada's future, our children: Patrick, Rory, Ellen, Geneviève, François-Yves, Louis, Courtney, Cameron, the two Alexes, and Lee. And one more: Viviane, conceived with the project in 1992.

The Challenge of Direct Democracy

Introduction

In October 1992 Canada's political leaders asked the country's voters to accept the Charlottetown Accord, a comprehensive package of constitutional amendments, the product of years of negotiation, consultation, and compromise. Voters rejected the Accord outright; they said No, simply halting Canada's formal constitutional evolution. But what did they mean when they did so? Would they have said Yes to any proposal? And did they really know what they were doing?

The first and second questions are critical to understanding the place of the 1992 referendum[1] in Canadian history. It is natural to wonder if the referendum foreshadows the *end* of that history, if the choices which now face the country are too stark. The third question is of universal interest, for the competence of electorates is critical to the very prospects of democracy, and the democratic prospect is an especially lively question in the 1990s. On one hand, peoples formerly under authoritarian rule struggle, not always successfully, to consolidate liberal democratic institutions. On the other hand, in both emerging and apparently consolidated democracies, party and parliamentary institutions seem under siege, are criticized for failing to deliver the good life or, worse still, for frustrating popular will and bottling up the very urge to democracy. Some of this frustration has been expressed in referendums, and, in using the referendum to chasten their leaders, Canadians followed a global trend. The referendum as an idea and an institution seems on the march. But is the referendum the final expression of the democratic urge, the ultimate test of faith in the people? Or is parliamentarism still the only practicable form of mass democracy, and is the impulse to referendums just a deception, a democratic cloak for recrudescence of Bonapartism? Is it a loss, not a vindication, of faith in democracy?

To extract the full significance of the referendum on the Charlottetown Accord, the three questions must be broached simultaneously. The answer to the first two questions is partly contingent on the answer to the last one. At the extreme, if voters simply cannot grasp a complex ballot measure, their vote will mean little, or at least it will not reflect the subtlety of the original proposal. But the last question cannot be posed in the abstract. Testing voters' cognitive or civic capacity requires specification of the alternative meanings an event might take on, meanings rooted inescapably in concrete context. This book, then, locates the 1992 referendum in peculiarly Canadian politics and history. But it also examines the Canadian event in a global context. And it puts at its very centre questions about how much voters knew, and what difference their knowledge made to the result.

THE STAKES

Broadly, two interpretations of the 1992 event offer themselves:

– Voters yielded to raw sentiment, held the constitution hostage, took a bargain that was both delicate and necessary and made it a lightning rod for unthinking rage. Rage was directed at elected politicians, more particularly at one elected politician, Prime Minister Brian Mulroney. Underneath rage at politicians was repudiation of vulnerable minorities, a manifestation of the worst kind of cultural nostalgia. The 1992 referendum was a profound blunder, as indeed any referendum would be in country such as Canada. Worse, rejection of the Charlottetown Accord has so confined the country's constitutional options as to make it ungovernable, possibly threatening its very integrity.
– Voters made a considered, reflective judgment and decided that negatives in the Accord outweighed positives. Voters may even have saved the political class from itself, from an ill-considered logic which leaders could not escape unaided; voters cut the constitutional Gordian knot. Even if politicians lost control of the event, mass and elite tacitly conspired to give Canada a necessary purgative.

The truth may lie between these extremes, or may embrace parts of both images.

To whom then was the result a No? Clues could be found in the content of the package. At the Accord's heart were key concessions to the government of Quebec. Voters outside that province may have had these concessions especially in mind, or may have indulged a visceral rejection of French Canada more generally. The package also accommodated other groups, but may have succeeded only in making those groups – and all group recognitions, all minority guarantees – the target. One price of getting players outside Quebec on board was to make potentially far-reaching changes to the upper chamber in Canada's parliament, the Senate – changes which threatened to reduce Quebec's power at the centre. This may have been too much for Quebeckers, on one hand, but too little for advocates of change, on the other. The suspicion nags, however, that voters knew little and cared less about these rather abstruse issues in bicameralism; perhaps demands for Senate reform lacked a popular base.

Other possibilities lie outside the package. For example, elites made arguments about consequences, about the general necessity of compromise and merits of this particular one, but were such arguments simply rejected? If so, were they rejected simply because the political elite made them? Canadians, as we have just said, were not alone in seeming to slap their leaders down. Is there in fact a crisis of leadership, for which the 1992 No result was just a symptom? Does the event shed light on the sources of elite/mass cleavage? Or was the problem with one part of the elite, Prime Minister Brian Mulroney and his Conservative government? If the Mulroney government was targeted, one possible reason may have been the economy. The Charlottetown Accord was presented in a period of deep economic recession. It might have become a lightning rod, a vehicle for economically motivated protest against government policy.

If the No vote was a rejection of the whole political elite in general, not just of Brian Mulroney or the Conservative party, what were they all doing wrong? One possibility lies in the logic of forming governments: all governments are coalitions of minorities. This is transparent when votes are counted by a proportional representation (PR) formula. Only rarely can a single party form a majority coalition; thus almost all governments are usually complicated, somewhat incoherent coalitions. But coalition-building is also essential in first-past-the-post systems. Here, coalitions are usually built in the electorate at large. Voters may resist the logic of coalition-building, however, and see it as betrayal, not fulfilment, of mass democracy's central principle – majority rule. Such a perception may be especially powerful if many voters assume that some "natural" majority exists, and that such a majority can be blocked from rule only by devious means. In this perception lies much of the appeal of referendums, which are seen as a means to cut through coalition-of-minorities obfuscation.

And the same perception may have been one basis for rejection of the Charlottetown Accord. The Accord and the elite proposing it may have both been rejected as a package. If so, this double-barrelled rejection may also contain the seeds of the 1993 election, the most cataclysmic in Canadian history.

Along the same lines, the Canadian experience may shed special light on the rough ride European unification continues to encounter: on the mixed reception of the Maastricht Treaty, the continued repudiation of membership in some places, and "Euro-scepticism" in others. Running through these events seems to be an elite/mass cleavage rather like the Canadian one; certainly, in many European referendums, carefully wrought elite initiatives have been rebuffed. The European experience also includes dramatically successful initiatives, but the most successful of all are frightening: the earliest uses of the plebsicite, in France of the 1790s, led to authoritarian rule; Bonapartist consolidation of power by means of plebiscites is part of Europeans' anti-referendum lexicon. Could Bonapartism be just the flip side of mass resistance to hard-won elite compromises? Does a No vote such as Canada's in 1992 indicate a robust civil society at the grass roots, or is it just a training ground for assaults on constitutionalism?

This ugly side of the referendum experience takes us straight to questions about electoral competence. How well informed are voters? What difference does information make? The key contribution on the empirical record is Converse's 1964 article, "The Nature of Belief Systems in Mass Publics," which documents a widespread lack of political information and questions the reality behind the appearance of ostensible public opinion. Converse's basic arguments have proven highly resistant to frontal attack. But recently challenges have been mounted *in*directly: voters' ignorance of substantive policy is conceded, but ignorance, it is claimed, does not negate the possibility of consistent electoral choice. One argument posits a *low-information rationality*,[2] which says that ignorance is no barrier to consistent policy choice by individuals. A second argument might be styled *aggregationist*: even if many individuals get their own choices wrong, such errors cancel themselves out and the pivotal votes are cast by relatively well-informed individuals. If either type of argument really works empirically, the case for frequent consultation is strengthened and Bonapartist fears seem less compelling.

Canada's 1992 referendum was not only compelling, it was well documented. Most importantly for this book, the authors engineered early release of sample in place for a prospective election study. This represents, as far as we know, the most comprehensive investigation of opinion, intention, perceptions, and actual behaviour in the 1992 Canadian event, or indeed, for any referendum or referendum-like vote anywhere in the world. It is the only survey which allows scholars – ourselves and others – to reconstruct the dynamics of voters' referendum preferences. Moreover, 1992 data are linked to data collected during the 1993 election.[3]

The first three chapters of the book are in the nature of background. Chapter 1 considers direct democracy as a general phenomenon. Emphasis lies on how voters assess complex documents when information is costly, the central problem in the elite-mass nexus. From consideration of this problem emerges a basic estimation model for the rest of the book.

Chapter 2 describes the background and nature of the Charlottetown Accord and supplies narrative of the campaign. From narrative emerge specific questions about interpretation of the event.

Chapter 3 considers the Charlottetown Accord as a bargain – whether it made sense as one and how voters responded to it as a bundle of "carrots" – by examining support and opposition for key elements in the Accord, in Canada as a whole and by region, with special attention to the contrast between Quebec and the rest of Canada.

The next four chapters focus on Canada outside Quebec. Chapter 4 investigates voters' response to general arguments for and against the Accord. If the substance of the Accord dangled "carrots" before voters, general arguments were "sticks" with which to beat those same voters. The question here is whether voters can be brought to reason beyond the specifics of an agreement, from ends as well as means. Can voters deliberate?

Chapter 5 goes to the elite-mass nexus and examines one low-information-rationality claim – that voters can locate a ballot measure by triangulation, by asking who is for it and who is against it. But how aware in fact were voters of elite interventions and how did that awareness evolve? Could voters organize perceptions of intervenors? In particular, did voters see the pro-Accord coalition as inclusively as the coalition's members saw themselves? The lead role in this chapter is played by the most important actor the pro-Accord team failed to capture, Pierre Trudeau.

Chapter 6 looks at polls and expectations. Some voters may have made their own decisions contingent on choices by other voters. For example, if most voters were unwilling to accept the Accord, why should any single voter embrace it? The event was closely polled and these polls may have fed voters' expectations. Did expectations, in turn, shape reality, as another low-information-rationality argument proposes?

Chapter 7 looks at group membership and group sentiment. It considers both raw feeling and refined conceptions of Canada's group basis, and relates sentiment in turn to the country's demographic and class structure. Support and opposition cut through traditional partisan divisions, and, instead, followed a class divide, especially along educational lines. This naturally begs a question first raised in chapter 1: were Canadians perched higher on the class ladder more likely to vote Yes because they knew better what the country needed?

In the remaining chapters, Quebec re-enters the field. Chapter 8 looks at Quebec alone, by replicating those elements of the rest-of-Canada estimation that make sense for Quebec, modifying factors and estimations as required. The most important point is that the threshold for success in Quebec was very high, almost impossible to step over.

Chapter 9 addresses head-on the central questions about direct democracy, and discusses voters' cognitive capacity and style. How much did voters know about the Accord? What difference did knowledge make to the overall chances of a Yes vote? Did knowledge affect the very structure of reasoning about the document? Do the same conclusions apply for Quebec as for the rest of Canada? Here all low-information-rationality and aggegationist arguments get an extended hearing.

Chapter 10 combines evidence from low and high – from mass response in 1992, from the "high politics" of 1992, from Canada's earlier experience with plebiscites, and from the experience of other countries – to address an obvious question: was it all a terrible mistake?

Chapter 11 extracts conclusions from the previous ten chapters, partly to interpret the referendum as an event in Canadian history, but mainly to consider the general challenge of direct democracy.

1 The Challenge of Direct Democracy

One key opponent of the Charlottetown Accord was Preston Manning, leader of the Reform Party, a new and apparently growing political force. Reform presented itself as a populist movement, sympathetic in principle to direct democracy, including the referendum. When the time came to announce his position, Manning summarized it with a clever double entendre, "Know More." This sounded like "No More," and played into voters' constitutional fatigue. But it also suggested that the more voters learned about the Accord, the less they would like it. This suggestion carried a subtext that suited Reform perfectly: an image of democratic action in which voters know best and elites, even when they act in good faith, cannot be trusted. In 1992 this image had wide currency and may have made the referendum necessary. It presents direct democracy as a challenge to elites, embodying as it does the claim that direct votes inject common sense into the process, even allowing common sense to triumph. And it raises questions of *motive*: Do incentives embedded in ordinary politics lead elites astray, and is direct democracy the necessary corrective?

But direct democracy also evokes at least two other images, both unflattering to voters. Sometimes voters seem like curmudgeons, unwilling to countenance change even when the status quo is no longer sustainable. The mirror image is voters as dupes, too easily led, even to the point of voting for dictatorship. If the "curmudgeon" and "dupe" images differ in relation to the status quo, they converge in raising the question of competence. In each case, voters seem incapable of realizing interests that, in a more reflective mode, they would recognize as their own. The challenge of direct democracy, on this view, is not so much to elites as to voters themselves: How can electorates be brought to think the way elites do, or believe they do? Do elites retain any role in guiding such popular reflection or deliberation as occurs? If the first image turns on motivational differences between mass and elite, the curmudgeon and dupe images turn on a cognitive claim, that the electorate lacks the ability for reflective decision-making.

At stake, arguably, are the prospects for democracy. Pushed to the limit, the "common sense" image calls representative institutions in question. If elites can never be trusted, what basis remains for representative decision-making, for the complicated, Madisonian fabric of indirect democracy?[1] Lurking behind the image is the spectre of Carl Schmitt's 1926 critique of parliamentarism. He claimed that the association between parliamentary institutions and democracy is merely contingent and that, concomitantly, a dictator can embody democratic aspirations as well as a parliament does, better even. Schmitt's critique eventually led him to support Hitler as the "democratic" solution to the problem of Weimar parliamentarism. The second and third images, of curmudgeons and dupes respectively, call in question democracy of any sort, parliamentary or plebiscitarian. At a minimum, they imply that voters lack civic capacity, the ability to transcend their immediate wants. Worse, they suggest that voters lack the intelligence to act on even narrow definitions of their interests. The Charlottetown Accord invited voters to look beyond narrow sectional or ethnic interests, and its rejection raises concerns that voters could not look beyond their own selfish concerns. Yet the Accord also presented a complicated bargain with elements apparently addressed to a broad spectrum of specific interests, and it was advertised as containing something for everyone. Its rejection may also suggest that many voters lacked the ability to identify even their own piece of the pie. But these propositions presuppose that the Accord was indeed what the country needed, that its virtues, if not immediately obvious, were nonetheless apparent to those with eyes to see, that those who said Yes did so clear-sightedly.

By implication, those who said No invoked a wholly different calculus from those who said Yes. Much of the folklore of referendums and plebiscites is based on votes framed on single issues, more precisely on questions which are contrived to seem simple, even when the underlying reality is complex. So framed, direct votes threaten the delicate coalitional bargaining that complicated polities, especially bi- or multinational ones, require. They can be opportunities for raw majoritarianism, when what is required is either coalitions of minorities or true deliberation. The Charlottetown Accord did embody a delicate bargain, of course, as have constitutional or quasi-constitutional votes in many places. But the track record for voting on such multidimensional propositions is chequered, and rejection of the Canadian initiative was not an isolated instance. The suspicion lingers that rejection of the specific agreement was also a rejection of the very logic of coalition-building – that however complicated elites saw the situation to be, voters made the question simple for themselves.

This chapter begins by elaborating on the three images of direct democracy. It then unpacks each image, first presenting the question in terms of voters' competence, then turning to voters' motives, specifically to how motives might vary as we go up or down the competence ladder. From this emerges a model to organize analysis in the rest of the book. Given that the Charlottetown Accord was the product of a broad elite consensus, on one hand, and was manifestly rejected by the broad mass of voters, on the other, the model is framed in terms of the relationship between political knowledge and the probability of assenting to the elite's initiative, of casting a Yes vote.

IMAGES OF DIRECT DEMOCRACY

Common Sense and Majority Rule

Preston Manning invoked a model of democratic choice that makes two critical assumptions: that voters are well equipped to decide for themselves; and that elites are not to be trusted.

Voters will sometimes reject ballot measures, sometimes accept them, but the target is always elite arrogance. Illicit features of the status quo will be swept away while prideful, insensitive elite initiatives will be blocked. The model originated in US populist rhetoric, but has a long-standing Canadian pedigree as well (Laycock, 1990).[2] Its apparently widespread acceptance in the years before 1992 helped force the hand of Canada's elite and necessitate the Charlottetown vote. All along it figured prominently in the rhetoric of opposition to the Charlottetown Accord. This was certainly true on the political right, as with Preston Manning. But as it became clear that the Accord was going down, opponents on the centre and left suppressed their fears and joined Manning's chorus.[3]

This model insists that voters truly do command the information they need. The relevant knowledge does not necessarily involve technical mastery but certainly includes common sense. Thus differences among voters in what might be called encyclopedic knowledge of politics should be irrelevant to the vote. Instead, differences between mass and elite must turn on differences of motive, and, on this model, elite motives are inherently suspect.

Voters themselves, ideally, derive and apply common sense *without the encumbrances of special interests*:

... the Man of Good Will was abstracted from association with positive interests; his chief interests were negative ...

... far from joining organizations to advance his own interests, he would dissociate himself from such combinations and address himself directly and high-mindedly to the problems of government. His approach to politics was, in a sense intellectualistic: he would study the issues and think them through, rather than learn about them through pursuing his needs (Hofstadter, 1955, p. 261).

Indeed, citizens play their role more effectively the more isolated they are from the blandishments of elites, where elites include not just elected officials and their advisers, but also those private interests with whom public actors are tempted to conspire. Idealized citizens are the yeomen, mechanics, and homemakers who suffer through obfuscatory discussion at the town meeting, finally stand up, and cut to the heart of the matter.

In doing so they uncover the elite treachery behind the complexities. Majority-rule elections do not suffice to guarantee majority-preferred policy outcomes, since parliamentary majorities do not always coincide with electoral ones. Even when majorities do coincide, the parliamentarians in question change when they reach the capital. They enter into refined debates among themselves, into a closed conversation preoccupied with different issues from those weighing on ordinary folks. They become susceptible to lobbying by special interests who pay the costs of electioneering with surplus extracted – by capitalists through asymmetric market relations, by union leaders through closed-shop arrangements – from ordinary voters. Most generally, they court votes and approval from strategically placed minorities, and sell out the interests of the country's natural majority. Critical to this model is the assumption that such a majority actually exists.

Voters as Curmudgeons

That voters too often foolishly reject elite initiatives is sometimes presented as the lesson of Australian experience, where voters seem

unwilling to accept even the modest centralization necessary to realize their own policy preferences. In Australia all proposed constitutional amendments must be put to popular vote and almost all
fail. The routine failure is commonly blamed on the difficulty of the
voter's task: the questions are inherently complex; the Australian
constitutional document is arid and has not produced a popular
cult; schools teach little about it; campaigns are too short; parties
obfuscate the issues (Aitken, 1978, pp. 135–6).[4] Put crudely, the implication is that Australian voters are too ignorant to be led, and
that the status quo is sacrosanct when it has no right to be. The Australian example may be tainted by the tendency for that country's
parties to divide over referendum issues, a point to which we return
below.

But even where elites coalesce, voters may still resist. Echoes of
Canada's 1992 vote can be heard in recent European experience. In
1972 three countries voted on joining the European Community. In
Denmark, Norway, and Ireland, major parties supported membership, but only in Ireland did the measure pass easily, with no disturb-
ing of party-system waters. Norwegians rejected advice from a wide
majority of MPs and from all major-party leaders and voted to stay
out. The Labour-Conservative joint campaign discredited both parties. In Denmark the largest parties urged a Yes and a clear majority
of voters took their advice, but the campaign was fractious and may
have contributed to the dramatic fragmentation of the Danish electorate in 1973 (Luthardt, 1993, p. 62).

In 1992 the Maastricht Treaty produced referendums in Ireland,
Denmark, and France. The treaty reconstitutes the representative
foundation of the Union and promotes monetary integration and social policy coordination. It is sweeping, technically worded, and impenetrable. Once again, only in Ireland was referendum passage easy.
In Denmark leaders of all mainstream parties urged a Yes vote, while
No advocates were an awkward coalition of left and right, of groups
outside the mainstream. The issue around which opponents coalesced, significantly, was a simple tribal one: maintaining Denmark's
freedom of action, especially in relation to the German behemoth next
door (Christiansen, 1992). The No side won. In France, the broad centre of the elected elite supported Maastricht strongly. Opposition
came from the far left and right, some of the latter from inside the
governing majority. The vote passed, but only just, and the narrowness of the result may have weakened the party system.

In 1994 Norway tried again with roughly the same alignment of
forces as in 1972, with no more success (Pettersen, Jenssen, and Listhaug, 1995).

These cases can be interpreted as suggesting that voters are unwilling to recognize that the status quo, even if comfortable, is no longer tenable. Equally, they are unwilling to recognize that a ballot measure, although promising little comfort, nonetheless represents a defensible change, arguably the minimum tenable shift. To accept it is risky but to reject it is riskier still. Sometimes an outright majority acts this way and so unwittingly puts at risk its own political-economic framework. Even if only a large minority does this, the consequences for later politics can be dire.

Voters as Dupes

The third model is like the second in positing that voters cannot learn, but this time ignorance leads them not to reject initiatives but to accept them foolishly, to be dupes. This is the French and Bonapartist model: ignorant voters too readily acquiesce in the consolidation of executive power, even in attacks on democracy itself. Sometimes this acquiescence is cloaked in democratic garb, as in Charles de Gaulle's personalization of the Fifth Republic presidency. At other times, voters just rush directly to their chains, as with the founding of France's First and Second Empires. In the fledgling, unconsolidated democracies of eastern Europe and the former Soviet Union, referendums have become a cottage industry, as strategically placed actors attempt to circumvent each other by direct but manipulatory popular appeal (Brady and Kaplan, 1994). Here, leaders and followers seem constantly on the verge of painting themselves into constitutional corners. Generally, where the referendum is readily available, the elements of the status quo most necessary to a liberal constitutional order seem chronically at risk. Early in the 1992 campaign, fears of this sort, that Canadians would be bullied into being Brian Mulroney's dupes, preoccupied many of the Charlottetown Accord's opponents.[5]

REFLECTION AND DELIBERATION, MASS AND ELITE

In both the curmudgeon and dupe images, either voters lack civic spirit or referendums suppress what spirit they have. Missing is anything resembling *deliberation*:

Discussion is not only like war: it is also like love ... The will of a majority does not prevail when it is merely the formal will of mathematical majority. It prevails when it has been attained in a spirit, and when it has thus attained a content or substance, which does justice to the whole of the community and satisfies its general and universal character. The *spirit* which does justice to the whole of the community is a spirit which induces the majority to make concessions to the views of the minority, at the same time as it asks the minority to make the greater concession of accepting, or at any rate tolerating, the trend of its own view. The *substance* or content of any majority-will which does justice to the whole community is a substance or content which incorporates elements drawn from the whole … If the spirit of discussion – which is a spirit of giving as well as of taking, of learning as well as of teaching – is present from beginning to end, there is a genuine reason for thinking that the opinion of the majority, intrinsically and inherently, will possess quality and value (Barker, 1942, pp. 67–8).

Referendums, allegedly, cannot meet Barker's definition of deliberation, but must instead be occasions only for naked mathematical majorities, for mere opinion. Mere opinion – according to Elster "isolated and private expression of preferences" – is the antithesis of deliberation. It lacks the uncertainty about implications and outcomes that fuels true deliberation (Manin, 1987), which leaves open the possibility of "tranformation of preferences through public and rational discussion" (Elster, 1986, p. 112). And its moral status is feeble in the same way that opinion polls are. The majority can be predetermined by the question, and subtle reframing of the issue can make the majority look very different, even reversing the apparent polarity of the outcome. Where this can occur, the moral standing of any particular referendum majority must be in doubt (McLean, 1991).

Representative forums, conversely, offer the possibility of deliberation (Fishkin, 1991). They can be sites for true exchange of views, in which a participant can be both listener and speaker in fairly quick succession. Physical proximity and repeated interaction allow common views to emerge, in interests and in a definition of the underlying situation. If there exists a "strategy-proof" majority – a majority not contingent on the starting point of the process – much time and mutual forbearance may be required to identify it. Representative bodies may not always act to find such majorities. Yet only they have the competence, where competence means not participants' native ability but properties of the forum itself – time and repeated interaction. If no natural majority can be found, even a representative forum can be manipulated (Riker, 1982). But actors engaged in legislative play at least possess relatively full information (if they don't have it at the outset, interaction helps them acquire it) and can anticipate manipulatory initiatives. Most critically, they can construct forms of delegation that serve the majority interest (Krehbiel, 1991; Kiewiet and McCubbins, 1991).

But if representative institutions have the potential to be sites for deliberation, how likely are they to deliberate in fact? In a parliamentary democracy with strong parties, such deliberation as occurs is likely to be in camera, within parties. Exchanges between parties are designed not to minimize differences but usually to magnify them. When differences are minimized, it is not as the end result of open deliberation but as the product of a tacit bargain. Commonly, the tacit bargain reflects the desire of all parties to attract certain blocs of votes, as each party seeks to build a coalition of minorities. If the appeal of this strategy testifies to the weakness or absence of "natural" majorities, the symbolism is appalling: representatives claim the right to decide on behalf of the whole because only they have the opportunity for true deliberation. But instead of truly deliberating, they merely bargain. Parties' very silence on certain questions naturally makes observers – voters – wonder if the real agenda is not hidden.

Each image captures part of the truth, then, but no one model captures all of it. Sometimes the status quo wins and so electorates cannot be just dupes. Sometimes the status quo loses and so electorates cannot be just curmudgeons. Electorates cannot comprise only persons "of good will": the disheartening willingness of voters to surrender their own liberties or the liberties of certain fellow citizens has made "plebiscitary democracy" a term of disdain. If referendums rarely meet the test of deliberation, more explicitly deliberative bodies – parliaments – rarely do either.

As worded, each image is a caricature, each demands acceptance on faith, and no critical tests among them are possible. To get anywhere, the images must be unpacked, and doing so requires us to consider four elements in the mass-elite nexus. Two refer to cognition:

– First is voters' own *competence*. The scholarly record on political knowledge and sophistication confirms that competence is indeed problematic, that many citizens know next to nothing about the political order, and that the proportion who can reproduce the barest semblance of intellectually consistent policy reasoning is small. But some citizens surely know more than others, and knowledge may not be a necessary condition for consistent collective choice.
– Second, how *hard*, how cognitively demanding, is the ballot question? Perhaps voters resist saying Yes to hard questions. Conversely, easy questions – ones made to seem easy, at least – may invite a rush to positive judgment. Then again, perhaps the issue is not questions, but answers.

The next element bridges cognition and motivation:

– How *one-sided* are *signals* about the question? Do all high-profile intervenors support one side only, or are powerful signals being sent
from both sides?
The final element is about motives only:
– Are an intervenor's incentives only to tell the truth about a ballot
measure, or does he or she face incentives to lie? Generally, how
credible are the sources of the signals for and against the ballot measure?

The place to start is with voters themselves.

THE QUESTION OF COMPETENCE

The Problem

Empirical work on elections, public opinion, and mass belief systems
raises serious doubts about voters' fitness to hold in trust the very institutions constituted in their name. Out of these doubts has emerged
the "theory of democratic elitism," which gives a stronger rationale
for *representative*, as opposed to *direct*, democracy than the traditional
ones of time and geographic scale. One ground for doubt concerns
values: elites seem more likely than the rank and file to affirm democratic values; indeed, they seem to be the only true repositories of
such values (Stouffer, 1955). This problem is seen as incomplete so-
cialization into the culture of democracy, where the cultural focus is
on procedural guarantees against majority tyranny. This is a perspective we return to below. The rest of this section focuses on the other
ground for anxiety: on majorities' lack of self-awareness.
    If one concern is that voters pursue unworthy ends, the other is
that they are unable to make consistent connections between ends
and means. Converse (1964) has stated that most citizens know little
about political questions, especially about remote and abstract ones.
When voters are asked what they like or dislike about candidates and
parties, few volunteer anything that resembles the application of any
ideas to politics. Propositions which seem intrinsically linked intellectually evoke little linkage empirically; voters exhibit little effort toward intellectual consistency, nor do they always give the same
answer when a question is repeated. Most distressing, citizens who
have firm attitudes rarely change them, while those who seem to
change have no definite attitudes to begin with; what appears as
change is nothing more than randomly generated response. From this
Converse concludes that much ostensible "public opinion" is little
more than "non-attitudes." All this fuels doubts about the moral

standing of almost any majority that happens to appear, in survey data certainly, possibly even in real life.

Not surprisingly, these views have been challenged. Achen (1975) argues persuasively that the case against voters' civic competence, based on surveys, errs in attributing to voters a weakness more properly attributed to measures; correction for attenuation due to measurement error makes ideas appear more integrated and stable than Converse claimed was the case. Survey questions that attempt to fit complex policy questions to respondents with modest political knowledge *must* be fraught with error. But this is hardly reassuring, as it just testifies to the elite-mass gap in another way. As Sniderman et al. (1991, p. 17) point out, the difference between Converse and Achen is not so much methodological as ontological. Converse assumes the problem is with respondents and estimates how wide the civic gap is; Achen assumes the problem is with measures and estimates how great the measurement error is. This controversy aside, there is no escaping the conclusion that some voters simply do not possess the information necessary for minimally consistent choice. And many voters whose measured positions on policy questions seem stable do not support those attitudes with much information (Smith, 1989).

Some argue that the empirical basis of these claims is time- and place-bound, peculiar to the United States in the late 1950s. But most attempts to argue that things were different at other times and places have foundered. There is no persuasive evidence, for instance, that Americans became ideologically more constrained as the temperature of US politics rose in the 1960s.[6] A direct comparison with what is usually regarded as an ideologically motivated electorate, in France, suggests that French citizens are about as remote, cognitively, from the political elite as US voters are (Converse and Pierce, 1986).[7] Canadians are no more constrained by ideology than Americans (Johnston, 1986).

Others argue that the empirical claim is fundamentally misconceived, that it reflects a situation which could hardly be better designed to induce apathy. The opportunities for active political engagement are presently so few and so unsatisfying that indifference is only to be expected. Conversely, the argument goes that a regular diet of serious democratic responsibility would awaken a so-far dormant civic capacity (Pateman, 1980; Barber, 1984). The Pateman-Barber claim does seem plausible for face-to-face deliberative decision-making and evidence exists on the capacity of rank-and-file citizens to rise to the face-to-face challenge (see, for instance, Mansbridge, 1980). For mass-participation choices, however, the case is harder to make. Indeed, rational choice models imply precisely this: the number who vote is so large that the probability any individual will affect the result is tiny; it is thus irrational for voters to invest much in political learning, unless they happen to have a taste for the game; the rational action is to be a free rider, to let others bear the cost of deciding; this motive, once generalized, yields an apathetic electorate (Downs, 1957). If this model helps explain current apathy, it also holds out scant hope for change on the mass-participation front, as referendums would be at least as vulnerable as general elections to free riding. Certainly, the record for referendums is not encouraging. Direct turnout comparisons within jurisdictions indicate that participation drops off for direct ballots relative to candidate ballots (Cronin, 1989). The jurisdictions in which direct ballots are most ubiquitous, such as Switzerland and certain American states, tend to have chronically low turnout for all votes, direct or representational. Although frequent referendums are unlikely to have induced the low turnout, neither can they be said to have stimulated participation.

But is all this evidence and argument really relevant? Does individuals' cognitive competence matter to the whole electorate's capacity to decide rationally? Two broad lines of argument to the contrary can be discerned. Some individuals clearly know more than others, but substantive knowledge and intellectual modes of reasoning are not absolutely necessary to get a voter to the "correct" position, as defined above. Even substantively ignorant voters can get to the right position, they just get there by non-intellectual means. Arguments on these lines exemplify *low-information rationality*. On the other hand, some individuals are clearly better than others in getting to their own "correct" position, the position they would adopt were they fully informed. But when votes are summed up, the collectively correct outcome prevails; that is, the apparent majority is also the true one, even when many individuals choose the wrong side. These arguments may be called *aggregationist*.

Low-Information Rationality

Under this general rubric cluster three conceptualizations of a process by which uninformed voters can come to consistent judgments. Voters can learn from each other through published opinion polls; they can employ internal reasoning strategies of varying degrees of sophistication and, critically, unsophisticated strategies can be as efficient as sophisticated ones; and they can get outside help.

Polls as Orienting Devices. One piece of potentially relevant information is fairly easy to acquire: readings of how other voters intend to vote from published opinion polls. Even where poorly informed voters have different substantive interests from better informed ones, the former can use polls about party or the popularity of the ballot measure to orient themselves to the choice, or so McKelvey and Ordeshook (1986) conjecture. For this method to work, voters must have a sense of where they themselves sit relative to the rest of the electorate, such as on the left or on the right, pro-Quebec or anti-Quebec. Then, once a poll is published, voters can update their sense of how far from the status quo a ballot measure sits. On the basis of this updating, some voters then change their own vote intention, and this change is reflected in the next published poll. This next poll provides a further opportunity for updating, and for further (presumably fewer) shifts of intention, yielding another (presumably smaller) measured aggregate shift. The process should continue until voters get the choices properly fixed: "Since polls are themselves a function of citizen perception and preferences, we can think of an equilibrium as a poll which does not change when individuals condition their behavior on the information conveyed by the poll" (McKelvey and Ordeshook, 1986, p. 914).

A roughly parallel argument was made by Bartels (1988): among the things polls can do for voters is tell them how much to like a candidate. This logic can extend to ballot measures. Two questions arise immediately:

– *Do low-information voters rely on polls more than high-information ones do?*
– *Can polls play low-information voters false?*

Alternative Reasoning Strategies. The literature on belief systems in mass publics posited that poorly informed individuals cannot make consistent choices. If consistent choices require conscious commitment on substantive policy, the assumption is probably warranted. In fact, Converse (1964) had relatively little to say about the vote. Subsequent decades have seen political scientists embark on numerous, generally plausible accounts of policy-based elections. One of the most striking instances preceded the 1992 referendum by a mere four years. In Canada's free-trade-driven election virtually every voter came to an interpretable position on the issue and about 90 per cent of those with a position cast a consistent vote (Johnston et al., 1992). If the 1988 result is at all representative, many voters must get to approximately the "correct" position by means other than sophisticated ratiocination. The likely alternatives were canvassed by Sniderman et al. (1991).[8] In their opinion, some voters do employ *ideological* modes of reasoning and their numbers are not trivial. But a substitute for ideology exists, and this substitute may be no less effective for being crude: *feeling* about groups. Feeling about groups can help voters locate parties – and groups themselves – on dimensions that are essentially ideological, even if voters do not recognize the dimensions as such. However, if ideology and feeling are different mainsprings of choice, each mainspring can also express itself by alternative routes. Some voters incorporate feelings and ideas into a *hierarchical reasoning chain*, entertaining arguments of intermediate generality. Others may take the basic motive right to the choice, without intermediate steps.

Consider what a hierarchical chain looks like. The best place to start is in the middle, with an argument of intermediate generality. A chain's middle link is a consideration which is immediately relevant to the final choice but which also looks back to a more general consideration, an idea or a feeling. The intermediate argument is commonly shaped as a *heuristic*, a stylized story which helps interpret the situation for choice. The most common heuristic is a victimization story, which the voter accepts or rejects. If a policy delivers benefits to a group that voters see as mainly victimized, they might support the policy. If they think the group has itself to blame, they might oppose the policy. Either way, the causal attribution to the source of the problem is critical to the view of remedies; this is the final link in the chain.

But what attribution are voters likely to make, what kind of story are they likely to summon up or accept? This is a question about the chain's initial links and this is where master ideas and feelings come in:

First consider how the victimization heuristic might be governed by a master *idea*. A voter on the ideological left probably sees victimization as pervasive, and many aggrieved groups count on the left for support. Voters on the right resist appeals from victimization and instead emphasize personal responsibility. Voters who tend not to see victims in general should be relatively unlikely to see any particular group as victimized, quite apart from how they feel about the group.

Now consider how heuristics can be sorted by *feelings*. Even voters ideologically susceptible to appeals from victimization might resist imputing victimization to a group they dislike. Conversely, even voters who generally resist victimization arguments might make an exception for a group they like. A role for ideology does not preclude a role for feeling, and we can readily imagine voters coming to judgment by summing up ideas and feelings.

How this applies to the Charlottetown Accord will be discussed later in this chapter, but some basic questions are already starting to come into focus:

- *What groups matter for voters' assessment of the Accord?*
- *What master ideas does the Accord engage?*
- *What intermediate arguments sort the choice?*
- *In particular, are there any victims on the scene?*

How voters decide is likely to depend on how much information they have. Information conditions the structure of choice in two ways. First, where well-informed voters employ multiple motives – ideological as well as affective – poorly-informed voters typically consult only feelings. Second, where well-informed voters sift their multiple motives through an elaborate logical hierarchy, poorly-informed voters take only feelings straight to the bottom line. In any given vote, then, more than one reasoning process is likely to be engaged. What voters mean may depend, then, on how much they know about the question. The implications of such heterogeneity for voting on the Charlottetown Accord will be considered below, when we look at differences between questions.

Here let us close with a lingering question raised by Sniderman et al. Arguably, their strongest claim is that feelings are efficient substitutes for ideas. However, their work shows only that it is possible for feelings to substitute for ideas. They find poorly educated respondents connect feelings to choice about as efficiently as well-educated ones do. They also find that when respondents are asked to locate parties and groups from left to right, even among poorly educated ones *average* locations are basically correct. But both of these findings stop short of proof that low-information voters as *individuals* are as efficient as high-information ones. Feelings alone may still be less efficient than feelings combined with ideas. And low-information voters, taken all together, may get locations right on average, but the individuals may be all over the place, less constrained by reality than high-information voters.[9] The question that remains, then, is:

- *Did low-information voters connect their own interests, however they defined them, to the vote on the Charlottetown Accord as efficiently as high-information voters did?*

Outside Help: The Role of Intervenors. In the simplest case, to vote No on a ballot measure is to vote Yes to the status quo, whatever one thinks about the status quo in some absolute sense. The ballot measure is not, then, considered in the abstract but in relation to things as they are now. At the beginning of a referendum campaign, all voters face the task of figuring out how big a departure from the status quo the ballot measure represents (Lupia, 1992). Voters can start by asking who set the agenda, and who really wants the proposal to pass. The change embodied in the measure must be worth the agenda-setter's while, otherwise it would not have been proposed. This suggests that the change is not trivial. If one knows the agenda-setter's general political orientation, then one should also be able to guess the direction of change. If that orientation is not known, as is commonly the case with privately sponsored initiatives, then a voter cannot even guess the direction.

To locate the ballot measure with some exactness, voters need to go beyond the agenda setter and ask who else has taken a position on the proposal. All intervenors, even ones the voter does not like, are potentially useful (McKelvey and Ordeshook, 1986; Lupia, 1992). This means, though, that how one feels about the intervenor should affect how one reacts to the intervention. Crudely, voters can mentally line up supporters and opponents, discern where support stops and opposition starts, and conclude that the measure must lie somewhere near that boundary. Then, voters can consult their own feelings about supporters and opponents, and combine feelings about intervenors with knowledge of the support/opposition boundary to assess whether the measure will make them better or worse off.

All this is to say that interventions *can*, in principle, facilitate the choice for low-information voters. But do they have this effect in fact? Conceivably, becoming aware of an intervention is itself a cognitively demanding task, one which requires the same sort of understanding as does mastery of substantive arguments. The harder it is to become aware of interventions, the more might prior differences in information-processing capacity actually be compounded, not mitigated. The question that lingers from 1992, then, is:

- *Did interventions overcome the cognitive demands of the Charlottetown Accord and help narrow informational differences in the vote, or did interventions, by placing cognitive demands in their own right, only widen pre-existing differences?*

Aggregationist Arguments

Empirical Version. If "non-attitudes" truly lead to random response, random error (in respondents' own behaviour, not in measures) must also be offsetting: for every voter wrongly choosing one side there must be another voter wrongly choosing the other side. This leaves the field effectively in control of those who know what they are doing. The most forceful statement of this view is Page and Shapiro (1992).[10] Their argument shifts from the individual to the aggregate, and claims that an empirically observed distribution is identical, within sampling error, to the distribution that would emerge were everyone fully informed. Outcomes are still vulnerable to the wording of the question, not from voters' incapacity, but as a reflection of the intrinsic logic of unconstrained majority rule. This vulnerability exists even when all voters are perfectly informed (Farquharson, 1969). The "measurement error" created thereby is systematic, not random. And random error, to come back to the point, should not matter.

Analytical Version. At bottom, this empirical claim is an intuitive re-statement of the Condorcet Jury Theorem, which states that "the group, deciding on the basis of majority rule, is more competent than the average individual and, quite possibly, more competent than the 'best' (most competent) individual" (Miller, 1986, p. 177). The theorem assumes that, on average, an individual's probability of giving the "right" answer is greater than 0.50. It need not be much greater than this; all that is required is that an individual be slightly more likely than not to be right. If the decision is then made by simple majority voting in a group, the likelihood that the group choice (which can be based, of course, on a very narrow majority) is correct exceeds the av-erage likelihood that an individual is correct. The larger the group the wider the difference and, as group size grows, the group's chance of getting it right exceeds that for the group's smartest member. The logic that produces this result is exactly analogous to the logic of random sampling: the larger the sample, the less the sampling error.

In its classic form, the theorem presupposes the existence of a "cor-rect" answer, by analogy to the problem facing a jury in a criminal trial – hence the theorem's name.[11] The defendant must be either guilty or not guilty of the allegation. But the theorem can be extended to situations in which there is no single correct answer. All that is re-quired is that there be a correct answer for each voter, where correct is a now-familiar notion: what this particular voter would choose if he or she were fully informed. In a binary choice, there must a majority whose true interests lie on one side and a minority whose true inter-ests lie on the other. Extended to this situation, the theorem asks: given voter ignorance, what is the probability that the majority actu-ally revealed in a vote is the true majority, the one which would ap-pear were everyone fully informed? In ideal circumstances, the probability that the true majority prevails is still larger than the typi-cal majority's actual size; the correct side should win most of the time, if only narrowly. And this should become more certain, the larger the voting body. The difficulty lies with what constitutes ideal circum-stances. Where voters in the majority are more competent than voters in the minority, or where majority and minority are equally compe-tent, the theorem delivers the goods. But what if individuals in the mi-nority know their interests better than individuals in the majority? In this situation, minority rule can regularly prevail. The surest guarantee of the successful operation of the Extended Jury Theorem, then, is *no covariance between information and direction of opinion.*

Having presented it as a factor, Miller considers such covariance no further. Subsequent work, including Page and Shapiro, takes Miller if not as absolutely dispositive, then at least as greatly reassuring.[12] In our view, however, the link between information and direction of opinion is absolutely crucial. And it is, as Bartels (1990, 1995) reminds us, ultimately an empirical question, one still largely unaddressed. Bartels challenges us to consider the possibility that substantive information is still a necessary condition for deriving opinions that comport with our true interests, and that supplying voters with information might change their opinions. The basic questions, then, are:
– *Is there an overall, whole-electorate relationship between information and direction of opinion?*
– *Do voters with a given profile of politically relevant characteristics think differently if they know more?*
If the answer to either of these questions is yes, then we should to hesitate to accept claims that mere aggregation covers voter ignorance.

QUESTIONS AND ANSWERS

Not all questions will place the same demands on voters. Some issues are technical, impenetrable to voters lacking prior knowledge. Some questions have many dimensions, yet must be assessed as a package – in other words, voters must ask if they like the things they like enough to offset the things they dislike. Some questions may turn less on their intrinsic attractiveness or repulsiveness than on their fit to the times – for example, a disagreeable measure may nonetheless be necessary to avert an even more disagreeable alternative, and Hobson's choices are hard choices. But some issues, conversely, are "easy." Voters cope best with questions about symbols, especially if the symbols embody a familiar theme, and if the issue concerns ends rather than means.

It is tempting to suggest, then, that one pattern running through global data on direct democracy is the sheer difficulty of the question. Moreover, this pattern may help us sort out the relative appropriateness of the three images with which the chapter opened:

– The "dupe" image may be fed by historical experience with questions that are easy to say Yes to. Bonapartist moves typically involve an appeal to voters' self-love. Sometimes voters are encouraged to compare themselves to a culturally devalued outgroup. The group may be completely outside the society, possibly an historic enemy or oppressor. Alternatively, the group may be sociologically intermingled with the local majority but susceptible to treatment as a scapegoat, to being described as a parasite on the majority host. In either case, voters can readily get to a position on the question by consulting their feelings. Sometimes voters are encouraged to see themselves as put upon by culturally arrogant elites. In a similar but less sinister vein, voters may be attracted by proposals which seem to (and may in fact) empower them. Therefore they are likely to endorse direct election of the executive, or proposals to institutionalize direct democracy, which will expand the scope for their own further involvement in legislation. Often, strategically minded elites pose questions to which the easy answer is Yes.

– The "curmudgeon" image may be fed by questions that are hard to say Yes to. This did seem to be true of most examples in the earlier discussion, such as Australian constitutional measures and moves toward European unification. The ballot measures were generally highly technical, defensible (indeed, comprehensible) only when all their parts were taken together. Sometimes, hard questions are unavoidable. Australians have no choice, if their constitution is to be amended, and this was often true in European examples. Sometimes, though, hard questions may be put specifically to elicit a No.

– The "common sense" image, the one most favourable to direct democracy, contends that, in the final analysis, almost all political questions are easy. Invariably, it is asserted, they can be settled by reference to a few moral principles of the kind parents teach to children, or to a simple *cui bono* query. Indeed, this proposition is one of the very props of democracy, for the larger the number of issues susceptible to commonsensical determination, the larger can be citizens' direct role. At the same time, claims that the issue is truly complex are a sure guide that someone in the elite, or some academic in elite pay, is trying to cloud the issue.

From differences among questions it is one step back to differences among voters. If there really is such a thing as a hard question, then perhaps only the best-informed voters have the ability to say Yes to it. If there is such a thing as an easy question then perhaps everyone can be brought to say Yes. It would be tempting to leave this as a tentative generalization, which accounts for both the overall success rate of hard and easy measures and for differences across measures in the cognitive basis of response. The problem is that many questions are hard and easy at the same time. For example, measures that are considered hard often propose territorial unification or political centralization. This is true of many failed Australian measures and was always true of hotly contested European Union ones. If unification or centralization is the issue, then hard measures may only be the flip side of many successful easy ones, for centralization is vulnerable to being characterized as taking power away from the people. In such instances, reasons to say Yes are not just hard to fathom, reasons to say No are easy to find. The opposite is true of many apparently easy questions. The empowerment offered by Bonapartist measures is more apparent than real, for instance, as these measures tend to be the most centralizing of all. But to grasp that fact takes some cognitive power; reasons to acquiesce are more easily grasped.

Perhaps, then, there are no hard or easy questions, just hard and easy answers. If the hard answer is Yes and the easy answer is No, the Yes is unlikely to succeed but well-informed voters are more likely to give it. If the hard answer is No and the easy answer is Yes, the Yes is likely to win and only the best-informed will resist.[13]

The Charlottetown Accord seems to fit this account perfectly. One thing the Accord did not do was propose centralization; if anything it promised the opposite. But it certainly presented a technical face. Some of its language consisted of quasi-legal terms of art, in that some parts rested on assumptions unwritten and unspoken, most readily recognizable to citizens with legal training. And certain parts made sense only when read together with other parts. The Charlottetown Accord was certainly multidimensional and most of its specific components were opposed by electoral majorities. For most voters, a Yes vote would have required, at a minimum, transcending dislikes to realize likes. Many voters, we argue, liked nothing whatsoever in the Accord, and for such voters to say Yes would require them to conclude that its failure would still be worse than its success. Failure might, for example, lead to the country's breakup, an outcome far worse, at least to some, than the constitutional entrenchment of individually disliked elements. To say Yes to the Accord arguably required grappling with technical legalisms and multidimensional trade-offs. At a minimum it required comparing one imaginary alternative to another. To say No, in contrast, seemed easy. For all the Accord's complexity, it ought to have evoked feelings about groups, for at its core lay constitutional recognition of strategically placed groups. It did seem to play to minority consciousness, although equivocally so. Certainly, it did not appeal to simple majoritarianism. The Accord was, cognitively speaking, hard to say Yes to, easy to say No to.

At this point, differences among answers dovetail with the differences among voters identified by Sniderman et al. If reasons to say Yes to the Charlottetown Accord were hard to grasp while reasons to say No were easy to understand, the Accord's supporters should have come disproportionately from the best-informed. Getting to Yes required an ability to deal in abstractions and a positive orientation to certain traditionally devalued outgroups, both things promoted by education and information.[14] Getting to No required little in the way of abstraction. It required only negative group references. If the information-Yes vote relationship proves indeed to be positive, then one reading of the event is that the Charlottetown Accord was a test which most Canadians failed. The questions that emerge, then, are:

– *Did Yes and No voters differ qualitatively? Did Yes voters employ ideas as well as feelings and did they reason hierarchically? Did No voters rely only on feelings and reason in only a minimally structured way?*

The story cannot end at this point, however. In 1992 getting to a Yes vote meant coming to the conclusion favoured by the elite, and voters who know more about a complex public question also resemble the elite which poses the question in the first place. This brings us to two considerations in political leadership: the clarity of the elite signal; and the credibility of the signal's source.

ELITE DIVISION AND COHESION

Why should elite cohesion or division matter at all? This discussion flows from Lupia's model (1991, 1994, 1995) of agenda-setters, intervenors, and cue-taking. The identity of the agenda-setter is critical to that model, as are the identities of intervenors who line up for and against a measure. What if virtually all key players line up on one side?

Elites coalesce because they believe this increases a measure's chances of success, implicitly mimicking Lupia's model. The record suggests their belief is warranted. Almost all pertinent evidence comes from Switzerland, the United States, and Australia.[15] In Switzerland and the United States, elite-initiated constitutional proposals almost always pass; in Australia they almost always fail. Swiss and American measures almost always enjoy consensual elite support; Australian ones almost never do. Further to the point is variation across kinds of ballot measure within Switzerland and the United States, between constitutional and non-constitutional issues, and between elite origination and non-elite origination.[16] In Switzerland most elite-originated constitutional measures actually do carry, and such measures are more likely to pass than either constitutional proposals originating outside the elite or non-constitutional proposals originating inside it (Aubert, 1978, p. 44). Similarly, in the United States private initiatives almost always fail, while measures that originate in formal constitutional processes usually pass (Magleby, 1984). And in both countries what distinguishes the most successful class of measures, constitutional ones, is elite consensus. Often consensus is inescapable, as constitutional measures must clear extraordinary legislative hurdles before they can be referred to the electorate.

But is elite consensus an independent factor in a measure's chances of success? Do voters take consensus to signal that the measure is compelling, worthy of support? Two alternative explanations for the observed elite consensus–popular success relationship are plausible.

- *Innocuousness:* Elite consensus rarely forms around a measure which is contentious, or which envisages a large shift from the status quo. Thus, among possible constitutional measures, only innocuous ones, typically, clear the threshold for popular referral; big changes remain bottled up. If the measure is really innocuous, voters might be able to discern this for themselves and say Yes anyway. Big non-constitutional changes, which require only simple legislative majorities or which are placed on the ballot by private initiative, should be transparently *not* innocuous and so get voted down. On this account, the elite consensus–Yes vote relationship is just a byproduct and elite consensus supplies no signal in its own right. The Charlottetown Accord may be only an exception that proves the rule: it was manifestly not innocuous, and it was shot down.
- *Popularity:* Elites sometimes respond to pre-existing popular majorities. On one hand, measures likely to lose are suppressed. One might ask, for example, why the Meech Lake Accord was never referred. In answering this question, it does not suffice to appeal to Canada's lack of plebisicitory history. Two national plebiscites had been held; the referendum possibility was raised in the 1980–2 constitutional crisis, and the 1980 Quebec referendum supplied a kind of precedent. The 1988 election might have turned on the Accord had but one party raised the issue (Johnston et al., 1992, chapters 3 and 8). The simplest interpretation is that all parties wanted the Accord, or feared opposing it, but all reckoned that popular referral would doom it.[17] In contrast, ineluctably popular measures commonly receive elite endorsement as a matter of self-defence. A good example is directly relevant to the difference between the Meech Lake and Charlottetown accords. In 1991 the British Columbia legislature adopted an enabling bill for referendums and the government authorized that a plebsicite on the desirability of further direct votes be conducted during the general election later that year. The measure was proposed by the Social

Credit government, smarting at adverse popular reaction to its too-ready endorsement of the Meech Lake Accord and hoping to force the hand of the NDP, a party historically hostile to plebiscites, as is the labour and social democratic left elsewhere. In the 1991 climate, however, the NDP felt compelled to support the Social Credit measure, as it was bound to pass and the party was unwilling to let itself be cornered.[18] The contrast between non-referral of the Meech Lake Accord and the British Columbia example points up a pattern of strategic referral–non-referral, which, again, could produce an elite consensus–referendum success relationship wholly as a by-product.

Although both explanations must be true some of the time, the record still suggests that elite endorsement helps proposals and that consensual endorsement helps most of all. The fact that in both Switzerland and the United States even elite proposals not backed by consensus outperform private ones seems telling.[19] Most telling, though, is the Australian example. Australian references seem relatively innocuous, do not embody bigger shifts from the status quo than Swiss or American referrals.[20] Yet they fail, and critical to their failure is the fact that they get caught up in the toils of party division. The few which do have bipartisan elite support are not overwhelmingly likely to pass either, but only they have any chance at all (Sharman and Stuart, 1981).[21]

Certainly, broad elite support is often seen by agenda-setters themselves as a pressing necessity. This was the widely drawn lesson of the 1975 United Kingdom referendum, where voters were asked if they wished to stay in the European Community. Although the governing Labour party was divided and the referendum was designed to relieve this tension, it seems critical that Labour's division was less within the cabinet than between front and back benches. The top leadership of all parties favoured membership and this quasi-consensus helped the Yes forces (Butler and Kitzinger, 1976). Finally, a striking articulation of this logic was offered by Pierre Bourgault, as part of his contribution to Quebec's post-1990 soul searching: "aujourd'hui un seul homme puisse empêcher d'atteindre la souveraineté. Si Robert Bourassa déciderait demain de faire l'indépendence, surtout quand on a vu le virage souverainiste de son parti, nous serions indépendants dans une semaine avec 80% des voix" (Lisée, 1994a, pp. 403–4)

Certain generalizations suggest themselves, then. First, if a measure originates outside the elite, contesting views may not be necessary for a voter to say No. Private sponsors face few sanctions for misrepresentation, and thus tend to be reflexively distrusted. The empirical evidence shows that their measures correspondingly tend to be voted down. Professional politicians, in contrast, face incentives to tell the truth. They engage in repeated play with other professional politicians, and their colleagues punish them for lying. Accordingly, politicians start with a presumption in their favour.[22] To assert that politicians are more credible than private actors is not to say that voters just follow any politician's lead. Credibility interacts with evaluation. I may give Preston Manning his due and allow not just that his opposition reflects a close and competent reading of the Accord, but that it is a truthful expression of his interests and those of his clientele; but since I happen not to be in his clientele, I personally take his opposition to indicate that I should consider supporting the deal. The critical thing is not that I like Manning, just that I see no reason for him to misrepresent his own true feelings about the document. If *all* politicians, ones I dislike and ones I like, support the measure, this is a cue that the matter is sufficiently pressing for politicians to sink their normal differences. Without elite contestation, I have no basis for resisting the proposal. Or do I? Best, perhaps, is to let the section end with the obvious questions:

– *Is elite cohesion a sufficient condition for a large departure from the status quo to succeed? Or is it just a necessary condition, not sufficient?*
– *Is elite division a necessary condition for a constitutional measure to fail?*

CREDIBILITY AND COGNITIVE CAPACITY

What if I distrust politicians as a class? The comparative and historical record suggests that elite consensus is usually a necessary condition for passage of measures that lack built-in popular appeal. That it might not be a sufficient condition was suggested by the Danish vote (and very nearly by the French one) on the Maastricht Treaty, by the most recent Norwegian rejection of membership in the European Union, and, of course, by the Charlottetown Accord itself. Although consensus is designed specifically to neutralize differences in evaluation of specific actors, this may only open the process up to a broader alienation from politics as a whole, and invite precisely the retributive populist response that makes many observers fear direct democracy in the first place. For when elites coalesce, many voters may suspect a plot against majority rule. The intensity of such suspicions, and thus of alienation from the process, may be inversely related to social advantage and cognitive capacity.

Certainly the empirical record hints at a positive relationship between cognitive capacity and willingness to follow the elite lead; support for consensual initiatives typically is greatest among more highly educated voters. This has emerged as the chronic European unification pattern: the elite decides that unification – either joining the Union to begin with or, once in, accepting further centralization – is the necessary thing; a cross-party coalition[23] forms to convey this point; sometimes the electorate agrees, sometimes not; but agreement is always more complete among highly educated voters than among poorly educated ones. This was the case in the 1975 British vote (Särlvik et al., 1976; Butler and Kitzinger, 1976), the 1992 French one (Collas, 1992; Habert, 1992–3; Luthardt, 1993; Tiersky, 1994), and the 1994 Norwegian one (Pettersen et al., 1995).

Two counter examples have been documented, but both bear out this rule by supplying variance on both variables: the elite divided, and educational differences in the vote were weak to nonexistent. In 1979 Scotland rejected a form of home rule by referendum. The issue was truly complicated as one could support the particulars of home rule for opposed reasons, and one could oppose it for opposed reasons. The parties were divided internally but also, and more importantly, against each other (Macartney, 1981, pp. 14–25, 36–41). The electorate split on party lines and, notwithstanding the question's complexity, no education-vote relation was apparent (Bochel and Denver, 1981, chapter 8).

Closer to home is the 1980 Quebec referendum. The question was whether or not Quebeckers wished to give their provincial government a mandate to negotiate sovereignty-association with the rest of Canada. A clear majority said No; almost all non-francophones said No and francophones divided roughly 50–50.[24] The hyphenation of sovereignty and association suggests at least two distinct dimensions in the ballot question. Certainly, voters were confused about what sovereignty-association meant. A further tension was between a desire for national self-assertion and a fear of the economic costs of such assertion (Pinard, 1980). In short, the task for voters was nothing if not difficult. But here, too, education was not a factor in the choice and the critical fact seems to be that debate was organized on party lines (Pinard and Hamilton, 1984; Blais and Nadeau, 1984; Pammett et al., 1984).

It is awkward that both these examples concern political devolution or disintegration. Could this be the real basis of contrast with elite-consensus examples, where so many of the latter concerned centralization in some form? We think not, for if that were the primary basis of the contrast, then the education-Yes relationship in Scotland and Quebec should have been reversed, not merely neutralized.

The most obvious reading of the total pattern is that the consensus-division pattern in referendum voting corresponds to a distinction now drawn in the literature on public opinion formation, between mainstream and polarization effects. In the "mainstream" case, two patterns come together: the elite coalesces around a measure and the measure gets its greatest support from the best-informed (Zaller, 1992, 1994). Evidence for the effect goes back at least five decades, to Cantril (1944), but what it signifies remains unclear.

We can imagine three plausible interpretations, each with its own moral implication:

– The conjunction may just reflect each group's cognitive mastery, which leads each to the same conclusion. Both political leaders and well-informed voters see fairly clearly what the situation requires, and because recognition involves cognitively difficult tasks, these are the only two groups who grasp the need. But if this is the process, then elite consensus as such carries no independent significance, is not a signal in its own right.

– If elite consensus is indeed an independent signal and if the voters most sensitive to it are the most educated, then the only logical cognitive connection is mere exposure to elite argument, unaccompanied by judgment. The standard interpretation goes something like this: the cognitive gradient reflects not a differential grasp "of the nation's true interests," but rather the "indoctrinating effect of exposure to mainstream elite discourse" (Zaller, 1994, p. 190). If this is a cognitive story, it is a thin one; education or information simply helps one read the cue cards more quickly: "the politically educated are not better analysts of complex situations but are simply more aware of what official ... policy is" (Gamson and Modigliani, 1966, p. 188).

– Cognition may play an even smaller role than the slight one just outlined. Is it possible that, at least with the burden of information pumped out in the superheated atmosphere of a referendum campaign, many normally ill-informed voters get the elite message but actively reject it? The cognitive gradient may overlap an affective one: sociological or cultural factors that inhibit general acquisition of political knowledge also make one less supportive of the political elite. If one dislikes politics, for instance, one should also dislike politicians and avoid political information. But if one feels compelled to make political choices, if only in self-defence, one should attend to the sources of directive cues. Where all or most leaders send the same cues, dislike of the elite should fuel rejection of the cue. But to reject it, one must receive it, and so the truly operative gradient is not cognitive but affective.

If the third model is at all operative, what fuels the alienation at its core? One possibility is that satisfaction or resentment with life in general follows lines of social advantage or disadvantage. Politicians happen to be counted among life's winners and so are obvious targets of resentment for those who have reason to feel resentful. Other winners may be similarly resented, but they rarely present themselves as targets. Note, though, that voters who respond with mere resentment to an elite-consensus cue are not necessarily playing the cue-taking game. The content of the ballot measure may be irrelevant, and the measure merely a passive vehicle for transmitting punishment to the political class.

A more subtle but no less resentment-filled possibility does involve cue-taking, and this may be especially applicable to the 1992 case. Generalized unhappiness aside, why might a voter express disgust with the whole political class? One possibility lies in the tendency of parliamentary parties to suppress certain kinds of controversy, to avoid questions that make party politics – and perhaps society as a whole – explode. In many countries, Canada prominent among them, parties assiduously avoid overt racial or ethnic appeals. Two sources for such avoidance come to mind; each engages a subtly different response, but both engagements produce an apparent cognitive gradient in acquiescence.

First, political elites understand the complexities of multiracial or multicultural societies, or at least have a heightened appreciation of their explosive possibilities. They tend also to be more tolerant of groups that are outside the mainstream or otherwise culturally devalued (Sullivan et al., 1982; McClosky and Brill, 1983). Elite consensus commonly signals deliberate avoidance of the explosive issue, and well-educated voters, themselves relatively sensitive to the larger issue, get the message in the particular instance.

Second, certain ethnic groups are strategically located for the plurality-election game. Quebec's historic role as a pivot for governments (Johnston et al., 1992; Bakvis and Macpherson, 1995) makes francophones a key interest, even ones outside Quebec. Groups whose immigration history is mainly post-World War Two also tend to be critical, located as they are in urban swing ridings (Wood, 1978). Parties seek to attract these groups, but the imperative of also seeking other voters makes the whole process somewhat covert, and no party seriously interested in forming a government has an incentive to defect from this process. This time, though, it is *low*-information voters who "get the message," and if they generally resent the politics of ethnic accommodation, they may take cross-party consensus to signal the centrality of such politics to the proposal at issue. This, of course, is a restatement of the central feature of the "common sense" image of direct democracy.

All the foregoing implies elite consensus, when only one powerful cue can be heard. However, if the elite divides, education or prior information commonly drops out as a factor in referendum voting. Easiest, perhaps, is when division is along traditional party lines. Only if highly educated or highly knowledgeable voters *identify* with parties or leaders on the Yes side should the knowledge-Yes vote link remain; in this case it would not be intrinsically cognitive, but instead would be essentially affective. If well-educated voters identify with No advocates, the relationship should reverse: knowing more should seem to produce a No vote. If a link between political knowledge and identification with one side or the other is absent, no simple knowledge-vote relationship need appear.

What might appear is an *interactive* relationship: the more you know the greater should be the consistency between predisposition and action. The hinge in the interaction is the predisposition. If you identify with the Yes forces, knowledge should increase your likelihood of taking their cue and voting Yes yourself. But if you identify with the No forces, knowledge should increase the likelihood of a No vote. This interactive pattern has been dubbed by Zaller (1992) the "polarization effect." But then, information can sharpen cleavages, even when the core of the elite all hums the same tune. Even if we find that, overall, information induces a Yes vote, supplying more information to someone who starts off disaffected may provide that person with better, more informed reasons for saying No.

The mainstream versus polarization distinction seems tailored for Canada in 1992. Outside Quebec, the party elite coalesced and so the process should have been mainstream: identification with any specific party should matter little to the Yes vote. Instead, response should reflect a generalized ability or willingness to take elite cues. In Quebec the elite divided roughly as it had in 1980 and so the operative process should have been polarization: voters' primary identification should be with one or the other contesting party, not with the elected elite as a whole.

This leaves the following questions:
– *Did the information-vote relationship differ between Quebec and the rest of Canada?*
For the rest of Canada a mainstream effect may have emerged. In Quebec, however, a more plausible expectation is for polarization.
– *If there was an information-vote relationship, did this stem from intrinsically cognitive differences, or did it just reflect background sociological factors, as indexed, for example, by education?*
If the real story is educational, and if real effect of education is not really cognitive, then it seems natural to ask:

– *Did those who knew more – or were better educated – vote Yes just because they* identified *with the elite?*

Identification need not be so much positive as absence of negatives: highly-educated voters are less likely than less well educated ones to believe that politicians are all crooks or liars. And highly-educated voters are less likely to be offended by minority-coalition building. Hence:

– *If there was an educational or informational gradient in the Yes vote, did it reflect greater willingness to accommodate minorities?*

In the last few questions, we have danced around the functional link between education and information. It makes sense, though, to come right out with the following query:

– *Was the effect of knowledge different from the effect of education?*

Finally, we need to pose questions about possible interactions between knowledge and other factors:

– *Did knowledge narrow or widen group differences?*

– *How did knowledge interact with the agenda-setting and intervention process? In particular, did knowing more make intervenors less necessary, or did it make their effect more efficient?*

The last question shades into being about low-information rationality, and brings us almost full circle.

MAKING SENSE OF THE VOTE
BY MAKING SENSE OF THE ACCORD

Figure 1–1 pulls all these considerations together in a rough schematic of how voters might make sense of a complex document and come to judgment. Exposition of the schematic is easiest if we start with the vote's most immediate sources and work up the chain.

Closest to the vote are *specific elements* in the proposal and *general arguments* on its behalf. Specific elements refer to substantive features of the ballot measure. General claims vary from simple ones about whether a given province or group won or lost to complex arguments that invited voters to reason as elites do (or believe they do): that is, to consider the consequences of *not* accepting the package; to transcend immediate personal or group stakes, and to see the deal as a whole or accept half a loaf.

Links among general arguments and specific elements are represented as reciprocal. For certain general arguments, response probably reflected support or opposition to specific elements. For other general arguments the reverse was probably true. For still others, general-specific links might have been truly reciprocal: some voters accept a general argument because they support a specific element, while others accept a specific element in which they have no intrinsic

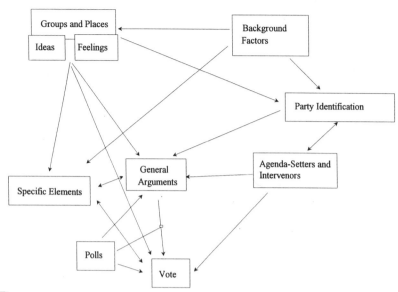

Figure 1–1
Reasoning about the Accord: General Schematic

interest as part of a package they support for general reasons.[25] It might seem to follow from our earlier discussion that response to general arguments should precede opinion on specific elements, in the spirit of a hierarchical reasoning chain (Sniderman et al., 1991). Some general arguments about a hastily announced constitutional package may indeed articulate abiding ideological or group-benefit themes, and so precede opinion on specifics. Other arguments may refer to the fit between measure and crisis. But at least one plausible general argument – that the voter's province was, on balance, a winner (loser) in the deal – seems absolutely to follow specifics, not lead them. Figure 1–1 summarizes all this complexity by evasion, with double-headed arrows. Detailed consideration of reasoning about the Charlottetown Accord must await chapter 4.

Polls are presented in Figure 1–1 as having three effects: on the vote itself, on acceptance/rejection of general arguments, and on the relevance of general arguments to choice. That they *can* have an independent effect is now on the record.[26] They might have mattered to voting on the Charlottetown Accord in particular for three reasons, each reflected by a causal arrow in Figure 1–1:

– First is the possibility outlined earlier in this chapter, that voters use polls to locate the ballot measure substantively. This is the basis for

the hypothesized direct effect on the vote (McKelvey and Orde-shook, 1986; Bartels, 1988).
- Second, polls might matter to the plausibility of certain general arguments, arguments based on fears about how other voters, Que-beckers especially, might react to a No vote in the rest of the country. This argues for the link from polls to certain attitudes, although most attitudes ought, in fact, to be unaffected by polls.
- Third is a possibility created by the fact that a simple national majority would not have sufficed to pass the Charlottetown Accord; a more complex formula was necessary. Thus, how much effort voters in one province were required to invest in their decision might depend on the balance of opinion elsewhere: if the Accord was obviously going down in Quebec, for example, why should voters in British Columbia bother to grapple with its complexities? This would weaken the link between all substantive considerations and the vote, a relationship represented in Figure 1–1 by an interaction term.

Now move another step up the reasoning hierarchy, to *agenda-set-ters* and *intervenors*. Although voters' response to an agenda-setter or intervenor may originate in the deepest recesses of Canadian history, agenda moves and interventions should be effective precisely to the extent that they are sharply etched against this background. They should thus be fresh and immediate in the voter's mind.

The most obvious condition for a voter's response to an agenda-setter or intervenor is where, if anywhere, he or she fits into the *party* system. But interventions themselves can affect voters' views of parties. Most interesting is when an intervention is contrary to what the historical record predicts. Such an intervention can be especially useful in building and splitting coalitions; it represents genuine information. It can also come as a betrayal and so may undermine long-standing party alignments.

Further in the background is *group sentiment*, with two parts: feelings and ideas. These are obvious factors, given the group bargaining that produced the Charlottetown Accord. But as Sniderman and his colleagues remind us, group feeling is the most universally available link in a reasoning chain. And group feeling is an abiding source of party preference. Mere feeling does not exhaust the relevance of group sentiments to the Accord, however. *Ideas* about groups in general, conceived separately from feelings toward particular groups, may have mattered. Ideology in some more general sense was not available to govern the 1992 choice, given all-party support of the Accord. But a document manifestly about a polity's group life was likely to engage general ideas, not just feelings, about groups.

Group sentiment cannot be detached from the structure of group membership (*background factors*). To the extent that interests were engaged in the Accord, simple membership ought to have been a factor in opinion on its elements. Group membership, like group sentiment, also informs party choice.

Not everything in the background is linked directly to everything in the foreground. There is no particular reason why background factors should have any direct impact on willingness to accept a general argument. But background certainly should influence opinion on those specific elements that refer to groups. Party identification need have no direct effect on opinion about specific elements, but should be intimately involved in accepting or rejecting general arguments made by parties' leading figures.

Where Figure 1–1 lays out the general schematic, Figure 1–2 outlines plausible effects on the schematic from substantive knowledge of the Accord. Discussion earlier in this chapter suggests two generic effects, main and interaction. Main effects take two forms:

- Simplest is a *direct* effect of knowledge on the vote itself. This tests for the existence of a mainstream effect: the more you know, the more likely you are to vote Yes. At the same time it also tests Preston Manning's opposite proposition, that to know the Accord was to dislike it. Absence of a relationship would point to the dominance of some kind of polarization.
- In *indirect* effects, the more one knows, the more supportive one is of minority rights in general, the more one likes (the less one dislikes) particular minority groups, and the more one likes (the less one dislikes) politicians, and the more open one might be to both specific elements in and general arguments for a complex proposal.

Interaction effects come in five forms, involving:

- *Background factors.* Does knowledge reduce group differences in the vote or widen them? If there is a national interest, a "right" answer for everyone, knowing more should reduce differences. If, conversely, groups have basic conflicts of interest, knowledge might actually widen group differences (Bartels, 1990, 1995).
- *Feelings about groups.* The less you know, the less should the impact of feelings about groups be mediated by opinion on other elements in the setup; instead feelings should operate on the vote only directly.
- *Ideas about groups.* The more you know, the more important ideas should be, absolutely and relative to feelings.

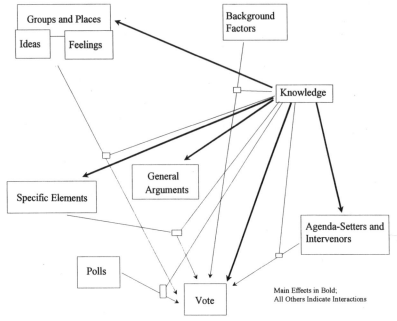

Figure 1–2
Reasoning about the Accord: Impact of Knowledge

- *Feelings about intervenors.* If you basically like the intervenor, then knowing more might incline you all the more to follow his or her lead; knowledge makes you aware of the basis, perhaps even the direction, of the very intervention. The flip side of this logic applies to an intervenor you basically dislike: the more you know the more you should be repelled by the intervention.
- *Polls.* If we observe that published polls mattered to the formation of preferences, this too must be fitted into the picture of political cognition. On one hand, processing poll information can be intellectually demanding and only relatively well-informed voters may be up to the task. On the other hand, if voters read polls only to find out what to think, polls should be most important for uninformed voters (McKelvey and Ordeshook, 1986).

The model should help us clarify a basic difference between Quebec and the rest of Canada: knowledge of the Charlottetown Accord should matter less in Quebec than in the rest of Canada as a main-effect factor in the vote. The Quebec elite divided roughly on party lines. Outside Quebec, the central players coalesced and removed the overt partisan basis of choice. If Canadians outside Quebec are like voters elsewhere, knowledge – or, perhaps more tellingly, education or other sociological factors associated with knowledge – should induce support for the elite as such. In Quebec the elite was not at issue and so knowledge – or, again, education – need not have been a factor. Among Quebeckers most available to the Yes, however, the structure may be quite like that in the rest of the country.

2 Coming Through Charlottetown

The seeds for the 1992 débâcle were sown a decade earlier. The process that ended with the Charlottetown Accord began as an attempt to close gaps left by a settlement entrenched in 1982. At various points, negotiations stalled as attempts to satisfy one interest provoked opposition from others. Satisfying one seemed to require satisfying all, hence the delicacy and complexity of the bargain ultimately reached at Charlottetown. At critical junctures the exact sequence by which certain elements got included forced other, probably fatal, inclusions.

1982: UNFINISHED BUSINESS?

If the failure of the Accord reaffirmed how hard it is to alter Canada's constitution, the very attempt indicated the intensity of pressure for change. The pressures arose, arguably, from an earlier round of constitutional innovation, the crisis of 1980–2. That crisis began as an attempt at consensual deal-making, in order to deliver the renewal of the federation promised by victorious No forces in Quebec's 1980 referendum. The attempt foundered in late 1980, whereupon the Trudeau Liberal government embarked on an essentially unilateral[1] drive to patriate the British North America (BNA) Act, with an amending formula and a charter of rights attached to it. Ultimately nine provinces agreed to a modified patriation package, which came home as the Constitution Act, 1982 and an altered and domesticated BNA Act, now styled the Constitution Act, 1867.

The 1982 settlement left at least two hostages to fortune. First, even though the 1980–2 crisis began, ostensibly, as an attempt to conciliate Quebec, it was never approved by Quebec's provincial political elite and it embodied elements that pointedly contradicted the main thrust of Quebec language policy. Second, it gave constitutional recognition to Canada's Aboriginal peoples but, apart from promising further conferences, was silent on land claims and self-government, the heart of the Aboriginal agenda. It thus raised Aboriginal hopes without providing means for their fulfilment.

No less critically, the 1982 settlement did not address a representational deficit, real or alleged, in Canada's central institutions. Over the 1970s, westerners, especially Albertans, railed at their exclusion from power at the centre. The Liberal party, the natural party of government before 1984, had a very weak western base. Canada's single-member plurality electoral system compounded the weakness, and in 1980 denied the Liberals so much as a single seat west of Winnipeg. Given the dominance of the executive in Canada, absence from the ranks of the governing party means, in effect, taxation without representation.[2] Making matters worse was the fact that some of the most searing taxation issues of the 1970s and early 1980s related to natural resources, the foundation of the western economy. And the continuing constitutional preoccupation with Quebec evoked its strongest backlash in the west. Questions of representation thus became a cottage industry in the region. The most frequently proposed change was to the Senate and by the mid-1980s the government of Alberta had committed itself to thoroughgoing Senate reform, embodied in its "Triple-E" (equal, elected, effective) proposal. There was a real question about how important representational questions truly were, but by emphasizing them repeatedly, western politicians created a hostage of their own.[3] Momentum for Senate reform was not halted by the election of a western-dominated Conservative government in 1984.

Responding to these pressures was difficult, however, because of two key elements in the 1982 settlement. First, under the 1982 amending formula change to certain parts of the constitution required consent by Parliament and every provincial legislature. If a package contained so much as one element subject to this unanimity rule the whole package would, for political reasons, also be subject to unanimity, lest the deal come unstuck. The unanimity rule, obviously, raised the threshold for change and empowered potential veto groups. The fact that legislatures, not governments, were the custodians for change was widely believed to signal the beginning of a more open and consultative era. Second, the Charter of Rights and Freedoms both responded to and nurtured an emergent rights agenda,[4] especially outside Quebec, and converted the 1982 settlement from mere rectification of an historical anomaly into something valued for itself. Henceforth, anything which threatened the Charter provoked resistance. As part of the Charter was aimed precisely at language policy, attempts to vindicate Quebec's claims ran headlong into the new Charter constituency.

The 1982 settlement also inhibited change by mere force of example. Although no referendum was held, the 1980–2 crisis had a plebiscitory feel. The federal government sought to break a constitutional impasse by proposing a package whose key features were popular with the electorate at large. Ottawa successfully presented itself as more in touch with mass sentiment than any other player. Groups hitherto excluded were mobilized through a public committee process to support the package and even to modify it. Subsequent changes behind closed doors seemed only to prove the consultative rule, as these changes were modified still further to accommodate a last-minute, mass mobilization by women's and Aboriginal interests. The lesson seemed clear: elite bargaining should *accommodate*, not supersede, deeply felt popular sentiment.

For all that, provinces and other interests felt forced to adopt stratagems contrary to the spirit of 1982. The three key agendas – of Quebec's provincial elite, of Aboriginal peoples, and of certain smaller provinces – could no longer be considered in isolation from each other, if they ever could, as one excluded party could veto proposals by another. All would have to be included or none would. Including all required delicate negotiations, best done behind closed doors. But then closed-door negotiation has been a way of life for Canada's political leaders. The fact that there are only ten first ministers makes deal-making a realistic possibility. Also critical is the fact that first ministers can deliver on commitments to each other, as each provincial government usually dominates its legislature. This domination seemed to render the distinction between government and legislature a hollow one.

THE ABORIGINAL AGENDA: RECIPE FOR FAILURE

The 1982 settlement required that a constitutional conference on Aboriginal matters take place within a year and this conference led to a package[5] which Parliament and all provincial legislatures except that of Quebec ratified. Quebec's refusal was not motivated by the Aboriginal issue itself but partook of a general refusal to countenance the 1982 settlement. The amendments were small, in any case, and did not address the hard question of self-government. One amendment was a commitment to invite Aboriginal leaders to deliberate with first ministers on further proposals. Three more conferences were held from 1984 to 1987 and with the return of Robert Bourassa to power in Quebec came the return of his province to the table. But key provincial actors had no real desire to proceed and the conferences led nowhere. In particular, first ministers disagreed fundamentally with Aboriginal leaders over how self-government should be recognized – up front as a matter of principle, with the details left for later, or only after agreement had been reached on its specific form.[6]

The end of this first post-1982 phase portended key features of the next one. Bourassa refused to attend the last Aboriginal-rights conference, in March 1987, to protest slow progress on Quebec's demands. The contrast between the protracted public commitment to Aboriginal questions and the seeming foot-dragging on Quebec was not to be missed. In fact, public negotiations on Aboriginal questions were going nowhere, while private negotiations on Quebec's agenda were just about to bear fruit.

DROWNING IN MEECH LAKE

May and June 1987 saw two first ministers' conferences which produced what seemed at first to be a constitutional miracle – reconciliation of Quebec to the 1982 settlement. The package, the Meech Lake Accord, corresponded to proposals first made in a 1985 Quebec Liberal party policy document and reaffirmed by the now Liberal government at a 1986 conference at Mont Gabriel. Quebec asked for five things: recognition as a "distinct society" within Canada, to mitigate restraints by the Charter on the will of Quebec legislative majorities; restoration of the province's veto over constitutional amendment, widely assumed to exist before 1982 and arguably gambled away in the late stages of the crisis; enhanced power for Quebec over immigration; the right to name three civil law justices from the province to the Supreme Court of Canada; and an end to Ottawa's unilateral spending power.

By the standards of earlier negotiating positions, these seemed decidedly moderate demands and the other provinces proved responsive. Most pointedly, in the 1986 "Edmonton Declaration" the provinces agreed to give priority to this "Quebec round," and to refrain from bootlegging their own agendas onto it. They did not, however, just accept Quebec's demands. Turning the Mont Gabriel package into the Meech Lake Accord required two basic further steps, each of which reflected constraints imposed by the 1982 settlement. Some demands had to be generalized to all provinces, as a reflection of the fact that some of Quebec's demands required unanimous consent. Things which could not be generalized had to be adjusted in light of the coalition which had formed around the Charter.

Four of the five demands could be generalized. Quebec got its veto, but so did everybody else. The immigration demand was met by entrenching an earlier administrative agreement and offering similar entrenchments to other provinces. Quebec got to nominate three justices to the Supreme Court, but the federal government retained final say. Meanwhile all provinces got the right to submit names, although places on the bench were not formally reserved for any other province. The federal government agreed to make its spending in areas of exclusive provincial jurisdiction subject to provincial consent. Seven provinces had to agree for a program to be established and any of the (up to) three dissident provinces could establish its own program and receive the fiscal equivalent, provided the program met national objectives. There was much debate over this element and some adjustment of it, as many feared that limiting the spending power would undercut the federal government's role in social programs, which would eventually wither. On the other side it was argued that this clause represented the first formal acknowledgment of the spending power's very existence.

The one concession which could not be extended to other provinces was the distinct society clause, as any extension would gut it of practical significance. Here the challenge was to adjust it to the Charter. As worded it became an interpretive clause, not a trump that Quebec could play unilaterally, but still a potentially powerful argument before the courts. Also incorporated in the clause was a recognition of official language minorities, not something Quebec sought. But Quebec was able to get a deal that treated official language minorities and the francophone majority in Quebec asymmetrically: while minority interests were *protected*, francophone majority interests were to be *promoted*.

On top of all this, a hesitant move was made on Senate reform. By April 1987 Don Getty of Alberta could no longer maintain to his own constituents that this must remain the Quebec round. That month, he committed himself to raising the Senate at the next round of deliberations. One suggestion going the rounds was to give provinces power of appointment, to create an incentive for Ottawa to devise a new second chamber. In the end, a parallel was drawn with the new method of Supreme Court appointment: provinces would prepare a short list of nominees and the federal government would make the ultimate appointment. Ottawa retained the right to reject all names on a given list and call for another one.

Although the Accord was at first greeted warmly, things did not work out according to plan. A three-year ratification window was adopted and Parliament and eight legislatures ratified the Accord in fairly short order. But in two provinces things came unstuck quickly. In New Brunswick, Richard Hatfield suffered one of the worst defeats in Canadian history. Frank McKenna, the victor, had expressed doubts about the Accord and did not feel bound by his thoroughly discredited predecessor. In Manitoba, commitment to the Accord was in doubt from the beginning and Premier Howard Pawley warned other first ministers that an elaborate public hearing process would be required. Before hearings began his government fell and the ensuing election yielded a minority Conservative government. The most startling gains, though, were made by the Liberal party, whose leader, Sharon Carstairs, made opposition to the Accord the centrepiece of her campaign. Defeat also licensed New Democrats to voice their own doubts. Although the new Conservative premier, Gary Filmon, was not particularly opposed to the Accord, his ability to act was limited. Alone among premiers, Filmon lacked the basic attribute of an executive-federalism deal-maker – domination of his home legislature.

Filmon's task became even harder in December 1988. In that month the Supreme Court struck down the commercial sign provisions of Law 101, Quebec's charter of the French language. The political theatre that ensued was fatal for the Accord and drearily familar from decades of earlier history. To Quebeckers, the decision was a pointed example of the power of Pierre Trudeau's charter to strike at the wishes of that province's majority. That Bourassa had promised bilingual signs in the 1985 election got lost in the shuffle. This time, in any case, Quebec could fight back. Section 33 of the Constitution Act, 1982 allows provinces to invoke a "notwithstanding clause" in legislative preambles to shield statutes against certain parts of the Charter of Rights. Normally, the clause cannot neutralize court rulings expressly on official language minority rights. But the signs decision was not about official language rights. Rather, the court acted under the Charter's general guarantees of speech, here extending them to commercial speech. The Quebec government thus could respond by sheltering new restrictions under the notwithstanding clause. The reaction outside Quebec was violent. The new measure, Law 178, was taken to indicate what the distinct society clause really meant and, indeed, to foreshadow precisely what would be in store once the Accord was entrenched. Some commentators who had gone along with the language restrictions in Law 101 objected to the new ones, even though they were less restrictive. What had changed was the context in which they were adopted. Whereas Law 101 was passed by an avowedly sovereignist government before 1982, when few challenged the power of provincial majorities, Law 178 seemed a direct assault on the liberties now secured by the Charter. What is more, the Bourassa government which passed Law 178 had just supported the Conservatives and the Canada-US Free Trade Agreement in the November 1988 election. Where in the 1960s and 1970s Quebec nationalism struck many on the English-Canadian left as a progressive force, it now seemed unmasked as just another manifestation of political reaction.[7] On the English-Canadian right, the new sign law simply reinforced resistance to all concessions to French power.[8]

Finally there emerged Clyde Wells as premier of Newfoundland. Wells had been a legal adviser to the federal government during the 1980–1 crisis and represented it in constitutional litigation against his own province. He was a formidable advocate of a centralized federation, of the values in the Charter, and of Senate reform. Shortly after his government was formed in 1989 the Newfoundland legislature rescinded its ratification of the Accord, dropping the number of ratifying provinces to seven.

There matters more or less stood as the ratification deadline, 23 June 1990, approached. The lack of forward movement in the nonratifying provinces led to the creation of a committee under MP and sometime cabinet minister Jean Charest, which canvassed opinion mainly outside Quebec. The committee made two proposals of lasting importance. First, out of the Manitoba task force hearings (the ones Howard Pawley warned would be necessary) there emerged a counter to the distinct society clause, a "Canada clause." Charest and the Mulroney government both mentioned that this might be added to the Accord as a preamble. Second, it was proposed that the Accord make further Senate change subject to the unanimity rule, a proposal that angered westerners. Charest recommended that, if after some period no changes were made under the unanimity rule, Senate modifications would revert to a non-unanimous formula.

The committee met a mixed reception. The Canada clause was vetoed by Robert Bourassa,[9] but it resurfaced after 1990. A ministerial crisis was triggered, ending with the defection of Lucien Bouchard and some other government members. Bouchard and his former Conservative colleagues, together with two former Liberals disgusted at the selection of Jean Chrétien as leader, formed the Bloc Québécois.

To try and break the impasse, the first ministers were summoned one last time. In a week-long final meeting, the existing text of the Accord remained essentially unchanged, as Bourassa could not retreat from what were clearly his province's minimum conditions. The only room to move was on the hitherto suppressed Senate dimension. Here spring 1990 anticipated summer 1992. Picking up on the Charest committee and speaking for the government, Conservative Senator Lowell Murray suggest a three-year window for keeping the Senate under the unanimity rule, whereupon Senate reform would move to a special 7–50 formula: seven provinces comprising a majority of the population, of which one must be Quebec, two must be from the west, and these two must include at least 50 percent of the region's population, and two must be from the Atlantic region (no population provision); Ontario would have no veto. Thence discussion moved to a proposal by Joe Ghiz of Prince Edward Island: allow the two biggest provinces to retain their twenty-four Senate seats; give all other provinces but Prince Edward Island ten seats; give Prince Edward Island five. This would allow the seven medium-size provinces to dominate the chamber. The problem was obvious, however: Quebec's proportion would drop, a disastrous outcome for what was still described as the "Quebec round." The impasse was resolved by Ontario, which surrendered six seats, and New Brunswick and Nova Scotia, which surrendered two each. These ten seats were then given in twos to Newfoundland and each western province; each medium-size province would thus have eight seats, almost half the Ontario share. Prince Edward Island, the smallest province, retained its long-standing share of four, and thus had exactly half the seats of any middle-sized province. For Canada outside Quebec, the scheme seemed to be a workable compromise between overrepresenting small provinces and not forcing the seeming absurdity of setting Prince Edward Island equal to Ontario. Best of all, Quebec retained exactly its former share in the upper house. With the Senate logjam broken, the two remaining holdout provinces, Newfoundland and Manitoba, agreed to present the Accord to their respective legislatures. In each province, however, there was a hitch.

For Manitoba to meet the three-year deadline, MLAs had to give unanimous consent to expeditious treatment of the Accord. This was not forthcoming. The procedural blow, refusal of unanimity, was struck by the legislature's one Aboriginal member, Elijah Harper. The complete exclusion of Aboriginal issues from the Meech Lake Accord had come back to haunt the process. Harper was, in a sense, repaying Bourassa for the latter's boycott of the fourth conference on Aboriginal constitutional issues. If in March 1987 the preoccupation with Aboriginal questions contrasted with stalemate on Quebec ones, in June 1990 the opposite seemed true. In the end, the deadline arrived and the Manitoba legislature simply could not proceed.

In Newfoundland, the hitch was that Clyde Wells agreed to refer the matter but not to make a recommendation, at least did not guarantee to recommend a Yes. The House of Assembly did hear representations, including from the prime minister, and was getting ready to vote. Once it became clear that Manitoba was not going to proceed, however, Wells decided to spare his own House the agony of making a pointless decision. His overall strategy and the immediate circumstances of the decision remain controversial. But it was final, as was the outcome in Manitoba, and all the negotiations in 1986–7 and the last-minute moves in June 1990 came to nothing.

FROM MEECH LAKE
TO THE PEARSON BUILDING

The Process in Quebec

With the collapse of Meech, Quebec went into a sort of splendid isolation. In the National Assembly the premier asserted that Quebec was master of its fate: "Quoi qu'on dise et quoi qu'on fasse, le Québec est, aujourd'hui et toujours, une société distincte, libre et capable d'assumer son destin et son développement" (22 June 1990). Two days later, the feast of St-Jean-Baptiste, now officially the Fête Nationale, witnessed an enormous outpouring of nationalist feeling. Over the summer, poll readings of sovereignist sentiment soared (Cloutier et al., 1992). Bourassa vowed to avoid eleven-sided negotiations and, indeed, finessed the question of negotiation in any form. Over the next several months some in Quebec saw the province as girding itself to decide on sovereignty. Others saw Quebec as formulating its conditions for continued adhesion to Canada. Either way, the sovereignty option seemed back on the table.

Quebeckers' consultation with themselves took place in two principal forums: the Bélanger-Campeau Commission (officially, the Commission on the Political and Constitutional Future of Quebec), which comprised much of the province's elite; and the Constitutional Committee of the Quebec Liberal Party, known as the Allaire Committee. Although the Allaire Committee had been only a minor appendage to the party, it reported first (29 January 1991) and set the tone for what followed. Allaire proposed to move the Quebec position far beyond Meech; most important was its demand for a transfer of twenty-two powers. It is doubtful that Bourassa took this demand seriously, but for tactical reasons he made the Allaire report's demands his own. Among the tactical considerations was the overwhelming support given the Allaire proposals by the party's youth wing, led by Mario

Dumont (Russell, 1992, p. 159ff). Later, when Quebec had to consider the offer actually made by the rest of Canada, the hard line of the Allaire report lurked in the background.

The Bélanger-Campeau Commision reported on 29 March 1991 and made two key points. It argued that only an offer fully binding the federal government and other provinces merited consideration by Quebeckers; there should be no repetition of the Meech débâcle. It proposed what came to be the timetable for further deliberation in the country as a whole: a deadline of 26 October 1992 and a Quebec referendum on that date. If no binding offer was forthcoming or if the offer was transparently contemptible, the vote would be on sovereignty. This Quebec timetable became the Canada-wide one. The first step in setting the timetable was the passage of Law 150, which proposed a sovereignty question only. This was an extraordinary sequence of events, but it may have contained a trap for the nationalists. On one hand, the commission's proposal for a referendum on sovereignty was remarkable given the publicly federalist commitments of co-chair Michel Bélanger. On the other hand, the fact that even sovereignists on the commission signed a final report alluding to offers from the rest of Canada empowered Bourassa to negotiate, or at least to entertain such offers.[10]

Significantly, the two-year isolation did not start well, for reasons that looked back to Meech Lake and forward to Charlottetown. The summer of 1990 was the hottest since 1885 for Aboriginal-white relations. The bitterest conflict occurred in Quebec, at Oka, just as the province was absorbing the rejection of the Meech Lake Accord. The Oka dispute became an armed stand-off lasting several weeks. The one fatality in the dispute was an officer of the Sûreté du Québec. In a collateral confrontation, Mohawks nearer Montreal blocked a major bridge.[11] Oka seemed to portend more clashes, given that Quebec's development strategy envisaged hydroelectric power development in areas yet to be covered by agreements with their Aboriginal inhabitants. Support, at least in the abstract, for Aboriginal interests seemed widespread in the larger community. Clearly, Aboriginal peoples were arriving as a constitutional force, although support for their interests was not accompanied by equally widespread understanding of what these interests were.

Outside Quebec: The First Public Phase

The federal government got from the collapse of the Meech Lake Accord to the agreement at Charlottetown through wide popular consultation. The failure of Meech seemed to deliver the message that the people at large would no longer tolerate being excluded from deliberation over their own constitution. This time they would be consulted, even if it was only to bore them to death. Various forums were established and the ultimate consultation, a referendum, was aired. But in 1990–1 the question of how the process would conclude was finessed.

Two early post-Meech forums staked out ground that the federal government later evaded. One was the Spicer Commission (officially A Citizens' Forum on Canada's Future), which went the populist route and became a sounding board for all sorts of pent-up rage. The report confirmed that an offer to Quebec was still going to be a hard sell outside that province. On the other hand, the commission's small-scale deliberative forums expressed far less vituperative opinions than those revealed by self-selected calls to its 1–800 number. About the same time a joint House-Senate committee, chaired by Senator Gérald Beaudoin and MP Jim Edwards, considered the amending formula. Among other things, the committee urged the federal government to arm itself with the power to hold a referendum. Initially, nothing came of this suggestion.

A third, executive-level process involved extensive polling and elite negotiations, and led to the federal government's own proposals, tabled as "Shaping Canada's Future Together" in September 1991. These proposals addressed, more or less, most of the questions outlined earlier in this chapter.[12] Significantly, the core proposals did not require unanimous provincial consent. Key elements from the Meech round were brought forward. A genuflection was made toward Aboriginal self-government but, as before, no move was made toward recognizing self-government as an inherent right, to be accepted in principle before its modalities were specified. And a directly elected Senate overrepresenting small provinces – but not giving each province equal representation – was proposed. Two new elements also got injected into the debate, one by inclusion in the proposals, the other by exclusion.

To get something in return for giving some powers away and perhaps to create a bargaining counter, Ottawa demanded enhanced powers over the economy and the right to strike down barriers to the interprovincial flow of commodities, capital, and people. Concern over interprovincial barriers was growing, thanks especially to competitive pressures unleashed by the Canada-US Free Trade Agreement. But most protagonists of enhanced federal power over the economy, including the power to strike down provincial barriers, did not command concentrated political power themselves.[13] It was natural, thus, to suspect that Ottawa's own emphasis on the economic union was as much tactical as sincere.

But striking down interprovincial barriers, even as Ottawa proposed once again to back off its spending power, raised fears on the left. There thus emerged a demand for a "social charter," a bill of social and economic rights. As some provincial barriers to trade are justified in terms of mitigating the effects of either economic adjustment or chronic disadvantages, a social charter might ensure that governments did not use the rhetoric of the market to escape their responsibilities. At the same time, the jurisdictional decentralization that seemed inevitable to accommodate Quebec invited the perverse logic of fiscal federalism: small or poor provinces would be unable to resist pressures to undersupply services, relative to what their electorates would strictly prefer.[14] A social charter might force their hands. Its strongest advocates were the NDP provincial governments, especially the Rae government in Ontario. But in September 1991 no concession was made to this interest.

Hints were dropped of an all-Canada referendum. Quite apart from concerns to give constitutional change popular legitimacy, there may also have been a deeply strategic reason for an all-Canada popular referral: to force Quebec and the rest of Canada to vote on the same question. Otherwise Bourassa might frame questions for Quebeckers whose main purpose would be to outmanœuvre the rest of Canada. One possibility was that Bourassa would pose two questions. The first would present the rest-of-Canada package along with Quebec's additional demands; the second would ask if sovereignty is the preferred alternative should the rest of Canada rebuff the demands in the first question.[15] At this stage such strategic reckoning went nowhere and talk of a Canada-wide vote was scotched by the Conservatives' Quebec caucus, which feared that a federal referendum would seem to hijack Quebec's own initiative. At this point no thought appears to have been given to tailoring a rest-of-Canada vote to the one inside Quebec. Although the federal government eventually found a way around this problem, the time required for it do so indicated remarkable insensitivity to the West, since British Columbia and Alberta had already committed themselves to direct votes on any further constitutional proposals. These provinces' commitments and Quebec's own initiative meant that 45 percent of Canadian voters would vote on a package, one way or another.

In the meantime, public consideration of the proposals fell to yet another joint House-Senate committee, originally chaired by Senator Claude Castonguay and MP Dorothy Dobbie. The joint committee nearly broke up in a welter of partisan bickering. It was reconstituted in November 1991, with the resignation of Senator Castonguay and his replacement by Gérald Beaudoin, co-chair of the earlier committee on the amending formula. Beaudoin-Dobbie, as the committee was now called, was supplemented by five conferences, each on a segment of the proposals and sponsored by a nongovernmental agency. This seemed to get things back on track. The committee presented its report, *A Renewed Canada*, on 28 February 1992.

Back Behind Closed Doors

At this point provincial governments, temporarily sidelined but still the gatekeepers of constitutional change, resumed pride of place. On 12 March 1992 provincial ministerial representatives and representatives of key Aboriginal organizations began translating these public phase deliberations into an agreement that enough governments could live with to satisfy the requirements of the amending formula. The shift to first ministers may have allowed interests associated with the Liberals and NDP to weigh more in the balance than they had before, as these two parties controlled most provinces. The two parties aside, however, the circle of consultation abruptly shrank.

Ambiguity shrouded two key players. Quebec was still officially aloof. If continued absence made sense in terms of Quebec's self-stylization as awaiting offers but otherwise maintaining its dignity, it may have compromised the process fatally. Actors holding Quebec's proxy (Ottawa, Ontario, and Alberta by turns) seemed to have trouble discerning what Quebec's irreducible minimum was,[16] while interests opposed to Quebec felt all the more empowered. As for Ottawa, two questions hung over its representative, Joe Clark, minister for constitutional affairs. Was he really acting on government authority or was he freelancing? Did the prime minister even want him to succeed? As represented by Clark, Ottawa no longer seemed to worry about defending a position; the essential thing was the agreement itself, any agreement. Notwithstanding referendum commitments in three provinces, little thought seems to have been given to the saleability of the package to the general public. But then, the multilateral package may not have been intended to be the thing referred. It seems pretty clear that key Ottawa actors, notably the prime minister, expected Joe Clark's version of the endgame to fail. Once it became obvious that agreement was impossible, Brian Mulroney would step in with something like the September package. If seven of ten premiers could not agree to it or to something similarly narrowly conceived, then perhaps a referendum could force their hand. The government secured passage of Bill C-81, which enabled it to conduct referendums on its own terms,[17] including in fewer than ten provinces. Mulroney indicated that, should the premiers not agree by 15 July, he would make a written proposal on that date.[18]

Fear of pre-emption seemed to lead the premiers and Joe Clark to forestall Brian Mulroney, to force his own hand. The first ministers were now so immersed in their own process that they seemed not to see that a referendum shadow was lengthening anyway. Even less did they see that the prospect of a referendum should have disciplined their bargaining. The deal struck on 7 July 1992, the "Pearson accord," was patently unsaleable in Quebec and yet for the moment stood as English Canada's offer to that province. At this package's heart was a concession to Alberta that few would have predicted: a Senate in which each province was equally represented. Seats were to be filled by direct election under a proportional representation (PR) formula, the Single Transferable Vote. On most legislation this Senate would have a veto, although certain questions would require extraordinary Senate majorities to overturn the will of the House. What started as Don Getty's wishful thinking about the Triple-E had now been endorsed by Ontario, a province with much to lose from such a Senate, and by the federal government, at least by Joe Clark.[19]

Not only did the Pearson accord fail to give more jurisdiction to Quebec in its own right, but it also promised to reduce drastically Quebec's power at the centre. Robert Bourassa would almost certainly prefer the status quo to any conceivable lineal descendant of the Pearson accord. But he could not realistically submit the accord just to have it trumped by the status quo: presenting Pearson as the best possible deal would only validate sovereignists' argument that the Canadian system was unworkable. Under Law 150 if he did not put some relative of Pearson to the Quebec electorate, he would have to put sovereignty to them. At that point, polls still suggested that a majority would endorse sovereignty over the status quo (Lisée, 1994b, p. 274). By this time Bourassa himself had put aside any sovereignist pretence and wanted to avoid any choice which might favour a sovereignist outcome. Now he was forced to come to the table and try to overturn the Pearson deal.

FROM THE PEARSON BUILDING
TO CHARLOTTETOWN

The accord ultimately signed at Charlottetown on 28 August 1992 reflected the specific sequence of choices over July and August and makes sense only in light of the 7 July deal. Most importantly, Charlottetown sought to minimize the damage done by the Pearson concessions on a revised Senate. Equal representation in the Senate, once on the table, could not come off. The challenge shifted to drawing the representation rule's teeth. If what emerged neutralized the Senate – it is not clear that it did – it also created a huge hostage to fortune.

Direct election of senators was finessed. Where the Pearson accord envisaged direct election by PR, the Charlottetown Accord left the matter for each province to decide for itself. Direct election was a special problem for Quebec, as the provincial government was anxious that any new senators from the province be its agents.[20] Even if Bourassa conceded direct election, PR would still be unacceptable as it would undermine a logic which had served Quebec well: the plurality formula facilitates bloc-like behaviour by Quebec voters and has helped make the province the pivot for making and breaking governments (Johnston et al., 1992; Bakvis and Macpherson, 1995). Quebec hoped to reproduce the bloc logic in the Senate. All this was a bit vague, however. The Charlottetown Accord did not stipulate in so many words that choice of senators was anything other than by direct election. Perhaps sentiment for direct election would be so overwhelming, even in Quebec, that provinces would be forced to adopt the Pearson system. Then again, the logic of faction might force other provinces to follow Quebec and constitute their own Senate delegations as blocs. In any case, the principles of direct election and PR had been compromised.

More critical, however, was another set of changes, at the heart of which was a guarantee for Quebec of 25 percent of seats in the House of Commons. The logic of the guarantee was tied to how the Charlottetown Accord proposed to resolve House-Senate disagreements. The sliding-majorities system envisaged in the Pearson accord was replaced by a tripartite division of policy areas. At one end, natural resources initiatives (Alberta's abiding concern) could be blocked absolutely in the Senate by a simple majority for the negative; at the other end, the government's budget, the essence of Westminster-style confidence, was immune to Senate veto;[21] and for all matters in between, House-Senate disputes would be resolved by simple majority in a joint sitting. MPs would greatly outnumber senators but much would depend on how closely each house divided and on how sharply the representative foundations of each house diverged. This brings us to changes in the makeup of the House.

Senate representation had been equalized by shrinkage; where provincial delegations in the old Senate ranged from four to twenty-four seats, now each delegation would number only six. At the next step, any province losing Senate seats was exactly compensated in the House. This actually brought the House close to its original constitutive principle, representation by population. But given the original motives behind Senate reform, the symbolism was exactly wrong. Under the basic scheme, as Alberta and British Columbia each started with six senators and thus suffered no representational loss, neither would gain anything in the House. It was symbolically necessary to boost their House representation. But the boosts actually given were small and still left Alberta and British Columbia less well represented in the new House than in the old. Arguably, no imaginable shift could have sufficed, as the basic compensation scheme gave Quebec and Ontario thirty-six seats (eighteen each), a gain roughly equal to each westernmost province's standing share. The symbolism was disastrous; what started as an attempt to increase western power ended up looking like further reinforcement of central Canadian domination. Maybe the Senate really would evolve into a Triple-E on the Getty model and this would truly shift power toward the smaller provinces, but maybe it would not. The primary fact about any Senate proposal is that mere mention of the name invokes disgust, even in the West. Meanwhile, voters are habituated to thinking of power being derived from seats in the House. And there, the balance had just shifted dramatically *toward*, not away from, the large provinces. The meagre compensation that Alberta and British Columbia received just rubbed salt in the wound.

Any abstruseness that lingered around this argument was banished by the next move: Quebec was guaranteed 25 percent of House seats, roughly its historic share. Even if joint House-Senate sittings were the new power centre, Quebec would still carry its traditional weight and this weight – itself a bone of contention – was guaranteed *never* to drop.[22] Precedents were widely cited, such as the existing Senate floor for small provinces, the tradition of buffering intercensal representational losses, and the deliberate overrepresentation of rural areas. The examples were weak, however. Most had little effect and none guaranteed any province a percentage share. The arithmetic of the 25 percent guarantee, especially combined with the probable continuance of the other devices, would inevitably tell most heavily against a fast-growing province, since guaranteeing a floor for Quebec meant guaranteeing a ceiling for British Columbia. Even where rapid growth was not a consideration, the 25 percent guarantee smacked of special privilege and stirred tribal memories.

For all that, Bourassa faced an even bigger credibility challenge than Harcourt of British Columbia or Getty of Alberta. The gap between his government's apparent official position – acceptance of the Allaire report's demand for radical decentralization – and the Charlottetown Accord was wide. How could he explain away the fact that he accepted tiny jurisdictional gains while the official platform of his party listed twenty-two powers that ought to be transferred? The likely explanations would only be embarrassing: that he did not care about division of powers himself; that he presented his demands too late in the process; most critically that he presented them only *after* extracting the costly 25 percent guarantee.[23] His own party, at least, gave the Accord what seemed like an overwhelming endorsement on the weekend of 29–30 August 1992. This may have been the most critical step, for it ensured that his government would survive, whatever the outcome of the referendum. And he did secure the endorsement of Claude Castonguay, whose articulation of Quebec's interests ought to have been very credible. Set against this, Bourassa could not win over his party's most audible nationalists, Jean Allaire and Mario Dumont. Allaire resisted the Yes at the August convention and made his support for the No official on 3 September. Mario Dumont also opposed the Yes in August and formally endorsed the No on 8 September.

At first, the clearest winners at Charlottetown appeared to be Aboriginal peoples. Their very presence at the table was unprecedented and their representatives won what had seemed unthinkable only months before: recognition of an inherent right to self-government. But how much did they really win? And did all members of the Aboriginal communities want what their negotiators sought?

BACK INTO THE OPEN

By the time the Charlottetown Accord was drafted, a referendum seemed all but inevitable. Bill C-81 had broken the conceptual logjam and a referendum outside Quebec could be wedded to the process inside that province. Early indications were that the Accord was popular. Nonetheless, it was bound to provoke rhetorical battle on several fronts. On specific elements in the deal, the following became key questions:

– Was it a victory for Quebec, with the distinct society clause, veto, 25 percent guarantee, and concessions on the division of powers? This interpretation would be a positive inside Quebec but elsewhere made the Accord vulnerable to claims that it was yet another sellout to French power. Alternatively, was the Accord a humiliating loss for Quebec, with a weak distinct society clause, no more than cosmetic movement on the division of powers, a veto which both came too late and gave other provinces power over Quebec as surely as it gave Quebec power over them, and a dangerous shift in power at the centre that no shuffling of House seats could disguise?

- Did change to the House and Senate bring the representative system more in line with regional demands? But if so, did this threaten Quebec's interests? Or did Senate reform just add another layer of politicians, when all the public really wanted was abolition of the old institution?
- Did the Accord finally bring justice to Aboriginal peoples and enable them to resurrect indigenous forms of government? Or did it expose others to injustice – including Aboriginal women – by compromising the Charter and entrenching little oligarchies? Then again, did it give too little to Aboriginal peoples, even as it confirmed their subordination to federal and provincial law?[24]

Also invoked would be general claims. Much of the case for the Accord rested on the necessity of compromise. But was this the best possible one? A well-crafted compromise would allow the country to move on to other questions. The argument that this compromise was the best feasible one referred to the number of players who had to be conciliated, given the rules of amendment (provincial governments) and given a reading of who carried special moral authority (Aboriginal peoples). Players who were sceptical about Quebec's claims nonetheless accepted that realization of their own constitutional ambitions required accommodating Quebec. Advocates of the Quebec agenda accepted that realizing it required accommodation of strategic interests outside Quebec. To say this, however, is also to admit that the compromise had the defect of its virtues: arguments for the Yes in Quebec could readily become arguments for the No in the rest of the country, and vice versa.

Was the compromise even necessary? Here the argument went as follows: if the Accord failed, the constitutional crisis would continue; the country would probably split; the split would be bad for the economies of both Quebec and the rest of Canada; a split might engender further splits; and any split might deliver both (all) parts into the hands of the United States. Critical to the argument from necessity was the credibility of secession by Quebec combined with a fear of its effects. Not everyone feared the effects of secession. Nor did everyone take the secession prospect seriously. A familiar script in English Canada has Quebec always asking for more; secession threats are merely bluffs waiting to be called.

SOME GROUND RULES

Bill C-81 allowed Ottawa to conduct a referendum in any set of provinces and on any question it chose. The British Columbia and Alberta governments deemed that the intent of their own legislation was fulfilled by the national referendum.[25] This allowed Ottawa to make the process in the rest of Canada substantially parallel to Quebec's but to leave the Quebec vote in the province's own hands. Most importantly, Quebec could not be flooded with money from outside. Quebec's legislation (not Law 150, but a permanent statute, the one under which the 1980 referendum was fought) limited each side to one committee, formed out of the division on the question in the National Assembly, and imposed the same spending ceiling on each committee. The federal legislation, in contrast, was permissive: it limited what an individual committee could spend but imposed no ceiling on the number of committees. The only attempt at equalization lay in the provision of free and equal broadcast time to each side; paid broadcasting was another matter. Subject to these different rules, the same question was put to electorates inside and outside Quebec on the same day.[26]

Strictly speaking, the Quebec campaign was shorter than the federal one. Quebec law required twenty days to lapse between the end of debate in the National Assembly and the commencement of campaign hostilities and set a twenty-eight-day minimum for the campaign. Exactly this sequence ensued, as the Charlottetown process laboured under the Quebec time constraint. The federal law did not impose a waiting period but required a campaign of at least thirty-six days. Counting back from Quebec's date meant that the federal campaign lasted eight more days than Quebec's.[27]

The referendum had no legal force, except possibly in Alberta. Despite universal agreement on what to call it, the vote was in fact a plebiscite, just as in 1898 and 1942.[28] The key players committed themselves to respecting the wishes of the people, but no guidelines existed for how the people's votes should be counted. Early in the campaign, Joe Clark pre-empted the matter by stating that each province had to deliver a majority for any government to be morally bound. This may have reflected the fact that some elements in the Accord required unanimous provincial consent. Even though one could imagine circumstances under which governments whose own electorates said No would agree to respect a preponderant Yes in the rest of the country, it may have been tactically necessary to say that each province must say Yes, to deter wilful defection by electorates in individual provinces. The unanimity rule may only have been a double majority requirement in disguise, a guarantee for Quebec. Be that as it may, Mr Clark's fiat set a very high threshold. At a minimum, everyone seemed to accept that there had to be a national double majority: if Quebec said No, there would be no deal, whatever happened elsewhere.

THE CAMPAIGN IN QUEBEC

And from very early on it seemed clear that Quebec would indeed say No. Although the first polls after the final Charlottetown meeting on 28 August suggested that Quebeckers were closely divided, it was not long before polls confirmed the strength of anti-Accord sentiment.[29] For the official campaign period the path of vote intentions appears in Figure 2–1.[30] The figure confirms that Quebec leaned to the No before the official campaign began. Nothing in the campaign seemed to have an interpretable effect and no trend manifested itself. There is a hint of an uptick after 12 October (the date of a debate between Robert Bourassa and Jacques Parizeau), but if there was a surge it quickly subsided. The last week may have brought a recovery; by voting day the Yes share seems to have been about ten points higher than a week before. The last surge, if it was one, did not suffice. In Quebec the campaign was over before it officially began.

Jean Allaire's early accession to the No camp may have hurt; certainly it came around the time that the Quebec Yes share began to drop. Although Allaire's move came as little surprise, it added credibility to the No side under circumstances which foreshadowed a critical theme later in the campaign. Allaire's career had been obscure before 1990, but his report helped him speak for the broad middle of the premier's own party. His credibility was further enhanced by the fact that he risked paying a price for supporting the No side, as any prospects for his advancement in the Quebec Liberal party would be blocked. And when he joined the official Quebec No committee on the 11 September, he did so on his own terms, for he signalled that his opposition was solely to the Charlottetown Accord and that his No was not a vote for sovereignty.

On the other hand, Bourassa gained a critical nationalist ally in Claude Castonguay. It was at Castonguay's urging that Bourassa had withdrawn assent to the Victoria Charter twenty years earlier. Castonguay distanced himself from the rest-of-Canada process the previous November when he resigned his co-chairmanship of the Castonguay-Dobbie road show. Most critically, perhaps, he opposed the Pearson accord. He was one onlooker who could say that the movement from Pearson to Charlottetown was great enough to justify a Yes without being accused of doing so just to save his own political position.

But then things took a dramatic turn for the worse, as a telling attack on Bourassa's negotiating skills came from his own advisers. The critical evidence lay in the transcript of cellular telephone conversations between the deputy minister of intergovernmental affairs, Diane

---

Campaign Chronology: Quebec

August

30 – Parti libéral du Québec convention endorses Accord

September

3 – Jean Allaire comes out for the No

7 – Société St-Jean-Baptiste warns that Accord will threaten Quebec language legislation

8 – Mario Dumont comes out for the No, releases anti-Accord document on Liberal party letterhead

   – Quebec's version of question tabled in National Assembly

14 – Quebec Superior Court grants ten-day injunction to prevent publication of Diane Wilhelmy transcript

   – André Tremblay, adviser to Premier Bourassa, allegedly tells Quebec Chamber of Commerce that Bourassa so exhausted by end of Charlottetown process that he had difficulty understanding nuances in English

17 – *La Presse* names André Tremblay as Wilhelmy's interlocutor

18 – Quebec trade unions come out for No

28 – Mulroney claims No will lead to end of Canada, rips up copy of the Accord

30 – injunction on Wilhelmy tape lifted

October

1 – Wilhelmy-Tremblay conversation published

2 – Mulroney lists "31 gains" for Quebec

6 – Chrétien and Bouchard debate on Radio-Canada

10 – legal text released in Montreal

12 – debate between Bourassa and Parizeau

13 – Quebec Chamber of Commerce declines to endorse Accord

16 – *L'Actualité* publishes Bourassa's briefing documents

19 – Jacques Parizeau says he would interpret a win by the No as indicating support for sovereignty

---

Wilhelmy, and an initially unnamed interlocutor, which surfaced on 14 September. Although publication inside Quebec was immediately enjoined, its existence was on the record and partial excerpts appeared outside Quebec. The transcript went on the Quebec record on the 30 September. The other participant in the Wilhelmy conversation turned out to be André Tremblay, the premier's constitutional adviser. Tremblay also got embroiled in a dispute over whether or not he told the Quebec Chamber of Commerce that the premier suffered from crippling fatigue in the late stages of the Charlottetown negotiations.

Athough most of this turmoil occurred before the official campaign began, the credibility question did not die. The transcript of the Wilhelmy-Tremblay conversation was published on 1 October. On the 6th, Moe Sihota, British Columbia's constitutional affairs minister, attempted to shore up his own government's image by claiming that Bourassa had lost at Charlottetown; this claim inevitably received wide play in Quebec. On the 16th *L'Actualité* published the premier's briefing documents; this revisited the Wilhelmy-Tremblay exchanges.

Moreover, the premier could not control debate about the consequences of saying No. The argument that saying No would hasten sovereignty was potentially potent, but its credibility rested at least in part on sovereignists' own actions. And the sovereignist organizers of the No took pains to reassure Quebeckers that *only* the Charlottetown Accord, not the fate of the union, was at issue. The terms under which Jean Allaire joined the No camp were carefully wrought to this end; he was assured that he would not have to compromise his federalist commitments. On the other hand, on 19 October Jacques Parizeau added some credibility to federalist claims about the gravity of a No by claiming that he would interpret such a vote as the first step toward sovereignty. His backtracking was immediate, however, and by the end of the campaign one could sense a general backing off, both inside and outside Quebec, from extreme versions of arguments from consequences.

In the campaign itself, Robert Bourassa was generally able to proceed with a free hand and most observers agree that he outperformed Jacques Parizeau in the leaders' debate on 12 October. But quite apart from establishing his credibility, Bourassa's task was truly daunting. The large sovereignist fraction of the Quebec electorate was simply not going to buy any proposal aimed at consolidating the Canadian union; for the Yes to win a bare majority in the Quebec electorate as a whole, the majority in the non-sovereignist camp would have to be very one-sided.

The struggle in Quebec was mostly between two centrally-led armies, in the spirit of Quebec's referendum law. The Fédération des femmes du Québec, like feminists outside Quebec, rejected the Accord. Otherwise, the obvious nonparty actors were either diffident or predictable. One diffident actor was the Quebec business community. Most active on the Yes side was the "Regroupement économie et constitution," led by Claude Beauchamp, but the Conseil du Patronat also supported the Accord unequivocally. But the Chambre de Commerce decided not to take a stand, and some prominent individuals urged a No. All three major Quebec labour federations, the FTQ, CSN, and CEQ came out clearly for the No on 18 September. This was no surprise, as all officially supported Quebec sovereignty. Awkwardly, the FTQ was a constituent member of the Canadian Labour Congress, which campaigned for the Yes.

THE CAMPAIGN OUTSIDE QUEBEC

Active Interventions

In the rest of Canada negative reaction appeared even before the Accord was reached. Then a broad array of interests came on side. But once the pro-Accord interests assembled, they fell on their collective face.

Mohawk leaders rejected the Accord even before its final shape was clear. They objected to the continued application of Canadian and provincial law to Aboriginal communities, an objection of long standing but fuelled by memories of Oka. Outside the Aboriginal community, the strongest initial reaction was in British Columbia. By agreeing to House and Senate changes, Premier Mike Harcourt tossed away any chance that his province would acquire power commensurate with its size. By Friday, 21 August, before negotiations moved to Charlottetown, British Columbia's hotline radio shows were dominated by negative reaction. Academic commentary in the region was also harsh.[31] Premier Harcourt's difficulties were compounded by his hasty commitment to gender equality for the BC Senate delegation. Opponents were aroused all the more, while many in Harcourt's own camp were offended by later suggestions that he might back off from the commitment.

But then the Accord's supporting coalition broadened impressively. Organized labour, the first element to join, promised to be strategically critical, as it was not a natural ally of the Conservative government. Union leaders worried about the economic union proposals; they feared that restrictions on provinces could be used to block interventionist schemes favoured by the movement. At the same time, labour leaders also reflexively opposed most proposals for reducing the federal role in social policy. The one thing of substance in the Accord that they would actually favour was the social charter, but the language was weak. Labour's endorsement would thus signal that the compromise was honourable, as the crisis was grave. Appropriately, the first indication was very diffident. On 31 August, Bob White of the Canadian Labour Congress (CLC) gave the Accord what he himself described as a "cautious endorsement" and the question of whether the CLC would actually campaign remained open. Part of the hesitation appeared to be out of concern not to provoke Quebec

Chronology: the Rest of Canada

August

21 – outline of constitutional agreement reached in Ottawa

– negative reaction to House-Senate proposals already apparent in BC and Alberta

– Mohawk leaders reject agreement

28 – Charlottetown Accord approved

31 – CLC leader Bob White gives cautious endorsement of Accord

September

4 – Ottawa announces wording of question

10 – John Turner speaks in favour of Accord in last day of debate in House

– referendum bill passes House of Commons, 232–12

13 – NAC comes out against Accord after weekend meeting, attacks Canada clause and restrictions on federal spending power

15 – Canadian Press reports that CLC will campaign for the Yes

18 – Business Council on National Issues comes out for Yes

21 – first official day of campaign outside Quebec

– Pierre Trudeau condemns Quebec "blackmail" in *Maclean's-Actualité*

– National Citizens' Coalition joins the No side, fears social charter

22 – announcement of national Yes panel

23 – Union of BC Indian Chiefs rejects Accord

– bands in Treaties 6 and 7 (Alberta) oppose Accord

25 – Royal Bank report predicts dire consequences of No

26 – Angus Reid poll indicates that Yes and No roughly tied nationwide

October

1 – Trudeau denounces Charlottetown Accord accord in speech at Maison du Egg Roll

3 – publication of Consensus Report

5 – Manning and McLaughlin in televised debate at University of Guelph

6 – Yes TV advertisements begin

– Moe Sihota (BC) claims that Bourassa "lost" on question of distinct society

7 – Clyde Wells campaigns for Yes

8 – Assembly of Manitoba Chiefs rejects Accord

13 – legal text officially published

– Native Women's Association of Canada asks court to block referendum

15 – debate between NAC president Judy Rebick (No) and past-president Lynn McDonald (Yes)

16 – Assembly of First Nations chiefs decline to endorse Accord

– *Globe and Mail* poll indicates that Yes is losing nationwide

17 – Angus Reid and Environics polls confirm that Yes is losing

20 – Native Council of Canada (off-reserve) endorses Accord

unions. Two weeks later, however, the CLC overcame its doubts and established a committee for the Yes.

This placed the union movement at odds with another player on the political left, the women's movement. Leaders of the movement had not as a rule made positive demands, comparable, for instance, to the demand for Aboriginal self-government. The only explicit positive demand was for gender equality in the Senate and this was reactive; Senate reform itself was hardly a priority for the women's movement. Instead, feminist leaders fought rearguard actions, to defend the Charter of Rights and kindred values. For the most part this meant exerting pressure to modify elements in the Accord which they would strictly have preferred not even come into existence. Once the Accord was struck the question became whether leaders in the movement could live with it and for most, the answer was no. The highest profile belonged to the National Action Committee on the Status of Women (NAC), which rejected the Accord after a weekend meeting on 12–13 September. NAC's official statement expressed concern about the Canada clause, which was deemed to place too much emphasis on the country's governments and made "no mention of individual equality guarantees from the ... Charter."[32] Worry was also expressed that groups not explicitly mentioned in the clause would be subordinated in their enjoyment of rights to groups which did gain mention. As well, NAC feared that the Accord's restrictions on the federal spending power would bar the path to a national child care program and would place existing joint programs at risk.

Just as the labour-feminist gap opened, labour acquired an unsettling ally – the Business Council on National Issues (BCNI). If the business community had an appointed role it was not so much to endorse the specifics of the Accord as to ruminate aloud on the implications of a No. For most business people the Accord was a disappointment. Its provisions for the economic union were weak and the social charter was more of a genuflection to the left than most in the business community would have preferred. Would they swallow their doubts sufficiently to endorse an agreement which at least held out the prospect of an end to political crisis? BCNI's intervention signalled that outside Quebec the answer would be mainly yes and the Council was soon joined by other groups representing large firms. Also prominent were chartered banks. Here, though, the most pointed intervention may have backfired: on 25 September, a Royal Bank of Canada report predicted that breakup of the country would produce a 16 percent drop in standard of living, a 15 percent unemployment rate, a $4,000 real income drop per capita, and a million-person outmigration to the United States. The Royal Bank numbers seemed wild and calculated to frighten voters, Quebec voters in particular. One prominent critic of the Royal Bank study was none other than Bob White. Ordinarily, rejection of a bank's conclusion by the country's senior labour leader would come as no surprise. This time, though, the contretemps was awkward, as Mr White was an ally in the referendum war. And the business community was not unanimous. The National Citizens' Coalition, a small-business-oriented group, opposed the Accord because of the social charter.

As all this was happening the official campaigns were getting under way. The official Yes panel, the Canada Committee, was carefully constructed to represent a broad range of interests. Especially prominent was June Callwood, of whose feminist credentials there could be no doubt and whose presence seemed aimed at the NAC. Sensitivity to the NAC was also visible in the Yes side's less official ranks. One of NDP leader Audrey McLaughlin's tasks was to address herself explicitly to NAC's concerns, which she did most notably on 24 September. Also important was Lynn McDonald, formerly an NDP MP and, critically, a former president of NAC, who did the same in a 15 October debate with Judy Rebick, NAC's current head. Where Ms Rebick reiterated the theme that the Accord would block action on the feminist agenda, McDonald argued that the Accord was the very precondition for moving on. It may not have helped, however, that these two supporters were also past or present MPs. Were they expert feminist onlookers or were they just part of the pro-Accord coalition?

Another key fellow traveller for the Accord was Peter Lougheed, aimed at the West. Although Lougheed was a Conservative and thus suspect as too natural an ally for Brian Mulroney, his other reputation was as the most formidable advocate of western interests the country had ever seen. As well, Lougheed was already practised as an intervenor, having been a highly visible advocate of the Canada-US Free Trade Agreement in 1988. If such a person could say that the Charlottetown Accord was good enough for the West, many votes might be turned.

Peter Lougheed was, arguably, the counterweight to Preston Manning, leader of the Reform party. Reform, constituted around a rejection of politics as usual, had to oppose the ultimate expression of politics as usual, such as a multifacted deal like the Charlottetown Accord. If the triumph of the No ensured that the pot would continue to boil and linguistic tempers fray even more, so much the better for a party whose appeal, whatever its nominal program, was mainly sectionalist. Saying No was thus the easy and predictable thing for Manning to do. He appears, however, to have agonized about the matter for two weeks[33] before coming out for the No on 10 September, the day the House passed the referendum question.

The Reform claim is worth dwelling on at length. The first point was that the agreement was nothing of the sort: "All we have is something called a 'consensus report' – page after page of vague statements of principle, the meaning of which is unresolved." Where the Yes side argued that the Accord would enable us to move on, Reform argued precisely the contrary: "The truth is there is no final agreement – only a general framework for further constitutional negotiations." To underscore the point, the Reform statement itemized thirty-four areas requiring negotiation of yet more political accords, fourteen areas requiring first ministers' conferences, and twelve areas "so vague they require negotiation or court litigation." The Accord would institutionalize the very thing it was supposed to end.

Where the Yes side encouraged voters to say Yes to Canada, Reform argued that the true pro-Canadian vote was a No, because "Canada is worth too much to gamble its future by trading a flawed constitution we know for one that is largely undefined and completely uncertain." Here two claims are encapsulated: on one hand, the Charlottetown Accord represents change which is too great and yet unknowable; on the other hand, the status quo, even if not entirely satisfactory, is still tenable. In case there was any doubt, Reform called for a constitutional moratorium; by implication Reform was prepared to sacrifice its own commitment to Senate reform. Finally, Reform launched the astute double entendre, "Know More."

One other Reform rhetorical ploy was widely criticized but is important for our purposes. Manning regularly referred to the Accord as the "Mulroney deal," exactly the term used to describe the 1988 trade pact. His gamble was that voters would assess the agreement in light of their feelings – preponderantly negative – about the chief negotiator.

In publicity value, however, Lougheed and Manning were both overshadowed by Pierre Trudeau. Why might a deeply enigmatic figure out of the quickly receding past have any effect? To begin with, he remained the defining political figure for a generation of Canadians. Many felt at home in his Liberal party, constituted around the values in the Charter of Rights, including the Charter's particular version of French-English accommodation. His reading of the Accord's implications for the Charter could be very persuasive. The Charter was *his* legacy. Although it was shaped through a fairly open process, the document exists only because of his political will and acumen. As a lawyer he could deploy a superior understanding of threats to his legacy. Even former opponents might respond to his cue, as the Charter's symbolic power probably transcends its specific guarantees.

Perhaps the most critical question about Trudeau, however, is where he fitted in English Canada's response to French Canada. Unlike Preston Manning, he could not be accused of opposing the Accord out of generalized hostility to French Canadian aspirations. Even if he opposed much of what Quebec's provincial elite stood for, he was still for French Canada what Peter Lougheed had been for the West, the most formidable advocate ever. This suggests that his role was to detach Quebec's natural sympathizers from the Accord coalition. But a darker possibility was suggested by Bob Rae: "'He made anti-French feeling respectable' said Bob Rae ... Rae kept running into people during the referendum campaign who were using Trudeau's words to justify their anti-French sentiments" (Delacourt, p. 183).

The relative power of these contrasting models of Trudeau's impact may be critical to interpretation of the event. Pierre Trudeau hit the electorate twice. On Monday, 21 September, *Maclean's-Actualité* published his condemnation of the whole process of accommodating Quebec. Strictly speaking, the article was not a comment on the Accord, as it had been commissioned some weeks before. The implications were unmistakable, however, and early news broadcasts mistakenly presented it as about the Accord. Any doubt about where Mr Trudeau stood was resolved on 1 October by his speech at a Montreal restaurant, the Maison du Egg Roll. There he rejected the Accord outright. He said it would "institutionalize constitutional bickering," that it would create a "hierarchy of classes of citizens," that its distinct society clause and recognition of aboriginal self-government would make collective rights trump individual ones, and that it would spell the end of social programs in poor provinces. A Yes would ensure that "the blackmail [from Quebec] would continue."[34]

If this were not enough, the Aboriginal coalition came apart – or failed to congeal – as the campaign progressed. One key date was 23 September, when Treaty 6 and 7 bands from Alberta placed anti-Accord advertisements in major newspapers and the Union of BC Indian Chiefs came out officially for the No. On 8 October the Assembly of Manitoba chiefs rejected the Accord. This was uncomfortably close to the backyard of Ovide Mercredi, the principal Aboriginal presence in Accord negotiations and himself from Manitoba. Mercredi's political weakness was underscored by his own organization, the Assembly of First Nations (AFN) when the chiefs declined to support the Accord on 16 October. If some Aboriginal leaders believed the Accord gave them too little power, others in their communities believed it gave them too much. In particular, many Aboriginal women feared that the Accord blocked application of the Charter to self-governing Aboriginal communities and on 13 October the Native Women's Association of Canada sought an injunction to stop the referendum.

In the face of this criticism the Yes forces were hard pressed to establish just what it was they were asking people to say Yes to. The Accord was vague in many details and its official text was not available until 3 October. It was hard to insist on the necessity of the compromise if Canadians could not know what the compromise was. Lack of text, conversely, licensed critics to say what they pleased, as no basis existed for a refutation. To this end, the negotiators rushed to finish their work in time for voters to admire it.

Even more important was the legal text, which arrived in two stages. Official release was set for 13 October, less than two weeks before the vote. But the text was effectively released on the 10th, since the Bourassa-Parizeau debate in Quebec was scheduled for the 12th and Parizeau refused to debate non-existent text. Bourassa did not want to give Parizeau a pretext to avoid debate and so authorized early release. Thereupon, Manitoba also released the text. Officials in Ottawa did not resist early release in these provinces. Indeed, limited early release might have been tactically ideal. No one could say that text did not exist, that something was being hidden. But actually getting hold of it was still next to impossible and so the Yes forces enjoyed a long Thanksgiving weekend of favourable publicity.

Strategic Information: Polls

If even one provincial electorate threatened to say No, according to Joe Clark's formula, most arguments for acquiescing in the compromise would be undercut. Strategic information was thus at a premium. Although voters were unlikely to follow the race in every province or region, it is reasonable to conjecture that they could follow some polls, about the country as a whole or about Quebec perhaps. Although more detail on published polls can be found in chapter 6, suffice it to say here that two polling moments stood out in the campaign. On 26 September the Angus Reid group published the first indication that Yes forces faced a serious battle nationwide. Although trouble was evident in Quebec and British Columbia as early as the Gallup poll of 16 September, all earlier polls had indicated a strong Canada-wide edge for the Yes. The 26 September poll suggested that Yes and No were now running even. Then on 16–17 October three polls weighed in with clearly bad news: each indicated that the Canada-wide Yes share was shaping up to be only 44 or 45 percent.

Markets

September

17 – Bank of Canada rate jumps 0.20 to 5.34 percent

24 – Bank of Canada rate jumps 0.35 to 5.69 percent

28 – dollar drops 0.51¢, closes at 80.15¢ US

29 – interest rates on Treasury bills jump from 5.87 to 7.65 percent

– dollar drops nearly 1¢, but closes at 80

– rate on overnight loans rises from 4.75 to 12 percent, then settles at 6.5

– TSE 300 falls for third consecutive day

30 – Charter banks fix prime rates at 8.25 percent

– dollar rises .25 percent, closing at 80.24

– TSE 300 drops 87.6 points

October

 1 – Bank of Canada rate increased 1.93 points to 7.62 percent

– Goldman-Sachs and Moody's say No means only return to status quo

13 – dollar closes at 80.42

– Bank rate at 7.93 percent

14 – Standard & Poors cuts rating on Canada's foreign-currency debt from AAA to AA+

– dollar closes at $0.80 US

15 – Bank rate at 7.81 percent

22 – Bank rate falls to 7.37 percent

– dollar closes at 80.52¢

23 – dollar closes at 80.12¢

The Invisible Hand

If the country was really in danger of breaking up and if breakup would bring economic catastrophe, markets should have signalled this pretty quickly. And the markets did react to events in the campaign. They first signalled fear of a No, then shifted to acquiescence. The sharpest negative reactions were clustered toward the end of September, shortly after the first Reid poll hint that the No might prevail. On 28 September the dollar experienced its biggest drop between consecutive closings, a 0.51¢ fall, to 80.15¢ US. In the next day's trading the dollar dropped another full cent but rallied, with Bank of Canada help, to close at 80¢ US. The overall drop in September was about 3.5¢. Thereafter, the dollar fluctuated around 80¢ US and by 14 October appeared to be gaining strength.

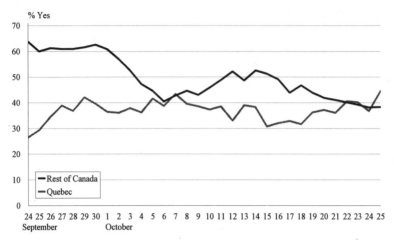

5-day moving average

Figure 2–1
Evolution of Vote Intentions

The dollar's late-campaign strength also reflected an aggressive move on interest rates. Anxiety was visible even before the official campaign began. Where on 10 September the bank rate sank to 5.14 percent, the next two weeks saw the rate edge up such that on the 24th it reached 5.69 percent, its highest level since early July. The next rate-setting day, 1 October, followed immediately on the exchange rate crisis and saw the bank rate surge to 7.62 percent. This surge had been anticipated on the 29th, the day the Canada-US exchange rate dropped one full cent before its closing recovery. That exchange-rate recovery was helped by a surge in another interest rate, the chartered banks' overnight-loans rate, from 4.75 to 12 percent. Although the overnight rate settled back to 6.5 percent once the currency stabilized, the surge in the bank rate itself followed immediately. It edged upward the next Thursday (8 October) to 7.93, then settled back to 7.81 (15 October) and 7.37 (22 October). The subtitle for a 14 October *Globe and Mail* story on the markets was telling: "Buyers seek stability as fears over referendum result ebb."[35]

THE VOTE: INTENTIONS AND RESULT

Figure 2–1 hints that Trudeau's intervention was decisive. Before the first weekend in October, prospects for the Yes outside Quebec seemed bright; there seemed to be a Yes: No ratio of about 60:40. Then the Yes lead collapsed, a drop that required no more than five days,

Table 2–1
The Yes Share by Region

Week	BC	Prairies	Ontario	Atlantic
24–27 Sept	41	60	62	
	(26)	(34)	(37)	59
28 Sept–4 Oct	44	59	63	(62)
	(55)	(105)	(88)	
5–11 Oct	31	41	44	48
	(45)	(82)	(126)	(37)
12–18 Oct	40	49	51	63
	(49)	(83)	(111)	(47)
9–25 Oct	39	32	38	61
	(47)	(98)	(146)	(60)

NOTE: Entries in parentheses are number of observations

from the 1st to the 5th. If anything, this *understates* the speed of the drop: a raw tracking – not smoothed by moving averages – suggests that the drop was *overnight*, between 3 and 4 October! The total collapse spanned 20 points, such that the Yes share outside Quebec bottomed out around 40 percent.

Table 2–1 indicates that the critical regions were Ontario and the Prairies; the Atlantic provinces always stayed on side and British Columbia never came on side. The table gives weekly readings, in deference to the fact that the daily number of interviews in each region was small. If in the opening phase Ontario and the Prairies looked rather like the Atlantic provinces, after the first October weekend, they looked more like British Columbia. Although the setback for the Yes was visible at least temporarily everywhere, only in Ontario and the Prairies did the shift matter to the final result. British Columbia was already in the No camp, and although the drop in the Atlantic provinces was about as great as in other regions, that region's starting point was just too high to permit a net reversal of direction.

In mid-October the Yes share made a partial recovery. According to the moving average tracking in Figure 2–1, the Yes share began a surge on the 10th, reached 50 percent on the 12th. The raw tracking has a shift to 50 percent between the 11th and 12th, staying roughly there on the 13th, moving up to 61 percent on the 14th. Shifts of this magnitude and duration are unlikely to be products just of sampling error.[36] The recovery was visible everywhere, according to Table 2–1, although it was greatest in Ontario and the Atlantic provinces, so much so that the latter region ended the campaign virtually where it began. Interpretation of the recovery does not come easily. It might have been driven by favourable publicity over the Accord's legal text. It might have been nothing more than a quasi-automatic decay in the impulse from Trudeau's "Egg Roll" speech.

Whatever its source, the recovery stalled and then went into reverse: the moving average tracking in Figure 2–1 indicates the beginning of the drop on the 15th or 16th; the raw tracking points to the same days.[37] On referendum day 45 percent voted Yes in the country as a whole. In Quebec the Yes share stood at 42 percent. In the Atlantic provinces the Yes held its 60:40 margin, although the No won narrowly in Nova Scotia. In the West the margin was 40:60 (in British Columbia 32:68). In Ontario the outcome was essentially 50:50.

3 The Charlottetown Accord as a Coalition

Day to day, politics is about building coalitions of minorities, about reconciling opposites. In this respect, the Charlottetown Accord was just day-to-day politics writ large. It had "something for everyone": it attempted to respond to the reality that various segments of Canadian society have different grievances and that these grievances are hard to redress all at once. Selling such a package required two qualitatively different kinds of claim, "carrots" and "sticks." General arguments were the sticks: all Canadians would suffer economically and politically should the Yes lose. Specific arguments were the carrots, and there were different carrots to win over, or at least mollify, different segments. Each section of the public should be able to identify its own gain, see itself as a winner, and so support the Accord. Members of the broad pro-Accord elite coalition were deployed across the country to deliver persuasive messages to their respective policy communities, by walking them through the bargaining logic, by highlighting precisely what the Accord offered them, and by arguing that gains were real and significant. Their task was to use their political capital, their status as opinion leaders, to convince each segment of the public that the referendum was a unique opportunity to consolidate gains.

Although the No campaign lacked the organizational coherence of the Yes side, its task was similar: present an alternative set of persuasive messages to derail the logic and disconnect links in the chain of reasoning served up by the Yes side. One counter-argument was that gains were illusory or insufficient. Another claim was that purported gains required unacceptable compromises. The No forces also tapped into the general uncertainty surrounding the agreement by suggesting that, far from bringing closure to consitutional haggling, the Accord would just set the stage for more negotiations, and thus more concessions.

This chapter focuses on the Accord as a bargain, on the carrots. It examines support for four elements: recognition of Quebec as a distinct society within Canada; Quebec's 25 percent seat guarantee; changes to the Senate; and recognition of an inherent Aboriginal right of self-government. The sticks, the general arguments – whether a voter's own province was overall a winner; the general quality of the compromise; the Accord as a necessary condition for moving on to other problems; whether fear of Quebec's separation was warranted, and if, conversely, Quebec would always ask for more – figure in the next chapter.

RECOGNIZING QUEBEC AS A DISTINCT SOCIETY

If recognizing Quebec as a distinct society signalled thematic continuity with Meech Lake, the long-run implications of doing so were as uncertain in 1992 as in 1987. In 1992 the distinct society proposal did not stand alone but was written into section 2(1), the "Canada clause," which originated in Manitoba hearings and was put on the national agenda by the Charest Committee.[1] The clause was intended to "express fundamental Canadian values" and "guide the courts in their future interpretation of the entire Constitution, including the Canadian Charter of Rights and Freedoms" (*Consensus Report*, p. 1). In essence, the clause was a list of principles clustered under the themes of "Unity and Diversity." The distinct society proposal appeared twice: section 2(1)(c) defined it, by stating that "Quebec constitutes within Canada a distinct society, which includes a French-speaking majority, a unique culture and a civil law tradition"; section 2(2) affirmed the "role of the legislature and Government of Quebec to preserve and promote the distinct society of Quebec" (*Consensus Report*, p. 2).

One difficulty in fathoming the clause's precise implications turned on context. Clauses surrounding the two distinct society items could be construed as constraining the scope of Quebec's distinct status. One commitment was to racial and ethnic equality (section 2(1)(e)). Another acknowledged Aboriginals as "first peoples" with concomitant, but undefined, status and rights (section 2(1)(b)). Then there were commitments to respect both individual and collective rights (section 2(1)(f)), as well as recognition of the "equality of the provinces" and the need to recognize "their diverse characteristics" (section 2(1)(h)), and gestures toward language and gender rights. Which rights or characteristics would prevail in the event of conflict? Would guiding principles in one part of the Canada clause travel with or impinge on others?

For the francophone majority in Quebec, the fear would be that the recognition was *too* constrained, that it might be trumped by some other Canada clause consideration. Opinion on the distinct society clause and the other three elements appears in Figure 3–1.[2] Positions in outright opposition to the thrust of the Accord are cast as negatives, for graphic effect. "Don't know" appears on the positive side because it has to go somewhere, not because we believe that indifference or ambivalence implies consent. The figure confirms that the *idea* of recognizing Quebec as distinct earned virtually consensual support: over 80 percent of all Quebeckers (not just francophones) supported it. And almost all Quebeckers had an opinion on the clause; the "don't know" percentage was small. Table 3–1 indicates Quebeckers' sense of constraint: a one-sided majority believed that the distinct society clause did not go far enough. Even among those opposed to the clause, the plurality position was to see it as too weak. The implication is that in saying yes to the clause, Quebeckers were doing no more than acknowledging their due; it remains to be seen whether the clause as worded materially helped attract support for the whole package.

Outside Quebec, debate about the distinct society proposal, indeed about the Canada clause as a whole, was conducted in the abstract language of rights. Critics claimed that the Accord would entrench a pecking order of rights, a charge that went to the ideological underpinnings of the entire document. That argument centred around competing notions of liberty and community that have long animated Canadian constitutional debates (Vipond, 1991). Far from resolving tensions between visions, critics claimed that the Canada clause actually made the tensions more acute. A central thrust of Trudeau's Egg Roll speech expanded on the same theme: "We are not equals according to this Canada clause. It all depends on where each individual stands" (Trudeau, 1992, p. 13). Trudeau worried that the Accord would create a hierarchy of civic categories, that official language minorities would be put at risk, and that women and racial, ethnic, and religious minorities would be deprived of true equality before the law. Even more troubling to Trudeau, the distinct society clause and other elements of the Canada clause would give collective rights priority over individual ones.

A. Distinct Society

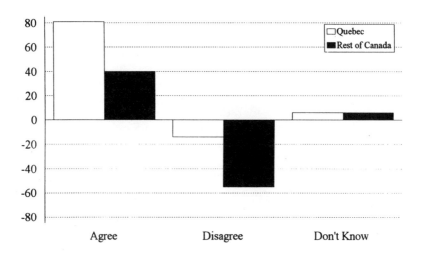

B. 25% Guarantee

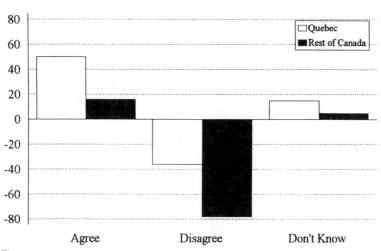

Figure 3–1
Support for Elements in the Accord

Reform opposition to the distinct society clause worked both sides.
One side mirrored the Trudeau critique: that the constitutional standing of a significant number of Canadians would be depend on "their
race, language and culture," that collective rights would dominate

C. Senate

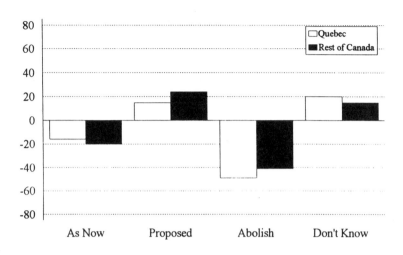

D. Self-Government

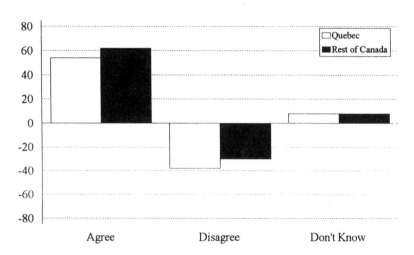

Figure 3–1 (cont'd)

individual ones. On this count, the distinct society clause, and the
Canada clause more generally, were "at variance with the Reform
Party's vision of Canada in which all Canadians are treated equally
in constitutional law regardless of race, language, or culture." On the

Table 3–1
Did the Distinct Society Clause Go the Right Distance?

	Quebec		Rest of Canada	
How Far?	Accept	Reject	Accept	Reject
Too Far	3	21	29	69
Just Far Enough	29	30	55	22
Not Far Enough	63	35	9	5
N	555	102	393	595

other side, Reform staked out surprising ground for the party of English Canada. Reform claimed that the deal did not satisfy the "legitimate aspirations of the francophone majority of Quebec" because the distinct society clause "has been effectively gutted by being placed in the Canada Clause where it is balanced by other sections." Following from this, the Accord would not "provide a strong antidote to Quebec separatism" because the distinct society clause as worded and located would "heighten rather than reduce Quebec's concern about its language and culture."[3]

For all this, the non-Quebec balance of opinion on the clause (Figure 3–1) resembled that from the Meech Lake years (Blais and Crête, 1991): reasonably closely divided but definitely negative. The gap between Quebec and the rest of Canada was wide, about 40 points: where outside Quebec 40 percent supported the clause, inside Quebec the figure was over 80 percent; the gap in opposition was roughly as great. As in Quebec, respondents in the rest of Canada seemed to know their minds on this question; the "don't know" percentage was very low. But in contrast to Quebec, according to Table 3–1, supporters of the clause typically thought that it went far enough. Indeed, a significant minority of supporters believed it went too far. That it went too far was the clear majority opinion among the clause's opponents.

Outside Quebec, the distinct society clause did not set regions against each other, according to Figure 3–2. Here, coding of opinion items is simplified for presentational clarity: if the balance of opinion is positive (more than 50 percent support among decided respondents), the bar appears above the zero line; if negative, below the line.[4] Closest to the 50 percent threshold was the Atlantic region, where supporters were roughly as numerous as opponents. In the two western regions opinion was negative but not, on balance, more

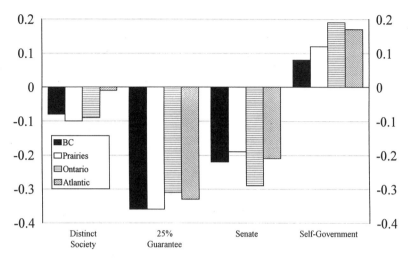

Figure 3–2
Support for Elements by Region, Rest of Canada

negative than in Ontario. Division on this question was primarily within provinces rather than between them. Most pointedly, Ontarians showed no more support for Quebec's core aspiration than did westerners.

THE 25 PERCENT GUARANTEE

The 25 percent guarantee was a qualitatively different issue from the distinct society clause in that it excited relatively little extended elite comment. For example, Pierre Trudeau did not mention it even once in his Egg Roll speech or in the question period and press conference after the speech. Similarly, it was only modestly prominent in Reform commentary. But the idea was easy to grasp. It was a simple but profound commitment that had direct implications for House representation of other provinces; it was part of a zero-sum game, so to speak. Outside Quebec, the clause was a rhetorical nightmare. It could not be justified in the majoritarian framework that serves as the official justification for Westminster-style responsible government. Indeed, it seemed only to institutionalize the peculiarly Canadian twist on responsible government – the traditional role of Quebec as pivot for governments (Bakvis and Macpherson, 1995; Johnston et al., 1992). To justify it proponents had to appeal to the Pearson-Charlottetown bargaining sequence, to present the guarantee as compensation for Quebec's loss of Senate seats.

Unsurprisingly, it polarized the country; a 40-point gap developed, roughly as wide as over the distinct society clause. But both inside and outside Quebec opinion on distinct society was 25–30 points closer to the approval end than was opinion on the 25 percent guarantee. Where on recognition as a distinct society almost all Quebec coalesced while the rest of Canada divided, on the 25 percent guarantee the opposite was true. Outside Quebec the balance in opposition was 78:16; in Quebec the balance in support was only 50:36. If Quebeckers were only diffidently supportive of the guarantee, they were also relatively uncertain about it: the "don't know" percentage was much higher for Quebec respondents than for ones in the rest of Canada and, among Quebeckers, much higher than for the distinct society clause. Opposition to the guarantee was only slightly higher in the Prairie provinces and British Columbia than in Ontario and the Atlantic provinces, according to Figure 3–2.[5]

SENATE REFORM

The proposed new Senate was difficult for citizens to fathom, as it packaged several concerns at once. Section 7 of the Accord authorized provinces to choose the mode of selection for their senators and section 8 proposed that the "Senate should initially total 62 Senators and should be composed of six Senators from each province and one Senator from each territory" (*Consensus Report*, p. 5). For Reform, the representational element was inadequate, particularly in its lack of a guarantee for direct popular election: "Election by provincial legislatures, if any provinces go that route, will probably be a farce; patronage will merely be transferred from the federal prime minister to provincial premiers." Even more critical for Reform was whether or not the new body would be effective, the third leg of the Triple-E. The crux of the matter was the provision for joint House-Senate votes: "on the vast majority of bills, defeat in the Senate will mean a second vote in a joint session of the Senate and the House of Commons, where 62 Senators will be overwhelmed by the 337 members of the House of Commons." In Reform's view, the new Senate would "not satisfy aspirations for regional equality or provide effective regional representation and balance in national decision making." Given the feebleness of the new body, Canada "would arguably be better off to leave the Senate as it is."[6]

If the Senate was a difficult issue for voters to fathom, it was also difficult to frame coherent questions about the proposals. We tried to cover the field with three questions. The first tapped judgments on the relevant imaginable alternatives: the Senate as proposed in the

Accord, the existing Senate, and outright abolition of the chamber. The second covered the representation issue that preoccupied delegations in the months before the Pearson accord: equal representation by province versus some allowance for provincial population differences. The third probed perceptions of the new chamber's likely effectiveness, by asking if its power seemed too great, too little, or about right.[7]

The new chamber attracted little support: 15 percent in Quebec, 24 percent in the rest of Canada. The existing Senate did almost as well as the proposed one: 16 percent in Quebec, 20 percent outside. Outright abolition of the Senate drew a wide plurality in both Quebec and the rest of Canada. Thus on the Senate Quebec and the rest of Canada, at least the totality of Canada outside Quebec, were not polarized. By implication, the Quebec elite's anxieties about the Senate were not misplaced: their mass base resisted the innovation. That Quebec voters greatly preferred outright abolition makes perfect sense, considering the provincial interest. Abolition of the Senate would kill all possibility of tinkering with the House-dominated system for which Quebec historically has been the pivot.

Conceivably, the non-Quebec data mask sharp differences among regions. In particular, Ontario may dominate and mask strong support for the new body in the West. Figure 3–2 indicates that this was clearly not the case, as the new Senate was opposed in each region.[8] Opposition was weakest in the Prairie provinces and strongest in Ontario, but in no region was there broad support. The one element of the Accord ostensibly designed to placate the West, then, did nothing of the sort. Is it possible that Ontario and the West opposed the new Senate for opposed reasons, Ontario because representation was equal by province, and the West because the institution, although grounded in equal representation, lacked effectiveness?

On representation, Figure 3–3 indicates that regions diverged roughly according to type: the Prairie and Atlantic provinces supported equality fairly one-sidedly; Ontarians gave a slight majority to unequal representation; and British Columbia leaned to the equal representation side but was roughly halfway between Ontario and the others. Considering the interests at stake, a bias toward equal representation is evident, in that even in the province with the most to lose equal representation attracted broad support.

If westerners secured their representational preference, did they recoil at the Senate's power limitations? Figure 3–3 also addresses this question, and the answer seems pretty clearly to be no. In fact, the data here are something of a morass. Like the campaign itself, our question asked voters to evaluate subtle power relations in an institutional

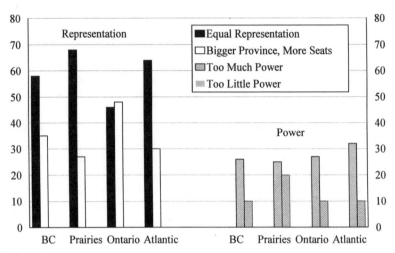

Figure 3–3
Representation and Power in the Senate by Region, Rest of Canada

context no one had ever seen. In this light, it is not surprising that 26 percent admitted straight off that they could not make a judgment and that another 29 percent said the setup seemed about right. Nonetheless, one fact about judgments on the new Senate's power seems solid: *there was very little pent-up demand for a more powerful Senate*. In each region more respondents said the new body had too much than said it had too little power. Only in the Prairie provinces did the "too little" share creep up to the "too much" one.[9] Elsewhere, the too much/too little ratio was 2.5:1 or 3:1; British Columbia was indistinguishable from Ontario and the region with the smallest provinces of all, the Atlantic provinces, was the most resistant to empowering the new body. Perhaps voters resisted increasing the power of the new Senate because they worried that it might not be directly elected. Our sense, however, is that this was not so; most voters outside Quebec seemed to assume the body would be directly elected, although this is only our impression. If we are right on this, then we must also conclude that opposition was not to the basic representation rule, for a majority did endorse equal representation, which was the rule actually embodied in the Accord. One final possibility is that voters rejected the Senate proposals because of the changes they entailed to the House, especially Quebec's 25 percent guarantee.

Table 3–2 brings all these considerations together. The dependent variable in the table is the 0,1 rendering of positions on the institu-

Table 3–2
Deconstructing the Senate, Rest of Canada

	(1)	(2)
REPRESENTATION:		
Equal	0.06*	0.04
	(0.03)	(0.03)
25% Guarantee	0.09**	0.09**
	(0.04)	(0.04)
POWER:		
Too Little	-0.01	-0.02
	(0.04)	(0.04)
Too Much	-0.23***	-0.23***
	(0.03)	(0.03)
REGION:		
Atlantic	–	0.09*
		(0.05)
Prairies	–	0.10**
		(0.03)
BC	–	0.07*
		(0.04)
Intercept	0.26	0.23
	(0.02)	(0.02)
R^2	0.06	0.07

Entries in parentheses are standard errors.
* $p < 0.05$; ** $p < 0.01$; *** $p < 0.001$

tion, 0 representing abolition or the existing body and 1 representing
the Accord's version, with non-response at 0.5. Two representation
considerations appear: equal versus unequal; and the 25 percent
guarantee that equal representation engendered. The power variable
appears as two terms, one for each side: respondents who said the
new body had too little power scored 1 on the corresponding term
and 0 otherwise; respondents who said the new body had too much
power scored 1 on the other term and 0 otherwise; the reference category for these two variables was no opinion or the judgment that the

proposal got power relations about right. Two terms allow for two plausible possibilities: asymmetry between sides; and a negative co-efficient on each side. We also allow region of residence to enter one estimation, to see how directly representing arguments affects provincial differences in support for the proposed chamber.

Representation considerations did account for some variation in support. Respondents who endorsed equal representation were about 6 points more likely to support the equally constituted body. But this is a tepid effect and it only shrinks when region enters the estimation. Shrinkage indicates that the idea of equality did not mediate the effect of region: westerners were not more supportive because they are more likely to endorse equal representation. Rather, supporters of equal representation were more likely to support the new body because they were disproportionately western residents. More important, and completely resistant to the regional control, is opinion on the 25 percent guarantee. Supporting this proposal increased one's likelihood of supporting the new Senate by 9 points. It is doubtful, though, that many non-Quebeckers supported the guarantee for itself. More likely, endorsement of the guarantee was a byproduct, not a cause, of accepting the compromise. A more substantive interpretation must be cast in the negative: that is, an unwillingness to accept the guarantee reduced one's support for the new Senate. All this said, endorsement of both equality and the guarantee, together with satisfaction with or ignorance of power relations, would still leave the likelihood of endorsing the new body well short of 0.50.[10] Of course, most respondents endorsed equality and rejected the guarantee, so the typical net effect was only slightly positive.

Much stronger was opinion on power relations, and, strikingly, all the action was on the "too much" side. The view that the new body had too much power virtually erased any chance of endorsing the change. This impact was not attenuated by regional controls. Saying that the new Senate had too little power, to begin with a less probable response than its opposite, had no effect. To the extent that the equation has a driving force, then, it lies in outright aversion to giving any variant of the Senate any more power. Significantly, there is no evidence that Canadians rejected the new Senate because it failed to live up to the Triple-E ideal. The opposite is more nearly true. And even respondents who declared satisfaction with the new Senate's power were highly unlikely to support the new body.

Opinion on power and representation, in its impact on support for the new Senate, cut through region. The two most impressive factors had coefficients untouched by regional controls. By the same token, coefficients on regions themselves correspond almost exactly to the differences in Figure 3–2. There were regional microclimates of Senate support – warmest in the Prairies and coolest in Ontario – but regional climatic differences represented little disagreement over substance, except perhaps mildly over representational equality.

The conclusion seems inescapable: voters outside Quebec, like voters inside that province, really had little use for Senate reform. The argument that voters rejected the proposed Senate as inadequate just will not wash. Support might have been a bit higher had Senate reform not entailed the 25 percent guarantee, but this too seems a stretch. The real story, it seems, is that voters never much wanted Senate reform. To the extent that leaders sincerely believed they were following popular sentiment in crafting that proposal, they acted on a misapprehension. It is true that a decade of published surveys showed a desire for Senate reform but the indication reflected more the constraints imposed by question format than a desire for real reform. A respondent who feels disgust with the existing Senate can hardly endorse the status quo when given a choice between it and some unspecified reform. Before the respondent has a chance to get to the real issue, the questioner is on to some other issue, perhaps to some specification on reform which presupposes a true willingness to embark on institutional transformation. The respondent is still blocked from registering disgust with the whole business. This is not to say that Canadians (outside Quebec at least), given a chance for full deliberation, would reject some true Senate reform. They might indeed conclude that Westminster-style majoritarianism no longer suits Canada, if it ever did. But they might as easily recoil from the potential gridlock that true bicameralism entails. At this point, Senate response in surveys seems under the control of opinion on the existing body and that opinion leads a large plurality to reject an upper house, *tout court*. The indication so far, then, is that the Senate had little chance of binding Canada outside Quebec to the Charlottetown Accord. And there is no evidence that this component of the Accord could have generated sufficient support for people to overlook, or set aside, any concerns they might have with other parts of the deal.

ABORIGINAL SELF-GOVERNMENT

More promising was Aboriginal self-government. One entire section of the Accord, part IV, was devoted to this issue. In addition, section 2(1)(b) of the Canada clause acknowledged that Canada's Aboriginal peoples "have the right to promote their languages, cultures and traditions and to ensure the integrity of their societies, and their governments constitute one of the three orders of government in Canada" (*Consensus Report*, p. 1). Section 9 aimed to guarantee Aboriginal representation in the Senate, section 20 mentioned an Aboriginal role in relation to the Supreme Court, section 22 spoke to Aboriginal representation in the House of Commons, section 40 provided for broad-gauged protection of Aboriginal cultures, and section 60 was designed to ensure Aboriginal participation in future constitutional amending procedures.

The Accord thus went further than any previous constitutional effort to address Aboriginal grievances. Even so, evidence that Aboriginal peoples were divided came early. Philip Fontaine, leader of the Manitoba Assembly of First Nations, argued that the proposals for Aboriginal self-government chipped away at traditional treaty rights. Members of the Assembly of First Nations Women's Group worried that, by shielding traditional Aboriginal rights, the Accord would undermine equality for native women. Other signs of discord emerged as direct challenges to Ovide Mercredi's authority. Leaders of the Mohawk Nation and chiefs of bands outside the Assembly of First Nations flatly denied that Mercredi spoke for them. Those not in open opposition to Mercredi and the Accord faced the problem of sorting out precisely what Aboriginal peoples had gained in the Accord. Section 9, which dealt with Aboriginal representation in the Senate, was silent on how many seats this meant. The precise relationship between Aboriginal groups and the Supreme Court, according to section 20, would be resolved at a future first ministers' conference. Aboriginal seats in the House of Commons had a similarly ephemeral quality. On the central issue of self-government there remained uncertainties to be resolved through negotiation. For some, like Keith Goulet, an Aboriginal MLA from Saskatchewan, statements of principle and assurances of future talks sufficed. They saw the Charlottetown agreement as an historic turning point. "You're looking at aboriginal people not only as consultants or advisers," he said, "We are now strategic builders of Confederation."[11] But for others, especially those troubled by the tentativeness of Aboriginal gains, the host of unresolved details made it difficult to distinguish symbol from substance. For them the dilemma remained: without critical details, was a Yes vote a justifiable leap of faith?

As the campaign began, a number of Aboriginal leaders staked out the claim that Aboriginal votes should be counted separately. Andrew Bear Robe, constitutional adviser to the Siksika Nation, captured that sentiment neatly and framed the issue in a way entirely consistent with the Accord's bargaining logic: "The self-government proposal is our part of the constitution. Aboriginal groups fought very hard for it, and it should be left up to us to decide whether we like it or not."[12]

Mercredi was of the same mind and he floated a thinly veiled threat to the effect that status Indians might even boycott the referendum. "If we can't identify the Indian vote," he asked, "why vote at all?"[13] When the logistical difficulties of counting native votes in urban areas became clear to everyone, the argument lost steam. As it did so, the potential for an Aboriginal veto subsided and the fate of the Accord, including the proposal for Aboriginal self-government, shifted into the hands of the non-Aboriginal majority.

And a clear majority of Canadians favoured that element of the Accord. Outside Quebec, according to Figure 3–1, supporters outnumbered opponents by a ratio of 62 to 30. Support was less one-sided in Quebec, at 54:38, but still seemingly decisive. In some respects, support for Aboriginal self-government comes as little surprise. It seems consistent with earlier indications of general sympathy on a range of Aboriginal issues (Gibbins and Ponting, 1978; Wohlfeld and Nevitte, 1990). In 1992 Aboriginal peoples seemed to enjoy a substantial reservoir of support. For example, when our respondents were asked "How much should be done for Aboriginal peoples," 78 percent outside Quebec said "much more" or "somewhat more." After the vote, respondents were asked "Should we go ahead with Aboriginal self government anyway?" The response was emphatic: nine out of ten said we should.

If Aboriginal support was wide, was it also deep? It is not difficult to muster sympathy in principle for a marginalized group, especially when little appears to be at stake. Specific proposals are another matter, however. Guaranteed seats for Aboriginals in the new Senate, for example, attracted less support than the principle of self-government and that principle itself received less backing than the most general statement of all, that more should be done for Aboriginals. The geography of support for self-government also hinted at political weakness: according to figures 3–1 and 3–2, the more immediate the experience of conflict, the less support for the principle. Support was highest in Ontario and the Atlantic provinces. It was markedly lower in the Prairie provinces and lower still in British Columbia, the other main site of confrontation in 1990. Indeed, support for self-government in British Columbia was about the same as in Quebec, definitely in the majority but not onesidedly so. Finally, consider a piece of evidence from a 1993 wave of the 1992–3 study. In the latter year we framed a question at the heart of self-government. Did this mean a relatively unencumbered right to legislate or should the right be constrained by uniformity of laws? Table 3–3 indicates that voters, at least by 1993, clearly meant the latter: among panel respondents the margin for uniform application of law was nearly 4:1.[14] Supporters of

Table 3–3
The Scope of Aboriginal Self-Government, All Canada (Quebec included)

	Aboriginal Self-Government (1992)		
Aboriginal Law (1993)	Support	Oppose	All
Make Own Laws	30	7	21
Same Laws as Others	68	93	77
N	850	463	1405

self-government were certainly more likely to concede an expansive right, but even in this group the clear majority favoured constraint. One might argue that this requirement was no more than what the Accord contained and that, further, respondents were endorsing not an entirely abstract proposition but self-government as recognized in the Accord. But then, what the Accord meant by self-government was a matter of disagreement.

SPECIFIC ELEMENTS AND THE VOTE

Element by element, support for the Accord's parts did not constitute a promising pattern. Only aboriginal self-government was supported in both Quebec and the rest of Canada. Quebec and the rest of Canada were also at one on the new Senate, but in opposition to it. On the heart of the package, the two Quebec elements, the country was deeply split. Although we do not present a table or figure on this point, it bears emphasis that these patterns revealed themselves throughout the campaign, from start to finish. *On no basic element in the Charlottetown Accord did opinion shift during the official campaign.*

What this meant for the vote appears in Table 3–4. The two leftmost columns indicate relationships on voting day, for Quebec and the rest of Canada respectively. As opinion stability in Quebec translated directly (at least over the official campaign) into vote stability, the voting-day estimation suffices for that province. Outside Quebec, in contrast, the vote evolved even as opinion on the Accord's substance did not. Hence, the two rightmost columns track evolution of the rest-of-Canada opinion-vote relation over the campaign.

In Quebec the picture is of offsetting negative and positive, with a perversity in between. On balance, the 25 percent guarantee appears to have helped the Yes. Other things equal, supporters were 16 points (coefficient of 0.16) more likely than opponents to vote Yes, and sup-

Table 3–4
Impact of Elements by Phase of Campaign

	Quebec	Rest of Canada		
			Intentions	
	Vote	Vote	24 Sept.–4 Oct	5–25 Oct.
Distinct Society Clause	-0.22***	0.29***	0.15**	0.24***
	(0.04)	(0.03)	(0.05)	(0.03)
25% Guarantee for Quebec	0.16***	0.20***	0.28***	0.27***
	(0.04)	(0.04)	(0.07)	(0.04)
Senate	0.37***	0.14***	0.07	0.23***
	(0.05)	(0.03)	(0.06)	(0.04)
Aboriginal Self-Government	0.00	0.15***	0.14***	0.06
	(0.04)	(0.03)	(0.06)	(0.03)
Intercept	0.40	0.13	0.34	0.20
	(0.05)	(0.02)	(0.05)	(0.03)
R^2-adjusted	0.14	0.21	0.12	0.20
N	673	1092	360	869

porters outnumbered opponents (Figure 3–1): 50 percent of Quebeckers supported the guarantee and that share multiplied by a coefficient of 0.16 yields a gain for the Yes side of 8 points. Conversely, opposition to the new Senate reduced the chance of a Yes by 37 points (coefficient of 0.37), and opponents greatly outnumbered supporters: 65 percent of Quebeckers opposed the new Senate (strictly speaking, preferred either the existing Senate or no Senate at all), and that share multiplied by the coefficient of 0.37 yields a 24-point estimated drop. As the balance tilted more away from the Senate than toward the guarantee and as the Senate coefficient was much larger, it is clear that events around the Pearson accord put the whole process in a deep hole. By extracting the 25 percent guarantee, Bourassa brought Quebec opinion part way back, but the gain was modest compared to the original loss. No further help was forthcoming from Aboriginal self-government, for which the coefficient was simply 0.

This left the distinct society clause, and its effect seems perverse: Quebec supporters of this concession were 22 points *less* likely than opponents to vote Yes. The perversity is only apparent, of course.

First, as Figure 3–1 indicated, Quebeckers' support for the distinct society clause was close to consensual. Those who opposed the clause – some non-francophones and extreme federalists among francophones – were likely to be in the Yes camp for other reasons, mainly fear of the consequences of rejection. Equally critically, among supporters of the clause, only 29 percent thought it went far enough (Table 3–1). Nearly two-thirds thought it supplied too little and supporters were twice as likely as opponents to assert this. For them, recognition of Quebec as a distinct society was the bare minimum, and so it hardly seemed like a concession.

In the rest of Canada the critical factors on voting day were the two Quebec elements. Other things equal, a supporter of the distinct society clause was nearly 30 points more likely than an opponent to vote Yes. But opponents outnumbered supporters by just less than 3:2. A supporter of the 25 percent guarantee was 20 points more likely than an opponent to vote Yes. On this element, opponents outnumbered supporters by over 4:1. Aboriginal self-government helped a little, in that supporters were more likely than opponents to vote Yes, and supporters outnumbered opponents. But the Senate contributed next to nothing to the Yes coalition: supporters were only modestly likely to vote Yes, and they were greatly outnumbered.

The Quebec/rest-of-Canada pattern suggests that as an exercise in traditional coalition-building, the Charlottetown Accord failed abjectly. Traditionally, a political bargain, a "logroll," gives each party what it wants intensely, and extracts only weakly valued concessions in return. As a logroll, the Charlottetown Accord was inverted: it gave each side either something it did not want or too little of what it did want, and demanded too much in return. Quebec won a key point in the distinct society clause but by 1992 this was taken for granted, the bare minimum. And as crafted in that year, the clause did not go far enough. The 25 percent guarantee was more novel and was helpful in itself. But the circumstances of its birth were fatal: it arose out of the Pearson accord Senate, and even the watered down Charlottetown version was too much for Quebec. Not only were Quebeckers opposed to the new body, they acted on that opposition. Voters in the rest of the country were almost as cool as Quebeckers to the new body, and the few who supported it were not very likely to act on that support. What moved voters outside Quebec were the key concessions to the other side.

For all that, voters outside Quebec were prepared early on to acquiesce in the Accord. What happened? The campaign shifted emphasis on elements to the disadvantage of the whole package and the Accord lost the benefit of the doubt:

- The factor with the greatest positive potential, Aboriginal self-government, never had a more than a weak link to the vote and after 5 October got decoupled from it. Before that date a supporter was 14 points more likely, other things equal, than an opponent to vote Yes. After 5 October the difference shrank to 6 points, although the original difference appears to have been restored by referendum day.
- Before 5 October a supporter of the 25 percent guarantee was 28 points more likely, other things equal, than an opponent to vote Yes. This difference held into the late campaign, although it shrank a bit on referendum day. This was bad news, of course, but it was bad news right from the start.
- Before 5 October the distinct society clause was less important than the 25 percent guarantee. After that date it rivalled the guarantee and on voting day it was somewhat more important. This shift is consistent with Trudeau's intervention, as he laid great weight on the clause. Increasing the importance of the distinct society clause was a key to undermining the Yes campaign.
- Before 5 October a Senate supporter was only slightly more likely than an opponent to vote Yes. After 5 October the difference became quite wide, although it narrowed on referendum day. It was not that Senate supporters became more likely to vote Yes. Rather, the intercept dropped and the sum of intercept and Senate slope remained roughly constant. As with opponents of the distinct society clause, so with opponents of the new Senate: they became less willing to go along with the deal.

Table 3–5 plots the unravelling of the Accord's rest-of-Canada support by phase, translating coefficients from Table 3–5 into vote shares. The top line gives the share for voters opposed to all four elements, based on Table 3–4's intercept values. Here is one indication of the Accord's loss of benefit of the doubt: before 4 October someone opposed to everything of substance still had one chance in three of voting Yes. This dropped to one chance in five after the 4th and was down to about one in eight by referendum day. At the other extreme, the handful of voters who supported everything in the Accord held the line: their Yes share slid by less than 10 points and was still over 90 percent on voting day. Groups in between traversed various courses. Least affected were voters who supported the key element for Quebec, the distinct society clause: at the outset, voters who supported only this element had a roughly 50:50 chance of voting Yes and, even at the end, their Yes share was over 40 percent. Next most resilient was support for the new Senate. Voters who supported only this had over four chances in ten of voting Yes early and this likelihood held into the late campaign. On voting day, however, the share was down to 27 percent, confirmation that the new Senate was just too peripheral a gain for voters who saw everything else as a loss. But the biggest disappointment must have been Aboriginal self-government. Voters who supported only this element, a large fraction of the electorate, had a close to 50:50 chance of voting Yes early on. After 5 October, however, this group's Yes share was cut in half. That it dropped no further would be small consolation to the Accord's architects. Combining self-government and Senate support (third line from the bottom) pushed the Yes share up but not, in the end, far enough. Indeed, a voter who supported both of these non-Quebec elements had the same Yes share (42 percent) as a voter who supported only the distinct society clause. *At the end support for some non-Quebec element could induce a Yes majority only in combination with a Quebec element.* Late in the campaign, a Senate-distinct society combination looked potent: among supporters of both, the Yes share actually grew after 5 October. But on voting day the share settled back to the early campaign value. The self-government–distinct society pair at first seemed more febrile but ended up being roughly as resilient. The critical element in each case, as already indicated, was the distinct society clause. This is most readily seen in terms of shifts in voting-day Yes shares. On that day, a voter opposed to every element was 37 points away from the 50-percent threshold. Supporting only the distinct society clause shifted one upward a full 29 points, to just 8 points short of the threshold. Adding just one non-Quebec element put the voter over the threshold. But supporting both non-Quebec things while accepting nothing for Quebec left a voter short of the 50-percent mark.

REFLECTIONS

For a document conceived so clearly and self-consciously as a bargain, the Charlottetown Accord was most peculiar. Typically, elements in a coalition of minorities appeal to the self-defined interests of pivotal actors, whose withdrawal from the coalition would doom it. It is odd, then, that the most widely supported element was a concession to one of the smallest groups. In sheer numbers, withdrawal of Aboriginal voters would be of virtually no electoral significance. Aboriginal peoples might have practical non-electoral clout, by threatening to take us back to the tense, occasionally violent summer of 1990. This probably weighed on many non-Aboriginal voters. But the implicit threat was also double-edged, as resort to unconventional politics could easily boomerang. For most voters in 1992, support for

Table 3–5
The Unravelling of Support, the Rest of Canada

	24 Sept.–4 Oct.	5–25 Oct.	Referendum Day
Oppose Every Element	34	20	13
Support Senate Only	41	43	27
Support Self-Govt. Only	48	26	28
Support Distinct Soc. Only	49	44	42
Support Self-Govt. + Senate	55	49	42
Support Senate + Distinct Soc.	56	67	56
Support Self-Govt. + Distinct Soc.	63	50	57
Support Every Element	98	100	91

Based on estimations in Table 3–4.

Aboriginal self-government must have been disinterested – only a recognition of a powerful moral claim. Whatever its exact basis, it was support for a concession to somebody else. But the same was true outside Quebec for the Accord's Quebec elements, and support for these was less common than for Aboriginal self-government. The clear evidence is, however, that supporting a Quebec element was absolutely critical to approving the whole package. Consider what this means. For someone outside Quebec, to support the distinct society clause can hardly mean liking the clause for itself. It must signal, rather, a disposition to compromise, to empathize with the other side's bargaining position or to care more about securing the whole package than about the arithmetic of its parts. As a narrowly conceived bargain, the Charlottetown Accord simply failed. If this was true outside Quebec, it was even more so in that province.

4 Beyond Coalition-Building

If the Accord was such a bad bargain, why did so many voters consider supporting it? Some may have suppressed doubts about specifics and accepted claims about the package as a whole. Voters were urged to accept half a loaf, the alternative being none. Voters were also asked to ponder the consequences of failure, to ask if the status quo was acceptable, even sustainable. If such arguments helped the Yes side at the start, they did not suffice at the end.

THE ARGUMENTS

Was one's province a winner or a loser? The crudest argument invited voters to focus on the general interest of their province, to conclude that the province had done well overall out of the deal. Negotiations bore the hallmarks of a first ministers' conference and this may have encouraged voters to consider how their own premier performed. The near-consensus of federal parties also worked to draw attention to provincial considerations, as citizens lacked nationwide partisan cues. Then there was the strategy of sending in favourite sons and daughters to explain how their province had won, and why Accord support was necessary to consolidate the gains. The contrast with the 1988 debate over the Canada-US Free Trade Agreement is instructive. On that occasion, parties divided sharply and these divisions were reflected in striking contrasts between party groups and weak contrasts among regions and language groups (Brady and Johnston, 1993). In 1992 the two federal parties provided exceptions that proved the rule:

both the Bloc Québécois and Reform opposed the deal but each was geographically concentrated.

Was the Accord the best compromise possible under the circumstances? By definition, an accord is a compromise, and evaluating a compromise entails stepping back from its specific contents and bringing general considerations into play. This entails more than just asking narrowly what is in the deal for me (us), as compared with others at the table; it also means accepting the necessity for accommodation among strategically placed or morally advantaged players. It seemed implausible, for instance, that virtually anyone other than a francophone Quebecker would enthusiastically embrace either the distinct society clause or the 25 percent seats guarantee for itself. Support for these elements outside Quebec would have to rely on transcendental reasoning, an appeal to an overriding logic. Voters outside Quebec might vote Yes because decades of communal conflict taught them that protagonists could not be satisfied by a simple solution. In that light, was the Accord basically fair? Did not some groups, such as Aboriginals and Quebeckers, have grievances that, on some principled grounds, had merit? And, all things considered, were the concessions reasonable? At a minimum, even if voters did not like the concessions, could they live with them? Were the long-run implications of rejection even worse? Was the status quo even tenable?

Might the Accord still allow us to move on to other questions even if it was not the best compromise possible? Constitutional matters dominated the public agenda for the better part of a decade, much to voters' chagrin. Many had no interest whatever in the constitution. Those who could muster some enthusiasm felt beaten down by seemingly endless rounds of haggling. Much comment on the Accord avoided its substance and emphasized instead the need to resolve constitutional uncertainty for the sake of the economy. More generally, constitutional preoccupations crowded many issues off the agenda. Voters might thus be led to vote Yes just to bring closure and move the constitution itself off the agenda.

Would saying No send Quebec the wrong message? In particular, would it increase the likelihood of secession? For elite negotiators, this question lurked behind all others. Reasoning proceeded on two levels, one substantive, the other procedural, but both favoured a Yes vote. On substance, two key elements (and other less salient ones) represented concessions to Quebec. Even if Quebeckers themselves were uneasy about the 25 percent guarantee, by 1992 recognition as a distinct society was firmly entrenched as the province's absolute minimum demand. Rejecting the Accord could thus be interpreted as rejecting Quebec, would stoke secessionist fires, and might sour prospects for Canadian federalism. Buttressing this logic were procedural considerations: what if Quebec said Yes and the rest of Canada said No? Quebec's Yes would signal both the importance of its own gains and its willingness to compromise. As long as a Quebec Yes seemed remotely possible, compromise-minded voters might have felt compelled to still their doubts just to avoid sending precisely the wrong signal. Of course, if it became clear that Quebec would not say Yes, then the procedural argument could turn on its head: Why risk signalling a willingness to concede prematurely? Would we validate worrisome non-Quebec initiatives which we now grudgingly accept because they are some group's price for accommodating Quebec, only to find that Quebec can live with them even less than we can? All this presupposes a willingness to accommodate Quebec, to accept that Quebec's demands were both legitimate in themselves and not the thin edge of a negotiating wedge.

Would saying Yes *send Quebec the wrong message?* In the rest of Canada Quebec is often described rather like a child: if you give it a small thing it comes back and asks for more. From this standpoint, voting Yes out of fear of Quebec secession would be a recipe for disaster, based on a misguided and naive reading of Canadian federalism, and would send precisely the wrong signal. Accepting the Accord would undermine federalism, not save it. To such an argument, how Quebec itself might vote was irrelevant.[1]

GENERAL CLAIMS FOR THE ACCORD

Three claims about the Accord's positive features are depicted in Figure 4–1. Each argument is presented as a "balance of opinion," rather as in Figure 3–2. If opinion on an argument favours the Accord, then the line is above the zero horizon. If opinion works against the Accord, the line is below the horizon.[2] One argument was unpersuasive from the beginning, and acceptance of all three diminished over the campaign:
– Most voters rejected the claim that their own province was a winner, and nothing in the campaign persuaded them otherwise. Early October events worsened opinion but their impact wore off. The campaign had no enduring effect on this general claim.
Each other argument lost ground:

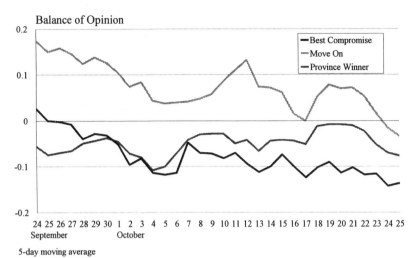

Balance of Opinion

Legend:
- Best Compromise
- Move On
- Province Winner

5-day moving average

Figure 4–1
Perceptions of the Accord

- The weaker claim was for the intrinisic merits of the compromise. This claim was accepted early on, but only by a tiny margin. By 27–28 September judgment was almost exactly in balance and apparently drifting down. The first October weekend saw the balance tip sharply,[3] never to recover; the distribution on 4–5 October persisted for the next three weeks. On the merits, voters rejected the compromise.
- More promising was the claim that the deal would allow us to move on the other questions. For almost the entire campaign most voters accepted this. The balance was especially favourable early on but, as with acceptance of the compromise, a downward drift was unmistakable. Even so, the balance tipped negative only at the very end. Unlike arguments for the compromise, opinion on the Accord's ability to move us on appeared to rally at various points.

These two characterizations of the compromise – that it was the best one possible and that it would facilitate moving on – were, unsurprisingly, closely related.

Table 4–1 makes this point in two ways. In the upper left of each cell is a column percentage, indicating, for each position on the Accord as compromise, whether voters believe the package will allow us to move on. This is the easiest way to present the strength of the relationship; supplementing column percentages is a table statistic,

Table 4–1
Two Readings of the Document

Allow us to Move on	Best Compromise			
	Disagree	Don't Know	Agree	
Disagree	60 32	20 3	13 5	39
Don't Know	9 5	26 4	3 1	9
Agree	31 17	54 7	83 28	52
	53	13	34	(1109)

Column percentages in roman, total percentages in italic.
Somer's d (symmetric) = 0.46

Somer's d. The link between arguments is revealed by comparison across rows. Of voters who rejected the compromise, only 31 percent believed the Accord would allow us to move on. In contrast, the percentage among those who approved the compromise was 83%. Where almost no one who approved the compromise thought that it would fail to settle things, a clear majority believed this among those who rejected the deal. The value of d for the table is thus very robust.

Now think about arguments as coalition-builders. For this, the relevant numbers are total percentages, which appear in each cell's bottom right corner. The Yes coalition's core consists of voters who accepted both arguments, 28 percent of the sample. Another 24 percent accepted the "move on" argument, even though they did not accept the "best compromise" one. This added up to a bare majority, but only because distributions were averaged over the whole campaign. By voting day, the sum was much less than 51 percent. What about voters who, though they rejected the claim about moving on, accepted the compromise as the best possible? These were very few, of course, only 5 percent of the total sample (less by voting day). To all intents and purposes, approval of the compromise's intrinsic merits nested inside agreement that the compromise, whatever its intrinsic merits, would close Canada's constitutional file. Acceptance of the latter defined the outer boundary of the potential pro-Accord coalition.

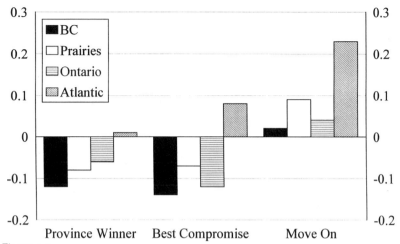

Figure 4–2
General Arguments about the Accord by Region, Rest of Canada

No characterization of the Accord created a powerful regional base, according to Figure 4–2.[4] Only the Atlantic provinces were distinguished for acceptance of pro-Accord arguments. In no other region did voters typically see their province as a winner. Only there did the balance of opinion (averaged over the campaign) favour the compromise. And Atlantic voters were by far the most persuaded that the deal would allow us to move on. If the Atlantic region was distinctive, no other region was. Especially striking is the similarity of Ontario to the western provinces. Only on the winner-loser criterion was there a clear East-West gradient and even so, Ontario was closer to the West than to the Atlantic provinces. On the other two arguments, Ontario rivalled British Columbia for alienation from the deal; Prairie voters were, if anything, modestly more forgiving.[5]

ARGUMENTS ABOUT QUEBEC

Arguments about Quebec never helped the Yes side outside Quebec, according to Figure 4–3. The figure's setup exactly parallels Figure 4–1. For visual clarity, coding of one argument – that Quebec always asks for more – is reversed. Here, unlike the other questions, agreement worked against the Accord. Reversal maintains the graphical logic of Figure 4–1: if the balance of opinion helped the Accord, it should appear above the zero horizon, otherwise, below it. Notice that for the entire campaign both arguments were below the horizon.

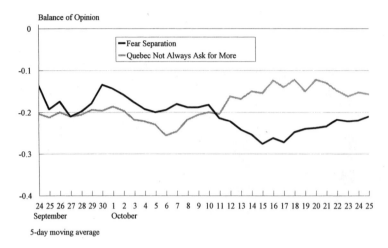

Figure 4–3
Perceptions of Quebec

Quebec's secession threat was never credible and, if anything, it became less credible over the course of the campaign. Accord advocates thus faced a fundamental difficulty: the negotiators' fear that, but for a comprehensive constitutional settlement, Quebec might leave, was simply not shared by the public at large. In no region did a majority fear Quebec's departure, according to Figure 4–4. The threat was most credible in Atlantic Canada, but even there most voters were unmoved. Ontarians, who also might reasonably fear disruption of central and eastern ties, were as unmoved as Prairie dwellers by threats.

Belief that Quebec would always ask for more was widespread, although less pervasive at the end than at the beginning. Claims that Quebec lost ground in 1980–2 and failed to recover ground in 1987–90 did not register. Voters invoked a simpler script to account for Quebec's demands: they saw them as part of a pattern of wanting more. And this perception knew no regional bounds; no differences appeared among the Atlantic region, Ontario, and the Prairie provinces. Only British Columbians stood out, as mildly less persuaded by this argument than voters elsewhere.

Opinion on the two Quebec arguments was not closely linked, according to Table 4–2. Among voters who saw Quebec as insatiable, 25 percent feared secession, as compared with 31 percent among more forgiving voters, only a 6-point difference. Somer's *d* for the

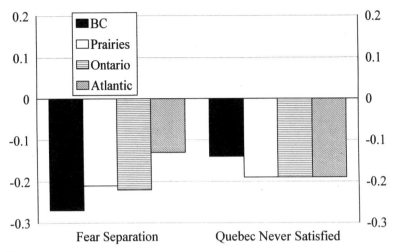

Figure 4–4
Perceptions of Quebec by Region, Rest of Canada

table is correspondingly weak. As sources of evaluation of the Accord, then, the two arguments were potentially independent, unlike the two positive arguments described earlier. But this independence could not have reassured Accord supporters. The coalition the questions' independence was most likely to help build was a negative one. As opinion on each question was one-sidedly negative, the mutual independence of the questions meant that a vast majority of voters outside Quebec could find at least one Quebec-related reason to say No. Nearly half the sample jointly affirmed insatiability and bluff. Twenty percent did not see Quebec as insatiable but also did not fear separation; saying Yes would have few ill Quebec-related consequences but neither would saying No. Another 17 percent did fear separation but also saw Quebec as insatiable; saying No might be fatal but saying Yes would not be much better, indeed might not even postpone further confrontation. The position of maximum sympathy, fearing separation and repudiating the insatiable image, was held by only 9 percent.

THE REASONING CHAIN

How did these arguments, together with opinion on specific elements, drive the vote? At issue here is the basic character and dynamics of the reasoning chains introduced in chapter 1. Figure 4–5

Table 4–2
Two Fears about Quebec

Fear Secession	Quebec Never Satisfied			
	Disagree	Don't Know	Agree	
No	67 20	58 3	73 48	70
Dont' Know	2 1	17 1	3 2	3
Yes	31 9	26 1	25 16	26
	29	5	66	(1109)

Column percentages in roman, total percentages in italic.
Somer's d (symmetric) = −0.06

elaborates on the sketch in Figure 1–1. We propose that relations among ideas and elements are a compound of *hierarchical* and *reciprocal*:

- Deep down, the point of the exercise was to accommodate Quebec. And Canadians' opinions on Quebec as a constitutional player pre-dated 1992. Hence, opinion on the two Quebec arguments should be wholly exogenous, a cause of opinion elsewhere in the system, never an effect. Specifically, general response to Quebec should affect response to the two specific Quebec elements and to the two most general claims for the deal.
- At the other extreme should be judgment on whether one's own province was a winner or loser. This is a judgment about the 1992 deal in particular, and so should reflect the deal's components.
- Inherently more complex should be the two most general arguments, for the quality of the compromise and the prospects for moving on. The more one approves any particular element, the more one should accept a general claim. Similarly, the larger the number of elements one supports, the more one should accept a general claim. But one might also accept a specific element only as a part of a generally approved package. Hence, causal relations between these two general arguments and the four specific elements are presented as reciprocal.

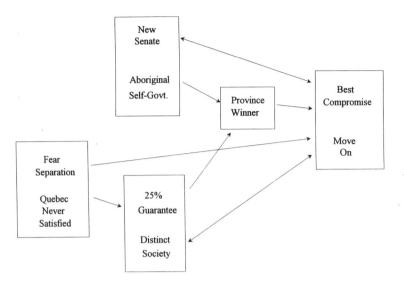

Figure 4–5
Reasoning about Specific and General: A Model

The complexities of Figure 4–5 have two basic implications for estimation. First, many relationships have multiple stages and, to do justice to certain factors, estimation must reflect those stages. Estimation
for impact at any stage is unlikely to do justice to the total impact
from factors at earlier stages. For instance, Quebec perceptions affect
opinion Quebec elements; Quebec elements affect opinion on provincial judgment; provincial judgment affects acquiescence in the "best
compromise" claim; the "best compromise" claim affects the vote.
Impact from Quebec perceptions will be masked by the fact that
some, perhaps most, is routed through opinion on the package's two
Quebec elements, and impact from these elements in turn will be
masked by impact from provincial judgment, and so on. This is not a
great difficulty, however. For truly interesting earlier factors, estimations can begin by omitting intervening variables; this "reduced
form" yields estimates for total impact. Then, as intervening factors
are added, we can specifiy the routes by which a background factor's
total effect is exerted.

Second, and more awkward, is the fact that some relationships are
reciprocal, as between each specific element and each of the two positive arguments. In a reciprocal nexus, estimation for impact in one direction will be confounded by impact in the other direction. Although

Table 4–3
Quebec: Background and Foreground

	Distinct Society	*25% Guarantee*
Fear Separation	0.08**	0.08**
	(0.03)	(0.02)
Queber Never Satisfied	-0.28***	-0.20***
	(0.03)	(0.02)
Intercept	0.59	0.28
	(0.03)	(0.02)
R^2	0.08	0.07

Entries in parentheses are standard errors
* $p < 0.05$; ** $p < 0.01$; *** $p < 0.001$

it would be nice to sort out all reciprocal links, this objective eludes us. Identification of reciprocal links requires replacement of direct measures of each variable with "instrumental" ones. Consider, as an example, links between distinct society opinion and acceptance/rejection of the "best compromise" claim. We need a measure for distinct society opinion close to the direct measure but not identical to it – one purged of any possible impact from "best compromise" opinion. We need a corresponding instrument, purged of impact from distinct society opinion, for "best compromise." To get such measures we need predictors for one variable which are not predictors for the other and in our data set no such predictors presented themselves. We cannot, then, truly separate reciprocal effects.[6] The causal minutiae in this domain are not, in any case, central to the general logic we wish to elucidate. What we shall do is estimate the impact of general arguments and the vote twice, with and without specific elements in the setup. With these two estimations, with evidence from Table 3–5, and some supplementary estimations, we can tell a very textured story.

GENERAL ARGUMENTS AND SPECIFIC ELEMENTS: ESTIMATION

The Quebec Nexus

Table 4–3 begins at the beginning, with the impact of Quebec perceptions on the assessment of the Accord's key Quebec elements. Strikingly, one Quebec perception is of little significance at this stage: fear played only a weak role in support or opposition to either the distinct

Table 4–4
Coming to General Judgment

	Province Winner	Best Compromise		Move On	
GENERAL ARGUMENTS					
Province Winner	–	–	0.37*** (0.03)	–	0.34*** (0.03)
Fear Separation	–	–	0.16*** (0.03)	–	0.17*** (0.03)
Quebec Never Satisfied	–	–	0.03 (0.03)	–	0.02 (0.03)
SPECIFIC ELEMENTS					
Distinct Society	0.16*** (0.03)	0.17*** (0.03)	0.11*** (0.03)	0.11*** (0.03)	0.05 (0.03)
25% Guarantee	0.26*** (0.03)	0.25*** (0.04).	0.14*** (0.04)	0.20*** (0.04)	0.09* (0.04)
New Senate	0.08** (0.03)	0.10*** (0.03)	0.07* (0.03)	0.13*** (0.03)	0.09** (0.03)
Aboriginal Self-Govt.	0.05* (0.03)	0.05 (0.03)	0.04 (0.03)	0.10*** (0.02)	0.09** (0.03)
Intercept	0.27 (0.02)	0.23 (0.02)	0.07 (0.04)	0.39 (0.03)	0.24 (0.04)
R^2-adjusted	0.14	0.12	0.25	0.09	0.19

society clause or the 25 percent guarantee. What mattered more – in the negative – was the view that Quebec was insatiable. This was particularly true for opinion on the distinct society clause: seeing Quebec as insatiable cut support for the clause roughly in half. The smaller coefficient on the 25 percent guarantee is partly a "floor" effect. Even among voters who did not see Quebec as insatiable, support for the guarantee was slight; little room was left for downward movement, and virtually no voter who saw Quebec as insatiable supported the guarantee.

Provincial Performance

Judgment on whether one's province won or lost was driven mainly by opinion on Quebec elements, not by opinion on non-Quebec ones, according to the leftmost column of Table 4–4. Most powerful was precisely the Quebec consideration that touched other provinces' representation claims directly, the 25 percent guarantee. Voters who disapproved of everything else crossed the 0.50 threshold on provincial assessment if they could be induced to accept the guarantee; of course, few voters did accept it. The distinct society clause was second in line although with a markedly less dramatic effect. Even so, it easily exceeded the impact of opinion on either the Senate or self-government. The tiny impact from Senate opinion may be the estimation's most notable aspect – the dog that didn't bark. If most non-Quebec voters judged their province's performance harshly, it was not because their premier failed to extract the right Senate. What premiers failed to do, in voters' eyes, was block Quebec.

Coming to General Judgment on the Accord

Judgment on the province was the most powerful single factor in acceptance or rejection of positive claims for the Accord. As this chapter's first section argued, this was precisely what the process encouraged. But this induction boomeranged: respondents tended to see their province not as a winner but as a loser. Voters who supported no element in the deal, who had the "wrong" perceptions of Quebec, and who saw their own province as a loser had no chance of approving the compromise. If all other things remained true, seeing the province as a winner moved the chances of approval up 37 points. Of course, voters who saw their province as a winner also tended to accept the distinct society clause, and such voters had about a 50–50 chance of approving the compromise.[7] Among voters who accepted the clause yet saw their province as a loser the compromise was approved by only about 15 percent. The story is almost exactly the same for response to the claim about moving on.

Fear played a role in summary judgment, but not a very impressive one. Those who feared secession were 16 to 17 points more likely to accept a general argument, other things being equal. This is a rather smaller direct effect than from judgment on voters' own provinces. And this direct effect is almost the whole story: recall from Table 4–3 that fear played little role in opinion on key Quebec elements. Of course, few voters actually were fearful.

At this stage the other Quebec perception – whether or not the province was insatiable – exercised no leverage on acceptance of positive arguments. This is not to say that the perception was irrelevant; its effect was just indirect, through acceptance/rejection of key Quebec elements and thence through winner/loser judgments. And among specific elements, Quebec ones dominated the field. When only specific elements enter estimation, Quebec coefficients are strikingly similar all across the table: over 0.20 for the 25 percent guarantee and around 0.15 for the distinct society clause. When general arguments also enter estimation, these coefficients shrink roughly in half, mainly as effects are absorbed through the winner/loser judgment.

If Quebec elements dominated the field, they did not absolutely control it. Attitudes to the Senate and to Aboriginal self-government played a visible role, especially in relation to the claim that passing the Accord would allow us to move on. Effects from each non-Quebec element were roughly as powerful as from distinct society opinion. And for each, impact on acceptance/rejection of the general claim was strikingly direct: neither coefficient shrank much when "province winner" entered the estimation. This may seem ironic, especially for Senate attitudes. The new Senate was explicitly designed to deliver something to the allegedly most recalcitrant parts of English Canada in return for their acceptance of Quebec elements. It could have divided English Canada deeply, precisely over provincial gains and losses. That it gave too much to some provinces and too little to others does not detract from the point. Indeed, to the extent that the Senate mattered outside Quebec, this sort of discrepancy should register directly at the provincial bottom line. Opposing (favouring) the Senate because it makes one's province a loser (winner) should produce a powerful covariance between these factors. A lack of covariance testifes to the Senate's weak relevance to the electorate at large.

What then of the fact that the Senate coefficient is larger in the "move on" equation than in any other, especially larger than in the "province winner" equation? Most likely, this indicates that voters tended to assess the Senate in light of the deal, not the other way around. Willingness to accept the Senate was part of a more generalized willingness to accept the Accord – to settle with one major self-identified interest, the Senate-reform constituency, the better to get on to other questions. Few voters saw themselves as part of this constituency but some were willing to concede its existence and legitimacy.

Aboriginal self-government probably had some of these characteristics as well. Certainly there was little sense in which non-Aboriginals could see Aboriginal self-government as serving their own, non-Aboriginal interests.[8] Intuitively, though, self-government seems subtly different from Senate reform. The mere fact that self-government received so much more support than the new Senate suggests it was freer-standing opinion. Moreover, few doubted that most Aboriginal Canadians themselves wanted self-government, even if the Accord's particular variant ultimately divided First Nations. For his part, Ovide Mercredi claimed to speak only for Aboriginal peoples. If he

Table 4–5
Quebec Perceptions and the Vote: Reduced Form

	Intentions		
	24 Sept.–4 Oct.	5–25 Oct.	Vote
Fear Separation	0.29***	0.28***	0.20***
	(0.06)	(0.04)	(0.03)
Quebec Never Satisfied	-0.29**	-0.25***	-0.17***
	(0.06)	(0.04)	(0.03)
Intercept	0.67	0.55	0.45
	(0.06)	(0.03)	(0.03)
R^2-adjusted	0.16	0.12	0.06
N	289	698	1111

represented them inadequately, it was because he asked too little, not too much. Senate reform advocates, in contrast, claimed to represent a large fraction of the very voters to whom their appeal was addressed. They also claimed that the Accord provided less than their clients really wanted. Few voters could know that both claims were essentially false.

THE VOTE

Perceptions of Quebec

Perceptions of Quebec were powerful factors in the vote, each with roughly the same weight, according to Table 4–5. Shifting from the anti- to the pro-Quebec extreme more than doubled the likelihood of voting Yes: a voter who did not fear secession and who believed Quebec was never satisfied had a 28 percent chance of voting Yes; at the other extreme, a voter who feared secession and did not see Quebec as insatiable had a 65 percent chance of voting Yes.[9] Unfortunately for the Yes side, nearly half the sample fell at the anti-Quebec extreme (no fear, insatiable), and most others were in the middle.

Over the campaign, Quebec arguments became both less helpful to Yes forces and less relevant overall. Figure 4–3 indicated that both perceptions shifted modestly in the anti-Quebec direction. At the same time, the vote difference between Quebec extremes also dropped. In contrast to the election-day gap of 37 percent, the gap before 4 October

Table 4–6
Overall Evaluations and the Vote: Reduced Form

	Intentions		
	24 Sept.–4 Oct.	5–25 Oct.	Vote
Best Compromise	0.45***	0.51***	0.39***
	(0.06)	(0.03)	(0.03)
Move On	0.34***	0.29***	0.22***
	(0.06)	(0.03)	(0.03)
Intercept	0.17***	0.09	0.11
	(0.04)	(0.02)	(0.02)
R^2-adjusted	0.40	0.45	0.25
N	289	698	1111

between extremes was 58 percent. In other words, 38 percent of voters who did not fear secession and who saw Quebec as insatiable intended to vote Yes; of voters with the opposite profile, 98 percent intended to vote Yes.

Overall Evaluation of the Accord

By voting day, according to Table 4–6, evaluation of the compromise itself was about twice as important as belief about whether the compromise would allow us to move on. A voter who did nothing more than approve the compromise still had a 50: 50 chance of voting Yes.[10] A voter who decried the compromise but still saw the Accord as allowing us to move on fell far short of the 50: 50 threshold. And by voting day, as Figure 4–1 indicated, this most powerful argument had long since lost majority endorsement. Most voters rejected the proposition that the Charlottetown Accord was the best we could do.

Early in the campaign, the move on argument carried more weight. It never quite rivalled the best compromise claim, but, given its general acceptance early on, the move on claim certainly started out being helpful; it was the best shot at mobilizing the feeling of constitutional fatigue for the Yes side. As acceptance of the claim dropped, so did its purchase on the vote decision. By implication, as the campaign progressed voters focused more and more on the inherent merits or defects of the agreement. As chapter 3 made clear, focus on the deal itself could only hurt.[11]

Table 4–7
Specific Elements, General Arguments, and the Vote

	Intentions		
	24 Sept.–4 Oct.	5–25 Oct.	Vote
GENERAL ARGUMENTS			
Best Compromise	0.35***	0.36***	0.26***
	(0.06)	(0.04)	(0.03)
Move On	0.23***	0.22***	0.14***
	(0.06)	(0.03)	(0.03)
Province Winner	0.23***	0.21***	0.12***
	(0.06)	(0.04)	(0.03)
Fear Separation	0.11*	0.12***	0.07*
	(0.05)	(0.03)	(0.03)
Quebec Never Satisfied	-0.13**	-0.08**	0.00
	(0.05)	(0.03)	(0.03)
SPECIFIC ELEMENTS			
Distinct Society Clause	0.04	0.12***	0.21***
	(0.05)	(0.03)	(0.03)
25% Guarantee for Quebec	0.03	0.04	0.07
	(0.06)	(0.04)	(0.04)
Senate	-0.02	0.11***	0.08**
	(0.05)	(0.03)	(0.03)
Aboriginal Self-Government	0.10	-0.01	0.12***
	(0.05)	(0.03)	(0.03)
Intercept	0.15	0.04	-0.06
	(0.06)	(0.04)	(0.04)
R^2-adjusted	0.48	0.53	0.35
N	289	687	1092

All Factors, General and Specific

Table 4–7 completes the case, with all nine considerations included. Most critically, the table indicates displacement of general arguments by specific elements. Most dramatic was the emergence of the distinct society clause. Before 5 October, with all general arguments controlled, opinion on the clause had no independent effect (coefficient of only 0.04). Thereafter, distinct society opinion acquired a discernible, highly significant effect, and on voting day its power rivalled acceptance/rejection of the best compromise argument. Senate reform followed a similar, if more modest path: invisible at first (of course, this was true without any general arguments controlled; see Table 3–4) but clearly visible in late campaign and on voting day. Opinion on the 25 percent guarantee never really got out of the shadows; notwithstanding its importance, it was clearly caught up in general arguments. Even so, its coefficient was larger on voting day than before, and it came close to meeting the usual test for statistical significance.[12] Impact from opinion on Aboriginal self-government followed a more tortuous path, but its role on election day conforms to the general point here: it played a more distinct role than before.

At the same time, all general arguments lost power. For four of five considerations, the loss, indicated by shrinkage in coefficients, was around 0.10. This pattern was already visible in reduced-form estimations, and Table 4–7 indicates that it also held for province winner perceptions. The weight of the evidence seems plain: the pro-Accord coalition was thrown increasingly back on the narrow logic of coalition-building, a logic whose tests the Accord failed.[13]

CONCLUSIONS

Appeals from fear were bound to fail. Voters did not share the elite's apprehensions about Quebec's secession – indeed, they countered them with an ancient tribal nostrum about Quebec's greed and deviousness. Instead, voters had to be persuaded that the Accord was the deal to end all deals. Voters may not have been fearful, but they were tired. If they accepted that the Accord would end Canada's chronic constitutional crisis, they might be prepared to stomach otherwise distasteful medicine.

Voters outside Quebec were simply not seized by fear for the country, perhaps because they had been taken to the brink too many times by the same leaders. Given the course of negotiations and – perhaps more critically – early moves by sovereignists to neutralize secessionist fear, it is hard to fault voters' judgment. We suspect, however, that the lack of secession anxiety reflected not so much the Charlottetown chronology as a deep-seated, long-standing complacency about Quebec. What Canadians outside Quebec were anxious about was Quebec's getting too much. That Quebec by 1992 was arguably a three-time constitutional loser did not register. Instead, the prevailing language, also time-worn, was that Quebec asks too much – and gets too much. Even if Quebec fails in its ostensible constitutional quest, it gets paid off in other ways, in bricks and mortar, in dollars and cents, and in language policies and other symbolic concessions whose costs are borne by the rest of the country. In part, these concessions reflect the quotidian logic of getting and keeping single-party majorities. In part, they reflect the very constitutional anxieties that elites feel but the electorate does not.

Early on, the claim that the Accord would let us move on attracted quite one-sided majorities. No other positive argument came close, neither claims for the compromise itself nor appeals to provincialist self-regard. By confronting the claim that the settlement would move us on, Pierre Trudeau and Preston Manning took a high risk. By alluding to the document's failure to settle disputes, they might inadvertently have validated the premise that the disputes were real and, by implication, that failing to address them would provoke further trouble. At a minimum, their attacks might only increase the relevance of the only factor working initially to the Accord's advantage. But with risk goes reward: Trudeau and Manning took on supporters' most potent argument, and if its very credibility could be undermined, the deal would be doomed.

Its credibility *was* undermined. As this happened, as acceptance of positive arguments went down, so did their very relevance. It is tempting to infer that these two shifts were functionally related. As fewer and fewer other voters accept a generalized claim about an agreement, the less that claim should matter even to those who still accept it. The claim becomes less a factual proposition – once this deal carries, it *will* deliver the following benefit – and more a hypothetical one – had this deal carried, it *would* have delivered the following benefit. One might go to the wall for the former proposition, but not for the latter.

Be that as it may, opinion on specific elements *gained* importance. But if the Accord could not sell for what it promised to avert, even less could it sell for what it delivered. The only specific element whose priming could help the Accord was Aboriginal self-government, but this was the only specific element to become less important after 5 October, although it did weigh in the balance on voting day. The Senate became more important, but its supporters were too thin on the ground. In its other details, the Senate story in this chapter complements the one in chapter 3. Senate opinion was only weakly related to judgments on whether one's province won or lost. This does not indicate province-oriented dissatisfaction with the proposed Senate; regardless of the strategic intentions of those who crafted the

Accord, the proposed Senate was mostly irrelevant to provincialist score-keeping.

What was relevant for that score-keeping was the Quebec agenda. And taken all together, the evidence suggests that provincial self-regard, as such, was a weak force. As a factor in the vote, province winner never matched the combined power of acceptance/rejection of the two positive arguments (Table 4–7). The fact that, on one hand, score-keeping was driven by Quebec-related opinions and, on the other hand, largely unmoved by the most pointedly provincialist feature of the non-Quebec agenda, the Senate, suggests that what is commonly paraded as provincial self-regard is nothing of the sort. The existence of provincial boundaries and the government-driven logic of constitutional bargaining may encourage voters to frame their judgments as a provincial balance sheet. We were certainly encouraged to frame the matter this way and once we had done so, respondents willingly took us up on the question. But the question presupposed more provincialism than the 1992 facts warrant; the province winner question was to a great extent just another conduit for sentiment that looked outward – to Quebec. Arguably, negotiators made the same mistake. They saw resistance to Quebec's demands as the flip side of a localistic consciousness; so to overcome resistance, they pandered to localism by constructing an allegedly localistic Senate. Just as few voters wanted the new Senate (or any Senate, for that matter), so were hardly any as localistic as elites imagined them to be. But if many, perhaps most, voters' vision extended beyond their province's boundary, even if most voters' Canada included Quebec, as the saying went, it did not include recognizing Quebec as distinct, as the homeland of a founding people.

5 Locating the Accord

How did voters reach positions described in the preceding two chapters? Some voters could figure things out for themselves, obviously, but for many, shortcuts were necessary. The most obvious shortcut was to listen to well-placed commentators: agenda-setters, the Charlottetown negotiators themselves; and key intervenors, both the formidable coalition that formed around negotiators and the scattered forces in opposition. To assess the value of each agenda-setter or intervenor, the key issue was where that person or group came from, where he or she was on the policy landscape. If voters could locate intervenors, they could also get some sense of the Accord's distance from the status quo.

Locating a document like the Accord thus requires a kind of triangulation, sorting out spatial relations among intervenors, identifying where they sit relative to each other and to the voter. Then voters must identify whether a given intervenor supports or opposes the proposal. Ideally, having identified all interventions, voters can then find the boundary between supporters and opponents. The ballot measure must lie somewhere near that boundary. This, of course, is the logic, associated with McKelvey and Ordeshook (1986) and Lupia (1992, 1994, 1995), outlined in chapter 1.[1]

But coalition-building around the Charlottetown Accord was designed specifically to mask that boundary, perhaps even abolish it. The coalition was intended to be inclusive on every imaginable dimension of political evaluation. For every opponent there should also have been a supporter nearby, nearby – that is, in political or ideological

Table 5–1
Ratings of Intervenors *(N=1109)*

SUPPORTERS	
Mulroney	30
Chrétien	47
McLaughlin	47
Premier	43
Lougheed	50
Unions	48
The Business Community	65
SUPPORTER AVERAGE	47
OPPONENTS	
Trudeau	57
Manning	42
The Women's Movement	63
OPPONENT AVERAGE	54

Note: Entry is average rating on a 0–100 point scale.

"space." If the coalition succeeded, if every opponent was "covered" by a supporter, then every voter should also have found a reassuring figure nearby, urging him or her to say Yes.

This chapter starts by elaborating on spatial reasoning and characterizing the space intervenors inhabited. Then it considers the visibility and clarity of interventions, whether intervenors succeeded getting their message through. Key interventions are assessed for their power, whether they had the intended effect, indeed whether they had any effect at all. Finally, we consider the structure of response, the fit between intervenor and intended audience.

POPULARITY OF KEY PLAYERS

The idea of "distance," then, is this chapter's abiding theme. A psychological proxy for distance is warmth of feeling: the warmer your feelings toward an object the less alienated you are from it, the more you identify with it, the less distant it seems. Start with simple distances, to flesh out the balance of proximities for supporters and opponents. Table 5–1 gives the average ratings on a 0–100 scale (where 0 indicates absolute disdain, 50 ambivalence or indifference, and 100 unqualified affection), for ten individuals or groups which, in advance of the event, seemed likely to play key roles.[2] Several outstanding elements emerged:

- Of all players, Brian Mulroney was by far the least popular. He was rated some 15 to 20 points below other individuals in the Accord coalition, nearly 30 points behind his arch-nemesis, Pierre Trudeau.
- With the possible exception of the business community, evaluation of the rest of the pro-Accord coalition was middling: average ratings approached 50. Distributions were not markedly skewed and so, although judgments tended slightly to the negative, almost as many respondents gave positive ratings as negative ones.
- By quite a margin, the most popular individual was Pierre Trudeau.[3]
- Mr Trudeau's chief ally in opposition, Preston Manning, was the second *least* popular national figure.[4] Mr Manning may have conceived powerful opposition language, but he was not well placed to utter it himself.
- Groups tended to get higher ratings than individual politicians, perhaps as a measurement artifact. Unfortunately for the Accord coalition, however, union leaders were the least highly regarded of the key groups, although they got almost as many positive as negative ratings.

How politicians played into the country's geography is revealed in Figure 5–1, with entries cast as deviations from national average ratings in Table 5–1. Most striking is the lack of a consistent sectional thread in leader evaluation.[5] For Pierre Trudeau the opinions of the 1970s persisted – least popular on the Prairies, most popular in Ontario – but otherwise his popularity had a broad sectional base; strikingly, he was almost as popular in British Columbia as in Ontario. Preston Manning was liked least in Ontario but was otherwise undifferentiated; striking was his lack of localized appeal on the Prairies.

All the foregoing pales in comparison with rating for the provincial premiers. The sharpest contrast was between the Atlantic provinces and all others: a 10-point difference from the national average, almost a 15-point gap with Ontario. Although not presented in the figure, differences within regions deserve mention. Highest rated of any individual were Clyde Wells of Newfoundland and Joe Ghiz of Prince Edward Island. Close behind were Frank McKenna of New Brunswick and Gary Filmon of Manitoba. In their own provinces these four premiers outshone Pierre Trudeau. The local contrast with

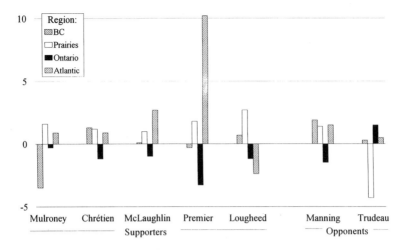

Entry is regional deviation from non-Quebec mean

Figure 5–1
Regional Differences in Evaluation of Intervenors

Trudeau was especially great for Filmon. The other premier with positive ratings was Roy Romanow of Saskatchewan. Donald Cameron
of Nova Scotia had the weakest standing in the Atlantic region, although even he beat the national average. That average was dragged
down by the three remaining premiers. Bob Rae and Mike Harcourt
fared badly, as Figure 5–1 indicates, Rae especially so. The figure
masks the worst performer of all, Don Getty of Alberta.

THE STRUCTURE OF EVALUATION

Average ratings are just the first step in characterizing how voters located the Charlottetown Accord. The language of distance and direction is a language of spatial coordinates. If voters are capable of
placing groups and politicians in a coordinate space, and if they can
identify which are supporters and which are opponents, then voters
can use the spatial pattern of support and opposition to locate the
Accord itself.

Start with ratings of political figures. A low average rating indicates
that most voters see the figure as distant from themselves and a high
rating that most see the object as close. For instance, Table 5–1 shows
that most voters felt distant from Mulroney and many felt close to
Trudeau. But even Brian Mulroney received some positive ratings and

Table 5–2
The Structure of Group and Politician Evaluation *(N=1109)*

| | Rotated Factor Pattern | | | |
	Conventional Politicians	Organization as Such	Left-Right	Trudeau Legacy
McLaughlin	**0.77**	0.17	-0.02	0.16
Premier	**0.72**	0.22	-0.04	-0.22
Chrétien	**0.61**	-0.06	0.34	0.36
Mulroney	**0.43**	0.11	**0.45**	**-0.46**
Business Cmty	-0.09	**0.72**	0.40	-0.17
Unions	0.33	**0.61**	-0.20	0.21
Women's Movement	0.21	**0.78**	-0.06	0.13
Lougheed	0.19	-0.03	**0.75**	0.01
Manning	-0.13	0.02	**0.65**	0.07
Trudeau	0.10	0.16	0.10	**0.84**

Method: Principal components factor analysis with varimax rotation

Pierre Trudeau received many negative ones. Did closeness to Trudeau imply distance from Mulroney?

To identify underlying evaluative dimensions, we employ factor analysis. This takes all the correlations among evaluations of objects and asks a series of questions: What single factor links evaluation of as many of the objects as possible? Once that first factor is extracted, what second factor explains most of the remaining variance? With two factors extracted, what third factor can we identify? And so on until as many factors are extracted as there are initial variables. So far, all that is accomplished is a rearrangement of deck chairs. But chairs are rearranged to maximize occupancy, and only some factors merit further scrutiny. Roughly speaking, the number of variables explained by a factor is indexed by the factor's eigenvalue; only factors with eigenvalues greater than one are worth retaining. The four factors presented in Table 5–2 account for 63 percent of all variance in evaluation. Once we identify the plausible number of factors, we "rotate" them to provide the simplest, most sharply differentiated explanation.[6]

In descending order of importance, according to Table 5–2, the rotated factors were:

1 Orientation toward *conventional politicians*. This is the core of the Accord's coalition and it seems to hinge on two characteristics. One is identification with the NDP: evaluation of Audrey McLaughlin has the highest loading; second highest is for evaluation of provincial premiers, and in 1992 the NDP presided over provinces comprising two-thirds of the non-Quebec sample. Second is *currently active* involvement in parliamentary or legislative politics: the three lowest loadings are for Manning, Trudeau, and Lougheed, individuals outside elected office; Brian Mulroney and Jean Chrétien, in contrast, loaded highly on this factor, although not as highly as the NDP figures.

2 Response to *organizations as such*. Although each organization was strikingly different and these particular organizations routinely sparred with each other, all three elicited fairly positive ratings.[7]

3 The classic *left-right* organization of political life. At one end were Preston Manning and Peter Lougheed, with Brian Mulroney close to them. At the other end was the labour movement, followed by the women's movement, the provincial premiers (recall that about two-thirds of this rest-of-Canada sample had an NDP premier in 1992), and Audrey McLaughlin. In the middle were Jean Chrétien and Pierre Trudeau.

4 Orientation to the *legacy of Pierre Trudeau*. Trudeau's ratings loaded on no other factor and no other ratings loaded on this factor as much as his did. This factor's other pole was anchored by Brian Mulroney's ratings. That fact and the rank order of loadings between poles defines the continuum in terms of what Trudeau-era Liberals and Mulroney-era Tories, respectively, stood for. Other actors, including the NDP, were a sideshow to the Liberal-Conservative struggle for control of historical-cultural interpretation.

Figures 5–2 and 5–3 locate actors on axes derived from Table 5–2. Loadings on factors indicate how much of a factor each variable carries. Take left-right as an example. In voters' eyes, Preston Manning and Peter Lougheed obviously have a lot of this factor. Brian Mulroney also possesses a lot but not as much as the first two. Jean Chrétien and Pierre Trudeau have even less, and so on. This logic allows us to use factor loadings to characterize the evaluative landscape; indeed, coordinates in Figures 5–2 and 5–3 are just loadings from Table 5–2. Thus, on Figure 5–2's horizontal left-right axis the union movement anchors the left and Peter Lougheed the right. On the vertical conventional politicians axis Audrey McLaughlin occupies the top position and Preston Manning the bottom.

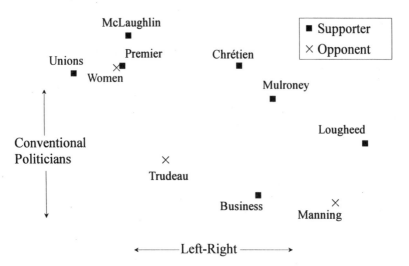

Figure 5–2
Evaluation of Intervenors I: Left-Right and Conventional Politicians

In factor analysis, the zero point is theoretically meaningless; to see this, consider left-right again. As this particular analysis presents it, the factor is mainly "rightness"; Manning and Lougheed have a lot, Audrey McLaughlin has only a little. The union movement gets a discernibly negative loading, but the whole continuum is displaced toward positive values, not an uncommon pattern in factor loadings. It makes no intuitive sense, however, to insist that McLaughlin occupies the centre of the spectrum. The centre must lie somewhere near Trudeau or Chrétien. To discourage too-literal interpretations of factor loadings, then, figures 5–2 and 5–3 suppress the zero point and the axes running through it. Instead, the figures bring out general spatial relations among key intervenors. To highlight relationships, boxes indicate supporters and crosses indicate opponents.

Did Charlottetown coalition-building succeed? Could supporters be found all over the landscape? Could a voter located almost anywhere find a supporter nearby and so be encouraged to conclude that the Accord was acceptable, even of positive benefit? At the same time, was every opponent shadowed by a nearby supporter or, best of all, surrounded by supporters?

Figure 5–2 locates actors in the space defined by the conventional politicians and left-right continua. The figure confirms that the pro-Accord coalition spanned the full range from left to right, from the union movement to Peter Lougheed. In this sense, the strategy be-hind the Accord succeeded spectacularly: a voter at left, right, or cen-tre could find an Accord supporter nearby. Almost the same was true on the conventional-unconventional continuum. Only Preston Man-ning was further removed from political conventionality than the mainly pro-Accord business community. The other pole, the conven-tional end, was positively saturated with Accord supporters.[8]

And for every opponent, a supporter lurked nearby. Most heavily covered was the women's movement, virtually surrounded by politi-cal kin. Less well covered were Trudeau and Manning. Trudeau was further from the nearest supporter (the business community) than any other opponent, Manning included. But the business community was closer to the unconventional pole than Trudeau, and Trudeau himself was only a little left of centre. If you collapsed either dimen-sion, Trudeau would seem surrounded. Preston Manning was closer to two supporters, the business community and Peter Lougheed, than Trudeau was to any. But he did anchor the unconventional pole; no one was further away than he from conventional politicians. If the left-right dimension collapsed, Manning would sit alone, uncovered to the south. But the business community would still be very close to hand. And Manning himself was not very popular. Figure 5–2 seems to reveal coalition-building success of the highest order.

But Pierre Trudeau's disruptive potential positively leaps out of Figure 5–3, where orientation to conventional politicians is supplanted by orientation to Trudeau's legacy.[9] Closest to Trudeau on both dimen-sions was Jean Chrétien. This is as it should be, for Chrétien was Trudeau's probable choice as successor in 1984, and his clear choice for Liberal leader in 1990. Recall that Chrétien's 1990 accession occurred in the superheated June that saw the death of the Meech Lake Accord. In-deed, the two events seemed functionally linked, both indicating the resurgence of a Charter-of-Rights coalition. Chrétien's location thus validates Accord supporters' concern to keep the Liberal party inside the coalition. Only he had much chance of neutralizing opposition by Trudeau. But if Chrétien was closer than anyone else to Trudeau, he was not closer to him on this dimension than to other members of pro-Accord coalition. As trustee of his own legacy, Trudeau was unchal-lenged. And his popularity, though not universal, was high.

VISIBILITY OF INTERVENORS

Voters' next step was to link the Accord to key actors. Linking it to in-siders – parliamentary figures and provincial premiers – should have been simple; these were the agenda-setters, after all. But for outside

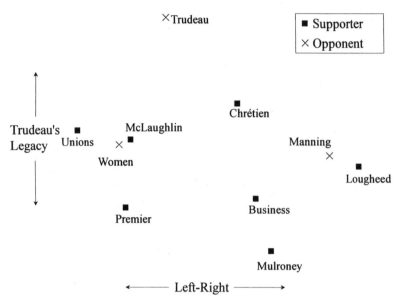

Figure 5–3
Evaluation of Intervenors II: Left-Right and Trudeau's Legacy

intervenors, including all opponents, awareness could not be taken for granted.

Awareness is tracked by day for individuals and groups in figures 5–4 and 5–5. The vertical scale is the number making the "correct" attribution as a percentage of all relevant possibilities: correct, incorrect, or no attribution.[10] Most attributions, if made in the first place, were correct. The largest percentage of incorrect was for the women's movement, but this is not surprising, as the movement was deeply divided. But given the position taken by the National Action Committee on the Status of Women (NAC) and the attention that position received, the relevant perception for our purposes was of opposition.

Among individuals, Pierre Trudeau was unquestionably the most visible for most of the campaign. Preston Manning rivalled Trudeau early and then again late. Peter Lougheed never came close to either:

– Lougheed may have been the great disappointment for the Yes forces. He had been a truly powerful spokesman for western interests and, of all individual supporters, it was Lougheed who came closest to covering Preston Manning. For all that, only one voter in

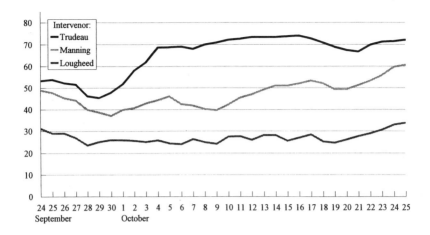

5-day moving average
Figure 5–4
Awareness of Intervenors I: Individuals

three identified his position correctly at the end, and for most of the campaign the proportion was more like one in four.

– Preston Manning was always more visible than Lougheed, although for most of the campaign not much more so. Manning initially lost visibility, probably a reflection of declining media treatment as his 10 September press conference receded into the past. But he gained visibility over October; his 5 October debate with Audrey McLaughlin may have helped. More important, we suspect, were his television advertisements. By the end, about 60 percent of non-Quebec respondents identified Manning as an opponent.

– All this was dwarfed by Pierre Trudeau, however. From the beginning about 50 percent attributed a No position to the former prime minister. Some of this may have been projection, perhaps from his role in killing the Meech Lake Accord. Some probably reflected awareness of his 21 September *Maclean's-Actualité* article, commonly reported as an attack on the Accord. In any case, awareness surged after his Egg Roll speech on the night of 1 October. The moving-average process in Figure 5–4 masks the speed of the surge and advances its onset. Recall that the speech could not have been a news story before the 2nd. In the raw tracking underlying the figure, the surge in awareness is overnight, from the 2nd to the 3rd, one day in advance of the collapse of the

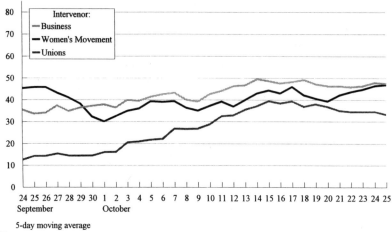

5-day moving average

Figure 5–5
Awareness of Intervenors II: Groups

Yes. By that day and thereafter, the percentage identifying Trudeau as an opponent was around 70.

Evidence on group interventions, in Figure 5–5, further confirms the importance of Trudeau and, possibly, of Manning. It does so indirectly, by showing that no group was outstandingly visible and no group supplied much in the way of short-term dynamics. All three groups did gain visibility – gradually, for the most part – such that by the end one-third to one-half the sample could make the correct group attribution. Most elite commentary focused on the women's movement, specifically on the NAC's opposition to the Accord. But the NAC was not more visible than the business community. Respondents picked up divisions within the women's movement: the percentage saying either that the women's movement supported the Accord or that the movement was divided grew over the campaign and ended up about 20 percent. Most of the time about half as many respondents said that the movement was divided or supportive as said it was opposed. Divisions in the business community were less widely seen.

Although visibility was regionalized, according to Figure 5–6, differences between regions were swamped by differences between intervenors. Typically, intervenors were most visible in Ontario. This was especially true for the women's movement, identified as opponents by about 10 percent more in Ontario than in the West, 20 percent more

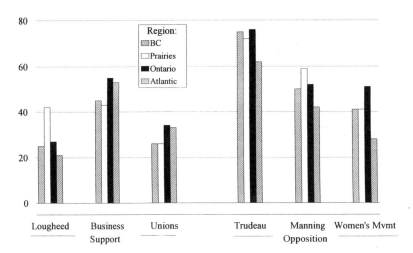

Entry is % making the indicated attribution

Figure 5–6
Awareness by Region

than in the Atlantic region. For awareness of Trudeau the boundary was between Ontario and the Atlantic provinces; westerners were nearly as clear as Ontarians on his position. Manning and Lougheed, the two western tribunes, were, appropriately, most visible in the West. But they were not equally visible in all four provinces: British Columbians were no more attentive to them than Ontarians were.

All this said, awareness was a strikingly national phenomenon. A highly visible intervenor was highly visible everywhere. Obscurity in one place was not offset by celebrity elsewhere. National visibility differences between intervenors were mirrored in local differences. Even within the Prairie region, for instance, Preston Manning was much less visible than Pierre Trudeau. Indeed, Manning was less visible in this, his highest-visibility region than Trudeau was in the Atlantic provinces, his lowest-visibility region.

IMPACT I: AWARENESS

All signs so far point to the centrality of Pierre Trudeau: of all opponents he was the least well covered by supporters; of all intervenors, he was the most visible; and of all intervenors only he experienced a sharp surge in visibility. But the most eloquent testimony to his influence is Figure 5–7, which juxtaposes awareness of Trudeau to the

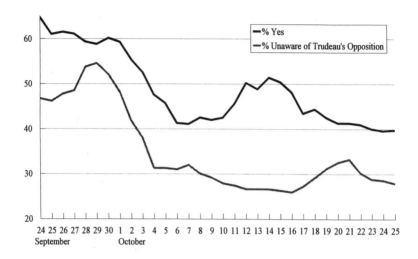

5-day moving average

Figure 5–7
Trudeau's Opposition and Voters' Support for the Accord

vote. The figure overlays Trudeau awareness from Figure 5–4 and the
Yes share outside Quebec from Figure 2–1. To make the point, the
awareness line is inverted (hence the labelling as % unaware). Both
series are five-day moving averages and so the suddenness of shifts is
understated; recall that, according to daily tracking, both the Yes-
share collapse and the Trudeau-awareness surge occurred overnight.
Smoothing does not mask the central point, that the shifts were absolutely parallel. First, the awareness surge and vote drop each spanned
20 points. Second, each shift occurred at exactly the same speed.
Third, awareness led vote shift by one day. The evidence in Figure 5–7
may be circumstantial, but we have never seen circumstantial evidence so powerful.

The argument is not that awareness of Trudeau was the whole
story of the campaign. But a comprehensive account must give due
weight to the Trudeau factor. After 4 October all further nuance in the
campaign has no Trudeau referent. Notice that Trudeau's visibility
made no more gains; the percentage aware of his opposition pla-
teaued around 70. Once stablilized, aggregate awareness of Trudeau
could account for no further net vote shifts. And two vote shifts were
visible: first, a temporary recovery and, second, a final drop.

Also important was the structure of support and opposition at any
given time. Was Trudeau important to these as well? The job of establishing this begins in Table 5–3. Here, vote intention[11] is regressed on

Table 5-3
Net Impact of Awareness

	All	BC	Prairies	Ontario	Atlantic
SUPPORTERS					
Lougheed	-0.02	0.06	-0.01	-0.07	0.08
	(0.04)	(0.11)	(0.08)	(0.05)	(0.14)
Business Community	0.04	0.14	0.08	-0.06	0.23*
	(0.04)	(0.09)	(0.08)	(0.05)	(0.10)
Unions	0.05	-0.05	0.04	0.05	0.30*
	(0.04)	(0.10)	(0.08)	(0.05)	(0.12)
OPPONENTS					
Trudeau	-0.15***	-0.07	-0.16	-0.17**	-0.26*
	(0.04)	(0.11)	(0.08)	(0.06)	(0.12)
Manning	0.08*	0.12	0.01	0.13*	-0.05
	(0.04)	(0.09)	(0.08)	(0.05)	(0.14)
Women's Movement	-0.03	-0.14	0.08	-0.01	-0.15
	(0.03)	(0.08)	(0.08)	(0.05)	(0.12)
Intercept	0.54	0.43	0.52	0.58	0.55
	(0.03)	(0.09)	(0.07)	(0.05)	(0.09)
R^2-adjusted	0.01	0.01	0.00	0.01	0.10
N	987	154	242	497	93

Entries in parentheses are standard errors;
* $p < 0.05$; ** $p < 0.01$; *** $p < 0.001$

variables, identical to those in figures 5–4 and 5–5, indicating awareness of each intervenor. Coefficients indicate *net impact* of awareness,
the difference made to the probability of a Yes vote by simple awareness of the intervenor's position.[12] In the national estimation, only
two intervenors stand out: Trudeau, and Manning. Awareness of
Trudeau had a clear negative impact on the Yes vote, net of all other
interventions. The coefficient is much smaller than the one-to-one
correspondence implied by the lockstep awareness-vote shifts of
Figure 5–7. There are several reasons for this and we shall explore
most of them in the next few pages. Suffice it to say here that only
Trudeau had anything like the impact an intervenor might wish for.

For most others, coefficients were of the correct sign but, Manning's aside, none were larger than ±0.05 and none significant by any test or criterion. Weak effects on the supporter's side might be expected; the Yes side lost, after all. But on the No side, some claims to have turned the tide, by the women's movement for instance, prove groundless. Preston Manning did have an effect, but not the one he intended: awareness of Manning's opposition helped the Yes rather than hurt it. The coefficient's perverse sign reflects the fact that Manning was not very popular, that more voters disliked him than liked him.

Conceivably, the national estimation overlooks strength in particular regions. Perhaps Manning helped the No in his home region, the Prairie provinces. Or the women's movement may have moved debate in metropolitan centres. The other columns of Table 5–3 address these possibilities. For the women's movement, strikingly, the smallest coefficient is for Ontario, where awareness of the movement's position was greatest. Only in British Columbia did impact from awareness of the women's movement come close to being statistically and substantively significant. At least the women's movement never had a perverse impact, unlike Preston Manning. Remarkably, nowhere did Manning have impact he intended. It might be small consolation that his effect was weakest in the Prairie provinces, that in his home region his impact was merely a nullity. His impact was greatest in Ontario, next greatest in British Columbia, and in both places, of course, he helped the side he was volubly working against.

Most influencable by far were voters in the Atlantic provinces. The overall power of the equation (as indicated by R^2) was far greater there than anywhere else, and several individual coefficients stood out. In that region no intervenor, not even Preston Manning, had the wrong effect. Both the business community and the union movement significantly helped the Yes forces, the women's movement may have helped the No side, and Pierre Trudeau had his biggest impact.

This brings us back to Trudeau yet again; the role – or lack of role – played by other intervenors places his contribution in perspective. His was the one intervention to slice through the electorate virtually everywhere. Only in British Columbia was his impact weak to nonexistent. His impact was as great on the Prairies as in Ontario, and on the Prairies Manning did not get in Trudeau's way.

Regions were not the only plausible lock gates for influence. It is also worth asking if certain intervenors had more impact in certain sociodemographic groups than in others, and if impacts shifted over time. Did the women's movement, for example, have more impact among women than among men? Did the union movement at least move union families? Did interventions matter more early, when overall awareness and knowledge were at a premium, or late, when interventions were most widely visible? Figure 5–8 addresses these questions, by presenting selected contrasts. Bars in the figure represent regression coefficients, exactly like coefficients in Table 5–3, indeed derived from identical setups. Four contrasts seemed worth making: by *phase*, before 4 October versus after that date; by *union status*; by *gender*; and by *party identification*. Four intervenors appear: Trudeau and Manning, because each was consistently important in Table 5–3; and the union and women's movements, because each claimed to represent readily identifiable constituencies. In the underlying estimations, Lougheed and business-community coefficients were also identified, but were not worth reporting.

The first lesson, in Panel A, is that, if anything, Table 5–3 understated Trudeau's importance. The whole-campaign coefficient of -0.15 averages two markedly different early versus late coefficients. In the early stages, when information was at a premium, awareness of Trudeau made a huge difference. This could not have been awareness of Trudeau's specific critique, since the Egg Roll speech was not given until the end of the early phase – indeed, it helped define phases. Rather, awareness was of his general post-1982 hostility to macro-constitutional tinkering, especially tinkering with his own legacy. For many, this awareness was fuelled by the *Maclean's-Actualité* article in late September. It is the drop in Trudeau's cross-sectional influence which indicates how completely he transformed the debate; at the margin, awareness of his particular intervention no longer mattered.

Such impact as the union and women's movements had also dropped from early to late. This is probably a close parallel to the pattern for Trudeau. When information is hard to come by, specific interventions can be telling, at least at the margin. As information spreads, many voters pick up substantive arguments from friends and neighbours or through social influence by opinion leaders, without necessarily being aware of the ultimate source. The pattern illustrates the "two-step flow" of communication and persuasion (Katz and Lazarsfeld, 1955). In the early campaign, opinion leaders picked up messages from elite intervenors, and the structure of vote intentions reflected first-round differences in direct exposure to elite messages. Later on, once leaders spread the word to followers, awareness of the original intervention ceased to matter.[13]

The exception to this general pattern is Preston Manning. Only he was more important late than early. As awareness of Manning's opposition spread, it slowed down the collapse of the Yes side. As voters who might otherwise have gone straight over to the No side located

A. Phase

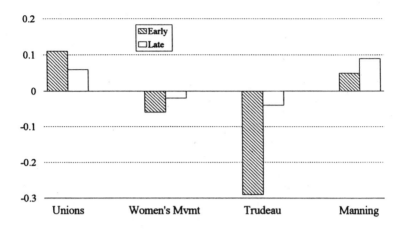

B. Union Status

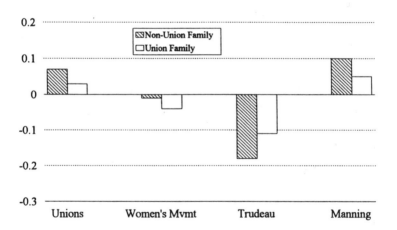

Figure 5–8
Selected Net Impact Contrasts

the Accord relative to Manning, they paused, perhaps, and asked themselves if his was the sort of company they wanted to keep.

Union membership did not make voters responsive to the union leaders' cues, according to Panel B of Figure 5–8. This is not because union voters were already more on side than non-members, and thus less in need of a push from union leadership. Notwithstanding lea-

C. Gender

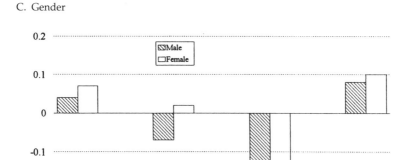

D. Party Identification

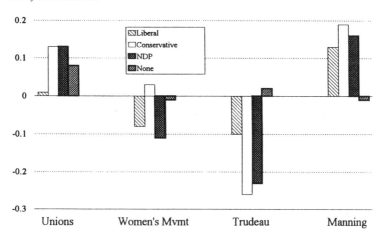

Figure 5–8 (cont'd)

ders' support for the Accord, union members were actually less likely than non-members to lean to the Yes.[14] Union membership seemed to render voters generally impervious to influence: Trudeau and Manning coefficients were also lower for members than non-members; only for the women's movement did the coefficient increase, and not by much.[15]

If the women's movement moved votes, the votes in question were cast by men. According to Panel C, awareness of feminist opposition made no difference whatsoever to women (the coefficient had the wrong sign, but was trivially small). Among men, there is a hint of effect: the coefficient, -0.07, is one-third larger than its standard error, and by a one-tailed test, has only 8 chances in 100 of being generated by chance.[16] Otherwise, women differed little from men; they were a bit less responsive to Trudeau, a bit more responsive (the wrong way) to Manning and to the union movement

Party identification,[17] in Panel D, made a modest difference, although not always in readily interpretable ways. Given Canada's partisan upheaval of 1993, the 1992 landscape is worth describing. The party system reflected in Figure 5–8 did not seem on the verge of breakdown. Canadians were as willing in 1992 as in 1988 to admit identifying with a party, and almost all identification outside Quebec was with one of the three traditional parties. Compared with 1988, the Liberal share (30 percent) was slightly larger and the Conservative share (22 percent) was slightly smaller, but these two parties continued to dominate identifications. The NDP remained well back (14 percent), but did not seem weaker than in 1988. Reform identification (6 percent) continued to be rare, and non-identifiers did not look like Reformers in disguise. Accord negotiators' concern to build a coalition embracing all three old parties was not misplaced.

But if negotiators hoped that all-party agreement would inoculate parties' supporters against outside intervention, their hopes were frustrated. Identification with a party made voters more responsive, not less, to external influence. For every intervenor but one, awareness moved nonpartisans less than partisans. The one exception is only partial; Liberals, but only Liberals, were less moved than nonpartisans by the union movement. The general pattern may reflect nonpartisans' general disconnection from politics.[18] It cannot be said that nonpartisans actively rejected the political class. If rejection were the motif, nonpartisan coefficients would have the wrong sign for Accord supporters, perhaps also for the women's movement, and would have big, properly signed coefficients for Manning, possibly for Trudeau. Instead, nonpartisan coefficients are just small substantively and insignificant statistically.

Among partisans the pattern defied easy interpretation. Awareness of union support increased the Yes share among New Democrats, which makes intuitive sense, and among Conservatives, which does not. Awareness of feminist opposition depressed the Yes share among Liberals and New Democrats; this makes sense in terms of both parties' historic positions and of the logic of Figure 5–2. Trudeau's impact was greater outside the Liberal camp than inside; the lesson here is not obvious. Finally, Preston Manning helped the Yes in all party groups, most of all among Conservatives and New Democrats. This may reflect the fact that Conservatives and New Democrats are disproportionately westerners (most importantly, not from the Atlantic provinces).

IMPACT II: FEELINGS

All the foregoing was about net effects, and it concerned groups and individuals who were not at the negotiating table. Now the tasks are both to unpack these interventions and to return agenda-setters into the consideration. Just as ratings of agenda-setters and intervenors underpinned the earlier factor analysis, so are they the driving force of this section's estimation. Not every player needs to be considered further or separately. Peter Lougheed's impact was so small that he now retires from view. Audrey McLaughlin, Jean Chrétien, and provincial permiers were close enough to each other on the factor analysis' principal component that they be can grouped, summarily, as "other leaders."[19] All other intervenors merit separate treatment, and so this section's analyses involve seven ratings, three for groups, four for individuals. To facilitate comparison with earlier estimations and to set the stage for later ones, ratings are compressed to a 0,1 interval.

It is not sufficient, in this instance, just to look at coefficients linking ratings with vote or vote intention, for a large coefficient does not necessarily mean that intervention by the corresponding person or group was itself decisive. Two barriers to straightforward interpretation lurk in the data. First, what if, for instance, the coefficient is of the wrong sign? Wrong in this context must not be confused with wrong (or perverse) as discussed in the previous section. Recall that Preston Manning had the wrong sign there – that is, despite his own intentions, awareness of his intervention increased the Yes share, reflecting his unpopularity. On this interpretation, the relationship between his ratings and the Yes vote should also be negative. But a negative relationship is not wrong for an opponent of the Accord, it is precisely the relationship that should hold. Wrong in this context means a *positive* coefficient for an *opponent* (the more you like the opponent, the more likely you are to vote Yes) or a *negative* coefficient for a *supporter* (the more you like the supporter, the less likely you are to vote Yes). A wrong sign in this sense indicates not that the intervention had a perverse effect but rather that the relationship was not generated by intervention-based triangulation at all.

But what if a large coefficient appears for an obscure intervenor? Early in the campaign, all intervenors, Trudeau aside, were obscure. This is not to say that they were politically inconsequential; in some cases, the opposite was true. But voters tended not to learn of their position immediately, and many voters never did. This was the lesson of figures 5–4 and 5–5. Only Pierre Trudeau's position was known to (or guessed correctly by) a majority of voters all along. Only Preston Manning joined him, and this became true just two weeks before the end of the campaign. No other individual or group position was ever clear to a majority of voters, although the business community and the women's movement came close at the very end. As with a coefficient of the wrong sign, a large coefficient attached to an obscure intervenor must reflect processes or factors outside the intervention. An obvious factor might be membership in a sociodemographic group that predisposes one to like or dislike a given intervenor and which at the same time predisposes one toward or away from the Yes.[20] This discussion directs us beyond simple regression of vote on feelings; feelings must be both related to awareness and conditioned on it.

Table 5–4 starts down the road of linking feelings to the vote. Some parts of the table seem straightforward; others demand refined analysis. By way of summary:

– Two consistently powerful positive coefficients make perfect sense, both in sign and power – those on Brian Mulroney and on other leaders.
– Three other intervenors always have the right sign, but the relative power of some coefficients is surprising. Feelings about the business community were always positively related to the vote, but did not become more so as awareness of the community's position spread. Feelings about Preston Manning were powerfully and negatively related to the Yes vote, and became, appropriately, more so as awareness of his position spread. But it seems odd, at first glance, that Manning's coefficients always were more powerful than Trudeau's.
– Two intervenors had the wrong sign, at least some of the time. The union movement never had the right sign, and the women's movement only acquired the correct sign at the very end.

Feeling about Accord negotiators was a big factor at every stage, bigger at the end than the beginning. Analytically, this is reassuring, for these took the most visible position of all. There can have been little confusion about the fact that the Accord was, collectively, "their" deal. Indeed, the deal belonged more to Brian Mulroney than he desired. It belonged even more to other leaders, however, in the sense that coefficients on their rating were bigger (by 0.20 to 0.30 points);

Table 5–4
Intervenor Evaluations and the Vote

| | Intention | | |
	24 Sept.–4 Oct.	5–25 Oct.	Vote
GROUPS			
Unions	-0.20	-0.17*	-0.17**
	(0.13)	(0.08)	(0.06)
Business	0.36*	0.15	0.23**
	(0.15)	(0.09)	(0.08)
Women's Movement	0.11	0.05	-0.13
	(0.15)	(0.09)	(0.07)
INDIVIDUALS			
Mulroney	0.42***	0.53***	0.49***
	(0.12)	(0.07)	(0.06)
Other Leaders	0.64***	0.86***	0.68***
	(0.19)	(0.11)	(0.09)
Trudeau	-0.09	-0.27***	-0.17**
	(0.12)	(0.07)	(0.06)
Manning	-0.50***	-0.62***	-0.67***
	(0.13)	(0.08)	(0.06)
Intercept	0.22	0.26	0.33
	(0.14)	(0.08)	(0.07)
R^2	0.17	0.26	0.21
N	287	683	1085

this is consistent with the facts and chronology of negotiation, as laid out in chapter 2.

If these facts are reassuring analytically, Accord supporters cannot have found them reassuring politically. Brian Mulroney was the single most unpopular figure on the entire landscape, and the positive coefficient means that his association with the Accord was highly damaging. Most other leaders were not hugely popular either. Indeed, certain premiers were downright unpopular, almost as badly regarded as Mulroney. But Chrétien and McLaughlin got middling reviews, and were highly regarded by some voters. Some premiers,

Atlantic provinces ones especially, were the most popular figures on the landscape. Here we see one possible explanation for the vote's rough East-West gradient.[21]

Feeling about the business community illustrates the problems of impact from an obscure intervention. The business coefficient was never that large, but its temporal shift makes the point. The strongest link existed when the community's position was least visible; as the community gained visibility, it lost power. The mildly powerful early-campaign effect must reflect not a considered triangulation between business leaders' express position and voters' feelings about business so much as a generally accommodative disposition toward constitutional tinkering amongst voters who also liked the business community. Later, this accommodative attitude was partly neutralized. It could not have been neutralized by the business community's own intervention, however; that should only have reinforced the disposition. Voters disposed to receive business-community cues must have heard rumbling offstage.

That rumbling could have been emitted by either Preston Manning or Pierre Trudeau. Big coefficients on the Manning rating might suggest he was the key. But awareness of his position was slow to spread. Early on, his link to the vote may have been more visceral than cognitive, as was true for feeling about the business community. The kind of person who liked Manning tended not to be constitutionally accommodating; accommodating persons, conversely, tended not to like Manning.

If Trudeau was the key intervenor, then why were his coefficients so weak? First, the coefficient grew as his visibility spread, exactly as it should if his active interventon was critical to voters' response. But there is a more telling assertion, which may seem surprising: there is, in fact, *no* simple relationship between size of coefficient and importance of intervenor. Recall one characterization of Trudeau in chapter 2: for English Canada, he remains identified as an advocate, not an opponent, of French-Canadian interests. Outside Quebec it matters little that his particular definition of those interests brings him in conflict with Quebec's provincial elite. Thus, voters anxious to accommodate French Canada/Quebec ought also to like Trudeau, not dislike him. So long as Trudeau remains silent, these same voters might give the Accord the benefit of the doubt, lean to the Yes. By itself this would produce a positive relationship between feeling for Trudeau and the vote. Conversely, highly knowledgeable voters should realize that Trudeau's vision clashes with principles contained in the Accord, and for voters taking this more nuanced view the feeling-vote connection should be negative. Coexistence of these contrasting relationships will produce a small net coefficient. Trudeau's power lay in his potential to activate opposition among English Canadians of good will, who are Quebec's natural allies. The very weakness of the overall coefficient testifies to his pivotal location. We return to this point, with evidence, below.

First, however, kindred – and complementary – points must be made about the union and women's movements. The union coefficient never had the correct sign. This does not indicate that union intervention actively hurt the Yes. But liking the union movement actually made a voter less likely to vote Yes, and so disliking the movement, a widely held position, should have helped the Yes. The union movement's natural supporters, the organized rank-and-file, were among the Accord's natural enemies, a point confirmed in chapter 7. Getting union leaders to endorse the deal might at least neutralize this opposition.

The story for the women's movement was the mirror image, at least at the beginning. Early in the campaign, the relationship between liking that movement and voting Yes was weakly positive.[22] Only at the very end did it turn negative. At every stage, women's-movement coefficients were weak. We know the movement never told powerfully in the balance, least of all among women. But we also see why Accord supporters worried about it. Feeling about organized feminism may have been politically akin to feeling about Trudeau: the more you like the movement, the more accommodating your disposition, on constitutional questions as on others. If the women's movement opposed the Accord, it might take some of the Accord's natural supporters with it. The movement failed to do this, but perhaps only because Pierre Trudeau got there first.

Now consider the feeling/vote connection with awareness controlled, in Figure 5–9. For the union and women's movements, awareness made little difference. The women's movement may have scored a small victory, as awareness of its opposition neutralized, or at least inhibited, its allies' natural accommodative attitude. The small positive ratings coefficient among voters unaware of the movement's position was driven toward zero among voters aware of the intervention. Neither coefficient was significantly different from zero, however. The union movement was utterly ineffectual in overcoming its allies' natural aversion to the Accord. Indeed, there is a hint that awareness of the union movement's position increased resistance to it.

Where awareness did matter was in relation to Trudeau and Manning. Among voters unaware of Manning's position, feeling about him was utterly unrelated to vote intention. Awareness, in contrast,

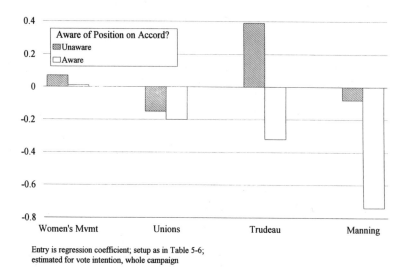

Entry is regression coefficient; setup as in Table 5-6;
estimated for vote intention, whole campaign

Figure 5–9
Impact of Evaluation with Awareness Controlled

unleashed a powerful negative linkage. Recall, though, that opinion about Manning himself tended to be negative, and so the negative coefficient helped the Accord more than hurt it. For Trudeau, the contrast between aware and unaware voters was just as great, and far more consequential. *Liking Trudeau impelled voters unaware of his position to the Yes side.*[23] To these voters, we suspect, Trudeau stood for accommodating French Canada, as did the Accord. *But voters aware of his opposition to this specific accommodation aligned themselves correctly.* Liking Trudeau pushed aware voters to the No, disliking pushed them to the Yes. Overall, aware voters outnumbered un- aware ones and the balance shifted dramatically in early October. This compositional shift explains Table 5–4's shift in the Trudeau rating's net effect, from none early to sharply negative late.

LESSONS

In many important respects, the pro-Accord coalition was well con- structed. Political leaders saw themselves as covering most poten- tial bases of opposition outside Quebec, and so did voters. Peter Lougheed, for instance, escaped close association with other present or former politicians, was popular in the West, and clearly rivalled Preston Manning as a bearer of business-community values. The union movement and the NDP covered opposition from the left.

Strikingly, the pro-Accord coalition controlled both the left and the right poles of debate. Although voters saw the heart of the coalition as conventionally partisan, it also included groups and individuals not tarred with the brush of political conventionality. But there was one actor left unmarked; the pro-Accord coalition simply could not come up with a serious shadow for Pierre Trudeau. Prominent Liberals were absolutely necessary to counter Trudeau but were obviously not sufficient.

For all that the coalition was broad, its constituent elements were not very popular. The extreme case was Brian Mulroney: in the twenty years that the 100-point rating device has been in use, no Canadian politician ever received ratings this low; Mulroney himself was rated some 25 points higher in 1988 (Johnston et al., 1992, chapter 6). The rest of the coalition (west of New Brunswick, at least) was not very helpful either, as the political class as a whole was less popular in 1992 than before. But then, not all opponents outshone supporters: Preston Manning was a case in point.

Only Pierre Trudeau enjoyed pan-Canadian credibility, at least outside Quebec. He was still recognizable and popular, more highly rated than any other present or former politician on the national stage and more likely to get a rating in the first place than anyone but Brian Mulroney. Only a few premiers matched his rating and they only in their own provinces. He was not classed as a conventional politician; only the relatively unpopular Preston Manning had less of whatever made a politician conventional. Yet Trudeau was not stuck out on an ideological limb: on the left-right continuum he was near the centre. His ideological distinctiveness seemed to have more to do with the values embodied in the Charter of Rights. Defence of the Charter was a key element in the post-1985 politics of accommodating Quebec, and Pierre Trudeau was the Charter's tribune. Thanks to all of this, voters paid attention to his judgment. Many guessed his position correctly even before he placed it on public display, and the surge in awareness of his position corresponded exactly to the collapse of the Yes. Yet his greatest popularity was with voters anxious to say Yes to constitutional accommodation, not with voters whose reflex was negative. So when Trudeau moved voters, he moved the Accord's natural supporters.

Quite possibly, Trudeau would not have been so prominent but for the supporting cast of other opponents. When we reflect on the language of the No forces, we are struck repeatedly by rhetoric originating with the women's movement, on one hand, and with Preston Manning, on the other. Mr Trudeau's own intervention picked up themes from both masterfully. Even if much of what the former prime minister said was derivative, had already been said, and would be said again, there is no gainsaying Figure 5–7. Others supplied the script, but it is unlikely that others could have delivered it as effectively as Pierre Trudeau.

6 Polls and Expectations: Further Explorations in Campaign Dynamics

If Pierre Trudeau was the biggest story of campaign dynamics, he could not have been the only one. The 20-point drop in Yes share induced by the Egg Roll speech did not last. According to Figure 2–1, about half the drop was erased within roughly one week. But if the total post-Egg Roll drop was not sustained, neither was the 10-point recovery. Something else came along to knock the Yes share back down. This chapter considers the possibility that reality fell prey to expectations, to voters' sense of the chances of a Yes majority.

Expectations might matter for reasons canvassed in chapters 1 and 2. As a reflection of polls, expectations might play a low-information role, supplementing the logic of agenda-setting and intervention in helping voters locate the Accord relative to themselves and to the status quo. This is the process outlined by McKelvey and Ordeshook (1986) and discussed in chapter 1. In their own right, expectations were made relevant by Joe Clark's statement that the Accord had to pass everywhere for it to pass anywhere. If the Accord's chances seemed reasonable, many voters might have concluded that the civic thing was to give the deal the benefit of the doubt, not let anxieties about specifics stand in the way of constitutional peace. But if the Accord's prospects were dim anyway, the civic requirement was less pressing, and voters could act directly on objections to specific elements. The final drop in Yes share outside Quebec did follow the first clear indication from polls that the Accord was not merely in trouble but was likely to lose outright.

Substantiating connections among polls, expectations, and the vote requires several steps. The first is to flesh out why in principle expectations might have mattered in 1992. Then comes the question, expectations of what? Of how Canada as a whole would vote? How certain provinces would vote? Next is to consider whether voters can derive expectations for any such voting units, and to ask if the most readily grasped units are really relevant to the overall choice. Finally comes the task of establishing if, at any point, expectations drove intentions.

WHY EXPECTATIONS?
EXPECTATIONS FOR WHAT?

Voters may have called Joe Clark's bluff. His claim that each and every provincial electorate must say Yes for Parliament and legislatures to be bound made the anticipated result in a voter's own province a potential factor in the choice, and it should have made other provinces relevant as well. But it is one thing to say that strategic information is potentially relevant. It is quite another to claim that voters can actually absorb and deploy such information.

That Canadian voters' expectations can help shape expressed preferences in general elections is now a matter of record (Johnston et al., 1992). It is also clear that electoral expectations are not wholly arbitrary, that they follow concrete indications about reality. Polls drive expectations, although voters can also revise expectations in the absence of polls, by introspection. True, expectations also embody wishful thinking: for instance, partisans tend to view their own party's chances more rosily than others do. Voters may have a weak tendency to make national inferences from regional information, but they do revise local expectations on the basis of national poll results. Dynamically speaking, these national-to-local revisions seem to make sense, but they can also lead voters astray. But all of this refers to a regularly recurring phenomenon, the general election.[1] Can voters apply expectations to a referendum?

First of all, expectations of whom? According to Joe Clark, every province should matter to every elector. So long as one province threatened to defect from the Accord, most arguments for acquiescing in the compromise would be undercut. It seems unreasonable, however, to expect voters to process information about each and every province. Indeed, it is prohibitively expensive for commercial polling firms to gather samples large enough to cover them all.[2] And it was never clear that the country would abide by Mr Clark's rule. The suspicion lingers that the real rule was the simpler, double-majority of Quebec and the rest in disguise. Still, any reasonable formula for acceptance of the Charlottetown Accord was bound to impose fairly punishing strategic demands on voters.

Three electorates struck us as worth asking about:

1 – Most immediate to the respondent was his or her *own province*. This was one route into the unanimity rule. Asking about the province also gives us potential leverage in understanding how respondents came to perceive the broader result. To what extent, for example, would they project from the anticipated provincial result to the national one?

2 – Would projection work the other way around? The simplest news presentation is a single, *national* number. Pollsters and media alike were wary of provincial breakdowns, given typical subsample sizes, and so coverage was dominated by national shares. The national number should have been especially important for shifts over time. Residents of British Columbia, at one extreme, and New Brunswick, at the other, probably differed all along in expectations for their own provinces and may have differed modestly, but along lines corresponding to provincial expectations, in their expectations for the national result. But *changes* in British Columbians' and New Brunswickers' expectations for their own province may have been driven by the updating of the national result.

3 – One province was worth asking everyone about: *Quebec*. Whatever the fine print for the rest of Canada, most observers understood that the Accord was, in a sense, bilateral, that rejection of the deal by Quebec was fatal.

Each expectation had a rhythm of its own, according to Figure 6–1.[3] All went generally down, but the sequencing was accordion-like: convergence, divergence, convergence, divergence. Sensibly enough, expectations were usually lowest for Quebec. Less sensible early on was the relative standing of the provincial and national expectations: before 5–6 October, expectations were higher for the national than for the typical provincial result. This was perfectly reasonable in British Columbia, but elsewhere the reverse ought to have been true: *all* other respondents lived in provinces for which expectations should have been *above* the national expectation, where the latter should have been depressed by knowledge of British Columbia and, more especially, Quebec. There seems, then, to have been a systematic bias toward either pessimism about the local result or optimism about the national one.

Certainly the national bias seems – with hindsight, at least – to have been toward optimism, and this is supported by bias in expecta-

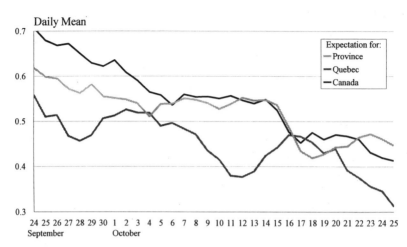

5-day moving average

Figure 6–1
The Evolution of Expectations

tions for Quebec. For Quebec, the average early reading was about 50: 50, at odds with what we know from Figure 2–1 and with publicly available evidence, reviewed below, from that province. It is tempting to infer that voters were sceptical of the poll evidence, that they discounted published indications out of Quebec. In any case, around 5–6 October, national and provincial expectations converged with those for Quebec, although expectations for all units were still slightly on the optimistic side. Then expectations for Quebec and the rest of Canada diverged again, as expectations for Quebec dropped dramatically. In the same period, expectations for respondents' own provinces and for the whole country stabilized, at a reading still modestly positive. Provincial and national expectations became, on average, scarcely distinguishable.

The final phase was ushered in around 16 October. Expectations for province and nation crashed rapidly, and thereafter were negative. Curiously, expectations for Quebec had surged, so that for a brief span the three expectations were once again indistinguishable. But then expectations for Quebec dropped again. By the end, respondents outside Quebec saw that province as highly unlikely to deliver a Yes majority and the arithmetically correct pattern emerged: Quebec at the bottom, Canada in the middle, one's own province on top.[4] The essential point, though, may be that all three judgments were pessimistic, realistically so.

PUBLICLY AVAILABLE KNOWLEDGE:
THE POLLS

By the standard set in the 1988 election, the 1992 poll record was strikingly meagre. The 1988 publication rate was thrice weekly, twenty-two polls in all. The same rate applied to the shorter referendum campaign would have yielded fifteen polls.[5] Instead, only twelve appeared, and this by an exceedingly generous count. Two (Reid and Environics) predated the official campaign; three were the Toronto *Globe and Mail*'s cumulative tracking, published each Friday in October; the other *Globe* reading (20 October) was a fairly obscure inside-page midweek story about its own poll. During the writ period only five polls aimed at a mass circulation audience appeared.[6]

Reporting of shares also differed from 1988. For elections, leaners are usually assigned to parties and undecideds are excluded from calculations; percentages for live alternatives thus add up to 100 and resemble the election-day count. For the referendum, reports seemed reluctant to draw attention to the bottom line, so the results usually appeared in fairly raw form. Yes and No percentages typically included undecideds in the denominator and the undecided share varied a lot from poll to poll. The extreme cases were the Reid (9 percent undecided) and Environics (27 percent) polls published on the same day, 17 October. Readers or viewers thus had to do some arithmetic for themselves.

As a rule, reports of polls leaners were assigned to a side. In at least one very prominent case, though, the issue may have been confused. Newspaper accounts of the Reid poll published on 17 October gave most prominence to initial response, in which only 33 percent (37 percent among decided) said Yes. Television coverage of the Reid poll hewed to the norm of assigning leaners, however; this produced a reading of 40 percent (44 percent among decided).

The strategic landscape changed on 17 October. Reid and Environics predicted a Yes loss Canada-wide. This was the first such indication for a mass audience, as Reid polled for the Southam newspaper chain and Environics for the Toronto *Star* and CTV. Attentive poll watchers might have gotten the message one day earlier in the Toronto *Globe and Mail* or on the CBC. But the *Globe*'s own circulation is limited and most television viewers must have been glued to CTV and the World Series. The CTV Friday supper-hour news in Toronto referred briefly to the *Globe* poll, but did not mention the newspaper by name and their national broadcast for central and Atlantic Canada was very late, delayed by the baseball game.

Table 6–1
Published Polls: National Results

Publication Date	House (Outlet)	Yes	No	Undecided	Yes/ Decided
September					
9	Environics (CTV/Star)	51	24	24	67
9	Reid (Southam)	58	25	17	70
16	Gallup (various)	42	29	29	59
26	Reid (Southam)	42	41	17	51
October					
7	Gallup (various)	41	41	18	50
9	Globe and Mail	40	43	17	48
16	Globe and Mail	36	45	19	44
17	Reid (Southam)	40	50	9	44
	Environics (CTV/Star)	33	40	27	45
20	Globe and Mail	39	46	15	46
21	Gallup (various)	40	50	10	44
23	Globe and Mail	37	47	16	44

The 16–17 October sequence was only the second major shift reported for the country as a whole. The other came in a Reid poll published 26 September. Before that date, the Yes seemed bound to win by a landslide. The Environics and Reid polls published 9 September pointed to a walkover everywhere. The Gallup poll published 16 September forecast the Yes defeat in Quebec and British Columbia,[7] but otherwise did not alter the national picture. The 26 September Reid poll was the first real indication of more widespread trouble: it placed the all-Canada Yes share among decided respondents at 51 percent. The next few polls confirmed roughly this picture: the 7 October Gallup poll and the 9 October *Globe and Mail* poll gave the sides roughly equal shares.

Table 6–2 indicates what could be learned about Quebec. Quebec opinion was tracked very closely, as chapter 8 reveals, but much of the work was done by Quebec-based firms and was reported, as far as we can tell, to Quebec audiences only. This chapter thus confines itself to Quebec subsample results in national surveys. Apart from the first two readings, these confirmed the picture in the Quebec-based polls. The first two polls gave the Yes a majority in Quebec and commentary, including by pollsters, on English-language news

Table 6–2
Published Polls: Quebec Results

Publication Date	House (Outlet)	Yes	No	Undecided	Yes/ Decided
September					
9	Environics (CTV/Star)	43	39	18	52
9	Reid (Southam)	49	38	13	56
16	Gallup (various)	31	48	21	39
26	Reid (Southam)	38	45	17	46
October					
7	Gallup (various)	32	46	22	41
9	Globe and Mail	27	54	14	33
16	Globe and Mail	27	53	15	34
17	Reid (Southam)	35	55	10	39
	Environics (CTV/Star)	35	51	15	42
20	Globe and Mail	33	50	15	40
21	Gallup (various)	30	58	12	34
23	Globe and Mail	35	50	13	41

programs was correspondingly optimistic.[8] The discrepancy between national and Quebec-based polls dissolved with the first
Gallup poll on 16 September. Thenceforth, voters outside Quebec
ought to have reckoned that the Accord was in trouble inside that
province. No subsequent poll showed the Yes even close to the No.
Nor was there any obvious trend. The lowest Quebec readings came
in the early October *Globe and Mail* reports and the 21 October
Gallup one.

PROJECTION, POLLS, AND EXPECTATIONS

How precisely did expectations reflect poll information? Did voters
employ other sources, including reflection on their own evolving intentions? Did other sources help or hinder voters in getting to the
right answer? Figure 6–2 juxtaposes published poll results and voters' expectations for Canada as a whole. In black is the 5-day moving
average of the national expectation, reproduced from Figure 6–1. Os-
cillating around it is the raw daily tracking, indicated by a dashed
line. Also appearing is the Yes share from the latest poll, and days on
which new polls appeared are boxed.[9]

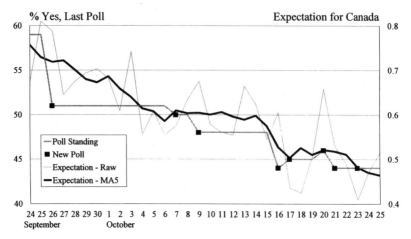

Figure 6–2
Polls and the National Expectation

The two discontinuities in published standings each moved expectations sharply. The first shift is masked by averaging, but is unmistakable in the daily tracking. No observation after 27 September was higher than either the 25 or 26 September observations. The other discontinuity is from 16 to 17 October. Every reading but one on or after the 17th was lower than every reading before that date.[10]

Figure 6–3 replicates Figure 6–2 for the Quebec expectation. There, the connection between poll information and expectations is either more complicated or simply less plausible than for Canada as a whole. Before 9 October there was no short-run dynamic link. Expectations for Quebec just oscillated around the midpoint. This may have been appropriate given that early poll returns themselves oscillated around a 40-percent Yes share for Quebec. The Reid poll of 26 September, which brought the first really bad news for the Yes side in the whole country, actually gave a more optimistic reading for Quebec than the immediately preceding Gallup poll. The first two *Globe and Mail* polls may have moved the strategic landscape, as they came in with Quebec Yes shares at under 35 percent. Just after the first *Globe* result, the Quebec expectation shifted permanently downward. Although a recovery began about 12 October, it was not sustained. Even at its highest point after 9 October, the expectation was, to all intents and purposes, never as high as in the early going. Meanwhile, the late recovery and collapse are hard to square with published polls. While

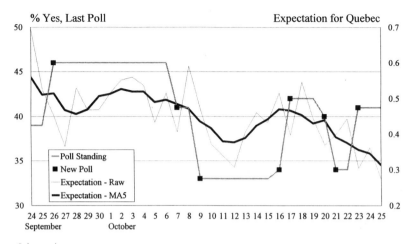

5-day moving average

Figure 6–3
Polls and the Quebec Expectation

it is true that three of the four post-16 October polls produced more optimistic readings for Quebec than either of the first two *Globe and Mail* polls, the recovery in the expectation for Quebec clearly pre-dated those more optimistic polls. The second-last poll reading, the Gallup on 21 October, was certainly a pessimistic account; but the expectation began its late drop before this poll was published. If the flurry of polls on the 16th and later did anything, they confirmed not that the Quebec Yes share had dropped but that it had not risen – or not risen enough.

Tables 6–3 and 6–4 bring various strands of this chapter together, to compare region of residence and current poll standing for their impact on expectations. Table 6–3 looks at the two most structurally similar expectations, for respondents' own provinces and for the whole country. Table 6–4 focuses on the expectation for Quebec; here the Canada-wide poll readings are compared with readings from Quebec alone. The two tables will also be compared with each other.

Poll variables correspond to updatings in figures 6–2 and 6–3. Each day a poll was published, the variable was updated to that day's Yes share, undecideds excluded. A simple, whole-campaign estimation would not be very persuasive, however, especially for national and provincial expectations. The national poll number went almost monotonically down, as did national and provincial expectations. The poll number could thus be just a trend term in disguise. For Quebec the problem is similar, just not so severe. Demonstrations are more convincing if they turn on *differences* between expectations series or, for Quebec, between national and provincial poll information. Also pertinent is timing: an implication of Figure 6–2 is that polls should carry more weight toward the end than the beginning. Accordingly, we present both whole-campaign and early/late estimations. Here the boundary between early and late is just the halfway mark in fieldwork. For these demonstrations, we have no basis in events, no Egg Roll, for dividing the campaign. Instead we adopt a statistical criterion – rough equalization of sample sizes.

For provincial and national expectations the following stand out:

- Regional differences were much sharper for provincial than for national expectations. This is exactly as it should be. Voters in a given province assessed a different electorate from voters in other provinces. In contrast, voters everywhere assessed the *same* electorate in deriving an expectation for Canada. That said, the national pattern did correspond weakly to the provincial one.
- The descending order of optimism was Atlantic provinces, Ontario,[11] Prairie provinces, and British Columbia. Least stable, relative to reality, were expectations in the Atlantic region.[12] That region traded places with Ontario, and never was as distinct from Ontario as reality indicated it should be. Prairie dwellers converged on British Columbians, a faithful reflection of the Yes collapse in the region (see Table 2–1).
- Regional differences did not diminish over the campaign. For the provincial expectation, this comes as no surprise. For the national one, we might have expected convergence as voters paid more attention to poll results.
- Voters did pay more attention to polls: early to late, poll coefficients more than doubled in size.
- Poll information may have had more impact on national than on provincial expectations, but only slightly more. The really striking finding is that national poll information drove provincial perceptions almost as efficiently as it did national ones.

In contrast to all this is the expectation for Quebec:

- Quebec perceptions were modestly more regionalized than the national expectation, but much less so than the provincial expectation. If the latter makes sense, the former does not. The mystery only deepens when one contemplates the specific pattern: the most optimistic was a region immediately adjacent to Quebec, the Atlantic

Table 6–3
Sources of Expectations for Canada and Respondents' Own Provinces

	24 Sept. –25 Oct.	24 Sept–11 Oct.	12–25 Oct.
A. RESPONDENT'S OWN PROVINCE			
BC	-0.30 (0.03)***	-0.28 (0.04)***	-0.31 (0.04)***
Prairies	-0.17 (0.03)***	-0.13 (0.03)***	-0.23 (0.04)***
Atlantic	0.01 (0.03)	-0.03 (0.05)	0.04 (0.05)
Poll	1.68 (0.26)***	1.39 (0.47)**	3.15 (0.84)***
Intercept	-0.21 (0.12)	-0.07 (0.24)	-0.86 (0.38)***
R^2-adjusted	0.12	0.08	0.14
B. CANADA			
BC	-0.04 (0.03)	-0.05 (0.04)	-0.02 (0.04)
Prairies	0.03 (0.02)	0.02 (0.03)	-0.10 (0.03)**
Atlantic	0.02 (0.03)	0.02 (0.05)	0.03 (0.04)
Poll	1.97 (0.24)***	1.36 (0.45)**	3.32 (0.80)***
Intercept	-0.40 (0.24)	-0.10 (0.23)*	-1.01 (0.74)
R^2-adjusted	0.05	0.01	0.03
N	*1302*	*678*	*623*

Entries in parentheses are standard errors;
* $p < 0.05$; ** $p < 0.01$; *** $p < 0.001$

provinces, and Ontario was scarcely less optimistic than the western provinces.

- Expectations did converge in the late campaign, although Atlantic residents still erred on the optimistic side.
- Polls helped shape Quebec perceptions but not very efficiently. The whole-period poll coefficient is comparable to that for provincial expectations. But expectations for Quebec depended more on early than late polls. Indeed, early on, national polls had more effect on expectations for Quebec than for respondents' own province or for the country as a whole! If there was a decisive poll, the most likely candidate would have been the Gallup one of 7 October. Thereafter, the Quebec expectation got detached from polls. Certainly, no simple poll story will cover the late drop in the expectation. For Quebec polls the apparent relationship at the end was even perverse: higher Yes shares induced lower expectations, and vice versa. The final collapse of expectations for Quebec did occur just as published polls registered a late recovery in that province, but the coefficient is so small and so unstable as to be virtually uninterpretable.

Table 6–4
Sources of Expectations for Quebec

	24 Sept. –25 Oct.	24 Sept–11 Oct.	12–25 Oct.
A. NATIONAL POLL INFORMATION			
BC	0.04 (0.03)	0.05 (0.04)	0.01 (0.04)
Prairies	0.04 (0.02)	0.05 (0.03)	0.03 (0.04)
Atlantic	0.11 (0.03)***	0.13 (0.05)**	0.10 (0.05)**
Poll	1.39 (0.26)***	1.61 (0.49)***	0.29 (0.84)
Intercept	-0.25 (0.13)	-0.36 (0.25)	0.25 (0.38)
R^2-adjusted	0.03	0.02	0.00
B. QUEBEC POLL INFORMATION			
BC	0.04 (0.03)	0.06 (0.04)	0.01 (0.05)
Prairies	0.05 (0.02)	0.06 (0.03)	0.03 (0.04)
Atlantic	0.12 (0.03)***	0.14 (0.05)**	0.10 (0.05)*
Poll	0.49 (0.20)**	0.43 (0.29)	-0.66 (0.38)
Intercept	0.22 (0.08)	0.27 (0.12)	0.63 (0.14)
R^2-adjusted	0.01	0.01	0.01
N	1303	678	625

– Generally, the information most relevant to Quebec expectations, from Quebec subsamples, had less effect than all-Canada shares. This comes out of a comparison of the top and bottom parts of Table 6–4. For the whole-campaign and early estimations, the Quebec-poll coefficient was one-quarter to one-third the size of that of the national poll.

The fit of expectations to polls was not simple. Focus on the latest poll and that alone makes most sense when the poll *contradicts* earlier ones, as happened with the 26 September Reid poll and the three 16–17 October polls. Other patterns in polls are also potentially relevant. For instance, *repetition* of a fairly clear result can induce mounting certainty.[13] Some of the gradual decline in all three expectations may have reflected gradually spreading awareness of polls, that did not so much change as repeat a negative message. The value of a poll may depend on its *timing*: late results ought to be more credible than early ones, for instance.

If poll information is not always sufficient to revise expectations, neither is it always necessary. Voters can revise expectations without external poll information. Under certain circumstances they can generalize from changes in their own intentions. For the Yes share to shift dramatically, many voters must undergo a conversion. If conversion reflects a dramatic event, citizens may naturally project from their own change to the electorate at large. Something like this must have happened after the Egg Roll speech. Even though no poll was published between 26 September and 7 October, expectations for the Canadian result dropped steadily.[14]

SELF-FULFILLING PROPHECY?

If expectations followed reality some of the time, did they also lead it? Were some voters willing to give the Accord the benefit of the doubt only so long as others were? Or were some voters looking to other voters to tell them what they should think about the document?

If so, it could only be the national expectation that would be able to shape reality in its own right. This conclusion is reached by elimination. In chapter 2 we raised the possibility that the Quebec expectation might be especially pivotal, but a closer investigation of the evidence undermines that expectation. Dynamically, perceptions of Quebec were laggard, updated too slowly to have any independent effect. The post-Egg-Roll vote crash did not follow any new information about the Quebec electorate's own intentions; indeed the crash preceded the first major decay in expectations for Quebec. Similarly, the crash after 17 October also preceded the final decay. Although poll coverage generally made a point of distinguishing Quebec from the national total, viewers seemed to get the message slowly and the picture was always murky.

Of the other two expectations, intuition leads us to the national one. News coverage of polls was overwhelmingly on national shares. Dynamically, voters probably made inferences *down* the ladder of aggregation, from national to provincial. The critical thing about the national expectation was its simplicity, both in itself and in the kind of external information it required. The cognitive demands of Joe Clark's unanimity rule may have been too great for voters, the costs to polling firms and mass media of meeting those demands may have been too high, or both. And at a critical point, the national expectation *anticipated* the vote.

That critical point was late, not early. Figure 6–4 overlays the national-expectations line from Figure 6–1, and the rest-of-Canada Yes-share line from Figure 2–1. Before the late October drop, the expectation line did not anticipate the vote line in a causally suggestive way. It is true that expectations dropped before the great post-Egg-Roll drop in vote intention. Perhaps Trudeau's intervention was rein-

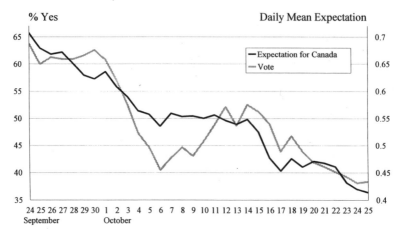

5-day moving average

Figure 6–4
Expectations and the Vote

forced by a spreading sense that the Accord was in trouble. But the drop was so gradual in this period that the main cause must still be attributed to the speech. Besides, although dropping, expectations were still clearly positive. The national expectation did not reach 50:50 until after the Globe-Reid-Environics deluge. From the Egg Roll speech to about 15 October, expectations only followed intentions, or even were detached to them.

But then expectations dropped suddenly, and clearly in advance of vote intention. The evidence, as with earlier demonstrations around the Egg Roll speech, may be circumstantial. But it surely seems telling. At this point, intention cannot cause expectation, not when the former lags the latter. The fact that expectation leads intention does not absolutely close the case, but it at least makes the causal link highly plausible. Also adding plausibility is the fact, established in Table 6–3, that expectations were so closely linked to external information at this point, and much more closely than before. And only at this point did the expectations line cross the vital 50:50 threshold. Earlier shifts made victory seem less probable, but the balance of probabilities, as perceived, still favoured the Yes. In a couple of days that perceptual balance tipped to the No.

More than vote intentions tipped with them; and so, for a second time, did the rhetorical basis of the campaign. The poll deluge did not discernibly affect the *balance* of opinion on any relevent argument. Recall from chapter 3 that opinion on specific elements was stable

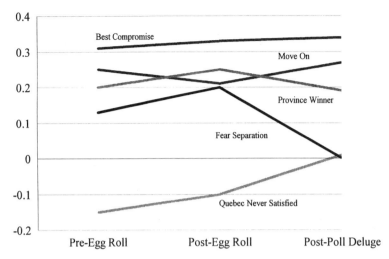

Figure 6–5
Egg Roll, Polls, and Impact of General Arguments

over the campaign. Chapter 4 indicated that balances shifted for four of five general arguments, for "best compromise," for "move on," and for the two Quebec perceptions. But none of the shifts was induced by events around 16 October. What did change, however, was the *relevance* of certain arguments. Figures 6–5 and 6–6 make the case.

Figure 6–5 gives values for coefficients on the five general arguments, extracted from estimations exactly parallel to those in Table 4–6. Vote intention was regressed on all five arguments and on all four specific elements, separately for the pre-Egg Roll period, the interim between Egg Roll and the poll deluge, and after the deluge. Coefficients on specifics are not presented as they do not contribute to the argument. Their pattern is familiar: larger coefficients after Egg Roll, no shrinkage after the deluge. The pattern is also familiar for the three positive arguments: no shrinkage, indeed no interpretable change.[15] But Quebec arguments were rendered irrelevant. Where the Egg Roll shift increased the relevance of fear (or lack of fear), the poll deluge utterly neutralized it. Fear of separation also happened to recede over the campaign (Figure 4–3), but the biggest story is that fear simply ceased to matter. So did perceiving Quebec as insatiable. Some neutralization of this claim occurred around the Egg Roll period, as its middle-period coefficient was smaller than its pre-Egg Roll one. The overall effect of the two Quebec coefficients did not change, though, thanks to the sharpened impact of fear. But like fear, insatiability became utterly irrelevant at the end.

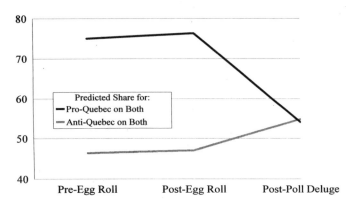

Figure 6–6
Quebec Perceptions and Vote Intentions

Figure 6–6 stylizes the change as shares in vote intention. Values were derived by setting voters at the mid-point on all other factors, neither accepting nor rejecting any positive argument, neither favouring nor opposing any specific element. This makes the electorate seem more positive on the Accord and more stable than it really was. But it brings out the impact from beliefs about Quebec starkly. Other things being equal, rejecting both negative claims induced a very high probability of voting Yes. Accepting both claims made one, on balance, unlikely to vote Yes, even assuming neutrality on other considerations. The difference between pro- and anti-Quebec extremes was about 30 points. The Egg Roll intervention did not change this at all. After the poll deluge, however, the 30-point gap utterly evaporated. To reiterate, the electorate did not suddenly become anti-Quebec at this point, nor, obviously, did it become pro-Quebec. What one believed about Quebec – positively or negatively – simply ceased to matter. Cause and effect here is very hard to disentangle, and we make no claim that the newly established irrelevance of Quebec-related general arguments was the key to late vote shifts. But the patterns in figures 6–5 and 6–6 are consistent with the general thrust of chapter 4: as the Accord went down, evaluation of the deal shifted from general to particular, from arguments about what would happen if the Accord succeeded or failed to arguments about what was in the deal itself.

REFLECTIONS

Taking expectations into account fitted the logic of the whole enterprise. Few things in the Accord were greeted warmly on their substance. Most had to be justified as part of the larger framework, as a concession to somebody else. If the overall willingness to bargain is weak, as indicated by a low Yes share in polls, then even voters truly disposed to make concessions on their own part may, so to speak, pull back from the table. Although the key bargaining relationship was between Quebec and the rest of Canada, non-Quebec voters were slow to plumb the depths of Quebec's rejection of the Accord. Once it became clear that the country as a whole was going to say No, however, a willingness to accommodate Quebec ceased to matter.[16]

7 Social Structure and Sentiment

Was the battle closely fought within the electorate's social and economic subgroups, or was the conflict mainly between groups? If group membership explained only a small part of the vote, did group sentiment pick up the slack?

Group-related attitudes can be very crude or quite sophisticated. The crudest sentiments in play were mere feelings, for Quebec in particular. Voters did more than just indulge feelings about Canada's group structure, however. They also entertained such thoughts as whether any groups have a distinctive claim, and whether decision rules should presumptively favour majorities or minorities. Either type of consideration – raw feeling or a conceptualized view of group life – could drive the vote, and each might reinforce the other.

Group membership, especially in "primordial" groups, has always been critical to Canadian party choice. However, the usual rules of partisan translation may not have applied in 1992, thanks to the inclusiveness of the pro-Accord coalition. This was precisely the intent of the cross-party pro-Accord coalition. If the gambit failed to secure its ultimate objective – a Canada-wide Yes to the Accord – did cross-party elite consensus at least move each party's mass base the same distance toward the Yes? And if long-standing divisions were overcome, did others take their place? Especially intriguing is the possibility that the Accord exposed a division usually only weakly expressed by Canadian parties – a gulf between classes. The Accord may have fallen victim to the deep, post-1990 economic recession. Alternatively, the deal may have tapped into the country's class structure; it may have gotten its greatest support among Canadian society's more fortunate members.

GROUP SENTIMENT

Raw Feeling

Potentially, many groups could have been engaged sentimentally in assessment of the Accord. But the pivotal feelings, we submit, were about Quebec. If the Accord clearly implicated Aboriginal Peoples, their key concession – self-government – was both consensually supported and of only limited relevance to the vote. Voters may have decided that the Accord was also about recognition of other specific ethnic groups, but our evidence suggests otherwise. Voters' ratings of "immigrants" as a social category were unrelated to acceptance of general arguments, to judgment on the Accord's content, and to the vote.[1] Feeling about Quebec, in contrast, seeped into practically every nook and cranny of judgment on the deal.

Table 7–1 puts feeling about Quebec in affective context.[2] Response to the province is best described as lukewarm, an average rating of 58. Compared to the responses to individual intervenors, this seems positively tropical, but places and groups clearly extract more warmth than individuals and even more than organizations. Among places and groups, Quebec finishes dead last, far behind respondents' own province (81) and Canada (86). This is no surprise, nor is it surprising that the designation English Canadians handily outperforms Quebec, given that many respondents apply it to themselves. Most telling is that Quebec clearly also trails immigrants. Few voters actively dislike Quebec,[3] but the province cannot call upon a deep reservoir of affection.

Notwithstanding all this, ratings of Quebec were heavily of a piece with ratings of other objects, including other groups and places, as indicated by Panel B of Table 7–1. For instance, feeling about Quebec was strongly positively related to feeling about both Canada ($r = 0.41$) and respondents' own province ($r = 0.40$). To be sure, Canada, English Canadians, and province were even more closely related to each other than any one of them was to Quebec. And Quebec was more closely related to immigrants than to the other three objects. But the dominant fact is positivity. One reading of generally positive correlations is that they reflect a common factor best characterized as misanthropy versus philanthropy: the more you like one group, the more you like other groups as well; the less you like one group, the less you like others. Most respondents, thus, do not parcel out their affections

Table 7–1
Feelings: Quebec versus Other Places and Groups *(N=1101)*

A. Mean Ratings

Canada	86
Own Province	81
English Canadians	79
Immigrants	66
Quebec	**58**

B. Correlations among Ratings

	Canada	Province	English Canadians	Immigrants
Quebec	**0.41**	**0.40**	**0.26**	**0.47**
Canada		0.64	0.48	0.37
Province			0.57	0.36
English Canadians				0.40

in zero-sum ways; in other words, they do not make tradeoffs between groups.[4] The critical factor, rather, is how much affection one can express for anything. The greater one's capacity for liking one's own group, the more capacity one also has for embracing the Other. Conversely, individuals who reject the Other rarely feel at one with their own. This pattern recurs in study after study of group feeling in Canada (Gibbins, 1977; Simeon and Elkins, 1980; Johnston, 1986: Johnston and Blais, 1988). Then again, the pattern may be a measurement artifact, a reflection of differential orientation to numbers. Some respondents may chronically employ high numbers and others low numbers (Knight, 1984; Green, 1988; Wilcox et al., 1989).

Group Recognition and Rights

If only one specific group-like object, Quebec, was sentimentally in play, voters might still have responded to group claims stated in the abstract. Three claims might have informed judgment on the Accord, even if supporters of the deal downplayed them. One refers to founding peoples, and its acceptance should encourage a Yes vote. The second refers to a presumption of equal treatment; this argument could cut either way. Third is the relative appeal of majority rule and minority rights.

Founding Peoples. Traditionally, the founders have been styled French and English, and Quebec provincial governments present themselves as the only effective advocate of the French interest. For French Canada, the claim compounds moral and practical considerations. Canada could not have been founded in its modern form but for agreement by French Canada, as represented by the francophone political elite of Canada East. As a claim about Canada's origins, this is a practical statement. Even if this exhausts the historical content of the claim, the claim still takes on a moral gloss, for agreements, once made, should generally be kept.[5] But reference to 1867 does not exhaust history: French Canada was present not just at the time of Confederation but long before – over a century before the Conquest of 1759 in fact – and this adds still more moral force to the claim. French Canada, in short, has a claim akin to an aboriginal right.

Claims of right by Canada's officially recognized Aboriginal peoples – Indians, Inuit, and Métis – are almost exclusively moral. Aboriginal peoples were not part of the Confederation bargain, and that exclusion is part of the current grievance. But their more general right to feel aggrieved at exclusion – and to have the exclusion and its effects remedied – reflects their presence time out of mind in Canada.

Equal Rights. Claims to founding-peoples status encounter another claim, which may or may not be hostile to them. Much is made of equality as a constitutional principle, especially with entrenchment of the Charter of Rights. On one reading, entrenchment of equality rights reinforces the claims of founding peoples, for among the categories protected against invidious treatment are aboriginality and language, which make sense only under the aspect of something like "foundership." Even if other protected categories have no element of foundership, the critical fact may still be that they at least refer to groups and categories as such, usually with an implication of ascription. It can be said that certain persons are what they are for reasons outside their control and have commonly been victimized thereby, and equality rights constitutionally recognized as such invite courts to vindicate claims based on membership in a group. Membership in a putatively victimized group, or a general posture of sympathy with victimization claims, might also make one more sympathetic to claims from founding peoples, and vice versa. Sympathy aside, groups not acknowledged as founders and with low current status might ally with founding peoples as a way of levering enhanced recognition of their own contribution and status, eventually if not immediately (Sachdev and Bourhis, 1991). In a way, this is the political logic of multicultural policy; philosophically multiculturalism coexists uneasily with special recognition of older, founding groups, but politically the two logics are each other's necessary support.

Sympathy for founding peoples may not suffice, however, if the document seems to crowd out other groups' claims of equal right. This was the gist of NAC president Judy Rebick's argument that the Accord was "a bad deal for women." She worried that the Canada clause would create "a hierarchy of rights." Provisions on equality for women were much weaker than those governing recognition of Quebec as a distinct society, Aboriginal self-government, and minority language rights. The physically disabled, the elderly, the poor, and homosexuals were not explicitly mentioned in the Canada clause at all, and, claimed NAC vice-president Shelagh Day, "those who aren't mentioned ... will have their rights downgraded." According to Rebick, "the mood among women in this country is like the mood of Aboriginal peoples after Meech Lake – we can't be treated this way."[6] A particularly powerful argument focused on recognition of an inherent right for Aboriginal self-government: would this license continued discrimination against aboriginal women?

Rebick nonetheless accepted the major premise, the Accord's group logic; her disappointment was that its coalition was insufficiently inclusive.[7] But the rhetoric of equal treatment can also cut completely against coalition-building, can undermine group logic *tout court*. Some argue that *any* recognition of groups, even historically disadvantaged ones, undercuts equal treatment of individuals. On this ground, treating all Canadians alike means rejecting even founding peoples' claims, such claims especially perhaps. This was precisely the implication of early invocations of equal-rights language in Canada, most notably by Dalton McCarthy in the 1880s and 1890s. When McCarthy spoke of equal rights he meant no recognition of, no granting of validity to, claims by Catholics and francophones. In a similar vein, he rejected any claim that real Indian and Métis grievances mitigated Louis Riel's guilt; to accept such a claim was to compromise the blindness of justice, a key to equal treatment. For McCarthy, separate schools, the Jesuits' Estates settlement, and demands for mercy for Riel threatened the legacy of the Glorious Revolution, 1688, and its Bill of Rights, 1689 (Miller, 1979). Was the Charlottetown Accord the Popish Plot of 1992?[8]

If such appeals gain power by attachment to defensible principles, the Popish Plot reference reminds us that the appeals commonly harbour an ethno-religious subtext, and that receptiveness to them is shaped by where voters sit in the ethno-religious pecking order. Most susceptible in 1992 to equal-rights rhetoric might be groups who detect in the Accord a positive threat to their place in that pecking order, who see themselves losing out in a reallocation of status (Breton, 1984). Canadians of British background might be on the horns of a dilemma: founding-peoples arguments place Canadians of British origin inside the magic circle vis-à-vis all groups of more recent provenance, but force them to cohabit with one (French) or two (French, Aboriginal peoples) rather *déclassé* groups. Given informal possession of the social high ground by Canadians of Anglo-Celtic background, their best strategic option might be to insist on no formal group recognition, but to insist instead that only individual rights should be recognized. Most susceptible of all, though, might be groups advantaged under the informal status quo but not qualified for official founder status. That "less deserving" groups claim founding status only rubs salt in the wound. Fitting this description might be groups which started to arrive before the Second World War. Closest fit of all might be for Canadians whose origins lie in the Protestant monarchies of northern Europe, culturally most similar to Canadians of British background but for whom memories of discrimination and social marginality – not to mention economic and physical deprivation – still rankle. What, meanwhile, of the old antinomy of Canadian life, Catholic versus Protestant? Notwithstanding the exclusively secular language of the 1992 debate, ancestral memories and habits might still help condition voters' reflexes.

Majority Rule/Minority Rights. Founding-peoples arguments refer to facts of history and require that groups be called by name. A more general claim refers to rights of all minorities, regardless of history and almost regardless of size. It is sometimes said that a democracy is defined by majority rule but judged by how well it treats its minorities. This is the nub of the issue described by the quotation from Sir Ernest Barker in chapter 1. In true deliberation, putative majorities and minorities attempt to internalize each other's arguments, the better to grasp and evaluate their claims. Sometimes the minority should yield to the appeal of greater numbers; minorities should not, for instance, wilfully jeopardize a framework whose continued operation would benefit them more than would its rupture (even if it benefits them less than it does the majority). Similarly, the majority should forbear when brute exertion of its will deprives a minority of something especially valued, particularly when the majority's own interest is not compelling. Members of a given majority should keep in mind that on some other issue they will be in the minority. Members of the current minority should imagine themselves in an eventual majority. Democratic practice thus cannot be identified just with majority rule, and minority rights can never be absolute. But it is worth asking a voter about his or her reflex: as a general proposition, abstracted from cases, would you emphasize minority protection or majority power?

Table 7–2
Group Recognition and Rights

	Founding Peoples?	Make Distinctions?		More Important?	
		No	Yes	Majority Rule	Minority Rights
None	**17**	94	6	65	25
Two	**11**	92	6	65	26
Three	**72**	91	9	59	31
Total	*(1111)*	**91**	**8**	**61**	**30**

Table 7–2 shows the response to three questions designed to cover these debates: how many (if any) founding peoples there are; whether we should make distinctions among Canadians; and the relative priority of majority rule and minority rights. Marginal distributions of the response to each question are in bold, down the leftmost column and along the bottom row. Strikingly, Canadians accept the idea of a founding people in overwhelming numbers and most extend the notion to include Aboriginal peoples. Fewer than one in five reject the idea completely. Only about one in ten confines founding status to French and English.[9] But in the very ubiquity of assent lies a problem: can a status so universally conceded count for much politically?

The first hint that it does not is the even more one-sided rejection of making distinctions among Canadians: the ratio of rejection to acceptance is over 9:1. The item's wording, "We should make no distinctions, we are all Canadians," combined with its agree/disagree format, probably invited overwhelming acquiescence. That we are all Canadians is merely a fact. But the margin is still remarkable, and it leaves little slack for covariance with attribution of founding-people status. Respondents who acknowledge three founding peoples are slightly more likely to permit distinctions. The fact that the discontinuity, such as it is, falls between recognizing two and recognizing three, not between recognizing two and recognizing none, suggests that the handful who are prepared to make a distinction intend it to lie between Aboriginal peoples and all others.

Potentially more consequential is the majority/minority reflex. Although majority rule is clearly the privileged value, by roughly a 2:1, the number of voters whose reflex favours minorities is not trivial – about three in ten. And the reflex is more apparent among those who recognize founding peoples than among those who do not. But that difference is slight, a maximum of 6 points. As with refusal to make

Table 7–3
Founding Peoples and Minority Rights: Coalition Possibilities

Founding Peoples	More Important			
	Majority Rule	Minority Rights	Don't Know	
None	11	4	2	17
Two	7	3	1	11
Three	43	22	7	72
	61	30	9	(1111)

Entries are diagonal percentages

distinctions, it falls between those who recognize three, as opposed to only two, founding peoples. The hint, again, is that the minority most requiring special consideration is Aboriginal, not French. But this is just fine print: even voters who recognize three founding groups favour majorities by an overwhelming margin; majority preference is just all the more complete among voters who recognize no or only two founding peoples.

Table 7–3 considers overlap between founding-peoples sentiment and majority/minority preference to assess coalitional possibilities. Entries are diagonal percentages, the number with a particular combination of attitudes on each dimension as a percentage of all voters. In the bottom-left cell might lie the key to victory. Could the Charlottetown Accord be presented as simply affirming what we all know, that some groups got here first, but that this did not thereby prejudice the interests of later arrivals? If so, the 43 percent who acknowledge three groups but who opt for majority rule might be corralled, as might the 7 percent who don't know which – majority or minority – to favour. All the better if those who acknowledge founding peoples detect a racist subtext in opposition rhetoric. The 22 percent who positively lean to minorities might vote Yes regardless. Conversely, what if the Accord is presented as hostile to minorities, in contrast with the more direct and explicit guarantees in the Charter? The core logic of the Accord was to empower Aboriginal persons and most francophones (the majority resident in Quebec) by expanding their decision-making power, not by making some named right justiciable. This would not help the non-francophone minority in Quebec, nor francophone minorities outside Quebec. Also unrecognized were persons, women especially, not historically assigned decision-making roles in Aboriginal communities. But then, what if the Accord is heavily

Table 7–4
Founding Peoples, Minority Rights, and Feeling for Quebec

	More Important		
Founding Peoples	Majority Rule	Minority Rights	
None	51	53	52
Two	53	49	53
Three	59	64	61
	57	61	

Entries are mean ratings

weighted to minority interests? If that becomes the dominant gloss, the big 43 percent battalion becomes at risk.

Most important for coalition-building is how these rather intellectualized ruminations fit in with feeling toward the biggest piece in the Charlottetown puzzle – Quebec. If recognition of founding peoples is unrelated to feelings toward Quebec, then founding-peoples sentiment is irrelevant, and it would have no coalition-building potential. But acknowledgment of founding peoples combined with good will for Quebec might cut through a lot of intellectual barriers, for instance, to recognizing the province as a distinct society. As it happens, according to Table 7–4, founding-peoples sentiment is strongly related to feeling for Quebec, more strongly than is the majority/minority reflex. The specific shape of the association defies easy interpretation, and may contradict a pattern identified earlier. Once again, the key discontinuity is between three founding peoples and two, not between two and none. We cannot supply a fully satisfactory account of this. On one hand, the main effect (and the effect within the majority-rule camp) is the war between philanthropy and misanthropy identified above: the more groups you recognize, the warmer you feel to one of the groups in particular. But voters who recognize only two groups are defined as recognizing only English and French. Why voters who concede founder status only to francophones should like Quebec hardly more (among supporters of minority rights, like Quebec even less) than voters who recognize no founding peoples is a mystery. Be that as it may, voters prepared to recognize three founding peoples – a group which constitutes an overwhelming majority – like Quebec much more than other voters do. That is the good news. The bad news is that feeling for Quebec in this group is still not very warm compared to feeling for other places and groups. An equally valid characterization is that voters willing to enter into some of the logic of group

Table 7–5
Founding Peoples, Minority Rights, and the Vote

Founding Peoples	More Important		
	Majority Rule	Minority Rights	
None	24	28	25
Two	38	32	39
Three	38	50	43
	36	45	

Entry is Yes vote share in each group

accommodation are merely lukewarm toward Quebec. Voters who resist the logic verge on being outright chilly.

Group Sentiment and the Vote

Each sentiment – raw feeling for Quebec, recognition of founding peoples, majority/minority orientation – was potentially relevant to the vote. Feeling for Quebec is the most powerful of the three, and before it is allowed to overwhelm the system, consider the joint effect of the other two, in Table 7–5. Overall, voters who recognized founding peoples were considerably more likely than others to vote Yes. This time, the consequential boundary was between recognition/non-recognition: voters who recognized three founding peoples were slightly more likely than those who recognized only two to say Yes. But far more impressive was the difference between two and none. But if recognizing founding peoples promoted a Yes vote, it did not ensure it; a clear majority of such voters still voted No. The most economical description of the pattern is that voters who absolutely repudiated the idea of founding peoples had very little chance of voting Yes.

Reflexive preference for minority rights helped the Yes. The document was seen, then, as concerned primarily with securing minority interests. But the difference between extremes was not as large as for recognition of founders, and this may reflect the fact that the document's stance vis-à-vis minorities truly *was* ambiguous; arguably it put minorities within minorities at risk. In contrast, the Accord clearly presupposed the existence of founding peoples; voters who did not share that presupposition could find little in it to like. Voters who recognized three founding peoples and emphasized minority rights as well were the most likely of all to vote Yes; indeed the balance settled right at the 50:50 threshold.

Table 7–6
Group Sentiment and the Vote

Sentiment	Coefficient	Standard Error
Feeling for Quebec	0.45***	0.06
Minority Rights	0.07*	0.03
Founding Peoples	0.12**	0.04
Intercept	0.01	0.05
R^2	0.08	

* $p < 0.05$; ** $p < 0.01$; *** $p < 0.001$.

Table 7–6 lets feeling for Quebec back into the estimation, and, as anticipated, feelings overwhelm ideas. All three measures are compressed to a 0,1 interval, to assist comparison of coefficients. Each is coded so that the side favouring the Accord scores one and the other side zero. Having no position on minority rights is scored 0.5, as is recognizing only two founding peoples. The difference between founding-peoples extremes is now estimated as 0.12, in contrast with the 17-point difference in Table 7–5. Some of this shrinkage reflects control for compositional effects buried in the cells of that table, but most of it stems from control for Quebec feeling. The same is true for shrinkage between majority/minority extremes, for which the coefficient now appears as 0.07 (compare this with the 9-point difference on the column margin of Table 7–5). Each coefficient is still significant, however; group-related ideas did play a role in their own right, independently of raw feelings, in the vote.[10]

But a much bigger part was played by group-related feeling, for Quebec in particular. The exact difference defies estimation, for reasons related to difficulty of measurement. Feeling for Quebec is probably easier to measure than conceptions of community. By the time respondents encountered the Quebec rating they had used the 100-point scale nearly ten times, and so the device was now familiar; furthermore, Quebec is an unambiguous stimulus. Voters may fill the Quebec vessel with all sorts of different associations, but variation in those associations is just what we are trying to capture. The idea of a founding people, in contrast, is conceptually highly demanding, and the specific expression is not street language, not outside Quebec at least; it has not acquired enough familiarity for its negative implications to fuel debate over – and produce resistance to – the term itself.[11] And as the item was in agree/disagree format, it did not supply a reason for rejection. Respondents who did reject the term knew what they were doing and behaved accordingly, but their numbers were small. The majority/minority distinction is more accessible, more regularly encountered in daily life, and the item was a forced choice. Not surprisingly, the minority-oriented share was larger than the share who repudiated founding peoples. But the vote difference induced by taking a majority/minority position was small.

That feelings outweighed ideas cannot just have been a measurement artifact, however. If, as we aver, founding-peoples language is not found on the street, then differences over who, if anybody, founded the country or over whether presence at the creation entails special claims are unlikely to be expressed or mobilized in popular debate. Feelings, in contrast, are found on the street. It should not surprise us, then, that gut feelings dominated choice. Intellectualized conceptions of the polity should be most powerful, we expect, among well-informed voters, as Sniderman et al. (1991) argue. That is a matter for chapter 9, however.

Table 7–6 makes it pretty clear, though, that the Accord faced a massive burden of proof. Start with a voter who abhors Quebec, recognizes no founding peoples, and affirms majority rule. Effectively, not one such voter said Yes, as the equation's intercept is indistinguishable from zero. Voters who accepted both arguments and were indifferent to Quebec (rating of 50) still had less than a 50:50 chance of voting Yes.[12] To reach 50:50, a voter who accepted both pro-Accord arguments must also rate Quebec at 67.[13]

Pathways to the Vote

Table 7–6 is a total-effects or reduced-form estimation. Figure 1–1 argued, however, that group sentiment drove party and leader evaluation, response to general arguments, and opinion on specifics. Figure 1–1 was silent on exact pathways, and Figure 7–1 begins to put flesh on the skeleton. It starts at the back, so to speak, by asking what happens to a group-sentiment coefficient as each layer of intervening variables enters the estimation. The leftmost bar is just the total-effect coefficient, transcribed from Table 7–6. Next to it is the coefficient from an estimation which also includes the four intervenor ratings from chapter 5 and dummy variables for party identification. Then comes the coefficient when the five general arguments are also included. Last comes the coefficient with specific elements added in.

Minority rights and founding peoples mattered less than feeling about Quebec, as we already know, and can be discussed without much ado:

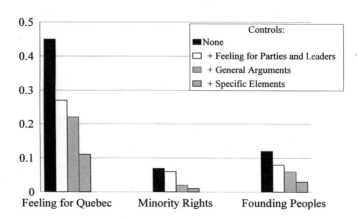

Figure 7–1
Pathways to the Vote: Group Sentiment

– Preference for *minority rights* has a simple structure. Controlling party/leader orientations hardly affects the coefficient; controlling acceptance of general arguments virtually eliminates it. By implication, minority preference is unrelated to party choice, and any relationship it might have to specific elements is caught up in general arguments.
– Impact from recognition of *founding peoples*, in contrast, is mediated by each prospective stage along the causal way. The coefficient shrinks a bit when party and intervenor orientation is controlled, a bit more when general arguments are controlled, and a bit more still when specific elements enter.

All this is small stuff compared with feeling for Quebec. Here two classes of mediating variables seem especially critical:

– The coefficient is cut nearly in half by *party system* controls. Canadians' response to the party system must be powerfully conditioned by their feelings for Quebec, historically the system's pivot for governments.
– The next biggest hit on the coefficient comes from opinion on specific elements. It is natural to suspect that this reflects the package's two Quebec elements – the 25 percent guarantee and the distinct society clause.

Only key mediating factors merit further detailed exploration. For minority orientation, general arguments are the key. For recognition of founders, a case could be made for stops all along the way, but this factor's overall weakness argues for fairly terse treatment. For Quebec feeling, emphasis should fall on the party system and on opinion on specifics, with a side glance at acceptance of general arguments. As feeling for Quebec drove so much of the system, it will get most of the attention.

Quebec feeling is intimately bound up with partisan feeling. This has been true for years, but by 1992 this truth had acquired an historically novel shape. In the past, Quebec divided the system right at its core, pitting Liberals against Conservatives, with the NDP a sideshow. Before 1984 only Liberals were at all credible in Quebec, even though their particular orientation to founding peoples' claims placed them at odds with Quebec provincial politicians. So complete was Brian Mulroney's post-1984 coalition-building success, however, that his party became at least as credible to Quebec as the Liberals were, probably more so. And as Mulroney pushed the Liberals aside, the NDP sensed an opening to unqualified major-party status and joined the binational coalition game wholeheartedly. By 1988 all three parties were effectively indistinguishable to voters on French-English relations. Their consensus on the Meech Lake Accord, for instance, took Quebec and language questions completely off the agenda (outside Quebec itself, at least) in the 1988 election.[14]

Table 7–7 and Figure 7–2 testify to the cross-party consensus. Table 7–7 tells a story about intervenors, with regressions of chapter 5's four intervenor ratings on Quebec feeling. The central contrast is between the two leftmost and the two rightmost columns, between Mulroney and "other leaders" on one hand, and Pierre Trudeau and Preston Manning on the other. Mulroney and the rest of the pro-Accord coalition were connected by voters to Quebec in exactly the same way. Considering that "other leaders" is, in partisan terms, a heterogeneous grab bag – Jean Chrétien, Audrey McLaughlin, and a collection of Liberal, Conservative, and (most importantly) NDP premiers – its sentimental convergence on Brian Mulroney, architect of the Conservative revolution, is remarkable. So is the contrast between these two ratings and the other two, especially with Preston Manning's.

Feeling about Quebec was simply unrelated to rating of Pierre Trudeau. This in itself is remarkable, given the utterly hegemonic domination of the Quebec electorate Trudeau wrought in the 1970s.[15] Of course, Trudeau did this by *opposing* language policies and constitutional initiatives originating in the province. And his opposition to Quebec provincial elites only sharpened as the 1980s progressed. Although he had retired formally from public life, his own early opposi-

Table 7–7
Feeling for Quebec and for Key Intervenors (N=1105)

	Mulroney	Other Leaders	Trudeau	Manning
Feeling for Quebec	0.15***	0.16***	0.05	-0.12***
	(0.03)	(0.02)	(0.03)	(0.02)
Intercept	0.21	0.37	0.54	0.49
	(0.02)	(0.01)	(0.02)	(0.02)
R^2	0.02	0.02	0.02	0.02

tion to the Meech Lake Accord arguably laid the foundation for much anti-Meech action which followed. Lines of political and personal affiliation to him could be detected in other key opponents, such as Deborah Coyne, Clyde Wells, and Jean Chrétien. But his opposition to Quebec provincial initiatives still did not link him positively to antipathy to Quebec. In fact the sign on the Trudeau-Quebec coefficient in Table 7–7 is positive; it is just not significantly different from zero. Trudeau cut through pro- and anti-Quebec sentiment.

Not so Preston Manning. Here we see the key anti-Quebec figure. And at this point, Manning also presented himself as the archetypal anti-political figure.[16] Feeling about Quebec encapsulated feeling about compromise, about politics as such. To like this anti-political figure was to dislike Quebec, the pivot for governments, the heartland of politics as usual.

This point is only reinforced by Figure 7–2, which shows that identification with a specific mainstream party was no longer associated with feeling toward Quebec. The fact that by 1992 Conservatives outside Quebec were no less affectionate than Liberals toward Quebec represents a profound negation of years of party history. Now, the best way to express disaffection from Quebec was to reject party identification altogether.[17]

The party coalition did not hold on referendum day according to Figure 7–3. True, non-partisans had the lowest Yes share by far, nearly 20 points smaller than the share among Conservatives, and this is fully consistent with the point just made. Among pro-Accord parties, however, only Conservatives managed to extract a Yes majority – and a razor-thin one at that – from their mass base. Next in line were Liberals, roughly halfway between Conservatives and New Democrats. New Democrats still outperformed non-partisans. The party-system story faces both ways. Party identification mattered a lot, and the Yes vote consisted very heavily of Conservative and Liberal identifiers,

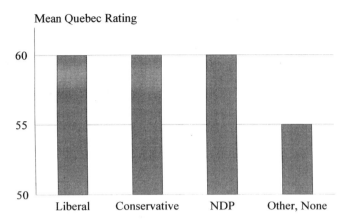

Figure 7–2
Party Identification and Feeling for Quebec

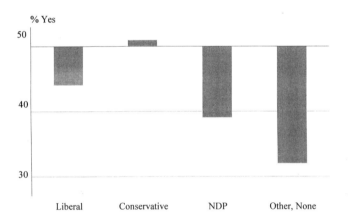

Figure 7–3
Party Identification and Vote

yet at the same time many Conservatives and most Liberals joined the ranks of the No.

Feeling for Quebec, along with other group sentiments, also operated on general arguments and specific elements, as Figure 7–1 implied and Table 7–8 specifies. The table relates each of the five general arguments and four specific elements to each of the three group sentiments, nine regression estimations in all, one estimation per row. For simplicity of presentation, only coefficients on sentiments appear; in-

Table 7–8
Group Sentiment and Considerations in the Accord

	Feeling for Quebec	Minority Rights	Founding Peoples
GENERAL			
Province Winner	0.29*	0.02	0.03
Best Compromise	0.27***	0.09**	0.03
Move On	0.13*	0.09**	0.19***
Fear Separation	0.15**	0.08**	0.08*
Quebec Never Satisfied	-0.56***	-0.06*	-0.06
SPECIFIC			
Distinct Society	0.67***	0.06*	0.14***
25% Guarantee	0.27***	0.05*	0.05
Senate	0.23***	0.01	0.06
Aboriginal Self-Government	0.34***	0.08**	0.19***

tercept terms, standard errors, and equation statistics do not appear.[18] Also for simplicity's sake, the table imposes no causal hierarchy. Party and intervenor orientations are not controlled, even though, as we know already, feelings about intervenors were very important determinants of opinion on the document. Some of what Table 7–8 registers as impact from feeling for Quebec will in fact be indirect, routed through intervenor ratings.[19]

Of the majority/minority orientation, not much need be said. Recall from above that voters took that orientation right to general arguments, and these arguments carried virtually all that orientation's impact on the vote. The orientation's impact was widely dispersed and weak at each site. Preferring minority rights made one modestly more accepting of the compromise, more persuaded that the agreement would facilitate moving on, more anxious about Quebec secession, and less cynical about Quebec's bargaining strategy. Substantively weak but statistically significant, coefficients also appeared for three of four specific elements. We suspect, however, that this is just a carryover from the primary effect, on general arguments.

Recognition of founding peoples was more focused. Among general orientations, its greatest impact by far was on seeing Canada move on. Conceivably, recognizing a bargainer as a founding people provided context for the bargain. These were legitimate claimants seeking their due; if their legitimate claims were satisfied they would cooperate on our common problems. Voters who rejected a founding-peoples claim might look upon the whole process with a cynical eye. To claim founder status was just another bargaining ploy; if we yielded to it here, we would be forced to yield again and again. Among specific elements, its greatest impact was in exactly the right place: on the two most widely supported founding-peoples guarantees – recogniton of Quebec as a distinct society and Aboriginal self-government.

Yet again, however, feeling for Quebec is the big story, with very significant impact on suppport for every specific element and on acceptance of most arguments. At the very heart of the matter was one perception – of Quebec as never satisfied – and one element – the distinct society clause. Liking Quebec had an enormous impact on whether or not one saw the province as insatiable. And so it should have. This argument is hardly amenable to proof, one way or the other. Indeed, our wording of the question was nasty, invited unreflective response. Yet the wording did seem to capture something in street discourse, and, of course, a clear majority of respondents agreed with it. To resist the claim, the most potent antidote was simple affection for Quebec. Feeling for Quebec was also critical to response to the distinct society clause. This proposal had been on the table, in one form or another, for five years, and although a majority of Canadians still opposed it, there was no dearth of prominent supporters. Feeling for Quebec powerfully conditioned acceptance of their cues.

At the other end, Quebec feeling had only a weak impact on the "move on" argument and, very surprisingly, on "fear of separation." Weakness in the "move on" coefficient may testify to power in the argument. Recall from chapter 4 that it was the only one with any promise for turning the rhetorical tide, the one argument clear majorities accepted virtually to campaign's end. And it was the one argument to look beyond the bargaining situation, the one argument to dissociate judgment from feeling about key protagonists – like Quebec or not, at least we could put this behind us. As for fear of separation, the weak coefficient implies that the argument was driven less by feelings about the thing itself than by perception of its likelihood. The critical issue was whether secession would actually happen if the Accord failed.

Now to effects of middling weight. The simplest interpretation is that these reflect response to the Accord as a package. The only consideration with specific Quebec content is the 25 percent guarantee, and this was no more driven by Quebec feeling than the others. Indeed, the link was hardly tighter than for approval of the new Senate. The Senate is, in a sense, the baseline. A voter could reach a position on Senate reform without consulting feelings for Quebec; this would imply a null coefficient. Given the way Senate reform actually entered the agenda, a more plausible expectation is that liking Quebec would make one oppose reform, disliking Quebec would make one favour it. To favour serious reform, especially to institute equal representation by province, means to jettison a binational foundation for government; this would surely be easiest for voters who actively disliked Quebec. Instead we see a robust positive coefficient. The sign of the coefficient, and the fact that four of the five considerations all attracted roughly the same size of effect – a coefficient around 0.25 on variables all scored on a 0,1 scale – leads us to see this as a byproduct of approval (or disapproval) of the whole deal.

Of middling coefficients, the largest was on Aboriginal self-government. Why should this differ from the others? Adding curiosity value is our sense, reported in chapter 4, that of all elements in the package, self-government was the most likely to win freestanding approval – that is, approval so one-sided that voters did not have to be strong-armed into accepting self-government as part of a package.[20] Yet here it picks up a robust effect from feeling for Quebec. The reason, we suspect, lies in a matter discussed earlier in this chapter. Feeling for Quebec can be thought of as having two components. One is specific to that province. The other is general to objects, especially to groups and places. To gauge approval of Quebec is to propose one of several functionally substitutable tests of philanthropic disposition. Few persons taking the test have much direct exposure to Quebec. To ask such people how much they like Quebec is to ask how much affection they can summon up for anything, including, to come back to the point, Aboriginal peoples.

SOCIAL STRUCTURE

Ascriptive Characteristics

Sentiment about groups was clearly important. Could the same be said for actual group membership? Figure 7–4 provides the first cut at this question, with the vote's ascriptive basis – that is, attributes mostly out of respondents' control, the givens in their lives.[21] Entries are Yes shares by group, and to bring out the balance of support/opposition, shares below 50 appear to hang from the 50 percent threshold, while shares above 50 appear stacked on it. As a practical matter, this isolates the handful of groups that said Yes.

On two dimensions, differences were tiny. Women and men differed hardly at all, and the direction of difference contradicted the

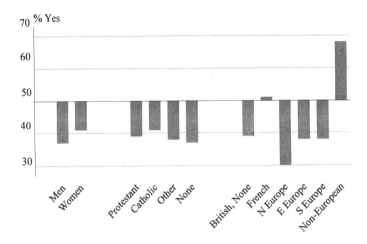

Figure 7-4
Vote and Social Structure I: Ascriptive Characteristics

hopes of the women's movement, as women were slightly more likely than men to vote Yes. Differences among religious groups were even smaller than between genders. This testifies to the cross-party consensus, for religion continued to be a key factor in party choice.[22]

On the third dimension, ethnicity,[23] some contrasts were dramatic. Canadians of non-European background were over twice as likely to vote Yes as Canadians of Northern European origin, at nearly 70 percent versus just 30 percent. Non-Europeans aside, the only other group to say Yes were French Canadians, and this by a tiny margin. For other groups – British or of no single ethnicity, Eastern European, and Southern European – the Yes share was just under 40 percent. Two questions seem worth pursuing here. What explains the distinctiveness of Northern Europeans, French Canadians, and non-Europeans? And why, given all the gender talk, were gender differences in the vote so weak?

Figure 7-5 traces pathways to the vote for the three distinctive ethnic groups, following roughly the logic employed for group sentiment in Figure 7-1. Each group's leftmost coefficient derives from a regression estimation that includes all ascriptive factors in Figure 7-4 and all class-economic factors in Figure 7-6 (below, yet to be discussed). The leftmost coefficient is, as in earlier estimations, a total-effect or reduced-form one. Each factor, including the three represented in the figure, is entered as a dummy variable. The coefficient thus gives the Yes-share difference (in proportions) between

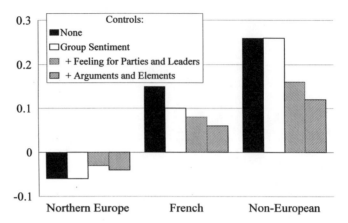

Figure 7–5
Pathways to the Vote I: Ethnicity

the indicated group and the reference category, which on this dimension is British ethnicity[24]; the difference between any pair of groups in the table is just the difference between coefficients. As all characteristics entered estimation, the coefficient represents a *ceteris paribus* estimate and may not correspond exactly to values implied in Figure 7–4. For instance, differences implicit in Figure 7–5 are typically smaller than in Figure 7–4, thanks perhaps to controls for religion or education. To the right appears the impact of intervening variables, controlled stage by stage on the logic of Figure 1–1: first the group sentiment variables, then party identification and intervenor ratings, finally general and specific Accord considerations. If the ethnic-group coefficient shrinks when a particular stage is reached, this indicates that factors at that stage help explain some of the link between ethnic group membership and the vote. If no shrinkage occurs, then that stage explains nothing about the original group difference.

For French Canadians each stage explains some of the original relationship, but the biggest shift is the first – control for group sentiment. The connections make perfect sense. French Canadians outside Quebec liked that province more than any other ethnic group did. Quebec just seemed less alien, and many still had ties of affinity to it. These voters also affirmed minority rights at a higher rate than any other group, except non-Europeans, and they were the one group in which more voters gave priority to minority rights than to majority rule.[25] These differences then translated into enhanced support for the Accord.

Smaller effects were also visible further along the chain. French Canadians liked Preston Manning much less than other groups did, gave him roughly a 10-point lower rating than other groups, and this helped push them to the Yes by way of repulsion.[26] For other intervenors French Canadians were not distinct, not even for Pierre Trudeau. Otherwise, French Canadians remained, as they have for virtually the entire twentieth century, an overwhelmingly Liberal group.[27] In 1992, however, this distinctiveness meant little, as Liberal strength only offset Conservative weakness. The two pro-Accord parties just negated each other, and NDP identification and no identification at all were roughly as common among French Canadians as among others. French Canadians were more prepared to acquiesce in Quebec-specific elements in the deal – more fearful of secession, less likely to see Quebec as insatiable, more in favour of the distinct society clause and the 25 percent guarantee.

Non-Europeans and Northern Europeans were not mirrror images either of each other or of French Canadians. Most strikingly, for neither other group did group sentiment explain anything. Northern Europeans did not like Quebec any less and non-Europeans did not like Quebec any more than others. Their respective aversion and attraction to the Accord thus was not an expression of raw feeling. Neither did these groups differ in willingness to recognize founding peoples, but then hardly any differences were visible on this consideration anyway. Non-Europeans gave higher priority to minority rights than every group other than the French, but most non-Europeans still yielded to majority rule. All this strikes us as notable for what is *not* explained. Canadians of North European origin might have epitomized resentment at the idea of founding peoples; they were too late to be founding peoples themselves, and had the most to lose from recognition of other groups as founders. Given old-world antipathies, these voters might also have liked Quebec least. A group-sentiment story for non-Europeans could also be easily constructed. But for both groups, the reasons for their distinctive vote shares lie further along the reasoning chain.

The key was party politics. Controlling party and intervenor orientation cut each group's coefficient roughly in half. Of all groups, non-Europeans were least likely, and Northern Europeans most likely to be non-partisan, where partisanship as such was one key divide in the Yes share. As well, Northern Europeans gave Preston Manning a higher rating than any other group did. Non-Europeans did the opposite, giving Manning his lowest ratings. For every other intervenor, however, non-Europeans anchored the high end, giving intervenors the highest ratings. This was true even for Trudeau, but was far more distinctively true for key pro-Accord intervenors – around 10 points higher for "other leaders," and 20 points higher for Brian Mulroney! Non-Europeans even rated Mulroney 9 points higher than they did Preston Manning. No other group actually rated Mulroney above Manning, although French Canadians came close. Of all Canadians, non-Europeans were the most incorporated into the party system, most loyal to the political class.

Non-Europeans' political incorporation carried through to willingness to entertain pro-Accord arguments. Non-Europeans were most likely to accept general claims for the necessity of the deal, and of all groups were the most supportive of Aboriginal self-government. Most distinctive, though, was their relative support for the 25 percent guarantee; only in this group could a large minority be said to have favoured it. Northern Europeans tended to be mildly less supportive of key features, but no less so than would be predicted from their relative aversion to party politics.

The ethnic-group basis of the Accord reaffirms some familiar patterns but contradicts others. The Northern European/non-European contrast is one basis of Liberal-Conservative conflict. But these two groups are small, non-Europeans especially so. Other groups also figure prominently in party politics and yet were quite indistinct on the Accord. The lack of contrast between Southern and Eastern Europeans illustrates this. Eastern Europeans have been something of a pillar for the Conservative party, while Southern Europeans exceed even French Canadians and non-Europeans in Liberal support.[28] No difference appeared between these groups and neither differed from Canadians of British background. In a way, this is not surprising. After all, political parties suspended their conflict for the duration of the referendum. But if certain ethnic groups converged, thanks to the partisan truce, why did others not converge?

The other great non-finding was the voting similarity of men and women. In part, this reflected conflicting pressures peculiar to the world of gender politics. Women's general orientations tilted them slightly toward the Yes, but certain features of the Accord pushed them in the opposite direction. Women were generally more sympathetic to minority claims and more likely to recognize founding peoples. Differences were not huge in this realm, but were always consistent. Women were slightly less alienated than men from party politics, slightly less enamoured of Preston Manning, slightly more positive on other leaders (one of whom, of course, was a woman). And women clearly worried more about Quebec separation and less about feeding Quebec's alleged insatiability. But women were less persuaded that their province was a winner and, perhaps most critically, less happy with the compromise. In this last difference we may see some impact from the NAC.

The NAC found itself in the difficult position of opposing the Accord on grounds that inclined voters at large in the other direction. For instance, women who knew the movement opposed the Accord were actually more likely than those who did not to endorse the Aboriginal self-government and distinct society proposals.[29] Awareness had its impact reinforced by feeling: among those aware of the movement's opposition, feeling toward the movement was positively related to endorsement of the proposals. At one point, Judy Rebick conceded that "nothing can be as odd as landing on the same side of the issue as the Bloc and Reform – other than having feminists working on two sides of an issue."[30] It would appear that, if anything, she understated NAC's predicament, for divisions – outright contradictions even – ran right through the movement's natural base.

The NAC had to substantiate the claim that women's specific interests were injured by the Accord, a claim based on subtle calculations of relative group advantage. Certainly, seeing women as losers in the deal reduced support for more concrete elements, notably Aboriginal self-government and the distinct society clause. Voters, female voters especially, were more likely to see women as losers if they were aware that the NAC opposed the agreement.[31] And women were more likely than men to see women as losers. But most voters, women as well as men, did not see women as an interest affected either way by the deal. Moreover, as chapter 5 indicated, only a minority of voters perceived the movement's opposition. A significant fraction – larger than for any other intervenor – placed them on the wrong side, and awareness spread mainly *after* most damage had been done.

Curiously, the NAC may have been helped by the floating of – and cool reception for – a proposal to guarantee female representation in the new Senate. The premiers of Ontario, Nova Scotia, and Saskatchewan all agreed to set aside half their provinces' seats for women. Mike Harcourt of British Columbia also signed on, until mounting criticism forced a retreat. Although the formal agreement embraced no quota, the representational cat was out of the bag. On this issue, the gender gap was quite sharp: 58 percent of women favoured some form of seat guarantee, compared to 45 percent of men. Mandating absolutely equal representation also divided men from women sharply, but in neither gender was there a majority for a strict 50 percent quota. The real effect of all this attention to the Senate, however, may have been to reduce overall support for the new model, and this in turn told against the Yes. Women were less likely than men to support the proposed Senate, perhaps for lack of a na-

tionwide quota. At the same time, the proposed Senate's natural supporters resisted quotas.[32]

Economics and Class

This section considers two functionally distinct but empirically over-
lapping possibilities: that the Accord fell victim to economic recession, and that its support reflected Canada's class structure. These
possibilities overlap to the extent that exposure to economic adversity
differs by class: the poor are not just poor, but also more at risk when
the economy sinks. The possibilities are distinct in the lessons they
teach about referendum voting in general.

Figure 7–6 lays out Yes shares, exactly on the model of Figure 7–4.
The two leftmost groupings address the question of short-term misfortune: one contrasts those currently employed with those currently
unemployed or laid off; the other assesses reports of change in financial well being over the preceding twelve months. The other three
groupings assess the abiding place in the social structure: unionized
or not; income; and educational attainment. In no group was there
much support for the Accord, but some differences stand out.

Economic misfortune clearly harmed the Accord's prospects, or so
it appears on first examination. Unemployed voters had the lowest
Yes share of any group examined so far. Voters claiming a worsened
financial condition were also markedly less likely to vote Yes than
voters reporting an improved or unchanged one. The difference was
not as sharp as for unemployed voters, and there was some overlap
between unemployed and worse-off categories. But the percentage
reporting being worse off was large by recent standards: 37 percent,
as compared with only 13 percent better off.

If short-term misfortune told against the Accord, so did permanent
disadvantage. But the measure of disadvantage was not income: voters with family incomes under $30,000 were less likely to vote Yes
than those higher up, but only slightly. And such income-vote relationship as could be gleaned was not monotonic.

Much more revealing was membership in the union movement.
Union families were more than 10 points less likely than non-union
families to vote Yes. Recall from chapter 5 that awareness of union
leaders' support for the Accord made only a small difference to the
vote and, moreover, that ratings of the union movement were negatively related to the Yes share, notwithstanding union leaders' endorsement of the Accord. Now we see what union leaders were
struggling against: a general effect from social disadvantage, leading
to a No vote.

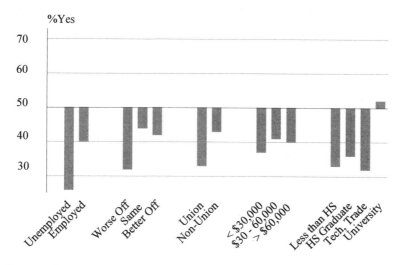

Figure 7–6
Vote and Social Structure II: Class and Economic Factors

The most striking effect of all, however, was from education. Here what stands out is not so much disadvantage as advantage. Where all non-university groups were uniformly for the No, university-educated voters were the only group in the entire array to vote Yes (if only barely), and the university/non-university difference was close to 20 points.

Figure 7–7 outlines the paths to the vote, by exact analogy to Figure 7–5. All class, economic, and ascriptive variables were entered into an initial estimation, and then sentimental, party system, and rhetorical considerations were added by stage. As before, the figure shows what happens to the indicated variable's vote coefficient. Also as before, the starting point (the bar labelled "none") indicates a *ceteris paribus* effect and usually implies a smaller impact than the gross differences in Figure 7–6. Only four groups merited further consideration: the unemployed (as contrasted with the employed), those financially worse off (as compared with those either better off or unchanged), union families (versus non-union), and the university-educated (as compared with, roughly, all other education-attainment groups).[33]

The impact from unemployment was mainly an expression of discontent with parties and leaders. Employment status made no difference at all to minority orientation and virtually none to recognition of founding peoples. The unemployed did like Quebec less than did

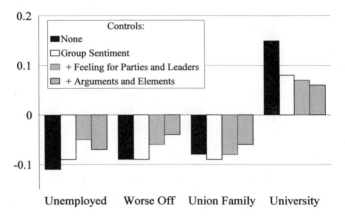

Figure 7–7
Pathways to the Vote II: Class and Economic Factors

those in work, a difference of about 9 points on our 0,100 scale, and this accounted for a small part of the total effect. Much more important, however, was the party system: controlling party factors cut the unemployment coefficient by more than half. Unemployed voters were distinct in two, reinforcing ways: they were less Conservative and less partisan. Indeed, aversion to parties ought, in a sense, to have produced an even more resounding No than it did, for adding substantive opinion on the Accord negates some of the effect of party controls. The unemployed translated less of their distaste for parties into distaste for the Accord's substance than most other groups did, but this did not stop them from still saying No.

Compare this with the pattern for the financially worse off (remember, this is a multivariate setup, so the "worse off" coefficient indicates impact from general misfortune independently of impact from the specific fact of unemployment). Being worse off did not sour voters on Quebec or on Canada's group basis, in that controlling group sentiment reduced the "worse off" coefficient not one bit. But, as with unemployment, economic adversity soured voters on the party system. Worsened conditions also reduced support for the Accord itself.

Impact from union membership was pretty raw. If anything, union families were disproportionately sympathetic to Quebec and to minorities, and they were not peculiarly alienated from party politics. On the other hand, they were less persuaded than others by the rhetoric around the Accord. When all the intervening factors were controlled, union families remained distinctively anti-Accord. We submit this as a fact, but can supply no further interpretation.

If group sentiment seems to have had only a negligible impact in relation to class and economic factors, the same could not be said for education. Most of the impact from university exposure was precisely sentimental: the total university coefficient was cut in half by including group-sentiment controls, and only modest further reductions were effected by further controls. University-educated voters rated Quebec roughly 10 points higher than other groups did and were about 7 points more likely to affirm minority rights.[34] Beyond this there is little to say. University-educated voters liked Trudeau a bit more than others and liked Manning a bit less than others, but these patterns, weak to begin with, offset each other. Education made no real difference to direction of party identification and hardly any to the overall likelihood of identifying with some party.

University education also had generally weak and partially offsetting effects in response to the rhetoric around the document. The most highly educated mostly accepted the compromise; they were the least likely to see Quebec as insatiable, but were also the least likely to fear secession. They were more supportive of each specific element, especially for the absolutely central one – recognition of Quebec as a distinct society. But the key was that, relative to other groups, university-educated voters approached the document with two strong presumptions in its favour: they liked Quebec more and they were more likely to give minorities the benefit of the doubt. These two inclinations did most of the work in leading highly educated voters to accept general arguments and endorse key elements.

A NOTE ON REGION

The Atlantic region was the only one to support the Accord wholeheartedly. Even Nova Scotia, which gave the No a slight edge, was effectively indistinguishable from Ontario, which goes down in history as having said Yes. What accounted for this region's distinctiveness? In this section we gather together factors described in earlier chapters and test their explanatory power with the tools exemplified in figures 7–5 and 7–7. Indeed, this section's demonstration, Figure 7–8, draws from the same underlying estimation as those two earlier figures.

First, recall the candidates for explanation:

– On specific elements, the Atlantic provinces differed little from the rest of the country (Figure 3–2). Certainly, the region favoured no element other regions opposed. The only element worth mentioning is the distinct society clause, on which Atlantic opinion was balanced, in contrast to decided opposition elsewhere.

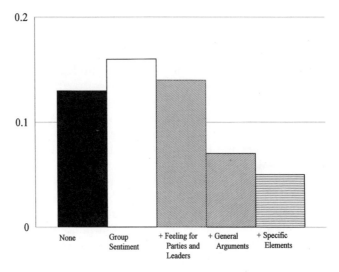

Figure 7–8
Pathways to the Vote III: The Atlantic Provinces

- On general arguments, the region was notably different on the arguments on both the best compromise the need to and move on. Residents of the region were also modestly more likely to see their province as a winner (Figure 4–2). Strikingly, Atlantic residents differed little from others on perceptions of Quebec, although they were slightly more likely to fear secession (Figure 4–4).
- The Atlantic region was more positive (or less negative) about certain figures in the pro-Accord coalition, in particular, about their own premiers (Figure 5–1).
- The possible missing link is group sentiment, which of course is this chapter's distinctive preoccupation, and to which we turn in a moment.

Many factors pull in the same direction, and given the staged character of reasoning about the Accord, the importance of one factor need not detract from the importance of another. Figure 7–8 presents the staged estimation.

Group sentiment played a disruptive role. Atlantic residents were not more pro-Quebec or more pro-minority than voters elsewhere. If such sentiments were a key factor, the Atlantic region would have been less distinct than it was in fact. Feeling for parties and leaders roughly compensated for group sentiment. But if party politics held the region in line, it did not account for the region's distinctiveness.

That task fell to the general arguments, which were more widely accepted in the region than elsewhere. The key arguments were about the compromise and the need to move on. Fear of separation could not have been the attitudinal key, and even less could perception of Quebec as insatiable or of the voter's own province as a winner have been pivotal. Finally, attitudes to specific elements added little to the story. The only specific element that could have mattered was the distinct society clause.

The basic story, then, is about Atlantic voters' greater disposition to compromise and greater desire to move on – orientations that helped them override objections to the deal itself. As a factor in the region, this orientation seems have been mainly freestanding. It is striking that Atlantic residents' acceptance of these arguments was not a direct product of the positive standing of the leaders – premiers especially – making the arguments. If that were the case, controlling parties and leaders would have produced a bigger reduction in the regional coefficient, relative to the further reduction effected by controlling general arguments. One possibility is that disposition to compromise is endemic to the region's political culture, and that overt expression of the disposition and positive ratings of politicians are each manifestations of that underlying cultural trait.

CONCLUSIONS

On the Charlottetown Accord, the electorate was not that deeply divided by its group life. True, the widest difference on a single dimension was nearly 40 points, but one group featuring in that particular contrast, non-Europeans, was very small. The numerically big battalions of the electorate tended to differ modestly. This is not unusual, in fact, and the 1992 result should be taken to confirm a general pattern, not even a peculiarly Canadian one. As Green puts it: "One of the most provocative findings in public opinion research is that tangible personal interests are seldom correlated with policy opinions ... although policies are invariably more costly to some individuals than to others, personal costs and benefits are poor predictors of how people wish the government to act" (1992, p. 128). The differences that do stand out rarely correspond to any obvious policy stake, nor do they follow the lines indicated by key intervenors or group leaders.

The heart of the matter was not so much membership as sentiment, toward groups and toward the party system. Orientation toward Quebec was most important; how voters felt about the province coloured response to the Accord itself, especially to its specific elements. But group-related attitudes went beyond raw feeling. Voters also detected two contestable propositions in the Accord's underpinnings: that Canada's founding peoples require special constitutional accommodation, and that minority rights should trump majority rule. At the same time, the Accord was the ultimate product of partisan compromise, and voters' response to the document was powerfully coloured by their orientations to parties and leaders. As the compromise took party differences mostly out of play, orientation to the system as such became the critical thing.

When group attitudes and party attitudes did mediate the impact from social structure, they did so in distinctive ways. For the most part, ethnic differences were unmediated by ethnic attitudes. Northern Europeans shunned the Accord and non-Europeans embraced it, but these polar groups were essentially undifferentiated by group-related attitudes.[35] Where they differed was in partisan incorporation. Northern Europeans, of relatively long standing historical standing in Canada, were the least loyal by far to the party system and to its personnel. Non-Europeans, mostly recent arrivals, were the most partisan and liked key political individuals the most. Roughly the same pattern held for most relevant forms of social disadvantage. The unemployed and those reporting worsened financial well-being did not express their distress through repudiation of Quebec or of minorities in general. What they did repudiate – or lacked the will to embrace – was the party system.

Rejection of the Accord was fuelled for some by a kind of tribal animosity, but for many others sentiment hardly seems tribal at all. It is true that the less one liked Quebec, the smaller the Yes share. Voters who disliked Quebec were probably offside from the very start; they detected that the Charlottetown Accord was about accommodating Quebec and rejected it accordingly. But such voters were not the strategic key to the result. Negotiators may have pitched the proposed Senate at this anti-Quebec interest, but chapters 3 and 4 made clear that this pitch rested on a misapprehension: negotiators mistook antipathy toward Quebec for a more generalized, more benign provincialism. Instead, the pivotal group looked to Pierre Trudeau, and these were not voters moved by antipathy to Quebec. To Quebec proper, these voters were indifferent; their concern was an honourable settlement, where the terms of honour were defined by Trudeau, not by Quebec's own elite. The Accord played into group sentiment, of course, but went down, ultimately, not because it repelled "Quebec haters" but because it could not hold the electorate's broad middle.

And group sentiment was most critical for the most highly educated, and here the story could not be one of crude tribal feeling. First of all, simple feeling did not do all the work for university-educated respondents; also important were more conceptualized opinions, especially about minorities as such. And second, the voters for whom group sentiment mattered most were also voters most accepting of claims by, so to speak, the Other. University-educated voters simply liked Quebec more and attached more weight to minority claims than others did. Conceivably, the university experience rubs the edges off group sentiment, exposes individuals to a wider world, and helps them grasp the logic of accommodation. Then again, getting to university, on one hand, and embracing outsiders, on the other, may be alternative manifestations of an underlying social competence and self-confidence.

We cannot settle this dispute but neither can we simply let it hang, for interpreting the role of education is central to interpreting the 1992 referendum and to assessing the challenge of direct democracy. In account after account, education is associated with interest, attentiveness, and political information. Formal education helps people sort through complicated arguments and find order in what for others is a disordered world (for representative statements, see Miller and Miller, 1976; Luskin, 1990; Dalton, 1988). And the Charlottetown Accord was nothing if not complex. If education's principal role was as a marker for political sophistication, highly educated voters should have been most adept at identifying their own interests, especially long-term ones, more persuaded by reasoned argument, and less influenced by media priming, symbolic flourishes, or the personalities of leaders (Iyengar et al., 1982; Knight, 1985). These arguments presuppose a *social learning* gradient, an index of differential absorption of messages about the seriousness of the crisis or at least of the seriousness of unresolved Canada-Quebec tensions. But, as chapter 1 argued, this is not the only available interpretation. The alternatives are canvassed in chapter 9.

8 Why Did Quebec Say No?

The Quebec campaign was over before it officially began. The province may have been prepared to say Yes for a very brief moment in the unofficial campaign during late August or early September, but otherwise the Yes share was well short of a majority. But if Quebec was almost always off side, its rejection of the Accord was never as one-sided as in, say, the West. In Quebec, there just was little room to move.

The weakness of campaign dynamics reflected the fact that half or more of the Quebec electorate was committed in advance to one side or the other; therefore it was bound either to accept or reject the deal, regardless of its merits. Non-francophones had powerful reasons to say Yes to the Accord, in hopes of blocking other Quebeckers' drive for sovereignty. Sovereignists had precisely the opposite motive, and could hardly accept a deal designed to frustrate their defining political objective. The real battle ground lay in the middle, among francophone non-sovereignists – a large group, but far less than the whole electorate.

This chapter begins by examining opinion dynamics in the unofficial campaign, relying on published commercial polls. Then comes consideration of the electorate's three blocs. Fixing the language boundary is easy, but demarcating sovereignists is not so straightforward. Sovereignty, although much discussed, remains a murky concept for voters at large. Even so, the attraction of sovereignty reflects an ongoing debate and sovereignty opinion is structured by voters' response to this debate. And sovereignty as such was not on the table in 1992. Even if one's aspiration for sovereignty was weak and on that account vulnerable to modest counter-argument, the Charlottetown Accord arguably blocked all conceivable moves toward it, and so was unacceptable. Running through the whole debate – and distinguishing the three blocs most sharply from each other – was group sentiment. In part, the pattern for Quebec mirrored that outside the province: where for the rest of Canada the prime mover was raw feeling for Quebec, in Quebec the key factor was feeling for Canada. Ideas also mattered, but the ideas at issue in Quebec were unique to the place.

DID THE CAMPAIGN MATTER?

The formal Quebec campaign – that is, the period in which paid advertising was permitted – started on 28 September, one week later than in the rest of Canada. But informally the battle began right after the Charlottetown Accord was struck, on 28 August. Figure 8–1 gives poll results to 28 September, as reported in the media.[1] Three periods suggest themselves:

– In the last week of August, five polls registered that Quebeckers were almost evenly divided,[2] with an average Yes share of 48 percent. Quebeckers may have briefly flirted with the Yes over the last weekend in August, as two polls indicated a majority for the Accord.[3]
– In the first half of September, when Quebeckers heard the exact wording of the question and heard basic arguments on both sides, the Yes share dropped below 50 percent. The drop seems to have been steady, from the Environics reading in the low 50s to the first Léger & Léger reading below 40 percent.
– After mid-September, the Yes share oscillated around 40 pecent. Léger & Léger readings were under 40 percent, others tended to be over that mark.[4] The simplest reading is that the Yes share bottomed out around 40 percent.

The difference between September extremes was 22 points, comparable to October shifts in the rest of Canada. This almost certainly overdramatizes the dynamics, however, as only one reading (Reid) exceeded 55 percent and the other extreme reading was by Léger & Léger, which usually tendered low estimates. The most obvious interpretation is that the Yes share dropped from about 55 percent to about 40 percent, over roughly two weeks and with no acceleration or braking.

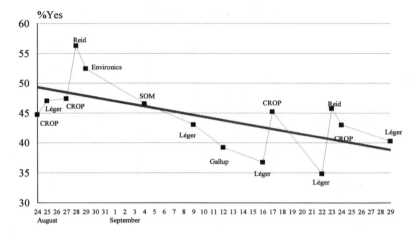

Figure 8–1
The Unofficial Campaign

No event stands out in Quebec as the equivalent of the Egg Roll speech. Support for the agreement started to erode well before the Quebec Superior Court injunction on 14 September against publication of the transcript of Diane Wilhelmy's conversation with André Tremblay. By that date the share was already bottoming out. Jean Allaire's public statement of opposition did predate the downturn, but Mario Dumont's statement did not. The most likely explanation is that the climate just shifted, although Jean Allaire may have given the critical initial push. Besides, the very earliest polls put Quebec in the No camp; the thing to be explained is not so much the drop from the Reid-Environics high point as how that brief high point was reached in the first place.

After 28 September, in any case, vote intentions moved little, in contrast with the rest of Canada, as Figure 2–1 indicated.[5] The lifting of the injunction on publishing the transcript of the Wilhelmy-Tremblay conversation on 30 September, Trudeau's speech at la Maison du Egg Roll, and the rise of the interest rate by two points on 1 October had no evident impact. The televised Bourassa-Parizeau debate on 12 October drew a wide audience (62 percent of our respondents), comparable to the Canada-wide audience for the leaders' debate in the 1988 election (Blais and Boyer, 1995). Bourassa won decisively, in the sense that 50 percent of our respondents thought he performed the best, compared to only 15 percent for Parizeau. Again, though, no movement in opinion was evident.[6]

THE THREE QUEBEC ELECTORATES

Quebec is not one electorate, but three, and should be analysed as such. Nonetheless, votes are counted for the province as a whole, and so the relative size of each part is critical, as is each group's willingness to turn out at the polls. Only one division, by language, corresponds to a census category. The other division, between sovereignists and all others, is explicitly political, and for that reason is commonly obfuscated.

Non-Francophone versus Francophone

As a minority within a minority, non-francophone Quebeckers arguably had the greatest stake in the success of the Accord. This interest bound anglophones and allophones (those whose first language is neither French nor English) together. According to the 1991 census, non-francophones[7] represent 18 percent of the total Quebec population, as well as of the population over twenty years old. As some non-francophones have not yet acquired Canadian citizenship, their share of registered voters is closer to 15 percent.[8] Offsetting this is a powerful drive to participate: non-francophones turn out at a higher rate than do francophones.[9] In our sample, non-francophones constituted 17 percent of those claiming to have voted.

Sovereignist versus Non-Sovereignist

Two issues shroud the boundary between sovereignists and non-sovereignists. One is the label itself. The term sovereignty dominates elite discourse, but other terms have been in play, often for specifically partisan reasons. The second is what Quebec voters think sovereignty means.

Four different terms have been used in opinion surveys: sovereignty-association, sovereignty, independence, and separation (Cloutier, Guay, and Latouche, 1992, p. 43). Separation carries heavily negative connotations and has been shunned in Quebec debate. Independence has a clear meaning, but again is not widely used in Quebec. It sometimes refers to the most radical of sovereignists, who want no economic association with the rest of Canada. This leaves the most commonly used terms, sovereignty and sovereignty-association. The latter is ambiguous on whether economic association with the rest of Canada is a necessary condition for favouring sovereignty. The same is true for sovereignty, at least as the idea has been used in Quebec debate, but the label still seems conceptually simpler. In any case, it is the dominant term in Quebec discourse, the least unsatisfactory, and the one we have chosen to use.

The second issue is whether Quebeckers really understand what sovereignty means. According to a CROP-*La Presse* survey published on 30 March 1992, 31 percent of Quebeckers believe that a sovereign Quebec would still be part of Canada. If some Quebeckers are confused about what sovereignty entails, the implication of such confusion is not entirely clear. Most importantly, if Quebeckers who think of themselves as sovereignist were told that a sovereign Quebec would no longer be part of Canada, would they still support sovereignty?

A proper answer to this question requires an experiment. Where half our Quebec sample was asked about support for "sovereignty," period, the other half was asked about "sovereignty, that is, Quebec is no longer part of Canada."[10] Results for francophones are presented in Figure 8–2. Asking only about sovereignty induces 60 percent to say they favour it.[11] Supplying a definition does three things. First, the "don't know" proportion declines substantially, from 10 percent to 3 percent. Second, it tilts the balance sharply against sovereignty, as support drops to 46 percent. In our view, the hard variant of the question better indicates genuine support for sovereignty, which means that surveys in Quebec routinely overestimate sovereignist sentiment among francophones by close to 15 points, by about 10 points in the electorate as a whole. Third, supplying a definition for sovereignty intensifies opposition. Among francophones, the percentage "very opposed" more than doubles, from 12 to 28 percent.

Apart from language, the socio-demographic bases of sovereignist sentiment are weak, according to Table 8–1. Among francophones, support for sovereignty is unrelated to gender or employment status, may be related to union membership, and is definitely but only weakly related to age, education, and income.[12] Most potent is a combination of age and low education: support for sovereignty is substantially weaker among those over fifty and those with less than a high school education. To a great extent these are the same people; about half the over-fifty group did not finish high school, and over-fifties constitute about half the less-than-high-school group. When schooling is not in the equation, the over-fifty coefficient is about one-third again larger, an indication that generational differences in educational attainment are part of what is at work here. Low-income voters, in contrast, are relatively supportive of sovereignty. The same also seems to be true of union families.[13]

More striking than differences, however, is their absence or weakness. In a way, this is consistent with the weak differences observed

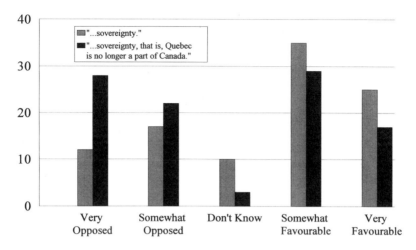

Figure 8–2
The Meaning of Sovereignty (Francophones Only)

for Accord support in chapter 7. The differences here are even weaker, but the sovereignty question is absolutely fundamental; it is much argued in Quebec, and opinion has had decades to crystallize. The weakness of cleavages in 1992 stands in sharp contrast to the pattern for the 1980 referendum, when youth (born after 1940), public-sector employment, higher education, and lack of religious commitment helped voters say Yes to giving the Quebec government a mandate to negotiate sovereignty-association with the rest of Canada (Blais and Nadeau, 1984).

The 1992 pattern was not wholly novel, however, for it corresponded to earlier findings for attenuation of social differences. Nadeau (1992) shows that the surge in support for sovereignty in 1990, in the wake of the failure of the Meech Lake Accord,[14] was accompanied by diminished cleavages, that recruitment to the sovereignist camp came disproportionately in groups of erstwhile weakness. By 1992 support had declined, but the decline evidently was across the board, and left sovereignty sentiment remarkably unstructured.

The factors making some francophone Quebeckers support and others oppose sovereignty thus must be mainly attitudinal and perceptual, and largely freestanding. Blais and Nadeau (1992) argue, for instance, that positions on sovereignty reflect tension between relative attachment to Quebec and Canada, on one hand, and concern over the economic consequences of separation, on the other (see also

Table 8–1
Support for Sovereignty among Francophones *(N =546)*

	(1)	*(2)*
Over fifty	-0.09*	-0.00
	(0.04)	(0.03)
Woman	-0.02	0.01
	(0.03)	(0.03)
Under $30,000	0.08*	0.06*
	(0.03)	(0.03)
$60,000 and over	-0.02	0.01
	(0.04)	(0.03)
Less than HS	-0.11*	-0.11**
	(0.05)	(0.04)
Trade School	-0.03	-0.04
	(0.04)	(0.04)
University	0.00	-0.01
	(0.04)	(0.04)
Unemployed	0.03	0.01
	(0.06)	(0.05)
Union	0.06	0.02
	(0.03)	(0.03)
Feeling for Canada	–	-0.69***
		(0.06)
Feeling for Quebec	–	0.41***
		(0.08)
Linguistic Threat	–	0.09***
		(0.03)
Economic Concerns	–	-0.30***
		(0.06)
Intercept	0.54	0.75
	(0.04)	(0.07)
R^2-adjusted	0.03	0.37

Entries in parentheses are standard errors;
* $p < 0.05$; ** $p < 0.01$; *** $p < 0.001$.

Pinard, 1980; Meadwell, 1993). For Dion (1992), the root of Quebec nationalism lies in concern about the fragility of the French language. The balance on each of these three factors appears in Figure 8–3 (non-francophone balances also appear, but discussion of them is post-

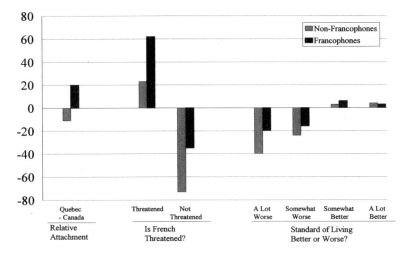

Figure 8–3
Considerations in Sovereignty

poned for now). Quebec gets a 20-point higher rating than Canada among francophone Quebeckers (and 60 percent feel closer to Quebec than to Canada).[15] Canada gets only a slightly higher rating among francophone Quebeckers than Quebec does in the rest of Canada.[16] Feeling about the two places are only weakly related: the correlation between the two ratings is 0.14, much smaller than between any pair of ratings in Table 7–1. These facts alone make sovereignty a serious option. That option becomes even more appealing when attachment to Quebec combines with fear for the language, and 61 percent of francophone Quebeckers believe that French is threatened inside the very province where it is the majority language.[17] On the other hand, concern about the economic consequences of separation weakens support for sovereignty. Thirty-five percent of francophones think their own standard of living would get worse (20 percent say "a lot worse") if Quebec separates; very few expect it would get better.[18]

Table 8–1 goes on to examine the role of these four considerations,[19] as well as what effect remains from background factors once feelings and perceptions are controlled. Most crucial are feelings of attachment, to Canada especially. Attitudes to Canada and to Quebec affect sovereignty sentiment separately, but the key is feeling for the country as a whole. On a common scale, moving a given distance has almost twice the effect for Canada feelings as for Quebec ones. Next in importance is fear for the consequences of separation. Moving from complete pessimism to complete optimism nearly doubles the chances of full support for sovereignty. According to Figure 8–3, francophones are more likely to see themselves faring worse than better from separation. Most, however, believe that a split with Canada will have no effect on their standard of living. Seeing French as threatened inside Quebec promotes sovereignist support. The marginal effect is small, but the balance of opinion is two to one on the side of threat. The division of opinion is serious, but the balance clearly favours sovereignist orientation.

Once these factors are controlled, age ceases to have any direct effect, and any hint of union distinctiveness also washes away. The year 1992 caught Quebec in the middle of an ongoing cultural shift, then, with emotional bonds to the rest of the country declining. The older generation likes Canada more and is more fearful of the consequences of separation. Older voters are also less fearful for the future of the language.[20] Age differences such as this admit competing interpretations: Do differences reflect *how much* voters have aged, their respective places in the life cycle? Or do they reflect *when* they came of age, what generation they belong to? Although, strictly speaking, longitudinal data are required to sort these effects out, three plausible (perhaps complementary) interpretations suggest a generational effect. First, older Quebeckers may be more aware of progress made by the French language over the last thirty years (Vaillancourt, 1988) and thus feel more positive about the future. Second, the fact that feelings for Canada are age-related fairly begs a generational interpretation, and generational differences in attachment suggest that older voters' lesser concern for the future of French reflects of a more lukewarm nationalism. Third, earlier research indicates that the demographic boundary in support for sovereignty is not fifty years of age, but birth before the early 1940s (Blais and Nadeau 1984); the stability of this pattern must be generational in origin, and leads us to suspect that collateral attitudes and perceptions have a similarly stable, generational structure. And the boundary falls exactly where generational interpretation says it should, between those who came of age before the Quiet Revolution and those who came of age during or after it. Age data mark a discontinuity in political culture.[21]

Income and education differences were hardly affected by these controls, however. High-school leavers' resistance to sovereignty may resemble the impact from age: lower education may increase resistance to novel, still-contested cultural forms. If so, education does not carry with it the more complex pattern of indirect effects that age does. The low-education group likes Quebec less but also likes Canada less; relative attachment cannot be the story here, then. The low-education group is relatively fearful of the economic consequences of separation, but is also more persuaded that French is threatened inside Quebec, again a saw-off. Roughly speaking, these observations also hold for low-income voters (many of whom are low-education voters as well, of course); for income, too, potential mediating factors are not arranged in a causally efficient way. Education and income are thus left to burn through directly. The positive association of one with the other helps undermine the class basis of sovereignty sentiment and contributes, ironically, to the socially unstructured field described above. There is also a hint in these data that social forces producing sovereignty sentiment are coming full circle, that older, pre-Quiet Revolution patterns of nationalist orientation are poking up. We return to this below, in discussing the francophone non-sovereignist vote.

The playing field was clearly tilted against the Yes forces. Non-francophones, with the most powerful reasons to say Yes, constituted less than 20 percent of the mobilized electorate, and of these a small fraction deemed themselves sovereignist. Francophone sovereignists, arrayed on the other side, were more than twice as numerous. By minimum estimate (as revealed by response to the "no longer part of Canada" treatment), sovereignists constituted over 40 percent of the total electorate. By maximum estimate (as revealed by response to the control), sovereignists made up close to half. Much might depend on which definition of sovereignty was operative as voters made up their minds on the Accord. But even by the hard, narrow definition, francophone sovereignists outnumbered non-francophones more than two to one. Moreover, not all non-sovereignists were outright federalists, and outright federalists might not have been impelled as powerfully toward the Yes as sovereignists were toward the No. The arithmetic is daunting: if we assign all non-francophones to the Yes and all sovereignists to the No, the Accord would require support from 73 to 85 percent of the key middle group to reach a province-wide majority.

According to Figure 8–4, almost all sovereignists did vote No, but not all non-francophones voted Yes. Instead, about one non-francophone in four voted No. Among allophones, the vote was more one-sided, 78 percent Yes;[22] among anglophones the Yes share was 71 percent. Conversely, only 11 percent of sovereignists could be tempted by the Accord. This leaves francophone non-sovereignists in the middle, and there the contest was extremely close. In the end, the No prevailed by thinnest of margins. Even a thin margin the other way would not have mattered, however: to carry the whole province, francophone non-sovereignists needed to be as enthusiastic as the non-francophones were.

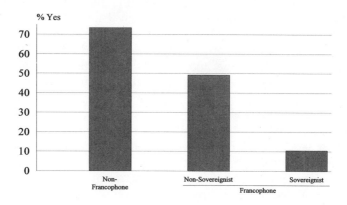

Figure 8–4
Vote by Bloc

FRANCOPHONE SOVEREIGNISTS: A SOLID NO

Strength of sovereignist commitment made a difference, but only a small one. Figure 8–5 brings this out in two ways – by controlling not just the direction of sovereignty opinion, but also its expressed intensity and the presence of experimental counter-induction. We expect Yes shares to fall off by intensity within the sovereignist camp, of course. But we also expect sovereignists' Yes shares to be smaller at each intensity level where that pro-sovereignist orientation is volunteered in the face of the counter-consideration: if you are prepared to favour sovereignty when the awful truth is laid bare, you must really mean it; for the same reason, you should already have figured out the full, anti-sovereignist signficance of the Accord. This proves to be true, but not impressively so. Most of the difference occurs among voters who claim to be "somewhat favourable" to sovereignty. Voters who are "strongly favourable" cast virtually no Yes votes in either treatment. Someone whose reflexive response is "very favourable" has very good reasons to say No. Some voters with this reflex will be pushed off it by the reminder of what sovereignty really means. For most, though, the counter-consideration will just temper their pro-sovereignty reflex, moving them from "very" to only "somewhat" favourable. Such voters still have plenty of reasons to say No.

The weakest sovereignists are those who make it only to "somewhat" favourable and only when no counter-consideration is invoked. These are the most vulnerable to counter-argument, but

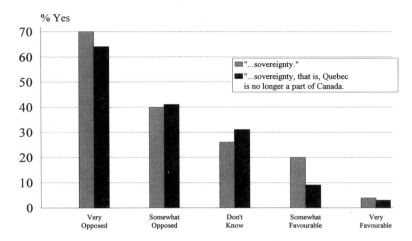

Figure 8–5
The Meaning of Sovereignty and the Vote (Francophones Only)

thanks to chance they have not heard ours. Some will hear such counter-arguments in the real campaign, however, and thus have a much higher chance of voting Yes than voters in any other apparently sovereignist category. But the largest sovereignist Yes share, the share among the weakest of the weak, was only 20 percent, smaller than the smallest non-sovereignist No share of 30 percent (among those "very opposed" to sovereignty even without being given a reason). Within the sovereignist camp, at its broadest definition, the maximum Yes-share difference is only 17 points (20 percent, control-condition somewhat favourable group versus 3 percent, treatment-condition "very" favourable group).

By implication, respondents on the boundary of sovereignist sentiment, who can be moved off the position by defining it clearly, still have much in common with respondents whose sovereignist commitment is more firm. Borderline voters can still be said to be proto-sovereignist, at least. This is confirmed by the most clearly ambivalent or indifferent respondents of all, those with no opinion. In each treatment, this group voted heavily No.[23] The effective discontinuity in impulse toward the Yes was not between hard-core sovereignists and all others. Rather it lay between hard-core federalists and all others.

Unsurprisingly, sovereignists and non-sovereignists differed most widely over whether Quebec had lost; 64 percent of sovereignists believed this, compared with only 32 percent of non-sovereignists. The overwhelming majority of sovereignists (89 percent) approved of the distinct society clause, but almost as large a share (75 percent) felt it did not go far enough. But this is window-dressing; the Accord was too small a displacement from the status quo – and threatened to block further displacements – for any self-respecting sovereignist, whatever they meant by the term, to accept.[24]

NON-FRANCOPHONES: A SOLID YES

Our estimate for non-francophones is roughly in line with other polls, but all polls disagree with analyses of official returns. St-Germain, Grenier, and Lavoie (*Le Devoir*, 23 February 1993, p. A7) put the non-francophone Yes share close to 90 percent (their exact claim is 88–89 percent). Drouilly (1993) puts it higher, between 91 and 100 percent, probably closer to 100. The truth probably lies somewhere between survey and estimates.

Surveys, for their part, may underestimate the non-francophone Yes share. As contact in Quebec is normally initiated in French, those not fluent in the majority language are systematically underrepresented, as they commonly break off even before they are offered an English interviewer. These same persons have the greatest stake of all in the success of a document binding Quebec to Canada.[25]

On the other hand, ecological analyses commonly overestimate individual-level relationships. In the case at hand, ecological analysis may fail to take into account "contextual" effects. In a contextual model, how likely a non-francophone is to vote Yes depends on the degree of reinforcement from friends, neighbours, and co-workers. This in turn reflects the proportion non-francophone in the (more or less) immediate environment. Non-francophones living in the western part of Montreal should have been stronger supporters of the Yes side than those living in francophone-dominated areas. But the same should be true of francophones in non-francophone areas. Within each context, differences should be smaller than total differences between contexts, as a matter of arithmetic. An alternative possibility is that francophones (and anglophones) make residential choices based on their opinions on sovereignty. Federalist francophones are likely to feel more comfortable than sovereignists among anglophones (they may be more comfortable speaking English, for one thing), and so are more likely to reside in predominantly anglophone neighbourhoods. Where this occurs, the language-vote relationship estimated on aggregate data will be biased upward, because of locational selection on the dependent variable. [26] Our guess is that the 90 percent+ estimate of the Yes share arrived by ecological analysis best applies to western Montreal, but represents an overestimate for the non-francophone community as a whole.

Be that as it may, non-francophone Quebeckers were solidly for the Yes. Why precisely were they so one-sided? Some of the answer lies in Figure 8–3, and the rest is to be found in Figure 8–6. Non-francophones like Canada more than they do Quebec, by a small but telling margin. They do not, on balance, see the French language as threatened inside Quebec. And they are much more likely to foresee financial reverses from separation; indeed, many fewer inhabit the middle ground on this perception than is the case among francophones.

Non-francophones were more sanguine about the deal itself: they were much more likely than francophone non-sovereignists to laud the compromise, to see it as a vehicle for moving on, and to see Quebec as a winner. The claim that the Accord was the best possible compromise under the circumstances found some resonance in both groups. Even among francophone non-sovereignists, 45 percent accepted the claim, slightly more than rejected it, a more favourable perceptual balance than outside Quebec. But an outright majority did not accept the claim and the margin was much smaller than among non-francophones. Most compelling for both camps was the claim that the Accord would allow the country to move on to other questions. Sixty-six percent of francophones accepted this claim and the margin was even greater among non-francophones.

The sharpest controversies on the deal revolved around whether Quebec had won or lost in the negotiations. Inside Quebec these were the stakes in the battle over the Wilhelmy-Tremblay transcripts. Between Quebec and the rest of Canada this was music for the dance around whether Bourassa had extracted huge concessions or had been shut down; it was this consideration that made Moe Sihota's comments in upcountry British Columbia such news in Quebec. Among francophone non-sovereignists, 34 percent said Quebec won, 32 percent that it lost – a perfect half-empty, half-full result, but a more positive one than in any other province. Among non-francophones opinion was sharply positive.[27]

One thing was agreed on by both language groups: neither foresaw Quebec's separation as an immediate consequence of failure of the Accord. This reflected the fact that, from the beginning, both camps in Quebec agreed not to raise the stakes of the referendum. Jacques Parizeau claimed that, although he would prefer a vote on sovereignty, as stipulated in Bill 150, he had no choice but to address the question as framed by the Liberal government, and so the referendum pertained solely to the merits and limits of the Charlottetown Accord. Robert Bourassa claimed that a No victory would create great uncertainty, which would be harmful for the economy, but did

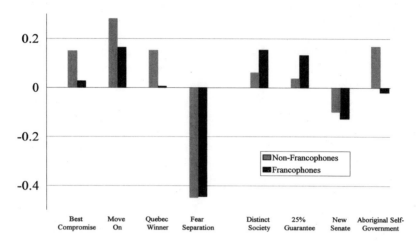

Figure 8–6
Considerations in the Accord (Non-Sovereignists Only)

not argue that a No would inevitably lead to sovereignty. And the visible presence of Jean Allaire and Pierre Trudeau in the No camp signalled that there were two federalist ways to say No.

Surprisingly, perhaps, non-francophones were not happier than francophones with most of the Accord's substance. They were less supportive of recognizing Quebec as a distinct society (although, unlike their counterparts outside the province, they were more likely to support recognition than not).[28] They were similarly less enthusiastic about guaranteeing Quebec 25 percent of the House of Commons seats. Still, most could stomach the measure. Neither language group found much to love in the proposed Senate. Finally, non-francophones, like voters outside Quebec, strongly affirmed the principle of Aboriginal self-government. Francophone non-sovereignists, strikingly, did not.[29]

Table 8–2 weighs all these considerations, casting the question as accounting for francophone/non-francophone differences within the non-sovereignist camp. It is a simplifed representation of the logic of Figure 1–1. First entered is the most basic demographic fact, the respondent's language. Then follow key questions of group sentiment: feeling for Canada and Quebec, perceptions of linguistic threat, and economic concerns about separation. Finally appear general arguments about the Accord (not including appeals to fear of separation, as none were made) and specific elements. Three stages suffice to make all the points about the non-francophone vote.

Table 8–2
Sources of the Francophone/Non-Francophone Difference (Non-Sovereignists only; N=356)

	(1)	(2)	(3)
Non-francophone	0.26***	0.14**	0.09
	(0.05)	(0.05)	(0.05)
Feeling for Canada	–	0.75***	0.53***
		(0.05)	(0.13)
Feeling for Quebec	–	-0.10	-0.15
		(0.12)	(0.12)
Linguistic Threat	–	-0.15**	-0.11*
		(0.05)	(0.05)
Economic Concern	–	0.32***	0.20*
		(0.09)	(0.09)
Best Compromise	–	–	0.25***
			(0.06)
Move On	–	–	0.03
			(0.06)
Quebec Winner	–	–	0.28***
			(0.06)
Distinct Society	–	–	0.11
			(0.06)
25% Guarantee	–	–	0.03
			(0.05)
Senate	–	–	0.00
			(0.06)
Aboriginal Self-Government	–	–	0.04
			(0.04)
Intercept	0.49	-0.12	-0.26
	(0.03)	(0.11)	(0.12)
R^2-adjusted	0.06	0.23	0.38

The leftmost column simply restates the group difference in Yes share, 26 points. Comparison along the top row indicates how much of the difference is explained by each succeeding block of intervening variables. About the half the group difference is attributable to basic sentiments and group perceptions. Most critical, once again, is feeling for Canada. Feeling about Quebec is not at issue. While it is true that non-francophones love Quebec less than francophones, this difference does not help account for the vote difference, not when feeling about the country as a whole is controlled. The latter is the operative sentiment: non-francophones love Canada more, and this difference tracked directly into the vote. That non-francophones were both less persuaded of linguistic threat and more persuaded that separation threatened their own livelihoods was also clearly involved. Opinion on the deal itself did the rest of the work. Most critical were that anglophones liked the compromise better and, concomitantly, were more likely to see Quebec as a winner. Belief that the deal might allow us to move on made no difference to the vote, even though it was sharply differentiated by language. No specific element made a difference to the vote, and thus to the group difference. Opinion on the distinct society clause came closest to affecting the vote, but this could not then account for the group difference. On the distinct society clause, as on the 25 percent guarantee, non-francophones were less accepting than francophones. If they were more likely than francophones to vote Yes, it was in spite of, not because of, opinion on these matters of substance. Only on Aboriginal self-government were non-francophones more supportive of the Accord, but this issue explained nothing of the vote and, by implication, none of the group difference. The language difference turned, then, on basic group sentiments and group-related perceptions, partly as these induced acquiescence in the overall compromise. Put bluntly, non-francophones voted for Canada.

FRANCOPHONE NON-SOVEREIGNISTS: ON THE FENCE

Begin by reconsidering Figure 8–5, which said less about sovereignist commitment than about the strength of anti-sovereignist feeling. Only among francophones "very" opposed to sovereignty did the Yes share approach the margin necessary to tip the province-wide result, and there only among voters who did not need to be told why they should oppose to sovereignty. Differences within the non-sovereignist camp were wider than between the group as a whole and either group on each side. Here, then, was the real battleground.

Analysis proceeds roughly as in the preceding section, stagewise, starting with socio-demographic factors and then working forward through sentimental considerations, and opinions on the Accord. One additional stage is considered: the competing roles of Quebec's key intervenors, Robert Bourassa and Jacques Parizeau. Neither intervenor mattered to blocs at the non-francophone pro-Accord or the sovereignist anti-Accord extreme, so compelling were other factors. But francophone non-sovereignists were divided over the merits of the two leaders. Many non-sovereignists rated Parizeau more highly than Bourassa. And the deal was Bourassa's to sell: he was the non-sovereignists' trustee; how well he was seen to discharge his trust would be critical to evaluation of the deal, and to the vote.

Background Factors

The leftmost column in Table 8–3 gives the total-effect coefficients. Only four coefficients appear, but the underlying estimation also included every factor directly represented in Table 8–1. None of the factors omitted from the table – unemployment and household income, as well as financial changes over the preceding twelve months[30] – had an effect remotely approaching statistical significance by the usual criterion.

Socio-demographic variables structured the vote even less than in the rest of Canada, consistent with the Quebec pattern for federal elections (Johnston et al., 1992, p. 91). Four divisions are worth signalling, however: older voters were more likely to vote Yes; university-educated voters also leaned to the Yes; union members were less likely than non-members to say Yes; and there is hint of a gender gap, wider at least than outside Quebec, as female Quebeckers seemed to resist the Accord. Only the first three crossed the conventional threshold of statistical significance, so they alone will get further discussion at this point.[31]

Voters over fifty were 29 points more likely than those under fifty to say Yes, other things equal. The university-educated were 22 points more likely than all others to do so.[32] If the first relationship corresponds to what we already know about the production of pro-sovereignty sentiment, the second is more surprising, for it reverses the older positive relationship between university education and nationalism (Blais and Nadeau, 1984). But the tendency here is in conflict with the earlier observation that *low* education inhibited sovereignist tendencies. Here we see high education doing something similar, moving voters away from the arch-sovereignist position on the Accord. This gives more food for thought about the social base of national sentiment in Quebec, a discussion we postpone yet again. Meanwhile, it should not escape notice that university education has the same effect in Quebec as in the rest of Canada, and as in European Union votes: it makes voters follow the lead of the political class. The same question is begged here as elsewhere. Does this reflect better information and a superior understanding of the real stakes, or do the university-educated just like – and resemble – elites more?

Table 8–3
Sources of the Vote among Francophone Non-sovereignists (Abstracted from Full Estimation; *N=241*)

	(1)		(2)		(3)		(4)	
SOCIO-DEMOGRAPHIC FACTORS								
Over Fifty	0.29***	(0.08)	0.19**	(0.07)	0.12	(0.07)	0.12	(0.07)
Woman	-0.10	(0.06)	-0.08	(0.06)	-0.08	(0.06)	-0.05	(0.06)
Union	-0.13	(0.07)	-0.10	(0.06)	-0.06	(0.06)	-0.06	(0.06)
University	0.22**	(0.08)	0.17*	(0.08)	0.12	(0.07)	0.11	(0.08)
GROUP SENTIMENTS								
Feeling for Canada	–		0.82***	(0.20)	0.54**	(0.20)	0.49**	(0.20)
Feeling for Quebec	–		-0.18	(0.20)	-0.21	(0.19)	-0.22	(0.18)
Linguistic Threat	–		-0.13*	(0.06)	-0.09	(0.06)	-0.09	(0.06)
Economic Concern	–		0.32*	(0.12)	-0.11	(0.12)	-0.08	(0.12)
INTERVENORS								
Bourassa	–		–		0.61***	(0.14)	0.36**	(0.14)
Parizeau	–		–		-0.33**	(0.12)	-0.27*	(0.12)
GENERAL ARGUMENTS								
Best Compromise	–		–		–		0.11	(0.08)
Move On	–		–		–		0.06	(0.07)
Quebec Winner	–		–		–		0.18*	(0.08)
SPECIFIC ELEMENTS								
Distinct Society	–		–		–		0.22*	(0.09)
25% Guarantee	–		–		–		0.06	(0.07)
New Senate	–		–		–		-0.01	(0.08)
Aboriginal Self-Government	–		–		–		0.03	(0.06)
Intercept	0.50	(0.08)	-0.12	(0.17)	0.12	(0.17)	-0.17	(0.18)
R^2-adjusted	0.09		0.23		0.32		0.38	

Group Sentiments

Just as attachments to Canada and Quebec drove sovereignty attitudes, so also these attachments were factors in the non-sovereignist vote. Quebec enjoyed a sentimental advantage: where 37 percent of francophone non-sovereignists were more attached to Quebec than to Canada, the opposite was true of only 14 percent; 47 percent were

equally attached to both. On the other hand, as with sovereignty attitudes, the key factor is feeling toward Canada. Indeed feeling for
Canada was even more important here than in the soveriegnty estimations of Table 8–1, and feeling for Quebec played virtually no role.
Whatever they felt about Quebec, many non-sovereignists evidently
saw support for the Accord as an expression of patriotism. Canada
was in a constitutional crisis, and they should support any deal that
would extricate the country from that crisis.[33]

Concern for the future of the French language in Quebec played an
independent role. Non-sovereignists were, of course, less anxious
than sovereignists, but were themselves divided on the question:
50 percent saw the language as threatened. And on Dion's (1992)
logic, even a non-sovereignist who sees the language as threatened
should hesitate over the Accord. Ironically, the heart of the matter
was the distinct society clause. It was vulnerable to being styled less
as recognition of the distinctive claims of Quebec's francophone majority than a commitment to the province's non-francophone minority, a validation – *not* a qualification – of the Charter's constitutional
entrenchment of Trudeau's language policy. Empirically, seeing
French as threatened in Quebec cut over 10 points from the Yes share,
other things equal.

Economic concerns about sovereignty played almost exactly the
same role here as in getting voters to a position on sovereignty itself:
a difference between extremes of roughly 30 percentage points. The
integrity of the country was at issue for many voters, even though it
had been taken off the agenda in a short-term sense. Non-sovereignists did not fear that rejection of this particular Accord was tantamount to saying No to Canada, or that rejection would give
sovereignists licence to proceed. But its entrenchment, pursuant to a
majority of Quebeckers saying Yes, would seriously undercut sovereignists' moral right to counter with a referendum on sovereignty. If
fencing sovereignists in was an absolute imperative, then doubts
about the Accord needed to be stilled. Conversely, if sovereignty did
not evoke great economic fear, the Accord could be considered on its
merits.

Group sentiment accounts for a good fraction of the vote's socio-
demographic basis. As already established, older voters love Canada
more, see less linguistic threat, and are more fearful of the consequences of separation. Controlling these factors reduces the "over 50"
coefficient markedly, although by no means reduces it to a nullity. Also
palpably reduced is the "university" term. Most important in this
group is the perception of linguistic threat: university voters were
much the least worried about the future of French in Quebec. By impli-

cation they were the least persuaded that continued adhesion to Canada was incompatible with the interests of the language community.

The group-sentiment package was also notable for what it omitted. As in the rest of Canada, orientation to founding peoples was not a factor in the vote. Unsurprisingly, Quebeckers were even readier than others to see two founding peoples, so much so, however, that there was little room for such recognition to cut into assessment of the document. From the Quebec perspective, in any case, the document was highly equivocal about founding peoples. Some parts of the Accord embodied a two-nations vision, the distinct society clause certainly, the 25 percent guarantee possibly. But other parts, most notably Senate reform, affronted the idea of a compact among founding peoples. The new Senate presupposed equality among provinces, a position vulnerable to attack as a betrayal of the 1867 bargain, as changing the rules in the middle of the game.

More surprising is the lack of impact from anything that might be construed as dismay over the federal-provincial division of powers. Decentralization has been a longstanding Quebec demand, based on the belief that francophones will always be a subordinate interest at the centre and that only a government francophones control outright can be trusted to defend their interests. Such a position – exactly the one Trudeau so vigorously attacked – naturally leads one to argue for devolution of power to Quebec certainly, to all provinces possibly. In the immediate background, of course, was the Allaire report, a key step in Quebec's internal constitutional consultation. The Allaire demand for many new powers was hard to reconcile with the reality of Charlottetown. As survey items on the division of powers are very hard to frame and produce very soft response, we attempted to get at the matter by a slightly indirect route, by posing the following: "Which government looks after your interests and needs the best: the government of Canada or the government of Quebec?"[34] Among francophone non-sovereignists, 38 percent chose Quebec, 18 percent chose Canada, and 44 percent could not tell. This confirms that even non-sovereignists have greater confidence in the provincial than in the federal government. More revealing, however, is that close to half cannot choose. And response to this question just did not make any difference to the vote.

Intervenors

The next stage confirms the centrality of Robert Bourassa. By referendum day his Quebec-wide mean rating stood at 45, similar to the average for other premiers in their respective provinces, not very good but not terrible either. His rating was lower than for both Jacques Parizeau (48) and Lucien Bouchard (49), but higher than for Trudeau (34), Mulroney (36) and Chrétien (31). Among francophone non-sovereignists more specifically, Bourassa's average rating was higher, 55, compared with 40 for Parizeau. Even so, 15 percent gave the two leaders identical ratings and another 29 percent liked Parizeau more.

Feelings about Bourassa were twice as important as feelings about Parizeau. At this stage in estimation, the premier stands out as the key object, the anchor for judgment on the Accord. Parizeau also mattered, independently of the premier, and including the two together in the accounting framework increases its predictive power by half, an R^2 shift from 0.23 to 0.32. Voters' age was important in assessment of the two leaders, and controlling assessments cut the over fifty coefficient dramatically, as it also did the university coefficient. Of course, university education and, even more, pre-1942 birth affected attachment to Canada, and this attachment also fed through to leader ratings. The more you liked Canada, the more you approved of Bourassa and disapproved of Parizeau. Controlling approval cuts the Canada coefficient sharply. The same happens to coefficients on linguistic threat and economic concern. The shift for the last is truly spectacular: with no control for intervenors, the coefficient is +0.32; with the control, it drops to -0.11. The negative sign may or may not merit interpretation; the critical fact is that fear of economic fallout from separation was intimately caught up in leader evaluation.[35]

As before, what is missing merits discussion. Unlike the rest of Canada, we exclude party identification and we consider no other intervenors, be they persons or organizations. In one sense, party identification had more impact in Quebec than in the rest of Canada, for reasons that are readily grasped. For a francophone Quebecker to identify with a federal party in the context of 1992 probably carries deeper meaning than elsewhere, for it indicates willingness to buck an anti-federal wave of opinion. But party identification adds little explanatory power when entered as a stage in its own right; by implication it is an indirect manifestation of group sentiment. And when Bourassa and Parizeau judgments are added, party identification is completely absorbed by them. It seemed easiest, then, to leave federal parties out, to leave the scene to the independently critical factors – group sentiment and intervenors' credibility.

Also missing are the arch-rivals in the campaign outside Quebec, Mulroney and Trudeau. Although Mulroney's mean rating in Quebec (36) was low, it was certainly better than in the rest of Canada and compared favourably with Trudeau's. But by 1992 neither was a pole of attraction for many francophones, and neither mattered much, at least not when feelings about the two provincial leaders were taken into account.

Jean Allaire and Claude Castonguay, potentially critical intervenors inside the provincial debate, also were shunted aside, at least they had been by the time the official campaign started.[36] Allaire is an especially interesting case. Fifty-seven percent of francophone non-sovereignists did not know that he had come out for the No, and awareness of his opposition made no difference to the vote. But he was the one unpredictable intervenor to declare himself in the critical period of early September. One possibility is that Allaire's announcement and the attendant news made many non-sovereignists aware of dissension in provincial Liberal ranks, even if they did not get Allaire himself in their sights and even if, unlike Allaire, they did not focus on the division of powers. The key is that dissension was within Bourassa's own ranks and that it was not from a predictable source; by the time our survey entered the field, impulses originating with Allaire had become fairly common knowledge, no longer attributable to Allaire in particular.

In the official campaign, groups were similarly not much at issue, or no longer were. Three merited consideration, the business community, unions, and the women's movement. The Quebec business community was mostly on the Yes side, and 34 percent of our respondents said business had come out for the Yes, and only 11 percent said the opposite. Second, the Quebec union movement was unanimously for the No; 47 percent identified the union position correctly, and only 9 percent the opposite. Finally, 31 percent of Quebec respondents were aware of opposition by the women's movement, and 9 percent made the opposite imputation.

These interventions may have made some difference. Awareness coefficients, estimated by analogy to the rest-of-Canada setup in chapter 5, were never impressive for Quebec. But we see what may be residue of these interventions back in the socio-demographic factors, in the leftmost column: union members and women leaned to the No, the most highly educated leaned to the Yes. This is circumstantial evidence, of course, but against a background of generally weak differences, the correspondence of mass response to elite indications is more exact than in the rest of Canada.

The Accord Itself

Considerations of substance all pointed to an intensely Quebec-focused decision. Among general considerations, only one directly affected the vote: whether or not Quebec was seen to have won at the bargaining table. The quality of the compromise and the necessity of moving on cut little ice, at least not in the company of other considerations.[37] Among specifics, the key was the distinct society clause, with the largest coefficient (0.22) in the last block. There is reason to interpret the coefficient cautiously, however. Consider what it means: it indicates the shift in the probability of voting Yes induced by movement from outright opposition (coded 0) to unqualified support (coded 1). Almost no francophone opposed recognition of Quebec as a distinct society. The effective ground of debate was between unqualified support and qualified support ("not far enough," coded 0.5). The impact of shifting between these alternatives was only 0.11. No other specific consideration made any difference whatsoever. Especially ironic is the lack of any effect from opinion on the 25 percent guarantee; the element overwhelmingly rejected and of considerable importance to the vote *outside* Quebec was of no help *inside* Quebec.

CONCLUSIONS

Some candidate interpretations of the Quebec result can be dismissed out of hand. Five non-findings are especially clear:

– Quebeckers did *not* ride a bandwagon, in possible contrast to some voters elsewhere. Only in early October did a majority in Quebec come to expect a No victory. Vote intentions shifted before expectations, and when expectations shifted, intentions remained stable.
– The Quebec No vote was not driven by the belief that other groups, especially Aboriginal peoples, had received too much at Charlottetown. A majority of Quebeckers approved of Aboriginal self-government. On this, sovereignists and non-francophones were indistinguishable from voters outside Quebec. Francophone non-sovereignists were less supportive, but did not act on their opinion. Aboriginal self-government was irrelevant to the Quebec vote, and Quebeckers' general perception that Aboriginal peoples were winners in the Accord did not make them see Quebec as a loser.
– Among non-sovereignists the No vote did not indicate support for a large devolution of powers to the Quebec government. Only 38 percent of francophone non-sovereignists put greater confidence in their provincial government than in Ottawa, and this made no difference to the vote. Non-sovereignists who voted No tended to be more Quebec-centred in their attachments and more fearful about the future of French. But this did not entail support for a large devolution of power.

– Trudeau's Egg Roll speech had no impact in Quebec, in marked contrast with the rest of Canada. Even non-francophone Quebeckers were unresponsive. Outside Quebec, we surmise, one source of Trudeau's power was that he spoke for some definition of a French-Canadian interest and, more generally, for linguistic minorities. But he was clearly no longer a tribune for the francophones within Quebec, nor even for the province's non-francophone minority.
– The economy played little or no role in the Quebec vote. Individuals' financial situation, whether they were unemployed or not, whether their situation had improved or deteriorated in the past year, whether they thought it would get better or worse in the coming year – all these were unrelated to the vote. Furthermore, the dramatic two-point interest-rate surge, the most spectacular jump in recent Canadian history, as well as the Royal Bank report predicting dire economic consequences from breakup of the country, just did not move opinion.

The Quebec result highlighted the existence of three distinct blocs of voters: non-francophones, francophone sovereignists, and francophone non-sovereignists. The first two groups were strongly cohesive in their voting behaviour, and sovereignists were most cohesive of all. For these two groups the crucial determinant was the sense of nationality, and there could be little doubt how they would vote. Sovereignists overwhelmingly rejected an agreement that confirmed Quebec's status as a mere province in the Canadian federation. Non-francophones overwhelmingly accepted an agreement that hemmed sovereignists in politically.

This left francophone non-sovereignists as the pivot, a role they evidently took very seriously. For them, the situation was complex, much as it was for centrist voters outside Quebec. Leaders of both camps lowered the stakes by agreeing that a No vote did not mean Yes to sovereignty. This was confirmed by the presence of federalists such as Jean Allaire in the No camp. On the other hand, they knew very well that sovereignists themselves would vote solidly No and that a No victory, although it would not lead directly to sovereignty, would increase the risk of its happening. A No victory would confirm that all attempts at further constitutional renewal had failed, that the idea of renewed federalism would lose credibility and would not be available as a counter-argument in an inevitable future referendum on sovereignty itself.

Whether or not one wished to block sovereignists' ambitions, was the agreement good enough for Quebec? Was it a price worth paying? These questions lay behind the extraordinary attention paid to the Wilhelmy affair, and makes one ask if the Yes could have won had it not happened. Certainly, Bourassa's credibility and the closely related matter of whether Quebec won or lost were absolutely critical to the vote among non-sovereignists. That being so, it is hard not to attribute some role to an affair which turned on privately expressed judgments on the premier by his closest advisers. But the drop in the Yes share predated the affair, which directs attention to the role of Jean Allaire. Allaire may have been critical twice over. His presence on the official No committee helped neutralize sovereignty as a question: this explains why the No forces were so eager to have him. But as he would gain nothing personally by it, why did he want to be there in the first place? The answer, of course, was his disappointment over the gap between the demands on the division of powers in the report which bore his name – and which Bourassa had accepted as his own – and what the premier had settled for at Charlottetown. Voters who reacted to Allaire's defection need not have cared much about the division of powers as such, but might well have agonized about the province's honour and dignity, to adapt Brian Mulroney's language; Allaire's defection suggested that the deal was dishonourable. This brings us back to Wilhelmy. We cannot pin a specific dynamic induction on the affair. But it appears with hindsight as the completion of the task begun by Jean Allaire's commitment to the No side. Allaire found the deal distasteful but, his report aside, he had been a bit player in constitutional matters and in politics more generally. Diane Wilhelmy, in contrast, was the premier's own choice as adviser on the constitutional file. And opinions imputed to her were not constructed for the record, but instead seemed candid. The affair may not have moved the Yes share down, but it may have undermined any possibility of moving the share back up.

And the francophone non-sovereignist Yes share had to go back up a long way for the Accord to carry in Quebec as a whole. It bears emphasis that *in the subset of Quebec voters potentially available to the Yes side, a majority did indeed say Yes.* The Yes was just not one-sided enough to overcome the hegemonic sovereignist No. Part of this non-sovereignist Yes majority, of course, was a precommitted group, made up of non-francophones. But about as many francophone non-sovereignists voted Yes as No, a more affirmative result than in most of the rest of Canada. No voters among non-sovereignists could not overcome misgivings about the agreement, as a compromise and for Quebec's particular interests, and were longer sure they could trust Robert Bourassa. They could afford to vote No, because doing so did not immediately imply separation from Canada. By the same token, many Yes voters, francophone and non-francophone, were simply saying Yes to Canada.

A casual reading of these data might lead one to conclude that the Quebec decision was overwhelmingly self-regarding. Among specific elements only one thing mattered – recognition of Quebec as a distinct society – which an overwhelming majority of francophones regarded as not having gone far enough. Views of the compromise were dominated by views of Quebec's place in it. Otherwise the only general claim that mattered was whether Quebec won or lost. Among intervenors, only the Quebec ones, Bourassa and Parizeau, mattered. The theatre of the unofficial campaign was entirely inside the family: Claude Castonguay on one side, Jean Allaire on the other; and the Wilhelmy verdict on the premier's energy level and ability to resist pressure. Among outsiders, the one who mattered most may have been an Indo-Canadian from Esquimalt speaking in Quesnel, British Columbia. Of course, he was speaking about Robert Bourassa, and confirming the Wilhelmy verdict.

But Quebeckers were no more focused on Quebec than outsiders were. Earlier chapters confirmed that the specific elements that mattered most were the ones that pertained to Quebec. When voters outside Quebec asked how their own province had fared at Charlottetown, their answers hinged in part on what Quebec extracted. Running through evaluations of the document were raw feelings about Quebec. For many these feelings were positive, in the end producing a Yes vote. But in Quebec, positive feeling for Canada had the same effect. This, of course, was the essence of the non-francophone vote. And its opposite was the essence of the sovereignist vote: sovereignists said No not for tactical reasons, to extract yet more out of the intra-Canadian process, but simply out of a desire to be done with Canada. When it came down to francophone non-sovereignists, feeling for Canada ultimately drove the result. In this group, more voters chose Canada than voters in the rest of the country chose Quebec.

9 "Know More": Education, Knowledge, and the Vote

University-educated Canadians were one of the few large electoral groups to vote Yes. This was true both outside Quebec and in Quebec's critical middle group, francophone non-sovereignists. But why? Did education produce political awareness and did awareness, in turn, promote a Yes vote? To put it crudely – and turn Preston Manning's admonition on its head – did university-educated voters say Yes because they did in fact "know more"? Canada in 1992 exemplified a pattern widely remarked empirically and commonly thought to reflect the operation of the mainstream effect identified in chapter 1. In its exalted version, the mainstream effect sees well-educated voters as most willing to recognize that the status quo is no longer sustainable and most able to accept that change, although painful, is necessary. In a less exalted form, well-educated voters merely receive the political elite's message uncritically, where poorly educated voters do not get it at all; knowledge, on this view, is not wisdom. Could it be, however, that *getting* the message is not the issue at all; poorly educated voters may still get the message, only to reject it. Central to each account is some notion of political knowledge and its relation to education.

Did knowledge itself, independently of social underpinnings, affect the vote? Did it help the Yes side, as much of the previous paragraph implies, or did it, as Preston Manning believed, favour the No? More generally, how did each argument identified in chapter 1 about knowledge-opinion-vote relationships fare? First there are low-information arguments:

- We have established a *prima facie* case that polls and expectations mattered at the end, roughly as predicted by McKelvey and Ordeshook (1986). Did they make a bigger difference to low-information voters, or did digesting poll information require a high-information background?
- We have established that both feelings and ideas mattered, and did so both inside and outside Quebec. Did their relative power vary across information levels, as Sniderman et al. (1991) predict?
- Both the Quebec and the rest-of-Canada electorates employed a decision hierarchy, from group sentiments on down to judgments on specific features of the Accord. Was the hierarchy more tightly integrated among well-informed voters? Indeed, did poorly informed voters employ considerations of intermediate generality at all?
- Did poorly informed voters, by whatever means, connect their interests to the vote as efficiently as well-informed voters did?
- Intervenors clearly mattered, as did evaluation of agenda-setters, much as argued by Lupia (1992, 1994, 1995). But did interventions overcome ignorance? Or could only knowledgeable voters take advantage of interventions, so much so that whole process actually compounded pre-existing information differentials?

Then there are aggregationist arguments (Page and Shapiro, 1992; Miller, 1986):

- Does knowledge affect substantive direction of opinion?
- Does knowledge alter the relationship between group membership and the vote?

The first task is to derive a measure of knowledge or information. With this measure in hand, we can then assess the impact of knowledge both as a factor in its own right and as a condition for the operation of other factors. Answering the questions in the previous paragraph requires us to work through the logic of Figure 1–2, along the following lines:

- *The knowledge-education nexus.* Is education's role essentially to impart political knowledge, which, in turn, promotes acceptance of the Accord? Or is the education effect not really a matter of superior knowledge at all, but instead an indicator of, say, class relations?
- *Group sentiment.* Do education and knowledge, severally or jointly, promote something like ethnic tolerance? Do they promote liking

for particular marginalized groups or affirmation of generalized notions of minority rights?
- *Support for the political class.* Does either factor promote liking for politicians, especially for those in the mainstream?
- *Acceptance of arguments and elements.* The most exalted version of the mainstream argument says that well-educated or knowledgeable voters most readily grasp *raison d'état*. This should show up in greater acceptance of general arguments. But then, rejection of general arguments may only reflect alienation from the conventional politicians who make the arguments.

These propositions are main effects. Also in play are interaction effects, where the operation of other factors (including education) are conditional on information:

- Does information narrow group differences, or widen them? If there is a national interest and information promotes awareness of it, then knowledge should diminish group differences. Conversely, if the only real interests are specific to groups, then information might actually widen differences.
- Information should condition how group sentiments affect the vote.
- It seems reasonable to propose that information tightens the link between feeling about intervenors and the vote. Indeed, we have intimations of this already from chapter 5.
- Does information connect opinion on specifics or on general arguments more closely to the vote? This would seem to follow if information imparts more structure generally to the choice. But perhaps low-information voters connect, say, group feeling very efficiently and this supplies structure in its own right.
- Does knowledge expand or compress impact from polls?

A KNOWLEDGE MEASURE

The best measures of political sophistication, information, or knowledge involve straightforward factual knowledge, "information holding" in Luskin's (1987) terms. Further, knowledge on particular political questions seems to stand for political knowledge more generally (Delli Carpini and Keeter, 1993).[1] And a factual-knowledge measure is ready to hand: the number of correct attributions to intervenors (based on the questions in chapter 5), for which basic distributions appear in Table 9-1. For the non-Quebec sample, the distribution is almost perfectly flat: about one-sixth of the sample appears in each of

Table 9–1
Overall Awareness of Intervenors

Number of Intervenors	Rest of Canada	Quebec	
		All	Francophone Non-Sovereignists
None	11	16	20
One	17	20	25
Two	17	22	21
Three	16	21	15
Four	16	14	14
Five	16	5	5
Six	7	<1	<1
N	1088	688	255

the middle five categories. The remaining sixth is split between extremes. Among Quebeckers the distribution is more bunched toward the low-information end, but not drastically so. This probably reflects the qualitatively distinct campaign in Quebec, which was more focused on rival party teams, less reliant on outside intervention.[2] With six possible intervenors, it is next to impossible for a respondent to guess all the way to the top or the bottom of the scale. The measure is, unfortunately, time-sensitive, as the average number of correct mentions increased over the campaign, as figures 5–4 and 5–5 imply. Respondents interviewed later in the campaign will seem more informed than respondents interviewed earlier. But of the total variance in the measure, the longitudinal part is actually very small. Consider the impact of the biggest short-term surge, the 20-point gain outside Quebec in awareness of Trudeau. This means that one respondent in five suddenly became aware of one intervenor in six, a shift on the 0–6 scale of 0.2 points. The average total gain over the full campaign was much less than one point. Longitudinal variance will be a source of measurement error – later respondents seeming to be slightly better informed than earlier ones – but overall measurement error in a 6-item knowledge measure is relatively small as survey measures go. Otherwise, from a measurement perspective, the index is wonderful; it spreads the sample out very efficiently.

As Table 9–2 makes clear, the level of information is affected by education. Earlier chapters indicated that education meant, to all and intents and purposes, university education, and so this chapter focuses solely on the university/non-university contrast. University-

Table 9–2
University Education and Information

	Rest of Canada	Quebec	
		All	Francophone Non-Sovereignists
Non-University	2.5	1.9	1.8
	(784)	(492)	(196)
University	3.5	2.7	4.6
	(327)	(196)	(59)

Entry is mean number of "correct" attributions to intervenors

educated respondents typically made one more correct attribution than non-university ones, although among francophone non-sovereignists the impact was nearly twice great. Measured against intuition the general effect seems small, and it would seem to be good news for the democratic prospect that education is not much of a requirement for political information-gathering. On the other hand, it may be worrisome that nearly half the voters in the rest-of-Canada sample were aware of only two intervenors or less. For most of these voters, on the arithmetic of chapter 5, Pierre Trudeau must have been the key source. Trudeau at least was located right at the strategic margin; if there was one intervenor to be aware of, it was he. His like may not be available for other votes, however.

EDUCATION, INFORMATION, AND THE VOTE

Figure 9–1 takes us to the bottom line, to the vote. Three electorates are distinguished: the rest of Canada, all of Quebec, and francophone non-sovereignists within Quebec. In each, information gradients correspond to education ones visible in earlier chapters. Information was very positively related to vote outside Quebec and among francophone non-sovereignists. In Quebec as a whole, however, virtually no relationship existed.[3] The preliminary reading, then, is that the information-vote relationship outside Quebec conforms to Gamson and Modigliani's 1966 mainstream model. In Quebec, the model looks more like one of polarization.

But do such interpretations hold up? Knowledge may truly be an active ingredient in the vote. Then again, the relationship may be only spurious: knowledge may not have an effect in its own right, but may function only as indicator of education, where education's true

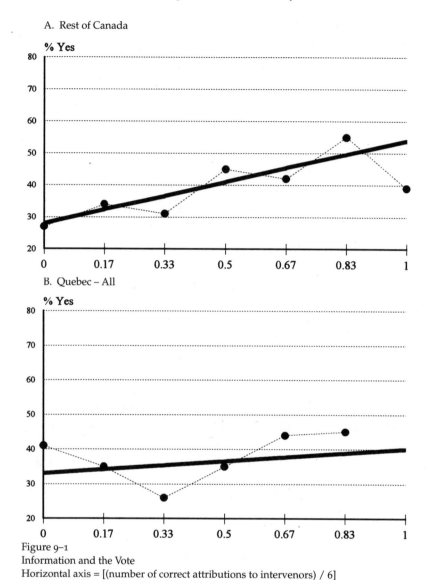

A. Rest of Canada

Figure 9–1
Information and the Vote
Horizontal axis = [(number of correct attributions to intervenors) / 6]

effect is not cognitive at all. Table 9–3 confronts the questions head on. Three estimations – vote on education only, on information only, and on both simultaneously – appear in each of the three sub-electorates. This covers the following possibilities:

C. Quebec – Francophone Non-Sovereignists

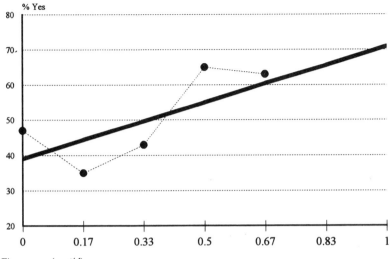

Figure 9–1 (*cont'd*)

- Education effects observed in chapters 7 and 8 may be truly *cognitive* in character. If so, if education facilitates information-gathering (even if education does nothing more than index prior differences in innate information-gathering ability),[4] then the education coefficient should shrink when information is added to the equation. This would indicate that information differences carry the real effect and in doing so, mediate background impact from educational differences.
- If education is mainly a *sociological* indicator, then controlling a cognitive variable like information should make no difference to the educational effect; education should remain as powerful as before. In psychological terms, such a pattern would indicate that education is a motivational, rather than a cognitive factor. In the cleanest case, the effect from information should shrink when forced to coexist with education. If information is only an indirect indicator of education and if information has no independent effect on vote direction, then controlling education should reveal the essential spuriousness of the uncontrolled information-vote relationship.
- If education and information both have independent effects, especially if controlling one hardly reduces the effect of the other, then we are faced with a story which is *both* cognitive and motivational.

Table 9-3
University Education, Information, and the Vote

| | Rest of Canada (N=1088) | | | Quebec | | | | | |
| | | | | All (N=688) | | | Francophone Non-Sovereignists (N=255) | | |
	(1)	(2)	(3)	(1)	(2)	(3)	(1)	(2)	(3)
Education	0.19***	–	0.16***	0.12**	–	0.11**	0.22**	–	0.19**
	(0.03)		(0.03)	(0.04)		(0.04)	(0.07)		(0.07)
Information	–	0.26***	0.20***	–	0.07	0.02	–	0.32**	0.25*
		(0.05)	(0.05)		(0.07)	(0.08)		(0.12)	(0.13)
Intercept	0.34	0.28	0.26	0.33	0.33	0.32	0.44	0.39	0.37
	(0.02)	(0.03)	(0.03)	(0.02)	(0.03)	(0.03)	(0.04)	(0.05)	(0.05)
R^2	0.03	0.02	0.04	0.01	0.00	0.01	0.03	0.02	0.04

Entries in parentheses are standard errors
* $p < 0.05$; ** $p < 0.01$; *** $p < 0.001$

With education controlled, the informational effect that remains can only be cognitive. With information controlled, the educational effect that remains must be mainly motivational.

Begin with the impact of education. In the uncontrolled case, equation (1), education has essentially the same, positive effect in the rest of Canada and among Quebec's francophone non-sovereignists, the now-familiar 20-point gap. In the whole Quebec sample, a smaller education gradient appears.

In two of the three uncontrolled information estimations, equations (2), information has a robust impact. Outside Quebec, the coefficient is slightly larger than the education one, and in Quebec the coefficient is nearly half as large again. The larger coefficients arguably overstate the power of information relative to education. Both variables are set here to a 0,1 range, but where for education every case lies at either the 0 or the 1 extreme, for information this is true of very few cases (Table 9–1). A rule of thumb for comparison is to cut the information coefficient in half, to capture roughly the interquartile impact. Overstated or not, information's effect in the all-Quebec sample was negligible.

Most important, though, is that controlling one affects the other only modestly. For the two strategic groups that really mattered, outside Quebec and among Quebec's francophone non-sovereignists, controlling information cuts about 0.03 from the education coefficient. Possibly, then, a small part of education's effect stems from development – or identification – of information-gathering skill. Most of education's effect must lie elsewhere. Conversely, controlling education has a larger impact on measured effect from information: in the two places where information matters, its effect shrinks by about one-fifth. This implies that some of the information effect is spurious, a byproduct of association with education. But if some is lost, most remains. Mainly, education and information just cut through each other.

Knowledge of politics did matter to the vote, and knowing more boosted the Yes, not the No. Impact as measured from knowledge is overwhelmingly likely to be real, not an artifact of other factors omitted from consideration. Cognitive capacity itself really promoted the interests of the pro-Accord coalition, and ignorance really inhibited them. But superior knowledge was not what made university-educated voters peculiarly likely to say Yes. This group was relatively likely to say Yes, of course, but not for reasons to do with information-processing ability. Rather, the Accord must have tapped well-educated voters' substantive values or identifications – their motives.

PATHWAYS TO THE VOTE

So far, education and information have been considered in the most general possible way, for total, or "reduced form," effect on the vote. Now we turn to the avenues by which these effects operated. As detailing every single pathway implicit in figures 1–1 and 1–2 would be tedious in the extreme, the following sections establish only the main points. Two basic forms of demonstration appear. First come estimations for information and education effects on key intervening factors. In each case, there is an obvious question. Were highly educated and informed voters generally more tolerant? Were they more supportive of the mainstream political class? Were they more acquiescent to elite arguments about the consequences of accepting or rejecting the Accord, or more supportive of its specific elements? Then follow accounts of what happens to total education and information effects on the vote as intervening factors – group sentiments, party and agenda setter-intervenor evaluations, and substantive opinions – are controlled, stage by stage.

Group Sentiment

Outside Quebec, information and education both affected group sentiments, but not every sentiment, and not all in the same way. Acceptance of the proposition that Canada has three founding peoples was so universal that neither education nor information made any difference. At the other extreme was feeling for Quebec; this was a highly differentiated sentiment, and both education and information produced affection for the province. For education this effect was reinforced by impact on minority orientation; university-educated voters were significantly more likely to give priority to minorities. For education, then, the two significant sentimental pathways were consistent and cumulative, helping the Yes. For information the story was more complicated, partly offsetting. If information made one like Quebec in particular more, it also made one support minorities in general less.

Roughly the same story can be told for francophone non-sovereignists in Quebec; indeed, the pattern is simpler, more consistent across factors. According to Table 9–5, the key mediating sentiments were feeling for Canada and perception of linguistic threat, and the story at this point was entirely about information, not education. For every group sentiment, effects from education had the same signs as effects from information, but none was statistically significant. For neither education nor information was feeling for Quebec a factor; approval

Table 9–4
University Education, Information, and Group Sentiments: Rest of Canada *(N=977)*

	Feeling for Quebec	Minority Orientation	Founding Peoples
Education	0.08***	0.07*	0.04
	(0.02)	(0.03)	(0.03)
Information	0.19***	-0.12*	-0.00
	(0.03)	(0.05)	(0.04)
Intercept	0.47	0.37	0.77
	(0.01)	(0.03)	(0.02)
R^2	0.08	0.01	0.00

Table 9–5
University Education, Information, and Group Sentiments: Quebec, Francophone Non-Sovereignists *(N=254)*

	Feeling for Quebec	Feeling for Canada	Economic Concern	Perceived Threat
Education	0.03	0.03	0.04	-0.09
	(0.03)	(0.03)	(0.04)	(0.07)
Information	0.07	0.14**	0.12	-0.57***
	(0.05)	(0.05)	(0.07)	(0.12)
Intercept	0.75	0.67	0.65	0.71
	(0.02)	(0.02)	(0.03)	(0.05)
R^2	0.01	0.04	0.01	0.09

of the province was so universal that feeling for Quebec simply could not differentiate voters within the province. The key feeling, of course, was toward Canada, and the more one knew, the more one liked the country as a whole. At the same time, information also neutralized perception of threats to French in Quebec. Information may have heightened concern over the economic consequences of sovereignty, but the coefficient in question was unstable. All group factors among francophone non-sovereignists were mutually reinforcing, all helped explain the information-Yes relationship.

Group sentiment bids fair, then, to account for much of the information-vote and education-vote relationships. Knowledge made one like the key negotiating partner – Canada or Quebec, as the case may be – and this induced acquiescence in the outcome of the negotia-

Table 9–6
University Education, Information, and the Party System: Rest of Canada *(N=974)*

	Cons	*Liberal*	*NDP*	*None*
Education	-0.04	0.06	-0.00	-0.02
	(0.03)	(0.03)	(0.03)	(0.03)
Information	0.09*	0.01	-0.02	-0.08
	(0.05)	(0.05)	(0.04)	(0.05)
Intercept	0.19	0.28	0.16	0.40
	(0.03)	(0.03)	(0.02)	(0.03)
R^2-adjusted	0.00	0.00	0.00	0.00

tions. Outside Quebec, this informational effect was reinforced by an exactly analogous one from education: part of what it means to acquire a university education is to embrace outside cultures and groups. The rest of the sentimental story mostly reinforces this simple effect from feeling; the signal exception is the negative rest-of-Canada link between information and minority orientation.

Intervenors and the Party System

Was identification with mainstream parties associated with either university education or information? As it happens, party identification was only weakly related to information, according to Table 9–6. Outside Quebec,[5] non-partisans were modestly less informed than partisans: moving from one extreme to the other on the information gradient reduced one's likelihood of non-partisanship by about 8 points, a statistically significant but substantively small effect. Among parties, information was highly selective, being associated only with Conservative identification, essentially as the mirror image of non-partisanship. Education was essentially unrelated to party identification, although there is a hint of a university-Liberal connection.

Outside Quebec, information also reinforced education in producing support for mainstream intervenors, but in a curiously backhanded way. According to Table 9–7, affection for the system's central players was mainly the result of education, not of actual political knowledge. And confusing the issue is the fact that university-educated voters' affection extended to Pierre Trudeau. Information in its own right did not make voters like Brian Mulroney or his supporting cast one bit more. What information did was make voters dislike Preston Manning (more likely, whatever facilitated information-

Table 9–7
University Education, Information, and Intervenors

	Rest of Canada (N=974)				Quebec, Francophone Non-sovereignists (N=242)	
	Mulroney	Other Leaders	Trudeau	Manning	Bourassa	Parizeau
Education	0.03	0.05***	0.04*	-0.03*	0.07*	-0.04
	(0.02)	(0.01)	(0.02)	(0.02)	(0.04)	(0.04)
Information	-0.03	-0.03	0.05	-0.12***	0.09	-0.07
	(0.03)	(0.02)	(0.03)	(0.02)	(0.06)	(0.06)
Intercept	0.30	0.46	0.54	0.49	0.48	0.42
	(0.02)	(0.01)	(0.01)	(0.01)	(0.03)	(0.03)
R^2-adjusted	0.00	0.02	0.01	0.04	0.02	0.00

gathering inhibited liking for Manning). The information coefficient on Manning's feeling thermometer was much the largest in the entire array, over twice as large as any other, from either information or education and on any intervenor. The education effect reinforced the information one, if only weakly. The story is potentially powerful and essentially a negative one: even if well-informed voters remained sceptical of mainstream politicians, they were even more sceptical of the newest outsider.

The Quebec pattern is weaker and less negatively toned. Information, as distinct from education, made no significant difference to assessment of either key intervenor. Education, on the other hand, did make one like Bourassa more, if not Parizeau less. The weakness of the Quebec pattern may be partly one of sample size: every coefficient is of the right sign, but all are unstable.

Arguments for the Accord

There is another striking effect of knowledge: knowing more did not lead voters to buy the general arguments for the Accord. If anything, it did the opposite. Among the most general evaluations of all, no information coefficient was significant, strictly speaking, and the largest one was negative: well-informed voters may have been relatively unpersuaded that the Accord would allow us to move on. University-educated voters were more likely than others to see their province as a winner; we do not know quite what to make of this, however.

Table 9-8
University Education, Information, and Arguments for the Accord

	Rest of Canada				Quebec: Francophone Non-Sovereignists			
	Education	Information	Intercept	R²-adj	Education	Information	Intercept	R²-adj
Best Compromise	0.04 (0.03)	0.07 (0.05)	0.36 (0.03)	0.00	0.11 (0.07)	0.13 (0.11)	0.45 (0.05)	0.01
Move On	0.05 (0.03)	-0.10 (0.05)	0.60 (0.03)	0.00	-0.04 (0.07)	-0.02 (0.12)	0.69 (0.05)	0.00
Province Winner	0.07* (0.03)	0.01 (0.05)	0.41 (0.03)	0.00	0.10 (0.06)	0.07 (0.11)	0.46 (0.04)	0.01
Fear of Separation	-0.00 (0.03)	-0.21*** (0.05)	0.39 (0.03)	0.02	–	–	–	–
Quebec Never Satisfied	-0.23*** (0.03)	0.02 (0.05)	0.74 (0.03)	0.05	–	–	–	–
Distinct Society	0.18*** (0.03)	0.15** (0.05)	0.29 (0.03)	0.05	0.07 (0.05)	0.01 (0.08)	0.63 (0.03)	0.00
25% Guarantee	0.05* (0.03)	-0.05 (0.04)	0.18 (0.02)	0.00	-0.04 (0.07)	0.26* (0.11)	0.57 (0.05)	0.01
New Senate	0.13*** (0.03)	0.16 (0.05)	0.15 (0.03)	0.04	0.06 (0.05)	-0.02 (0.09)	0.13 (0.04)	0.00
Aboriginal Self-Government	0.10** (0.03)	0.18*** (0.05)	0.53 (0.03)	0.03	0.00 (0.07)	0.11 (0.12)	0.44 (0.05)	0.00

The most powerful information relationship among the general arguments, however, did not help pro-Accord forces: *the more you knew, the less you feared Quebec separation.* At first glance, this might seem consistent with a strategy of using reason for the well-informed and bullying for the poorly informed. The problem with this interpretation is that even the most poorly informed did not, on balance, yield to fear: according to Table 9–8, the intercept in the "fear separation" estimation was only 0.39, indicating that even a voter who was aware of not one intervention was still more likely to reject the fear argument than accept it. High-information voters, meanwhile, may have learned that No forces in Quebec had deliberately lowered the stakes.

The other Quebec argument, the anti-Accord counter-claim that Quebec would ever be satisfied, was somewhat neutralized by education. On this question, university-educated voters were collectively on the fence.[6] Information (in contrast to education) made no further difference and, most pointedly, did not reduce acceptance of this anti-Accord argument.

Where both education and information did matter was to acceptance of the Accord's specific elements. The two factors had roughly similar effects across the array: where one mattered, so did the other. For instance, both schooling and information made voters more supportive of the distinct society clause, both induced acceptance of the new Senate, and both produced support for Aboriginal self-government. The only exceptions to the pattern involved the 25 percent guarantee: university-educated voters were slightly (and statistically significantly) more likely to accept the guarantee than others; information may have had the opposite effect, but the coefficient is not significant.

Among Quebec's francophone non-sovereignists, the structure was even weaker. There are hints of education and information effects among general arguments, but only hints. For specific elements there are not even hints, with one exception: information induced support for the 25 percent guarantee. This last relationship was, in fact the only clear, interpretable one in the whole Quebec field.

Neither inside Quebec nor outside, then, did knowing more make voters more acquiescent in the most general arguments for the Accord. Knowledge did not produce the worldiness allegedly necessary to enter into the spirit of compromise, it did not persuade voters of a link between the Accord and the need to move on, and it did not make voters see their own province as the winner. Most strikingly, outside Quebec, knowledge did not make separatist threats more credible; indeed, quite the opposite, it led voters to dismiss them. There was not, then, a broad information cleavage along "civic" lines.

The best-informed were no more likely than the worst-informed to see the situation the way mainstream politicians did. What knowledge – and education – did was induce acceptance of specifics.

Mediation of Effects

This brings us to staged estimations, in Table 9–9. The setups underlying the table correspond to staged estimations in earlier chapters. First appear "total effect" coefficients, reduced-form estimations. These are the effects to be "explained away" by intervening variables. Then come education and information coefficients when group sentiments are controlled. The key comparison for a given coefficient is with the total-effect coefficient in the line immediately above. The greater the reduction from the total-effect estimation, the more group sentiment explains the overall information-vote or education-vote relation. If, conversely, an information or education coefficient increases, then effects from this stage are perverse, work at cross purposes to the overall relationship. Next comes the party and intervenor stage. The logic of comparison at this stage is just an extension of the logic of the previous stage. If an education or information coefficient drops still more, then this stage provides further explanation of the total effect. By implication, not all the total information or education impact would have been captured by the preceding, group sentiment stage. If an information or education coefficient does not drop at this stage, then all party or intervenor mediation of the total effect would be derivative of the stage before, would reflect only the dependence of partisan attitudes themselves on group sentiment. This logic also applies to the last stage, for considerations in the Charlottetown Accord itself.

Outside Quebec, the story for information effects was very simple. Knowing more made a difference to group sentiments, as we know from Table 9–4, and this difference explains a major fraction of the total knowledge effect. Controlling group sentiment reduces the information coefficient by over one-quarter (from 0.20 to 0.14); further controls, if anything, nudge the coefficient back up. In this simplicity lie two oddities that must be underlined. First consider what it means when group sentiment does all the work of mediating the total information effect: *in fact, all the work must be done by feeling for Quebec.* Information did make voters like Quebec more; so far, so good. But information also made voters reject the generalized minority-rights claim, and we know from chapter 7 that this claim helped the Accord. The two sentiments thus worked at cross-purposes in mediating the total information effect. The implication of Table 9–9 is

Table 9–9
University Education, Information, and the Vote: Mediation of Effects

	Rest of Canada (N=984)		Quebec: Francophone Non-Sovereignists (N=242)	
	Education	Information	Education	Information
Total Effect	0.16***	0.20***	0.19*	.29*
	(0.03)	(0.05)	(0.08)	(0.13)
+ Group Sentiments	0.12***	0.14**	0.14*	0.05
	(0.03)	(0.05)	(0.07)	(0.12)
...+ Parties and Intervenors	0.10**	0.13**	0.10	0.07
	(0.03)	(0.05)	(0.07)	(0.12)
... + Accord Considerations	0.08**	0.15***	0.08	0.07
	(0.03)	(0.05)	(0.06)	(0.11)

that the offsetting of feeling by ideas was only partial, that by far the most important thing about information was its association with positive feeling. To know more was to like Quebec more; most of the rest was window-dressing. Indeed, the rest just confused the issue. Well-informed voters liked Preston Manning less (Table 9–6), but this must have been mainly derivative of his embodiment of anti-Quebec feeling; the feeling itself was the critical thing. Most strikingly, rhetoric around the Accord was unhelpful; although well-informed voters were relatively accepting of the Accord's specific features, they were least persuaded by the general arguments, most pointedly by appeals to fear.

For all this, the biggest fact about political information is that it cut through powerfully and directly to the vote. The total-effect coefficient loses about one-fourth of its total impact as intervening controls are added, but most of the impact remains direct, simply unexplained by the all the intervening elements. We return to this fact at the end of this chapter.

Impact from education was more textured, more staged. Again, group sentiments played a powerful role, as they alone cut 0.04–0.05 points from the education coefficient. In contrast to the case with information, however, further controls yield further cuts. No single stage cuts as much as the initial, group-sentiment one, but, cumulatively, further controls slice as much as the initial stage. Recall from Table 9–6 that university-educated voters rather liked pro-Accord intervenors; Table 9–9 implies that some of this feeling worked through to the vote, and exerted an effect over and above that from group sen-

timent. Similarly, education's impact on acceptance or rejection of Accord considerations fed through to the vote. Table 9–8 indicated that
education had no perverse effect on any consideration, in contrast to
information. University-educated voters tended to support each element in the deal, and also to dismiss the counter-claim that Quebec
always asks for more. Altogether, controls for intervening variables
reduced the education coefficient from 0.20 to 0.08.

The pattern for francophone non-sovereignists in Quebec resembled that for the rest of Canada, except for one key particular – the
overall power of group sentiment in relation to information. For education, the parallel between Quebec and the rest of Canada was almost exact. Controlling group sentiment knocked about 0.05 off the
total-effect, each further stage knocked some more off, and the last
stage left the direct-impact coefficient from education at 0.08, exactly
as in the rest of Canada. For information, in contrast, not only were
group sentiments the master control variables, but they carried almost the entire informational effect all by themselves. Merely controlling group sentiment caused the information coefficient to plummet
from 0.29 to an insignificant 0.05, while subsequent controls (as in the
rest of Canada) only fudge the issue slightly. Like the rest of Canada,
then, only group sentiment helps us to interpret the information effect. Unlike the rest of Canada, group sentiment alone explains virtually everything. In Quebec, the more knowledgeable the voter, the
more he or she liked Canada, the less he or she feared for the future of
French, and this combination of affection and confidence helped produce a Yes vote.[7]

INFORMATION AND THE GROUP BASIS OF THE VOTE

If we take as given that mastery of political knowledge generally
favoured the Yes, did it do so for all groups and places? This question
invites us to look at the interaction between information and the
vote's social-group basis. The following patterns are possible:

– Information could just *cut through* group differences, making all
  groups more supportive of the Charlottetown Accord by about the
  same amount. This would suggest that the Accord serves some
  general interest and that information promotes awareness of the
  connection, in competition with more specific interests which independently tug voters toward or away from the deal.
– Information could *widen* differences, by pushing generally opposed
  groups away from the Yes and generally favourable groups toward

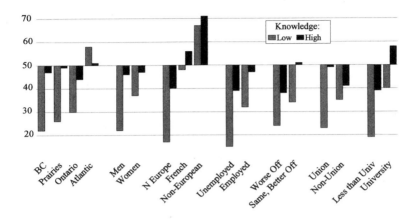

Figure 9–2
Impact of Knowledge on Group Differences in the Vote: Rest of Canada Only

it. This would suggest that nothing in the Accord really serves a general interest. Information just clarifies the deal's specific implications. The overall information-Yes relationship is simply a byproduct of the fact that winners, by good fortune, were better informed than losers; that helps explain why they are winners in life, if not in the 1992 vote.
– Information could *narrow* group differences, by pushing supporters down and opponents up. This would suggest that at least some arguments are general, transcending group membership, but are inherently contestible. Political knowledge alerts voters to the generality of the question and inhibits group-specific response, but does not, in the end, supply the answer to the general question.

Combinations of these three alternatives are also possible, reflecting a complicated texture of narrow and broad appeals, and, among broad appeals, overarching considerations juxtaposed to reasonable, agonizing doubts.

Evidence appears in Figure 9–2, for the rest of Canada only.[8] Yes shares are contrasted across key dimensions of social structure, conditioned on political information. The setup is very crude, as information is simply dichotomized at the median into high- and low-information groups, but the pattern is telling.[9] For the most part, the pattern embodies two characteristics: knowing more makes virtually every group more likely to vote Yes; and knowing more reduces group differences. The coexistence of these characteristics has a further implication, as a matter of arithmetic: Yes-share gains induced by information were greater in groups generally opposed to the Accord than in groups generally in favour of it. Although exceptions existed, getting above the whole-sample median on information tended to push all groups toward a Yes share in the mid to high 40 percent range.

Some of the cleavage compression is little short of astounding. For low-information voters the range across regions was over 30 points, for high-information voters the range was less than 10 points. This was the one dimension featuring convergence from both ends. Among poorly informed voters the gender gap was over 10 points, among the well-informed it was virtually non-existent and all the convergence was of males on females. The ethnic-group gap was over 45 points among the poorly informed, but about 30 points among the well-informed. This last figure is suspect as the number of well-informed non-European respondents was tiny. An employed/unemployed gap of 15–20 points became one of less than 10 points. A similar reduction occurred for the gap between those feeling worse off financially and those feeling the same or better off. The union/non-union contrast actually reversed: where poorly informed union members were more opposed than non-members to the deal, the opposite was true for well-informed members. Curiously, the one cleavage that did not seriously shrink with information was the university/non-university one! The 20-point gap remained roughly intact, as information just shifted both the university and the non-university distributions dramatically toward the Yes side. This reinforces the point that, although university-educated Canadians did know more than others (it would be shocking if they did not), it was not superior knowledge that produced their distinctive inclination to the Yes. University-educated Canadians evidently inhabit a different cultural universe from their fellow citizens, and the Charlottetown Accord may have been an authentic, if flawed, expression of that culture – a culture of group accommodation, almost for its own sake.

But if university-educated Canadians did not support the Accord out of superior knowledge, superior knowledge did nonetheless drive Canadians toward the Accord. After all the controls and alternative explanations are considered, it is difficult to dismiss the relationship as spurious, as reflecting the adventitious association of knowledge with some other, purely motivational factor. Even so, knowledge did not produce consensus. The convergence induced by knowing more was to, roughly, a 50:50 likelihood of voting Yes. In a sense, most groups started out with a strong bias against the Accord, as most group differences were in degree of negativity. Only in the Atlantic provinces and among visible minorities did the low-information presumption actually favour the deal. If information supplanted crude group-specific cues, it did so by alerting voters to the inherently contestible nature of the document; this at least got about one well-informed voter in two to say Yes, but it left one in two saying No.

INFORMATION, REASONING CHAINS,
AND THE AMPLIFICATION OF IDEAS
AND FEELINGS

Did Yes voters react to the Charlottetown Accord in a qualitatively different way from No voters? Asymmetry between sides of a question – or between answers – is a general theme in the comparative and historical record, and it is entirely possible that the Accord was, cognitively speaking, hard to accept but easy to reject. The analytic problem is that sides cannot be compared qualitatively; ultimately, all estimations require variance in the vote, require that a common model be used to predict whether or not a voter crosses the threshold between Yes and No. But we can approach the matter indirectly. It is now a matter of record that Yes voters were better informed, on average, than No voters. Moreover, these informational differences cannot be dismissed as mere artifacts of social position. Did better-informed voters, collectively more sympathetic to the Yes, approach the question differently from poorly informed voters, collectively leaning more to the No?

To evaluate this possibility, four areas must be canvassed in detail:

– Does knowing more amplify or suppress the power of raw feeling about groups? The principal contribution to the empirical record, Sniderman et al. (1991), leaves us with ambiguous expectations.
– Is knowing more a condition for mobilizing ideas, as opposed to feelings? Here Sniderman et al. are crystal clear: information *is* a precondition for ideas to matter. This is also argued by Zaller (1992, p. 28).
– Does knowing more amplify or suppress the power of feelings about agenda-setters and intervenors? Here, the literature on intervenors (McKelvey and Ordeshook, 1986; Lupia, 1992, 1994, 1995) is silent. Note, however, that chapter 5 has already made clear that awareness of a specific intervention unlocks the power of feeling toward the intervenor in question.
– Does information make the whole choice process more precise? Low-information rationality arguments (Popkin, 1992; Sniderman et al., 1991) imply that information is not a precondition for getting

voters to the right position, but Luskin's (1995) acerbic review suggests that, to the contrary, low-information choice is very imprecise.

The first two issues will be covered in the next section on group sentiment. Following this is an exploration of agenda-setters and intervenors. Finally comes consideration of the role of information in conditioning precision of the choice. Material for the entire discussion appears in Table 9–10 for the rest of Canada and Table 9–11 for Quebec.

Group Sentiment

In this section we take the now-familiar stagewise strategy and replicate it by information level. We focus, first, on the *summary effect* of group sentiment, the reduced form estimation, by information level. At this point, factors closer to the vote – feelings about agenda-setters and intervenors, attitudes to specific elements, and acceptance of general arguments – are omitted. For the moment it does not matter how, precisely, a sentimental factor's summary impact is mediated, the critical issue is whether the total effect of feelings and ideas differs by information level.

Second, we focus on the *mediation* process itself. Here the key is what happens to sentimental coefficients as stages are added. If sentiments are mediated more when information is rich than when it is poor, feeling coefficients should attenuate, as later stages are added, more among the well-informed than among the poorly informed. If this happens, then we may conclude, with Sniderman et al., that information makes reasoning more hierarchical.

The total effect of sentimental factors appears in the leftmost column of the two tables. Mediation of each sentiment is indicated by decay in its coefficient as we move rightward across the row. The first point is that information does not suppress the power of raw feeling. Outside Quebec, feeling toward that province is roughly as powerful, summarily speaking, in the high-information group as in the low-information one. In Quebec, information, if anything, unlocks the power of feeling, negative as well as positive, toward Canada. Recall, though, that, inside and outside Quebec, information is positively related to outgroup feeling. In other words, the role of group feeling is not merely tribal; negative emotions are not systematically more powerful than positive ones. For francophone non-sovereignists in Quebec, indeed, the opposite is more nearly true.

Information *does* unlock ideas. It was only among high-information voters that any potentially relevant conceptualizations of Canada's group life did matter. Outside Quebec, minority orientation and will-

Table 9–10
Mediation of Sentiments and Feelings I: Rest of Canada

Object/ Information	Demographics, plus group sentiments	... plus party identity and feelings about intervenors	... plus opinion on general arguments	... plus opinion on specific elements
Feelings about Quebec				
Low	0.37***	0.25**	0.23**	0.12
High	0.34***	0.14	0.09	0.06
Minority Orientation				
Low	0.06	0.06	0.05	0.05
High	0.10*	0.05	0.01	0.00
Founding Peoples				
Low	0.09	0.09	0.08	0.05
High	0.17**	0.10*	0.05	0.01
Mulroney				
Low	–	0.29**	0.19*	0.18*
High	–	0.47***	0.10	0.08
Other Leaders				
Low	–	0.60***	0.47**	0.43**
High	–	0.34**	0.10	0.04
Trudeau				
Low	–	-0.11	-0.12	-0.12
High	–	-0.37***	-0.19**	-0.17*
Manning				
Low		-0.19	-0.17	-0.15
High	–	-0.57***	-0.32***	-0.28***
Power of the Equation (R^2-adjusted)				
Low	0.08	0.17	0.26	0.28
High	0.11	0.30	0.46	0.47

ingness to recognize three founding peoples were significant factors in the informed choice, but they were of no account in the uninformed choice. As with feelings, ideas mattered most where they generally favoured the Accord. And, consistent with Sniderman et al., ideas mattered only where information was ready to hand.

Information also conditioned the expression of those ideas in the vote, again roughly consistent with the Sniderman et al. pattern. This comes out of comparisons across rows. The idea-vote link was simply

Table 9–11
Mediation of Sentiments and Feelings II: Quebec: Francophone Non-Sovereignists

Object/ Information	Demographics, plus group sentiments	... plus feelings about intervenors	... plus opinion on general arguments	... plus opinion on specific elements
Feelings about Quebec				
Low	-0.07	-0.06	-0.08	-0.09
High	-0.27	-0.31	-0.27	-0.43
Feelings about Canada				
Low	0.59	0.30	0.29	0.31
High	0.98***	0.59*	0.52*	0.60**
Economic Concerns				
Low	0.30	0.14	0.16	0.15
High	0.33*	0.07	0.08	0.04
Perceived Threat				
Low	-0.15	-0.14	-0.11	-0.14
High	-0.12	-0.05	-0.05	-0.02
Bourassa				
Low	–	0.67**	0.57*	0.52*
High	–	0.54***	0.29	0.23
Parizeau				
Low	–	-0.09	-0.06	-0.05
High	–	-0.49**	-0.32*	-0.34*
Power of the Equation (R^2-adjusted)				
Low	0.10	0.16	0.21	0.18
High	0.32	0.41	0.48	0.52

nonexistent for low-information voters, of course, and was always mediated for high-information ones. Outside Quebec, minority orientation and recognition of founding peoples had their greatest single effect on feelings about agenda-setters and intervenors, and in each case the first stage of controls cut the coefficient roughly in half. Each further stage cut a bit more, such that by the time the system was fully specified, no direct impact (at least none statistically significant) could be found. In Quebec, economic concerns primarily affected evaluation of Bourassa and Parizeau, and, again, did so most pointedly among the well-informed.

Information also conditioned the impact of feelings, although here the pattern is messier. The cleanest case is for high-information voters outside Quebec: feelings for Quebec were, for the most part, absorbed into evaluation of intervenors, and almost all the covariance left over was absorbed by substantive considerations. With all factors specified, feelings had no detectible direct effect on the vote. For low-information voters outside Quebec, mediation was slower and less complete. Only about half as much total covariance as among the well-informed was absorbed at the party-intervenor stage, and controlling general orientations made no further difference. Only when specific elements were controlled was any further mediation visible; for low-information voters a big fraction of feeling about Quebec went directly to Quebec elements in the Accord (for these voters, this was predominantly negative feeling shading into disapproval). And even with all factors specified, there remained a hint of a direct effect from feeling on the vote. A similar pattern appeared in Quebec, but the picture is clouded by instability of coefficients in the low-information group. In short, the low-high contrast for group feeling was not absolutely clean. Although at each stage, including the last one, low-information voters reasoned less hierarchically than high-information ones, it cannot be said that all poorly informed voters just took feeling straight to the vote, or even straight to evaluation of the distinct society clause or the 25 percent guarantee.

But the overall pattern is unmistakable. The basis for choice was more complex among high-information voters than among low-information ones. Whereas group feeling mattered at all information levels, only for well-informed voters did ideas also matter. If low-information voters also exhibited some hierarchical reasoning in connecting feeling to the vote, the pattern was clearer and more consistent among the well-informed. Information, thus, was a qualitative force which made reasoning about the Charlottetown Accord more textured. And complex, textured reasoning was, by implication, more common on the Yes side than on the No side.

Agenda-Setters and Intervenors

In the agenda-setter/intervenor realm, information usually amplified the effect of feeling, and did so especially strikingly on the negative side, according to the second column in tables 9–10 and 9–11. Where neither Trudeau nor Manning mattered to the rest of Canada among the poorly informed, each made a big difference among the well-informed. The same discrepancy emerged for Parizeau in Quebec. Among agenda-setters, the pattern was more chequered. Information clearly amplified the impact of feelings for Mulroney, although even among the poorly informed his impact was not trivial. Bourassa's impact may have been greater among the poorly informed, but the issue is clouded by the fact that his high-information coefficient was rather more stable than his low-information one. For other leaders, information may actually have dampened the impact of feeling.

But amplification of agenda-setter/intervenor feeling was clearly the overall story, as indicated by the R^2 gains at the bottom of the tables. Start with informational differences *before* agenda-setters and intervenors enter estimation. Outside Quebec, the explanatory power of demographic characteristics and group sentiment was only slightly greater in the high- than in the low-information group. For the well-informed, the slightly greater power of group sentiment (table 9–10 and 9–11, top rows) was partly offset by the weakening of group differences (implied in Figure 9–2). But once agenda-setter/intervenor feelings enter estimation, the low-high gap positively yawns. If the equation's power roughly doubles in the low-information group, it nearly trebles in the high-information group. In Quebec, gains are less dramatic but take the same form. Even without intervenors, Quebec's high-information voters employed group sentiment more efficiently, as indicated by an R^2 over three times as large (0.32, as compared with 0.10). Even so, the absolute explanatory difference widens from 0.22 to 0.25. At this stage (and at the earlier stage in Quebec) information did more than push voters to the Yes; it also helped voters make the right choice, given their group sentiments and given where they located each agenda-setter or intervenor. If this also helped some voters say Yes, for others it made clear that the right answer was No. Information helped feelings find the proper target. This anticipates general discussion of information and vote precision, which we address in the next section.

Finally, information conditioned how agenda-setter/intervenor feeling had its impact. For every intervenor, high-information coefficients shrink at each later stage. In three of six cases (Mulroney, other leaders, and Bourassa) the coefficient goes from being highly significant in reduced form to being indistinguishable from zero at the last stage, if not before. In two other cases (Trudeau and Manning) the coefficient is cut more than in half. In the last case (Parizeau), the reduction was still dramatic. For low-information voters, there was often no total impact for intervening voters to explain, of course. But where there was any low-information total effect to explain away, little actually was explained. Mulroney, other leaders, and Bourassa evaluations all affected the vote in the low-information group, but the coefficients were almost as large when every intervening variable was controlled as when none were.[10]

Explanatory Power and Precision

Finally, consider what happens across the rest of the bottom two rows of tables 9–10 and 9–11 as further stages are reached. Adding general arguments and specific elements makes only a small further difference to the model's explanatory power in the low-information group, but continues to make serious power increments in the high-information group. For low-information voters outside Quebec, adding general arguments boosts R^2 about as much as adding agenda-setters and intervenors; adding specific elements has little further effect. For their counterparts in Quebec, roughly the same is true, but the actual value of increments at each stage is even smaller. For high-information voters, adding general arguments boosts explanatory power dramatically outside Quebec, more than modestly inside Quebec. In each place, this stage takes the R^2 nearly to 0.50 and the next stage takes it essentially no further.

The low-information/high-information gap widens for two reasons. First, coefficients linking most general arguments to the vote are rather wider among high-information voters (not reported in a table). For instance, high-information voters were simply more likely to see evaluation of the compromise as relevant to the choice. They were not much more likely actually to approve of the compromise (see above, Table 9–8), just more likely to connect approval to a Yes vote and disapproval to a No vote. Second, well-informed voters were more likely actually to take positions on general arguments, to accept or reject the compromise, to see their province as a winner or a loser, and so on. Statistically, this expands the variance in the various independent variables in question, and this in turn increases their explanatory power.[11]

At the last stages, then, information made a further contribution to precision in the choice. Information helped voters find reasons to say Yes or No and then helped them connect those reasons to decision. Where information was lacking, choice was more random, less obviously connected to voters' interests, broad or narrow.

POLLS: COMPLEMENTS OR SUBSTITUTES?

One last question remains: did prior information make any difference to reception of new information in polls? Chapter 6 staked a strong if circumstantial case that polls moved the vote at the end, that the late surge of negative polls pulled the Yes share down one last time. Conceivably a voter would require considerable cognitive capacity to act on the poll information, to get the information in the first place, and

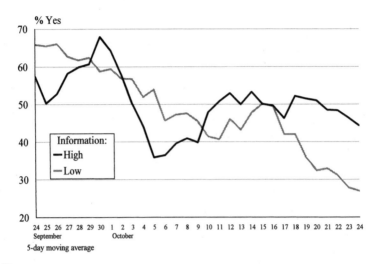

Figure 9–3
Information and Vote Dynamics: Rest of Canada

then see its relevance to choice. But a cognitively rich voter already had plenty of other bases for choice; this was the whole point of the immediately preceding section. If high-information votes were already well anchored and supported by substantive motives, they should not have been available for displacement by poll information.

The visual indication in Figure 9–3 is clear: *low-information voters, not high-information ones, responded to polls.* In the figure, voter intention (as opposed to the actual vote) is the issue. Only at the end of the campaign did there emerge the pattern that drives so much of this chapter – the strong positive relationship between information and Yes share. Down to the second-last weekend neither informational group was systematically more or less likely than the other to say Yes. High-information voters were the only ones to respond in any obvious way to Trudeau's Egg Roll speech; where the low-information Yes share gradually drifted down over the campaign's first two to three weeks, the high-information share dropped over 30 points in a few days. Then the high-information share moved up over 10 points, possibly to settle back a few points at the very end. The low information share continued to drift down a few days longer than the high-information one and then, with some lag, seemed to follow the high-information share back up. Down to about 16 October, then, low-information voters seemed to respond to the campaign with some lag, relative to high-information voters. The pattern was consistent with elements noted in earlier chapters and, generally, with a two-step flow of information and persuasion: well-informed opinion leaders get the message directly from broadcast media and then pass the message on. On or about 16 October, however, the pattern underwent a qualitative change. Low-information voters now seized the dynamic lead, as their Yes share dropped nearly 25 points. Again, the evidence is circumstantial, but the most obvious reading is that the barrage of negative polls either drove the low-information share down or allowed other factors to drag it down.

REFLECTIONS

University-educated Canadians said Yes but not because they knew more about the Charlottetown Accord than other Canadians did. University-educated voters did indeed know more about the Accord, but knowledge differences did not explain their vote away. If anything, the opposite was more nearly true; controlling education explained away more of information's effect than controlling information explained away education's effect. Closest of all to the truth, however, was that education and information were essentially independent of each other as factors in the vote.

What university education did was help non-Quebec voters identify with a culture of tolerance, the same culture that (according to chapter 7) the Charlottetown Accord drew upon. Whatever the legal-political arguments over the document's fine print, voters for the most part saw the Accord as an expression of the politics of group accommodation. Support for the deal was helped by liking for the component groups and by support for minority rights and recognition of founding peoples as general propositions, and university education promotes both orientations, particular and general. These group sentiments fed through to evaluation of agenda-setters and intervenors and to response to substantive arguments.

Although information, as distinct from education, also increased liking for specific minorities, it reduced support for minority rights in the abstract, and it also disarmed a key pro-Accord argument – fear of separation. Notwithstanding this offsetting between particular and general, the basic fact remained that the more voters knew, the more likely they were to vote Yes. Vote differences across the knowledge continuum rivalled those between education groups. But none of the total informational effect was explained by factors beyond simple liking for Quebec, and most of it remains unexplained.

One clue to the story of the rest of Canada might lie in the pattern for Quebec. As in the rest of the country, the Quebec story combines pure affect with more intellectualized orientations. Affect in this case is not for Quebec but for Canada as a whole, and both education and information increase it. The intellectualized orientation is the flip side of the minority orientation outside of Quebec: fear – or its absence – for the future of French in Quebec, which could be stylized either as fear of the anglophone majority in North America or of anglophone and allophone minorities inside Quebec. Either way, the operative sentiment is fear, and both highly educated and well-informed Quebec francophone non-sovereignists lack it. Both general patterns can be seen as a culture of *tolerance*, along the lines of the education effect outside Quebec. Both can also be seen as expressions of cutural *self-confidence* in that education and political knowledge alert one to the success of programs to promote French in Quebec – programs which for the most part are compatible with the larger federal scheme. This compatibility makes the larger scheme acceptable, indeed more likeable. Of course, the two readings on the pattern are not mutually exclusive; self-confidence can find expression in tolerance. This follows quite directly out of the Quebec data, but it also points us back to the pattern in the rest of Canada; well-informed voters outside Quebec may not be attuned to minority rights but neither are they fearful of particular minorities, and they are less fearful in general. If general lack of fearfulness was a precondition for Yes votes among the well-informed, then we have an irony: well-informed voters voted Yes not because they feared the Accord's rejection, for they rejected claims that the deal's failure would entrain Quebec's separation, but because they did not fear the consequences of its acceptance.

Information did more than shift the vote's direction. It also altered the vote's very basis, on several fronts at once:

– It reduced most group differences in the vote, mainly by raising the Yes share in groups predisposed against the deal.
– It made ideas more important relative to feelings.
– It made feelings about agenda-setters and intervenors operate more precisely.
– Similarly, it tightened the connection between substantive arguments, both general and specific, about the Accord and the vote.
– It made the overall reasoning process more hierarchical, by connecting ideas and feelings about groups to evaluation of agenda-setters and intervenors, and by connecting all of the foregoing to substantive considerations.
– In the late campaign it neutralized a bandwagon impact from the polls, as only low-information voters responded to indications that the Accord was doomed, by turning further against it .

These propositions are all about information as a condition for substantively based choice. Together with findings about the directional impact of information on substance, they point to unsettling conclusions about information and democracy.

In Canada in 1992 information was not directionally neutral. This compromises optimistic claims that error in public opinion formation is offsetting – that well-informed voters act, in effect, as tribunes for poorly informed ones. In point of fact, well-informed voters took different positions from poorly informed voters and evidently did so *because* they were better informed. This interpretation is buttressed by the observation that, as members of groups predisposed against the Accord learned more, the more pro-Accord they became; enlightenment did not just reinforce predispositons, it positively changed preferences. Alternatively put, the better informed were more likely to resist the temptation to vote No; the least informed went with the tide. Aggregationist arguments, claims that pooling information compensates for individual differences – in some cases, shortfalls – in cognitive capacity were not vindicated.

The failure of aggregation reflects, in part, a difficulty in the "low-information rationality" case. Feelings would be a more adequate substitute for ideas the more similarly two otherwise identical but differently informed voters felt about groups. Where the two felt the same way, feelings should bring each to the same vote, except to the extent that the well-informed voter was moved off that position by an idea. But the 1992 evidence suggests that the less you know the less you like outside groups. Where this is so, feelings do not merely substitute for ideas, they alter the direction of choice. If the poorly informed voter knew more, he or she would feel differently about the choice's group basis, and probably vote differently.

Aggregation aside, low-information rationality encounters a further difficulty in the connection of individual preferences to choice. It is true that outside Quebec low-information voters connected group feeling to the vote about as efficiently as did high-information voters, in the sense that feelings for Quebec had roughly the same predictive power at all information levels.[12] And low-information voters were more differentiated by another aspect of group life – group membership. But there the story grinds to a halt, for low-information voters availed themselves of few other sources of orientation. As a result, support or opposition to, say, the distinct society clause was less likely to be translated into the directionally correct vote among the poorly informed than among the well-informed. Relative to their own definition of their stakes in the outcome, as measured by questions about general arguments and specific elements, the poorly informed choice was quite random. *Feelings, in other words, did not close the gap, in translating interests into expressed preferences, between the poorly and the well-informed.* One reason they did not do so was that well-informed voters themselves had feelings, just as efficiently expressed as among poorly informed voters, and supplemented by other, relevant considerations. If the interest-vote connection fails at the individual level so regularly, then the argument is forced back on considerations of aggregation. And aggregation guarantees no miracles.

Another reason why well-informed voters got it right – where right reflected their own definition of their interests – was that they paid more attention to what cue-givers said. This might further compromise low-information arguments, in this case associated with Lupia (1992, 1994, 1995). Here the argument is that simple directional cues, especially if agenda-setters are matched by outside intervenors and even – perhaps especially – where intervenors do not share the voter's own interests, can be efficient substitutes for substantive information. In 1992 cue-givers did move voters, none more efficiently than Pierre Trudeau. Even Preston Manning's unintentionally perverse effect was, from this perspective, socially useful. But Lupia's argument is, at bottom, an "existence theorem," a proof that, under the right circumstances, an otherwise uninformed voter can get the choice properly framed. But such a theorem does not guarantee that this possibility is actually realized. If over 70 percent eventually claimed to pick up Trudeau's cue,[13] half the non-Quebec electorate was aware of no more than three key intervenors, and nearly half was aware of no more than two. For many voters, cue-taking was still very difficult, and for some effectively impossible. Given the distribution of awareness, it is not clear how much these interventions actually closed cognitive gaps. They may even have widened the gaps, for although cues may substitute for substance and so reduce cognitive burden, there remains the challenge of getting cues in the first place. Voters most likely to get a cue are least likely to need it, but they may still find it helpful and its helpfulness may compound their prior decisional advantage.

Did the electorate fail the test of direct democracy, then? The implications of preceding paragraphs, and of much of this chapter, are hard. It suggests that sharp informational differences exist; that knowledge changes attitudes and, in particular, promotes group accommodation, but that many voters, evidently for lack of knowledge, repudiate a politics of accommodation; and finally, that also for lack of knowledge, many voters fail to connect their own substantive opinions to the choice. When all is said and done, however, the 1992 vote did not divide the best from the worst informed. If the electorate failed a test, this was true even of its best-informed members. Although information raised the likelihood of a Yes vote, it never made such a vote overwhelmingly probable. If the Yes share among the very worst informed was around 30 percent (Figure 9–1), among the very best informed the share was roughly 50:50. The broad consensus among party elites and their closest allies was simply not mirrored in the electorate's most thoughtful and informed members. Ratiocination and positive group sentiment did no more than get this group to at least argue the question out. The arguments actually entertained in this group were roughly balanced, and produced a balanced division. This is shown most strikingly by Figure 9–2: yes, information boosted the Yes side's chances in almost every group; yes, information brought voters of diverse backgrounds to see issues in roughly the same way, drew them into a common debate, in contrast to the deep, raw divisions among those who knew little; but no, information did not produce consensus, it only clarified the lines of disagreement. While it does not do to wish away serious informational deficits in the electorate at large, neither, at least for 1992, does it make sense to blame the outcome on ignorance. Equally, it makes no sense to laud the outcome, which was a rejection of the elite's handiwork, as manifesting some deep, low-information rationality.

10 Simple Majorities in Complex Societies: Direct Democracy and High Politics

Was the referendum foolish, then? The vote on the Charlottetown Accord seemed only to continue Canada's dreary plebiscitory history. National plebiscites were held twice before, and hindsight regards each as an unhappy experience. They all gave the "wrong" answer, or the "right" answer in the wrong places, and each was deeply divisive. The dreariness is inescapable, for Canada, on this view, is precisely the sort of country that should never conduct national referendums.

Rule by simple popular majority presupposes underlying sociopolitical unity. Even when, as in 1992, a referendum's rules are supermajoritarian, direct votes are brutal in their transparency. Where a society is deeply split – "segmented" is a commonly used term – its continuing integrity may require consensual or proportional decision rules and elite accommodation, a pattern commonly referred to as "consociational" (Lijphart, 1968, 1977). Non-majoritarian decision rules reflect the moral diversity of the polity, the fact that it comprises more than one proto-nation or more than one moral community. Where communities are moral equals, one community has no right to swamp another merely by virtue of greater size, hence the resistance to straight majoritarian devices. At a minimum, power must be shared proportionally, where that is possible, or outcomes must favour groups proportionally over time. In the extreme, each group enjoys a veto, and the shareout must be equal across groups. So far, this describes the 1992 referendum rules, but it brings us to the other part of the process – elite accommodation. Elite bargaining is the necessary complement to non-majoritarian decision rules, for only by insider negotiation can inclusive bargains be struck. In the ideal case, once the elite bargain is struck no further action is required, as elites speak authoritatively for those whom they represent. Where elite authority falls short of this ideal, popular referral is still a bad idea, unlikely to close the elite-mass gap, on one hand, but highly likely to disrupt the fabric of compromise, on the other.[1]

Canada is often conceived of in terms like these. Consociational reasoning is embedded in the idea of founding peoples, with its purely moral (pre-existing occupation) and moral-practical (an essential party to the founding bargain) elements. It often lurks behind more general minority rights claims. Of course, acceptance or rejection of such a conceptualization was a critical division between the Yes and No sides in 1992, where well-informed and well-educated voters came closest to embracing the elite-accommodation view, but were divided and outnumbered. But such arguments also could be heard on other side. The strongest advocates of Senate reform, the proponents of the Triple-E, assumed that provinces are moral equals; only on such an assumption could placing Ontario and Prince Edward Island at the same level be anything other than absurd. Still, as this book makes clear, rejection of the Charlottetown Accord did not signal an embrace of the Triple-E ideal; more nearly it indicated complete rejection of consociational reasoning. Not only did voters reject a specific product of elite bargaining, but they also severely constrained prospects for future bargaining. The 1992 referendum opened a wound and guaranteed that the wound would stay open. On this account, the event only reaffirmed what many suspected – that referendums have no place in Canada, at least in the country as a whole, for in Canada there can be no winners in a referendum, only losers.[2]

To say this, however, is to imply, again, that in 1992 voters made the wrong choice. It also implies that such an outcome should never have been risked. Either the question – and so, inescapably, the constitutional bargain itself – should have been fundamentally different, or this bargain, once struck, should never have been referred. Could it be, however, that some semblance of the Charlottetown bargaining process and the referendum on the resultant bargain were both necessary? Almost regardless of result, both may have been inscapable purgative rituals.[3] As such, the referendum on the Charlottetown Accord will not be an isolated experience. For many referendums, the critical fact is their mere occurrence. From time to time elite accommodation breaks down and choices *must* be forced. In such periods, referendums can help governing parties – opposition parties too –

bring divisions out into the open. Or they can allow voters to vent frustration. From this perspective, it may not matter which side wins.

The 1992 vote, and its 1898 and 1942 predecessors, bear examination, then, for their role in blocking or smoothing the path of elite decision. For a referendum conceived as an elite-initiated mass consultation, the historical and comparative record[4] reveals at least seven possible objectives, some of which are mirror images. The first two illustrate direct referral as a *safety valve*, the "rubber life raft into which [a] party may one day have to climb," as James Callaghan once put it[5]:

- *Validating a shift of position*, abridging an earlier promise through a different and more recent genuflection toward popular sovereignty.
- *Externalizing party tension*, by a single move facilitating expression of intra-party division and compartmentalizing it. Sometimes this works, but sometimes it only brings divisions into bolder relief, deepens them, and hastens party breakup and realignment.

In the first two, the party is on the defensive, under pressure either from another party or from forces in history. Referendums can also be *offensive weapons*, as in:

- *Calling a bluff*, undercutting a claim made by one part of the elite that its position rests on a firm base of popular support, when it does not.
- *Substantiating a claim of support*, the mirror image of calling a bluff; showing that opinion on a measure is truly one-sided.

In each case, the real purpose is incidental to the question itself. The hidden agenda is to shore up the protagonist's general position by attaching it to an expression of majority sentiment, or to weaken the opponent by revealing the unpopularity of its position. In the latter case, opponents, on the *defensive*, can:

- *Decouple the issue* from party battle by seizing the initiative, and referring it themselves. Once the referral is made, voters need not vote against the referring party to send a signal on the specific referendum issue. This is not the same as externalizing tension, for the party benefitting from referral need not be internally divided, just dodging a bullet.[6]

The final two objectives, also mirror images, refer to the *substance* of the question:

- *Legitimating* a difficult initiative, by recommending it to the people and winning their acquiescence, in the interests of future constitutional harmony.
- From the opposite point of view, *delegitimating* an initiative, derailing action where the elite is seen as departing from majority will.

Of course, either of these objectives can overlap with more specifically partisan ones. Indeed, votes commonly serve two or more objectives, and because of this, even questions which ostensibly fail in their own terms can succeed on another level. Sometimes referendums, rather like Milton on his blindness, serve merely by being held.

The two earlier Canadian plebiscites illustrate some of these patterns and help set up discussion of the 1992 vote.

THE 1898 PLEBISCITE

Canada's first national plebiscite, in 1898, on prohibition of sale and consumption of alcoholic beverages, both externalized party tension and called a non-party bluff. The issue divided each party against itself and both tried to move it out of party politics. In government before 1896, the Conservatives temporized by establishing a royal commission. The Liberals, at their 1893 convention, committed themselves to a plebiscite. Politicians in both parties also hoped that the courts would take the problem out of their hands by declaring their regulatory actions *ultra vires*, but the courts did not oblige. The vote which then became politically inescapable was very close: a pro-prohibition majority of only 13,000 out of more than 540,000 votes. The Protestant-Catholic division was transparent and tribal passions were inflamed. Laurier was reluctant to impose prohibition on such a basis and referred to the low turnout of 44 percent in declining to act. He did not get off lightly. According to Craig Brown and Ramsay Cook, "There were ... those who viewed Laurier's inaction as yet another sign of the undue influence of Quebec and the Catholic Church on the Liberal government, which now stood in the path of Christian progress" (1974, p. 23).

It is hard to argue with Laurier's own reckoning in both calling the vote and then not acting on the result, however. The temperance crusade lacked an adequate base for its moral pretensions and the vote effectively disposed of the issue; certainly, the Laurier government was not haunted by it in the long run. Had the vote not been conducted, both parties' contortions would have continued, and the claims of the temperance advocates would have remained uncontested. Laurier thus externalized an issue that divided his own party, and called the bluff of an intensely moralistic and uncompromising interest group.

THE 1942 PLEBISCITE

The second plebiscite, in 1942, was on conscription for overseas service. In this case at least four purposes were served. Tensions inside the Liberal party were externalized, more or less. The issue was partly decoupled from the party battle; certainly a bullet was dodged by the Liberals and all possible advantage in the issue snatched away from the Conservatives. The depth of support for conscription was dramatically underlined, and the specific way in which support was substantiated facilitated the Liberal government's move off an earlier position.

The Mackenzie King Liberal government was constrained by its pledges in the 1939 Quebec provincial election and the 1940 federal one not to conscript manpower for overseas service. By 1942, however, pro-conscription pressure was mounting. Although Canada's first Gallup polls suggested that a majority favoured conscription, they also confirmed that the majority stopped at the Quebec boundary.[7] The government itself was deeply divided, just as it had been in 1898, and naturally hesitated.

The first job, however, was to dodge a bullet. The political dike burst when Sir Arthur Meighen made a public call for conscription. Meighen's moral power for English Canadians in 1942 was strikingly like that of Pierre Trudeau in 1992. The stage for Meighen's intervention was set by his resumption of the Conservative party leadership, resignation from the Senate, and his by-election candidacy on the pro-conscription turf of York South. The best way to head Meighen off was to hold a plebiscite, and the promise to hold one immediately took conscription off the York South agenda. This allowed the CCF, the only party contesting Meighen's bid for the seat, to concentrate on social policy. Social questions were a weak point for Meighen but, as early Gallup surveys also revealed, were an increasing preoccupation of the electorate. Meighen lost the election and the loss drained his moral authority. The immediate Tory threat to the government was turned aside, as the issue was temporarily decoupled from party politics. Not incidentally, the promise of the referendum also disarmed pro-conscription pressure inside the government.

There remained the plebiscite itself. If its mere announcement solved some of the government's problems, its outcome did not solve all the others. Although a clear majority voted to relieve the Liberals of their anti-conscription pledge, the overall result masked one-sided opposition in Quebec. The division resembled 1898 but was starker and emerged in a context of global crisis. The government felt licensed by the vote to take modest steps toward conscription, but still hesitated on its overseas application. Its pro-conscription members were hardly mollified by these steps and a high-profile anti-conscription minister quit. When the pressure for conscription peaked in 1944, the 1942 vote did not reconcile all anti-conscriptionists to the policy the government finally adopted nor did it speed the government along sufficiently to enable it to hold all its pro-conscription ministers.[8]

But if the 1942 vote, like the 1898 one, divided the country, it also, as in 1898, kept the Liberal party from cracking up. Given Canada's basic constitutional principles, such a split would have made the Liberal government unsustainable. In 1898 both parties benefited from the popular referral, as each was internally divided on the question; in 1942 only the Liberals were truly divided. But the relative coherence of the Conservatives in 1942 was deceptive; it reflected how narrow their base had become. No alternative to the Liberals was really imaginable under the circumstances, least of all an English-only coalition, similar to the one formed in 1917. Whereas in the late 1890s the party system was still in the throes of realignment and both parties enjoyed considerable support inside and outside Quebec and among both Catholics and Protestants, by 1942 realignment had been largely accomplished, significantly by the first conscription crisis in 1917 (Johnston et al., 1992, chapter 2; English, 1977). The plebiscite may have exposed divisions, but it is difficult to avoid the suspicion that they would have revealed themselves anyway, perhaps in even more virulent form.

Merely by being conducted, the vote released the government from its earlier pledge and thus allowed it to characterize its reversal as less than an outright betrayal of earlier commitments. It signalled to the government's Quebec supporters just how one-sided opinion was outside Quebec and thus undercut suspicions that the cabinet had a hidden pro-conscription agenda; it added credibility to the government's claim that it was only yielding to opinion and doing so only as casualty figures mounted. Even if the outcome still left the government in an uncomfortable position, it is difficult to imagine the government effecting the policy shift without the vote. And, of course, mere announcement of the vote undercut the very first, and possibly direst, threat to the government, from the formidable Arthur Meighen.

BACK TO THE FUTURE

The 1898 and 1942 votes revealed divisions that probably needed to be uncovered. Where 1898 stalled an initiative that needed to be stalled, 1942 unblocked action that an overwhelming majority believed necessary. What can we say along such lines about the referendum on the Charlottetown Accord? At one point or another, the sequence from Meech Lake to Charlottetown embodied every tactical move ever seen in referendum history, in Canada or elsewhere. Two key moves anticipated the whole process, indeed necessitated it.

Quebec: An Inescapable Referendum?

Robert Bourassa's creation of the Bélanger-Campeau Commission in the summer of 1990 was, we believe, virtually the only move available to him, if his objective was to evade a move to sovereignty. A vote directly on sovereignty at that point may well have carried, so poll readings in the period suggest. According to Cloutier et al., (1992), even the least popular wordings, "séparation" and "indépendance," returned majority support at key moments in 1990 and 1991.[9] Had Bourassa himself come out for sovereignty, it almost certainly would have passed, at least if Pierre Bourgault's logic was right.[10] And had a referendum been called, Bourassa would have felt extreme pressure to come out for the question his own government submitted. Equally, he would have felt pressure to oppose sovereignty. If, then, the immediate twin objectives were to avoid legitimating the sovereignist option itself and, in an emotionally overwrought climate, avoid delegitimating himself by opposing sovereignty, the appointment of a commission was necessary.

Although appointing the Bélanger-Campeau Commission had the virtue of avoiding a referendum in the short run, it was highly likely from the beginning that the commission would nonetheless propose one. Given that sovereignty was on the table, if only rhetorically, a referendum was bound to surface, as 1980 was universally accepted as a binding precedent. Even if the 1980 question was manipulative in its textual form, the rest of the process was deeply respectful of Quebeckers as a democratic people, designed to deliver roughly equally weighted interventions on the Yes and No sides. And in 1980 interventions, not wording, were decisive. If Quebeckers came away from 1980 wary of the divisiveness of referendums, they nonetheless saw the process as legitimate, and as their own.

If the possibility of sovereignty virtually forced a referendum onto the stage, once there, it also became the almost inescapable device for alternatives to a sovereignty question. And if Bélanger-Campeau's specific proposal contained a trap for nationalists (forcing them onto the rhetorical ground of considering offers from the rest of Canada), it also, potentially, contained one for federalists, especially unconditional ones in Ottawa. If the strongest people around Bourassa really wanted serious change to the federation, or if they really wanted sovereignty, the question actually put to Quebeckers could become the offer from the rest of Canada *plus* some further irreducible Quebec minimum. This then could produce an impasse, and set the stage for a move to sovereignty motivated – or justified at least – by a sense of having been rejected by the rest of Canada. In any case, before the summer of 1991 it was already clear that 25 percent of the Canadian electorate – that is, the Quebeckers – would vote on *something*. Would the other 75 percent accept not getting to vote on it as well? Then there was the question of what that something might be. For the federal government to control the question, they would, sooner or later, have to prepare for a referendum themselves.

British Columbia and Alberta Move

Ottawa may have hesitated, but its hand had already been forced by British Columbia and Alberta. In each province the ruling party felt badly damaged by its commitment to the Meech Lake Accord. For Social Credit in British Columbia and the Conservative party in Alberta, acquiescing in that Accord went against their popular bases and divided their legislative caucuses. For any future constitutional tension, a referendum was the obvious safety valve.

The Alberta government was especially vulnerable, for the Meech Lake Accord could be interpreted as compromising prospects of further change to the Senate, and thus seemed to fly in the face of one of Don Getty's earliest rhetorical commitments, to a Triple-E Senate. Weakened by a provincial election in early 1989, Getty tried to turn the Meech Lake Senate terms – provincial nomination, subject to federal approval – to advantage by calling an election to fill the next Alberta Senate vacancy. The venture blew up in his face as the winning candidate, Stan Waters, was a card-carrying member of Preston Manning's Reform party. The upper house was now a bully pulpit for Alberta and Reform opposition to all that Meech Lake stood for. Waters's direct election was a concession to popular sovereignty that made a referendum on further constitutional change the next logical step. The Alberta commitment was in place by spring 1991, not long after Bélanger-Campeau forced the issue in Quebec.

British Columbia was roughly in step with this timetable. The Social Credit government was under fire on many fronts. Its supporters tended to be reflexively anti-Quebec, and one way to secure their adherence was by guaranteeing them the chance to block any future pro-Quebec initiative. At this level, the referendum was a safety valve. At the same time, Social Credit dangled the referendum as a delegitimating device, acting out Dicey's 1890 prescription for blocking Irish Home Rule. For Dicey, the referendum was "the only check on the predominance of party which is at the same time democratic and conservative,"[11] a High Tory statement of the "common sense" logic outlined in chapter 1.

At the same time, the referendum was a move to undermine the NDP opposition. If the matter were solely one of referring a Canada-wide constitutional question, the NDP might sign on comfortably, even enthusiastically. Some of the most virulent criticism of the Meech Lake Accord in British Columbia had come from NDP supporters, and this criticism inevitably implicated NDP leaders for their support of the Accord. They might, thus, welcome referral as a safety valve for their own party. But Social Credit upped the stakes by offering a general-purpose referendum bill, reserving all power of referral to the government itself. This raised the spectre of manipulatory referrals, on one hand, and irresistible pressures for referral, on the other. Neither prospect appealed to social democrats; indeed, they were part of the reason why the left, at least in Westminster systems, had reflexively opposed the whole politics of referral. In effect, the left accepted Dicey's major premise – that electorates are conservative – only to reject the minor premise – that this conservatism is a good thing. Social Credit was mindful of precisely this when it tabled the bill. But New Democrats ducked: they supported the bill themselves.[12] When the British Columbia Legislative Assembly rose in 1991, that province too was pretty much committed to referring any future constitutional measure. Just to drive the populist point home, the very first referendums – mandating citizen-initiated referendums and authorizing the government to create a system for recall of legislators – were conducted along with the provincial general election later that year; both passed overwhelmingly.[13]

Legitimation by the Back Door

At this point, some form of referendum was inescapable, even if much of the political class denied the fact or was oblivious to it. Between Quebec and the two westernmost provinces, about 45 percent of the electorate was already bound to vote on constitutional change.

The three provinces might conceive the constitutional question in different ways, might even work completely at cross purposes. Indeed, the fact of a Quebec vote seemed to foreclose any creative response to the British Columbia and Alberta challenges, as the Conservative government's Quebec caucus blocked a referendum move in the late fall of 1991 (see above, chapter 2). But this could not be more than a holding action. Even though negotiations proceeded rather heedlessly of the referendum possibility – a point to which we return below – as negotiations approached their end, all participants seemed to embrace without hesitation the ultimate the necessity of popular referral.

In effect, negotiators were forced onto ground, prepared willy-nilly by the three provinces, of *legitimation-delegitimation*. Opponents of accommodating Quebec – whether out of hostility to Quebec proper or out of resistance to the rest-of-Canada baggage entailed by placating Quebec – now had the chance to reveal the unviability of "macroconstitutional" change, as Russell (1993) has styled it. Supporters of a constitutional settlement, unlike its opponents, had no great wish to make their own task more difficult. But if they really had something to sell, a successful sales venture might buy more constitutional peace than a process conducted entirely behind closed doors.[14] Most pointedly, if a majority of Quebeckers could be induced to accept the same package as voters elsewhere, sovereignists would find it very difficult to resurrect their particular project for years to come.

Externalization of Intra-Party Tension

For some opponents, especially inside the Liberal and New Democratic parties, delegitimation was the primary end, but externalization of party tension also was, or ought to have been, a consideration. For instance, opponents worried about the integrity of the Charter of Rights still tended to see themselves as Liberals or New Democrats and did not wish to break the country's party-system mould, or at least not their own party's place in it.

For other opponents, delegitimating the constitutional project may have been only secondary to smashing existing party alignments. A referendum would substantiate their claim that these insurgents, and not parties traditionally in control of the agenda, commanded the broad majority of constitutional opinion. This, of course, was the position of Preston Manning and Reform. It was also the position, implicitly, of Lucien Bouchard and the Bloc Québécois, although here breaking the party-system mould was necessarily linked to redefining the polity. On the other side of both these divides were mainstream Conservatives. A referendum might serve Conservative interests twice over: it might provide a forum in which residual Conservative party loyalty might be mobilized to buttress the Yes share; yet it might allow recalcitrant Conservatives to defect without threatening the government's survival. A Yes victory would neutralize further expression of constitutional discontent, for it would be won on ground chosen by opponents and would represent the settled opinion of the very people opponents had earlier claimed to represent. A No victory, in contrast, would be exactly what opponents wanted, and it would almost certainly halt the constitutional process. But such a result, even if it left Canada-Quebec relations in doubt, might at least get the Conservative party off the hook, as it might Liberals and New Democrats.

Some intimation of the consequences for the party system can be gleaned from tables 10–1 and 10–2, for the rest of Canada and Quebec respectively. Reading left to right, each table gives information about 1988 positions, 1988–92 turnover, and 1988–92–3 transitions respectively. In the leftmost column is the 1988 vote, including non-voting, as recalled by 1992 post-referendum respondents. Next appears the 1992 referendum vote within 1988 voting blocs. Finally appear 1993 vote breakdowns, within 1988–92 groups, where 1993 vote is from the post-election wave of the 1992–3 panel, and 1992–3 turnover comprises true panel changes, not 1993 recollections of 1992 behaviour.

Outside Quebec, party differences in 1992 vote roughly mirror those for party identification controls in chapter 7. Voters for each major party were markedly more likely to vote Yes than were 1988 non-voters and others.[15] But much of the difference was a product of turnout, as 1988 non-voters remained relatively unmobilized in 1992. Of 1988 non-voters who turned out in 1992, 29 percent voted Yes; the corresponding figure for 1988 Conservatives was 46 percent. Differences were proportionately smaller for Liberals and New Democrats; among active 1992 voters, 1988 New Democrats were only 7 points more likely than 1988 non-voters to vote Yes. In short, old-line parties could not deliver their followers, and gaps among old parties rivalled that across the summary voter/non-voter divide. Most telling of all, the Conservative party could not deliver a majority of its rest-of-Canada base.

Roughly speaking, the Conservative party broke in two at the Yes/ No divide.[16] A 1988 Conservative who voted Yes in 1992 was over twice as likely as one who voted No to stay Conservative in 1993. A 1988 Conservative who voted No was almost twice as likely as one who voted Yes to shift to Reform. Indeed, among these voters, Reform was the outright majority choice. The Reform percentage among

Table 10–1
The Referendum and the Party System: Rest of Canada

1988 Vote	1992 Vote		1993 Vote				
			Con	Lib	NDP	Reform	Other[2]/None
Con	Yes	42	**40**	27	0	28	5
	No	49	18	16	4	**49**	13
31	None	9	**41**	17	7	4	32
			29	21	3	**38**	8
Lib	Yes	38	10	**77**	2	6	6
	No	52	10	**63**	3	17	7
26	None	10	5	**44**	0	22	29
			10	**67**	2	13	8
NDP	Yes	31	9	33	**34**	13	11
	No	57	6	**32**	23	28	11
19	None	12	10	**39**	15	0	**36**
			8	**33**	25	21	14
None[1]	Yes	18	8	**41**	15	3	**31**
	No	45	13	29	5	25	**29**
21	None	37	3	26	4	6	**62**
			9	30	7	14	**40**

[1] Includes ineligible in 1988
[2] Mainly National Party

1988 Conservatives who voted Yes was not shabby either, but in this group about as many went Liberal as Reform. To No voters among former Conservatives, in contrast, the Liberal party had little appeal. 1988 Conservatives who voted No were also much more likely than their Yes counterparts to drop out or vote for some other party in 1993. This may indicate disgruntlement without outlet; they may have been Conservatives disgusted with their own party, unable to stomach any alternative (not even Reform, not even the Liberals), and so forced out of the system entirely. Note that the Yes/No 1993 turnout difference finds no parallel among either 1988 Liberals or New Democrats.

For Liberals, the Charlottetown Accord was hardly any litmus test at all. It is true that Liberal No voters were almost three times as likely as Liberal Yes voters to shift to Reform. But even among the No the Reform percentage was small. The dominant fact in Liberal turnover is that overwhelming majorities of both 1992 Yes and No voters among 1988 Liberals stayed Liberal in 1993. The least loyal (in contrast to the Conservative case) were 1988 Liberals who sat 1992 out, although even here a clear majority stayed with the party.

For 1988 New Democrats, 1992 was a divide twice over. First, the 1992 vote made a modest difference to a 1988 New Democrats' likelihood of staying NDP; the party held onto roughly one-third of its 1992 Yes voters, as compared with one-quarter of its No voters. Second, No voters were over twice as likely as Yes ones to shift to Reform. Even among No voters, however, more shifted to the Liberals than to Reform. Indeed, the probability that a 1988 New Democrat would vote Liberal was essentially unaffected by the 1992 vote; for 1988 New Democrats, 1992 polarized their own party against Reform. All this said, the forces working against the NDP in 1993 lay mainly outside the Charlottetown events, as a near plurality among New Democrats who followed the party line and a clear plurality among those who did not went Liberal in 1993, moved, that is, to another party in the Yes coalition. The most powerful factor orienting NDP defection, then, was party proximity on the left-right continuum, the continuum masked most efficiently by Charlottetown politics (see Figure 5–2)

In Quebec, divisions were, if anything, even clearer. First of all, the Conservative party absolutely failed to deliver the troops. A clear majority of 1988 Conservative voters voted No in 1992, whereas the Yes share in this group was barely larger than among 1988 non-voters, although markedly larger than among 1988 New Democrats. Here is a vivid indication of just how nationalist the Conservative Quebec base was.[17] The one party to deliver a Yes majority was the Liberal party, and 1988 Liberals constituted the majority within the Yes bloc.[18] The Liberals were, of course, the most full-bloodedly federalist party, and much of this Liberal Yes came from anglophones and allophones.

Within each party in Quebec, the Yes/No division prefigured 1993. Of Conservatives who voted No, the overwhelming majority went straight to the Bloc Québécois. Although a significant fraction of Conservative Yes voters also went to the Bloc (a 1988 Conservative who voted Yes was only slightly more likely to vote Conservative than Bloc in 1993), the vast majority stayed in the federalist camp, the largest single number going Liberal. Among 1988 Liberals, Yes voters stayed loyal to their party, while No voters were mostly likely to defect to the Bloc (although at a markedly lower rate than No-voting Tories). In sum, the Bloc inherited an overwhelming fraction of the No vote, the Liberals won a large fraction of the Yes, and a large minority of the Yes (especially among 1988 non-voters) also went to the Bloc. The Bloc emerged strengthened, the Conservatives exceedingly en-

Table 10–2
The Referendum and the Party System: Quebec

1988 Vote	1992 Vote		1993 Vote			
			Con	Lib	Bloc	Other[2]/None
Con	Yes	32	26	**35**	23	17
	No	62	13	10	**68**	7
33	None	7	–	–	–	–
			17	17	**54**	12
Lib	Yes	65	8	**78**	3	10
	No	31	15	24	**51**	10
26	None	5	–	–	–	–
			11	**60**	19	11
NDP	Yes	10	–	–	–	–
	No	76	0	5	**90**	5
8	None	14	–	–	–	–
			4	7	**69**	24
None[1]	Yes	18	0	**44**	42	14
	No	55	0	4	**78**	9
28	None	27	11	0	20	**69**
			2	12	**60**	26

[1] Includes ineligible in 1988

[2] Includes NDP

feebled, and the Liberals strengthened relative to 1984 but not relative to the pre-Mulroney era.

Did the referendum itself shatter the Conservatives? As a force in its own right, the referendum probably did not. The Conservatives had been weak in published polls for months, indeed years, before Charlottetown, and may even have bottomed out six to eight months before the referendum. Some of the party's weakness probably did stem from frustration with the chronic constitutional crisis, which was felt keenly in both the francophobe base outside Quebec and the nationalist base inside that province. Certainly, both Reform and the Bloc made serious advances in polls long before the constitutional crisis peaked. If the ultimate Conservative collapse was in part constitutionally driven, the referendum itself was probably only an incident along the way. And some of the collapse had other origins – in the GST controversy, the recession, and the incredible unpopularity of

Brian Mulroney. It is also possible that the Conservatives could have recovered. After Mulroney's retirement, the party's standing improved, so much so that they entered the 1993 campaign on at least a competitive footing (Johnston et al., 1994). That the ultimate collapse uncovered old constititional lesions yet again does not allow us to dismiss absolutely a potential role for the referendum in externalizing Conservative-party tension. But the potential was not realized.

If any party benefited from externalization it was the Liberals. Taking Quebec and the rest of Canada together, the Liberal party was at least as successful as the Conservatives in delivering Yes votes. And Liberals were least punished by their commitment to the Yes side, perhaps because that commitment seemed diffident.[19] The Liberals did lose Quebec No voters to the Bloc, but gained Conservative Yes voters in compensation. Outside Quebec, Liberals held onto both their Yes and No voters and made positive gains among both NDP and Conservative Yes voters. Again, though, we must be careful about attributing too much of this to the referendum. The critical thing about the Liberals is that they overcame their diffidence and did participate in negotiating the Accord and promoting the Yes. It may even have helped that their divisions over the Accord, exemplified by Pierre Trudeau's intervention, were unimpeachably federalist, indeed centralist. All this burnished their credentials as a party of national unity, the sole viable one left in 1993.

Calling Bluffs?

In a sense, bluffs were also being called, one unsuccessfully, the other perhaps successfully. The pro-Accord coalition gambled that opposition outside Quebec to the Meech Lake and post-Meech Lake agenda was weaker than its pretensions, that it resembled the purported temperance consensus of the 1890s. If actually forced to place their opposition to recognizing Quebec as a distinct society in the context of national crisis and to vote on it, rather than merely respond to opinion polls, voters might mute their objections – hold their noses, to use a recurring Canadian constitutional image – and say, however hesitantly, Yes. Many would resist this, of course, but a broad middle who disliked the distinct society clause for itself might nonetheless accept it if Quebeckers, in a parallel act, bound themselves to Canada. The strategy failed, of course. The rest-of-Canada bluff was not one after all.

Or so it has been portrayed after the fact. It is true that opinion on the distinct society clause was a major pivot for the vote (chapter 3); it would be bizarre if this were not so. But it does not follow from this that the clause to recognize Quebec as a distinct society is what killed the Accord. What was rejected in 1992 had much more than a distinct society clause in it. In some places Aboriginal self-government, notwithstanding general approbation, might have hurt. In others Senate reform might have hurt; it certainly did not help much. And Senate reform certainly did hurt in an indirect way, for it entailed further shifts in representation in the House of Commons, most notably the 25 percent guarantee.

The 25 percent guarantee, as chapter 3 also revealed, was among the most powerful factors in the vote and, of all factors, the one tilted most one-sidedly against the Yes. We cannot dismiss the possibility that without that guarantee the Accord would have passed outside Quebec – narrowly perhaps, but passed nonetheless. Recall from Table 3–5 that the referendum-day coefficient on the guarantee was 0.20 and from Figure 3–1 that nearly 80 percent of voters outside Quebec opposed this element. If nothing else in the system was disturbed, removal of the guarantee would add 16 percent to the Yes share. Of course, the guarantee came out of Senate bargaining, so removing the guarantee also effectively meant removing the new Senate. But as only slightly over 20 percent favoured the new body and as the Senate coefficient was only 0.14, the loss of support on this side of the ledger would be tiny (about 3 percent) compared with the gain (16 percent) on the other. The difficulty with this argument is its assumption about stability in coefficients: in particular, how much impact from the 25 percent guarantee would get absorbed into impact from the distinct society clause? The implication in the thought exercise is that by removing offending parts of the deal, we move the intercept up. This is tantamount to saying that many people who say they oppose recognition of Quebec as a distinct society (and who oppose Aboriginal self-government) would nonetheless vote Yes; we infer this because in the actual event opposition to the distinct society clause was only slightly more consequential statistically than opposition to the 25 percent guarantee. But removing the guarantee from the package may just shift the ostensible grounds of opposition. Opinion on both the guarantee and the distinct society clause was affected by feeling about Quebec, and feeling about Quebec was the biggest single background factor in the vote. Removing the guarantee might just have caused that Quebec feeling to flow through the more narrow channel of the distinct society clause, with little net effect on the overall prospects for a Yes. But not all the Quebec sentiment was negative, and Quebec sentiment was not the whole story of response to the Accord. It still seems reasonable to conjecture that the Accord would have come rather closer to passing, indeed might have received an outright majority, had the 25 percent guarantee (and the Senate) not been included. This line of reasoning implies that the original Meech Lake Accord had a better chance of passing in a referendum than did the Charlottetown variant which allegedly gave more to the rest of Canada.

It has been argued (Russell, 1993) that the 25 percent guarantee was an idea whose time just had not yet come, that its novelty denied it a serious airing. With time and serious debate, Canadians outside Quebec might have warmed to it. We think this is unlikely, and adduce the other Quebec element, the distinct society clause, as evidence. Recall the thought experiment in the preceding paragraph – an Accord without the 25 percent guarantee (and without the Senate) but with the distinct society clause. If the experiment made sense and the Accord did pass, it would still do so *in spite of,* not because of, the clause. The balance of support on the distinct society clause was not markedly different in 1992 from 1988 (compare Blais and Crête, 1992). If five years of exposure, debate, and fine-tuning failed to move opinion on the distinct society clause, which might have proved irrelevant outside Quebec, why should any amount of debate change opinion on the 25 percent guarantee, which was, beyond a shadow of a doubt, a zero-sum proposal to limit the political power of the fastest-growing provinces?

Had a guarantee-less Accord passed in spite of its distinct society clause, this would have been notwithstanding Pierre Trudeau's objections, for his objections were still heavily tied to that clause. By priming the distinct society clause, he added weight to objections already in place because of the guarantee. What if he had not intervened? It strikes us as unlikely that another intervenor would have picked up the slack. The women's movement had next to no effect, and was the most likely of all intervenors to be seen as split. Preston Manning ended the campaign with a visibility rivalling Trudeau's, but without Trudeau's ability to mobilize voters. Manning's turf had already been ploughed, as early oppositon to the Accord was heavily concentrated among Manning's natural constituents; they did not need him to tell them what to do. That he reflected their sentiments may have helped Manning and his party in 1993, but that is another story. The vote-shifting margin was not on the francophobic right but in the electorate's broad centre, among voters who had earlier responded to Trudeau precisely out of concern for the country's unity but also out of anxiety to square the quest for unity with deep-seated values. Such voters were, if anything, repelled by Preston Manning. But a clear signal from Trudeau that the Charlottetown Accord was the wrong response to the French-Canadian project would turn many against it. Figure 5–7 suggests that his net impact was 10 points, which took the deal from a comfortable majority to the razor's edge. This left support vulnerable to other influences. Had Trudeau not intervened, other factors might have reduced the Yes share; ballot measures generally do lose ground over campaigns. But without Trudeau, the Charlotte-town Accord might still have retained a cushion, enough support that general arguments, especially about moving on, would still be relevant. Also, the strategic considerations that told against it at the end might have been neutralized, perhaps even reversed.[20]

What if even Quebec's minimum were denied? Could it be that the real bluff called in 1992 was Quebec's? The 1992 vote itself was not about sovereignty, of course, but why it was not may be one of the event's central political facts. Sovereignists were eager to detach the No vote from the larger national issue. Of course, they were eager for a No to the Accord, as a Yes would prejudice the sovereignist project. But the critical fact is that they did not want the No to be rhetorically defined as to Canada itself: to sustain their own option they had to keep it off the table. Voters in the rest of Canada may thus be forgiven if they detected lack of nerve. Nerve was also lacking on the Yes side, as it too declined to play the sovereignty card. But this may have reflected anxiety as much about the saleability of the Accord as about sovereignty. If pro-Accord forces had styled rejection of the Accord as rejection of Canada, they might have extorted more votes for the deal, but they would also have risked sinking the country along with the deal.

The bottom line of November 1992 appears as Table 10–3. Quebec respondents were asked how they would choose, if forced, between sovereignty (where the term was defined as "Quebec is no longer a part of Canada") and "federalism as it is now."[21] The answer was as close to 50:50 as it is possible to get. Clearly, self-described sovereignists were not bluffing: 75 percent would choose a sovereign Quebec, a Quebec outside Canada. If it seems odd that 15 percent of sovereignists would choose Canada, note that 16 percent of non-francophones would choose a sovereign Quebec. The critical group, in any case, are voters who have doubts about sovereignty but who as francophones have an interest in shoring up the position of the one North American jurisdiction where they constitute a majority. Here too preference for the status quo over sovereignty was overwhelming.[22]

Do these data suggest that a Quebec bluff was called? At issue are three things. First is a conjunction of sampling error and context, the possibility that in late 1992 a narrow anti-sovereignist majority did not really exist. The second and third issues are mirror-image claims about persuasion for the longer run: How available are non-sovereignists for suasion in the event of no further negotiations? How

Table 10–3
Sovereignty versus the Status Quo: Quebec Voters Only

| | | Francophone | | |
Choice	Non-Francophone	Non-Sovereignist	Sovereignist	All
Canada as Now	81	68	15	47
Sovereign Quebec	16	20	75	44
Don't Know	3	12	11	10
	(115)	(252)	(291)	(659)

available are sovereignists for suasion in the event of a relatively pro-Quebec outcome of some future negotiation?

With a sample of this size, the standard error is ± 2 percentage points, and so the close result of Table 10–3 might be even closer still, possibly indicating a tiny sovereignist majority. This is a closer result than implied by most polls since 1980, but seems close to the norm for this late crisis period. The pattern suggests that Bourassa was wise to move the vote off sovereignty, for the mere fact of sovereignty as the question on 26 October 1992 would signal another breakdown in the Canada-Quebec relationship. Given that sovereignist passions had been deliberately cooled in the referendum campaign, the closeness of the result hints that Quebeckers, collectively, were not bluffing, and might have moved to sovereignty in the event of complete rebuff.[23]

What then of the longer run? If it comes to a vote on sovereignty versus the status quo, could more votes for Canada be teased out of non-sovereignists? Alternatively, could they be moved the other way? The answer, of course, depends on how unconditional their opposition to sovereignty is. Chapter 8 hints that for a critical number, opposition would not be absolute. A proto-sovereignist disposition could be detected inside the non-sovereignist camp. Some had only a mild affection for Canada, not all feared the economics of secession, and some believed French to be threatened in a Quebec inside Canada. The typical francophone non-sovereignist liked Quebec more than Canada, if only by a small margin. Although relatively fearful of secession's economic fallout, francophone non-sovereignists were less so than non-francophones. Most strikingly, among francophone non-sovereignists perceptions of threat to the French language were roughly in balance, and were almost exactly halfway between the perceptions of sovereignists, on one side, and of non-francophones, on the other.

Table 10–4
Support for the Status Quo: Francophone Non-Sovereignists *(N= 220)*

	Coefficient	Standard Error
Feeling for Quebec	-0.44*	0.18
Feeling for Canada	0.70***	0.18
Linguistic Threat	-0.08	0.06
Economic Concern	0.24*	0.11
Intercept	0.48	0.15
R²-adjusted	0.13	

*p < 0.05; ** p < 0.01; *** p < 0.001.

How these factors played into preference for the status quo in 1992 is presented in Table 10–4. On the two most powerful factors – feeling about Canada itself and economic concern – the balance of opinion favoured Canada. It is true that francophone non-sovereignists, on balance, liked Quebec more than Canada, but in an absolute sense this was a relatively pro-Canada group. And this group was very anxious about the economics of secession, even if not as anxious as non-francophones. The group's anxieties about language were not engaged in the choice, obviously a good thing from the federalist perspective.

What about suasion on the other side? The experiment in chapter 8 indicates that sovereignist ranks are thinned when the central element in sovereignty, separation from Canada, is spelled out. Even so the number remaining is formidable, and there may be little further room for movement. The real question about 1992, in any case, was not how many "real" sovereigntists there are, but whether *any* self-described sovereignists would accept a settlement which reaffirms the basic Quebec-Canada link even as it gives Quebec disproportionate power in the federation? If that number is small, then much of the Quebec argument is, once again, undercut. Arguments for the necessity of an asymmetric deal have two parts, and previous paragraphs considered only one part, the chance that federalist Quebeckers, if rebuffed, would vote to pull out of Canada. The other part is how likely sovereignists would be to accept a pro-Quebec deal. If this likelihood is low, then macro-constitutional negotiation seems also pretty pointless, involving the self-mutilation by the rest of Canada to no real end.

Putting all the evidence together hints that Quebec's hand – where Quebec voters were the hand – was objectively rather weak. Our reading of francophone non-sovereignists is that an overwhelming

272 The Challenge of Direct Democracy

majority, in 1992 at least, would vote to accept the status quo, if the alternative is sovereignty. Sovereignists, on the other hand, are highly unlikely to endorse any plausible constitutional proposal, out of the perfectly reasonable fear that doing so will compromise the ultimate objective. In this very peculiar sense, the 1992 referendum called Quebec's bluff. We should be absolutely be clear what we are *not* saying. We are not saying that Quebeckers will necessarily reject sovereignty, only that very few Quebeckers are really at the negotiating margin: most would either embrace the status quo or reject any imaginable alternative to it. And we are not rejecting the proposition that entrenchment of the Charlottetown Accord would have inhibited sovereignist moves; such moves would be hard to make in face of Quebec itself having embraced a pan-Canadian settlement.

A Failure of Anticipation

If success in 1992 would have spiked sovereignists' guns, rendering a sovereignty referendum infeasible, could such an objective have been pursued more shrewdly? From this point of view – their own central one, presumably – federalists mishandled the constitutional dossier. For all this chapter's talk about strategic uses of referendums, the most striking thing about the 1992 episode is how unstrategic it was.

In most accounts of referendum strategy, one detects threads recognizable to game theorists. Among the range of alternative possible equilibrium outcomes, key actors identify their preferred ones. In the jargon of the trade, they present the game to themselves in extensive form. Each actor reasons back from terminations of the game to see how, if at all, the preferred outcome can be reached. If only one can be reached, this will be identified as the "subgame perfect equilibrium" and all players, some resentfully perhaps, play their appointed roles.

Accounts of Ottawa's internal deliberations hint at such reasoning, most notably Norman Spector's 1991 thought exercise of working back from an imaginable late 1992 Quebec vote and the prime minister's spring 1992 ruminations and threats along the same lines (Lisée, 1994b, pp. 154, 289–91). Similar thinking was urged on Ottawa from the outside (Simpson, 1991; Johnston, 1991). But reasoning back from a referendum was not the dominant mode. Rather, the interests to be conciliated were always defined in terms of who was at the table, and the deal ultimately struck reflected almost exclusively considerations internal to the negotiation. Most critically, the Pearson accord had no serious prospect of success in the inevitable Quebec vote – indeed, it might have forced Bourassa to refer sovereignty as such – whatever its negotiators might have gleaned from noisy communications with him. But once a Senate with equal provincial representation was on the table, as it came to be with the Pearson deal, it could not be taken off. This then produced the further representational deal that so alienated the rest of country, especially the fastest growing provinces in the West. Of course, all deliberations about the Senate took pressures for reform of that institution seriously, when more pointed probing of popular bases of the constitution – probing inspired by a prospective referendum campaign – might have revealed the shallowness of opinion.

All this is easy to say, of course, and it is hard to fault a government for recoiling from a path which opponents would inevitably call Bonapartist (or words to that effect). Restraint was especially compelling given that an amending formula was already on the books, one controlled, more or less, by provincial governments. If any provincial government felt undercut by a referendum move on Ottawa's part, that undercutting could become a rhetorical factor in its own right, a basis for opposition to the ballot measure. But if it did, the protestation might not necessarily help the provincial premier making it. A provincial government, securely in control of the legislature which in turn holds the power to give or withold the province's assent, might refuse to follow its own electorate's dictates. But this too seems unlikely, even under the best of circumstances. Among the hardest provincial nuts to crack were British Columbia and Alberta, the very ones which by late 1991 had breached the referendum dike. In the end, this is the fact that makes Ottawa's 1991–2 movements the hardest to fathom. If Ottawa really wanted to secure Canada-wide approval for a constitutional package, they ought to have realized by late 1991 that almost half the electorate was already committed to voting on it anyway, and tailored the package accordingly. There were never any guarantees that even a tailored package would pass, but it seems that the key players did not even try to make it more acceptable. It is not enough to say that getting around Quebec's own referendum commitment was conceptually challenging. But that mere reference to Quebec's ownership of its own process in 1991 sufficed to brush aside commitments in place in Alberta and British Columbia indicates astonishing insensitivity in Ottawa.

They Also Serve Who Only Stand and Wait

This brings us full circle. After the collapse of the Meech Lake Accord, it was impossible not to try *something*. This point has already been made about Robert Bourassa. The succession of steps and objectives worked through over the last several pages started with Bourassa's need to temporize. Temporizing may have been a way of life for him, but doing so follows a grand – and useful – Canadian tradition. Sir John A. Macdonald was, after all, known with some affection as "Old Tomorrow." But Bourassa could not temporize alone, for that would force him down the sovereignty path. The rest of Canada had to labour mightily to make some sort of offer, if only as a token of the seriousness with which Quebec must be taken. The failure of the offer may leave the door to Quebec sovereignty open, and so there is some reason for federalists to lament, if not the failure of that particular Accord, then the failure to come up with a better one. But the very attempt served a larger objective – to keep sovereignty off the 1992 ballot, to allow passions to cool. If Bourassa's temporizing made a Quebec referendum more or less inevitable, so did it make a rest-of-Canada vote inevitable. As a necessary part of getting through the 1990–2 crisis, then, the referendum on the Charlottetown Accord served merely by being held.

11 Conclusions

The lessons of the 1992 referendum can be found at several levels. The most obvious question is: What did voters mean by rejecting the Charlottetown Accord? The answers to this question tell a story about Canadian constitutional politics. Rejection of this particular document naturally makes one ask if any measure would have passed. Would Canadians have rejected any proposal the political elite was realistically likely to make? This question shades into cross-national comparisons. The final question is the most general, probably the most enduring: Did Canadian voters really know what they were doing?

WHAT DID THE NO MEAN?

Did the rest of Canada say No to Quebec, to Quebec's demands at least? The answer must be yes, with qualifications. Four things argue for this conclusion:

- A majority of voters rejected recognition of Quebec as a distinct society, even after it had been watered down relative to the Meech Lake version.
- An overwhelming majority rejected Quebec's guarantee of 25 percent of the seats in the House of Commons.
- Most voters rejected arguments that failure of the Accord would lead to Quebec's separation, and affirmed the view that Quebec always asks for more. In other words, voters did not share the elite's belief that the country's integrity was truly threatened.

– The most powerful master sentiment was simple feeling for Quebec. This cuts both ways, of course, as positive feeling inclined voters to the Yes side just as negative feeling inclined them to the No, and positive – at least lukewarm – feeling toward Quebec was not in short supply.

Now for the qualifications. To say that voters in the rest of Canada disliked each Quebec element is not necessarily to say that they would reject a generally workable deal just because of one particular objectionable element. The problem may have been the compounding of objectionable Quebec-related features, especially piling the 25 percent guarantee on top of the distinct society clause. Perhaps they would have accepted, however reluctantly, a smaller package. Speculation aside, no evidence can be found that a majority outside Quebec was prepared to accept what were presented as Quebec's 1992 terms.

In rejecting the Quebec elements in the package, were voters affirming equality of provinces, a principle that enjoyed a vogue in 1980s constitutional discussion? We have no direct evidence, but hints can be teased out by indirect means. On one hand, a small majority favoured equal representation by province in a new Senate. On the other hand, voters rejected giving an equal-representation Senate more power. It might be argued that repudiation of the 25 percent guarantee was an affirmation of equality among provinces, on grounds that no province should get special constitutional treatment. But rejection of the guarantee is perfectly consistent with continued commitment to representation by population. The guarantee arguably offended against both equality of provinces and equality of persons. This ambiguous pattern suggests the following. Voters are unlikely to think about such abstractions as a matter of routine, and have little occasion to ponder the boundary between the two equalities. Outside Quebec, voters probably do affirm both equalities – of persons and of provinces. Quebec is threatened by equality of provinces, however, and the rest of Canada seems unlikely to acquiesce in any insurance policy written especially for Quebec. For decades Quebec's interests were covered by the principle of equality of persons: Quebec had so many persons that its share of House seats was huge, and it was pivotal to forming governments. The proper operation of this system required submerging the principle of equality among provinces (it is entirely likely, of course, that so long as no politician articulated the principle, it received little affirmation in the public at large). Various forces in the 1980s brought equality of provinces to the fore, however, in particular the 1982 amending formula, demands for Senate reform, and equal application of the Charter of Rights to all provinces. Now that parliamentary supremacy – where the House dominates Parliament – is under challenge, being pivotal in Parliament seems less and less a sure guarantee of Quebec's interests. And now Quebec is beginning to count for less in the House itself. If all this is true, the portents in the Charlottetown vote are not reassuring.

Was the vote a rejection of other ethnic groups, of minority rights in general? Here the answer is, once again, a mixed positive. In the negative, it must be said that voters supported the principle of Aboriginal self-government, and even believed that failure of the Charlottetown Accord ought not to stand in the way of recognition of this principle. But what did voters mean by such self-government? Our one piece of evidence from 1993 suggests that voters saw self-government for Aboriginal peoples as municipal in character, not as recognition of Aboriginal peoples as nations apart. More generally, most voters gave priority to majority rule at the expense of minority rights, and this position was not taken out of mere ignorance, for the best-informed were the most majority-oriented. And this orientation was a critical factor in the vote. It is difficult to avoid the conclusion that a populist, majoritarian procedure delivered a populist, majoritarian result.

Was the vote also a repudiation of the political class? For many voters, it must have been. First of all, evaluation of the pro-Accord coalition (not just of Brian Mulroney, of whom more in a moment) was an important factor in the vote. Non-partisans were most likely to say No, but most voters actively identified with a party also said No. Not even the Conservatives could deliver a majority of their 1988 base, and only a tiny majority of voters still identified with them in 1992 said Yes. A Yes vote required that voters still thought quite highly of the parties' current leadership. On this, the electorate was divided; the number who liked federal leaders and provincial premiers was not small, but disliking outweighed liking.

Very few voters admitted to liking Brian Mulroney. By 1992 he may have been the most unpopular prime minister in Canadian history. Certainly, his ratings on the 100-point "thermometer" scale were the lowest returned by any political figure since the device was first used in the 1970s. And evaluation of Mulroney was a factor in assessment of the Accord, independently of feelings toward the rest of the pro-Accord coalition. The vote must have been, in part, a repudiation of his leadership, ironically so in light of his own role in the events before July 1992. Moreover, divisions in the electorate over leaders, especially over Mulroney, foreshadowed the electoral events of 1993. One year after the referendum, the Conservative party split roughly where it had in the referendum itself. Even if the referendum was not the active force in inducing the split, it was a sensitive indicator of pressures inside the Conservatives' electoral coalition.

Whether the referendum was an active force in the 1993 result or merely a passive indicator of underlying forces is a very important question but beyond the competence of this book. We do know that on the eve of the 1993 vote the Conservatives seemed to have recovered some, if not all, of their 1988 position, and that the Reform surge originating in the late 1980s and early 1990s seemed to have stalled (Johnston et al., 1994). But the 1992 campaign may still have given Reform and Preston Manning priceless free publicity, on which the party was able to capitalize at the key moment in 1993. At the same time, the core issue in 1992, Canada-Quebec relations, had been since 1984 both the strategic opportunity for the Conservative party and the primary source of tension inside its ranks. In 1988 keeping this division off the agenda was critical to Conservative success. Its centrality to the politics of 1992 may still have rankled too much in 1993.

Finally, was the Accord a victim of the recession? The answer here also seems to be yes. Unemployed voters and voters reporting financial reverses in the preceding twelve months were disproportionately likely to vote No. Some of this may reflect ongoing class differences, of course. But other dimensions of class were controlled in our estimations and still these two characteristics burned through to the vote. Emphasis on the short-term nature of these effects is reinforced by the contrary tendency of an indicator of long-term economic differences – region.

All this has been about Canada outside Quebec. What of Quebec itself? The basic lesson about that province lies not so much in some summary judgment on what Quebeckers meant by voting No as in the proper way to think about Quebec: as an electorate divided into three parts, and subject to close, essentially partisan contestation. On almost any question, the effective battleground for Quebec is quite narrow, consisting as it does of francophone non-sovereignists, less than half the electorate. The relative advantage of No forces in 1992 – of anti-Ottawa forces more generally – in the other, precommitted component of the electorate is over two to one. Thus to carry a measure such as the Charlottetown Accord in Quebec as a whole requires a very one-sided result among francophone non-sovereignists in particular. Of the part of the Quebec electorate that was realistically available to vote Yes – francophone non-sovereignists combined with non-francophones – a clear majority did so. It is still worth asking why the pivotal francophone group did not rally more to the agreement. Some of the answer is sentimental: not everyone in this group loved Canada so much that they were prepared to buy just anything for the country's sake. Some of the answer was calculating: not every non-sovereignist believes that the economic consequences of sovereignty were so dire that any deal must be accepted to avert a split. In any case, by voting day both the Yes and the No sides claimed that sovereignty was not the issue. The deal itself did not give Quebec what it allegedly set out to get, an altered division of powers, but by then Quebec voters did not seem much troubled by that. The real fear may have been that the proposed Senate threatened a real alteration in the balance of power at the centre for which the 25 percent guarantee was no real insurance. In any case, the francophone non-sovereignist middle group was more pro-Accord than the rest of Canada was. Indeed, in being very closely split, this group uncannily resembled the best-informed voters outside Quebec.

WOULD CANADIANS EVER SAY YES?

We are not convinced that any and every post-1982 constitutional proposal is bound to fail, not even proposals with a modest bundling of elements. Our analyses suggest that removing the 25 percent guarantee might have brought the Charlottetown Accord closer to success. Of course, this also necessarily implies removing the Senate provisions, making the deal look much like its immediate predecessor, the Meech Lake Accord. But we stand by our intuition in chapter 10 that Meech might have passed if subjected to a real vote, rather than the hypothetical one of opinion polls. The Charlottetown Accord was simply too much. As well, most of the governments supporting it were unpopular, some deeply so. Some of that unpopularity reflected the constitutional preoccupation itself, to be sure, but by no means could all of it have done so. It did not help any of these governments, or the deal itself, that all of this struck voters as a diversion during the economic recession. Throughout this period a basic political fact had been Pierre Trudeau's continued presence in the wings. Had he not been available to walk on stage, his legacy might not have been so secure; this seems to be a direct implication of the logic of intervenors and voter cue-taking. In this respect, then, we do not accept the conclusions in Lusztig (1994), that Canadian constitutional negotiations are bound to fail.

More precisely, we are not convinced that they *were* bound to fail. We may now truly have witnessed a culture shift, but not so much before the Meech Lake process began as in and after that process. Closed-door negotiation, once something Canadians took for granted, has now acquired the status of a script, a heuristic, to borrow another chapter 1 motif. Any future package is vulnerable to being styled as yet another re-enactment of what is now widely seen as the "Meech Lake style" (Cairns, 1991; Jeffrey, 1993). Outside Quebec, mere invocation of the words "Meech Lake" may suffice to shut down further analysis of substance. Even if we are not absolutely convinced that every imaginable product of late 1980s–early 1990s controversy was bound to fail on referral, the accumulation of actual failure and the propagation of a folk wisdom may have made Lusztig's analysis self-confirming.

Of course, more than the Meech Lake style is at work here. Initiatives that work against the grain of majority sentiment are hard to sell, so Canadians' behaviour in 1992 was hardly peculiar. Electorates at large are culturally conservative, and analyses which imply that electoral change commonly bespeaks a thirst for cultural novelty are jejeune, to say the least. This was Dicey's point at the turn of the century. And any imaginable future constitutional initiative in Canada is as likely to work against the grain as the Meech Lake and Charlottetown Accords did. Many will find this cause for regret. But is the fundamental problem in the electorate? Some of the problem may lie in the amending formulas in the Constitution Act, 1982, which are essays in rigidity. But the problem lies mostly with the way the question is posed. It presupposes that the people are somehow to be faulted for reluctance to change, for carrying out the mission Dicey assigned them. If one believes in constitutionalism, however, rigidity is not unambiguously bad. A very strong presumption in favour of the status quo is one defining element in a constitutional culture. Of course, constitutions must evolve, they must adapt to circumstances. But rarely does such adaptation occur through amendment to the formal document. Rather, it occurs through bursts of creativity in the courts and through insensible, but no less potent, shifts in convention. Castigating the electorate for being slow to respond to pressure for formal constitutional change seems inconsistent in logic and is certainly unhistorical.

DID THEY KNOW WHAT THEY WERE DOING?

University-educated voters, and (among educational groups) only university-educated voters, voted Yes, by a small margin. They did not do so out of superior knowledge, however. They did usually know more about the Charlottetown Accord than less well-educated voters, but educational differences in knowledge seemed weak. And critically, controlling knowledge reduced the measured impact from education only slightly. Indeed, the control was slightly more powerful the other way: controlling education modestly reduced the measured knowledge effect. As factors in the vote, education and knowledge worked in the same direction, to favour a Yes vote, but did so independently of each other.

The educational gradient in the Yes vote did not seem to reflect mastery of what the situation required. Rather, university-educated voters were just relatively minority-oriented and relatively fond of Quebec, probably as part of a culture of tolerance in which political elites also share. If such a culture is necessary for Canada's survival, university education imparts mastery of the situation in its largest sense. But is this the same thing as grasping the immediate requirements of 1992? Does a general commitment to tolerance, in itself a good thing, require one to repress objections to the substance of a constitutional measure? It seems perfectly reasonable that tolerance be invoked as a reflex, a call to witness perhaps, but it is not the same thing as rational thought about the package.

In the educational finding also lies a more general caution. Much research on information and sophistication uses proxies for information, among these, education. Usually this is by default, as our understanding of how to measure information has matured only in the last decade and credible indicators are still in short supply.[1] Education can indicate cognitive capacity, but it also carries other baggage. That baggage is most likely to be engaged when tolerance is at issue, as with the Charlottetown Accord. But tolerance among university graduates is a cultural fact, not specifically the product of knowledge.

Information as such made a huge difference in 1992, and did so in many ways. Some claims about "low-information rationality" were not borne out, although some arguably were vindicated, at least not contradicted. Aggregationist claims did not fare well at all. Low-information voters evidently relied more on polls than high-information ones did, and the pattern seemed to vindicate the claim by McKelvey and Ordeshook that low-information voters could learn from high-information ones through polls. With a little over a week to go in the campaign, a deluge of polls shifted voters' expectations for the result dramatically downward, and with a small lag, the vote followed expectations. All this shift was attributable to low-information voters. But it did not make low-information voters converge on high-information ones; instead, they diverged. However, convergence across information levels is not an implication of McKelvey and Ordeshook's model, only convergence to an equilibrium, where the equilibrium vote distribution can be differentiated by information level. A reasonable inference is that polls reflected the weakness of high-information voters' commitment to the Charlottetown Accord, which then licensed low-information voters to go offside. Given that low-information voters were intrinsically less favourable to Quebec, this was not an inconsistent move.

This claim for a poll effect is based on aggregate evidence. Did poorly informed voters get themselves to the right position as efficiently as well-informed voters did, individual by individual? Sniderman et al. argue that poorly informed voters can get themselves to roughly the correct position – in other words, the position they would take were they better informed – by consulting their feelings. As a possibility this must be true. As an actual outcome, it was not forthcoming. To begin with, poorly informed voters were relatively unlikely to take a position on a matter of substance, either on a specific element or a general argument. Then, those who did take a position were relatively unlikely to connect it to the correct side of the vote. Moreover, the 1992 result must illustrate the more general case, for Sniderman and his colleagues are caught in another part of their own logic. They argue that well-informed voters also employ feelings, perhaps as efficiently as low-information voters do, but supplement feelings with more properly intellectual processes. Well-informed voters invoke ideas as well as feelings, and channel both ideas and feelings through complex, hierarchical reasoning chains. All this proved to be true for Canada in 1992. Indeed, we can claim not merely to have replicated Sniderman's structural claim, but to have gone one better. We have shown that their claim is true when the control is truly for information, not just for an education proxy. But the implication of this demonstration is incompatible with the claim that feelings adequately substitute for ideas. The more complex and hierarchical calculus used by high-information voters almost necessarily implies that their votes will express their own stakes in the outcome – however they conceive those stakes – relatively efficiently. The only way poorly informed voters could offset this is by linking feelings to the vote more efficiently than well-informed voters do. Sniderman et al. never argue that poorly-informed voters do this, and we never find this to be so. At the individual level, then, feelings do not make up for ideas, and poorly informed voters make much less consistent choices than well-informed voters do.

Did intervenors pick up the slack for poorly informed voters, as Lupia (1992) argues they can? Here too the answer leans to the negative. As with Sniderman et al., the debate is not over whether useful interventions are a possibility; they clearly are. Rather, the issue is one of outcome. First, how widespread was knowledge of interventions? Our sense is that it was very spotty and imperfect. It is true that 70 percent of the electorate was eventually able to locate Pierre Trudeau correctly. By the end, the percentage for Preston Manning rivalled

Trudeau, and Manning was a useful negative reference for many. But for many voters, one or the other of these was the only correct attribution. Of all intervenors, Pierre Trudeau was probably the most important to get a fix on, and it is reassuring that his relative visibility was commensurate with his importance in Canadian history. Given the sound and fury of the campaign, however, the overall incidence of intervenor awareness was not impressive.

Second, did it matter how many intervenors a voter could identify? It did indeed: the larger the number of intervenors a voter could locate, the more structured that voter's reaction to the interventions. If Pierre Trudeau was the only intervenor a voter could locate, the translation of his intervention into a consistent position on the Accord was still likely to be feeble. This follows from the spatial logic outlined in Lupia (1992): the more completely covered with intervenors the evaluative space is, the more precisely the ballot measure can be located. But just as referendum events can differ in how dense a distribution of interventions they evoke, so can individual voters in a given referendum differ in density of intervention points in their perceptual field. Unless awareness of interventions is very complete, it is possible that the actual process of intervention will only compound – certainly not overcome – pre-existing information differentials. Intervenors may only make the cognitively rich richer. There is no guarantee, and perhaps little likelihood, that intervenors constitute any more of a low-information rationality fix than raw feelings do.

So what, one might ask, if all that really counts is the aggregate result? This, of course, is the Page and Shapiro (1992) and Miller (1986) question. Two points are pertinent here, the overall information-vote relationship; and the interaction between information and the vote's social structural basis. Page and Shapiro seemed to regard the first as unproblematic, but Miller (1986) drew our attention to it. Certainly, in 1992 there was such a relationship: the more you knew the more likely you were to vote Yes. This relationship was not written in stone. It did not prevail at every point in the campaign, only at the end. And it did not come about because poorly informed voters were slow to catch up with well-informed ones; rather, poorly informed voters abruptly diverged from the others, evidently under induction from polls. Under other circumstances – perhaps even subtly different campaign dynamics for the Charlottetown Accord – the relationship might have been different, perhaps no relationship or even a reversed one. The critical point here is that an information-vote direction relationship cannot just be assumed to be zero, and thus Converse's (1964) original challenge just assumed away.

So what, one might still say. Perhaps well- and ill-informed voters just have different interests. Certainly, the information-vote direction connection by itself proves little. When, earlier, we discussed the structuring of the vote and how information facilitated that structuring, we talked only of feelings and ideas as they might relate to the vote, and passed over social sources of the vote. At this basic level, knowing more did not make social structure more important, nor did it improve the predictive power of vote equations with exclusively social structural factors on the right-hand side. At no information level did social factors supply much predictive muscle, but this is an ubiquitous finding (Green, 1992). What little there is to be derived from social position in coming to decision, knowing more does not clarify the interests associated with that position. Indeed, and this brings us to the point, in 1992 knowing more cut through social distinctions, markedly *compressing* group differences even as it dragged most groups' central tendencies in the Yes direction. By implication, information did not just clarify the interests embedded in a given group profile. Knowing more actively changed voters' calculus by taking them out of the group and into a larger forum.

A further implication of all this is that some voters deliberated, made a considered judgment on substance, and weighed positives and negatives carefully, as Noël (1994) argued. At the high end of the information continuum the calculus was complex. And this balanced calculus of individual-level decision yielded a collectively balanced result: well-informed voters split on the Charlottetown Accord. In this sense, rejection of the Accord truly did conform to Noël's model. The best-endowed voters did not rally to the elite consensus, neither did they utterly flee it; rather, some went along, others decided not to. Not every voter did this, of course. Voters with less information and less balance in the calculus leaned strongly to the No side. At the low end of the knowledge continuum, judgments were at once relatively raw, unfocused, and negative. There is a sense, then, in which the Yes and the No were qualitatively different, that No and Yes were answers to different questions.

For all that, the best and least-informed, although differentially attracted to the Yes side, were not polarized against each other. Poorly informed voters just dragged an overall negative result further down. It is conceivable that this group could have done the opposite had the signal from better-informed voters been unequivocally pro-Accord. Now, one factor anchored low-information voters to a No vote – relatively negative feelings toward Quebec – and this might keep such voters relatively hostile to all pro-Quebec initiatives. But a clearly positive signal from better-informed voters might at least have dragged the low-information Yes share up some, and, of course, what we mean by "positive signal" is a more one-sided Yes vote, itself a contribution to a possible overall Yes victory.

This brings us to a final point about the Charlottetown Accord: *it does not do to analyse the referendum vote as if the Accord itself was manifestly what the country needed.* Negotiating some kind of an accord was, from the federalist perspective, almost certainly necessary. Otherwise Bourassa would have been forced onto sovereignist ground. But this particular deal does not seem to stand the test of hindsight. It was true that at the very end of the campaign, the more you knew the more likely you were to say Yes. But "more likely to say Yes" did not mean "more likely than not to say Yes." The best-informed were in fact the most closely divided, and the pattern for the whole electorate was simply not one of partially realized consensus. Notwithstanding the lack of a split at the core of the political class, the overall pattern does not resemble any version of the mainstream effect (Gamson and Modigliani, 1966; Zaller, 1992). Certainly, by voting day Canadians were allowed to indulge themselves in a negativism that was partly tribal, partly (perhaps self-indulgently) anti-elite, and many Canadians took that permission and ran with it. It is also entirely possible that many of those same Canadians would indulge crude passions even for a more narrowly and more deliberately crafted measure, and in so doing would stand in the way of a constitutional measure more broadly supported by thoughtful Canadians. But in that event more thoughtful voters might win out. In 1992, thoughtful voters did not form a distinctive constituency for the Yes.

APPENDIX A:

Design of the 1992 Sample

DISTRIBUTION ACROSS PROVINCES AND WEIGHTS

To facilitate regional analyses, the 1992 study oversampled certain provinces. Outside Quebec, smaller provinces were oversampled relative to Ontario, and Quebec was oversampled relative to the country as a whole. The regional case was most compelling for Quebec as that province conducted its own vote and, more importantly, the two campaigns seemed likely to interact. Altogether, 1001 interviews were completed in Quebec during the campaign wave. Outside Quebec 1529 were completed, for an all-Canada total of 2530. For detail on the distribution of cases across provinces, see Northrup and Oram (1994), Table 2–2.

All analyses in this book used weighted samples, where weighting compensated only for probability of selection: down for oversampled provinces, up for undersampled provinces; down for small households, up for large ones. Compensation for household size is necessitated by the fact that the smaller the household, the greater one's likelihood of being contacted, as random selection was of telephone numbers. No correction for number of telephones per household seemed necessary. For analyses of the Quebec sample, only the household weight was required. For the rest of Canada and when Quebec and non-Quebec samples were combined, the household weight had to be multiplied by a second weight based on the census distribution of households across provinces. Weights were designed to reproduce the total number of cases in the analysis, so that inferential statistics employed the correct number of degrees of freedom.

DISTRIBUTION OVER TIME

Interviewing began on 24 September 1992 and roughly eighty interviews were completed each day. Clearance of the total sample was controlled so that the sample interviewed each day was indistinguishable from each other day's sample, within sampling error. By the fifth full day of fieldwork, completions settled in at roughly the campaign average. Completions thereafter had roughly the same profile, day-to-day: so many from that day's release, so many from the day before, and so on. This entailed a drop in response rate at the very end, with the rate for the whole sample being 65 percent. For many purposes, interviews conducted over this thirty-two-day span constitute a single sample, a 2530-person cross-section. But as daily replicates differed only in the passage of time – that is, day of interview was itself a random event – longitudinal comparisons are relatively easy.

A total of 2223 respondents were reinterviewed over the month following 31 October. These respondents were then folded into the sample released during the 1993 campaign. Of respondents who completed both referendum waves, 1434 were interviewed during the 1993 campaign, and of these 1312 were reinterviewed after the campaign.

Selected Items from the 1992–3 Canadian Referendum and Election Survey

refc2a: The referendum question asks, "Do you agree that the constitution of Canada should be renewed on the basis of the agreement reached on August 28th, 1992."

[If you do vote,] do you think you will vote *Yes* or *No*?

refc2d: [If you do vote,] do you think you will vote *Yes* or *No*?

refc3: Which way are you leaning: *Yes* or *No*?

refd1: Do you *Agree* or *Disagree* with the following statements.

No agreement will satisfy Quebec; they will always ask for more.

refd3: The agreement *is the best* compromise we can get under the circumstances.

refd4: The agreement will allow us to move on to other problems, like the economy.

refd5: Voting *No* to this agreement means saying *Yes* to Quebec's independence.

refd6: In the agreement, is Quebec a *winner* or a *loser*?

refd7: In the agreement, is [name of province] a *winner* or a *loser*?

refd9: Aboriginal peoples?

refd10: Women?

refe1, 2, 3: Which of the following do you prefer?

… The Senate *as it is now,*

… the Senate *as proposed* in the constitutional agreement,

… *or doing away* with the Senate altogether? [Order of alternatives randomly varied]

refe4: If you had to choose, should each province *have an equal number* of senators or should *bigger* provinces have *more* senators?

refe5: Does the agreement give the Senate *too much, too little,* or about the *right amount of power*?

refe6: Should women be guaranteed seats in the Senate?

refe7: Should women be guaranteed half the seats in the Senate?

refe8: Should Aboriginal peoples be guaranteed seats in the Senate?

refe9: Do you *agree* or *disagree* with the *proposal* to recognize the right of Canada's Aboriginal peoples to govern themselves?

refe10: Do you *agree* or *disagree* with the *proposal* to recognize Quebec as a *Distinct Society*?

refe11: [In return for losing most of its Senate seats,] Quebec has been guaranteed one-quarter of the seats in the House of Commons [regardless of its population]. [Two randomizations]

[Quebec Only]

refe12: In your opinion, is the French language threatened in Quebec?

[Outside Quebec Only]

reff1: In [province], is it *very likely, somewhat likely, somewhat unlikely* or, *very unlikely* that the *Yes* side will win?

[Whole Sample]

reff2: What about Quebec?

reff3: In Canada as a whole?

reff7: In your opinion, if the *No* side wins in *both* Quebec *and* the rest of Canada: Will Quebec separate from Canada?

[Quebec Only]

reff11: What is your opinion on Quebec sovereignty [that is, Quebec is no longer a part of Canada]?

[Outside Quebec Only]

reff12: What is your opinion on Quebec separation?

[Whole Sample]

reff14: If Quebec separates from Canada, do you think your standard of living will get better, get worse, or stay about the same as now?

reff15: *A lot* better or only *a little* better?

reff16: *A lot* worse or only *a little* worse?

refg1a: I'm going to name *some* people and groups who *might* take a public position on the constitutional agreement, for each can you tell me *as far as* *you know* if they have taken a *public* position on the agreement. First, has *Pierre Trudeau* taken a public position on the agreement?

refg1b: Has he come out *for* or *against*?

refg2a: Has *the business community* taken a public position on the agreement?

refg2b: Has it come out *for* or *against*?

refg3a: Has the *women's movement* taken a public position on the agreement?

refg3b: Has it come out *for* or *against*?

refg4a: Have *union leaders* taken a public position on the agreement?

refg4b: Have they come out *for* or *against*?

[Outside Quebec Only]

refg5a: Has *Preston Manning* taken a public position on the agreement?

refg5b: Has he come out *for* or *against*?

refg6a: Has *Peter Lougheed* taken a public position on the agreement?

refg6b: Has he come out *for* or *against*?

[Quebec Only]

refg7a: Has *Claude Castonguay* taken a public position on the agreement?

refg7b: Has he come out *for* or *against*?

refg8a: Has *Jean Allaire* taken a public position on the agreement?

refg8b: Has he come out *for* or *against*?

[Whole Sample]

refh1: Which government looks after your interests and needs the best: the government of Canada or the governemnt of [name of province]?

refh2: I am going to name some people and ask you how you feel about them on a thermometer that runs from 0 to 100 degrees. Ratings between 50 and 100 are positive. Ratings between 0 and 50 are negative. You may use any number from 0 to 100. How do you *feel* about *Pierre Trudeau*?

refh3: How do you *feel* about *Brian Mulroney*?

refh4: How do you *feel* about *Robert Bourassa*?

refh5: *Jean Chrétien*

refh6: *Audrey McLaughlin*?

[Outside Quebec Only]

refh7: How do you *feel* about [name of premier]

refh8: *Preston Manning*?

refh9: *Peter Lougheed*?

[Quebec Only]

refh10: *Lucien Bouchard*?

refh11: *Jacques Parizeau*?

[Whole Sample]

refh16: Canada has two founding peoples, French and English.

refh17: Canada has three founding peoples, French, English, and Aboriginal peoples.

refh18: We should make no distinctions, we are all Canadians.

refh20: Which is more important in a democratic society: *letting the majority decide*, or *protecting the needs and rights of minorities*?

refh26: I'd like to use the thermometer again. Just as a reminder the thermometer runs from 0 to 100 degrees. Ratings between 50 and 100 are positive. Ratings between 0 and 50 are negative. You may use any number from 0 to 100. How do you feel about *Canada*?

refh27: How do you feel about *Quebec*?

refh31: The *women's movement*?

refh32: The *business community*?

refh34: *unions*?

refi1a: Thinking of federal politics, do you usually think of yourself as a Liberal, Conservative, NDP, [Reform/Bloc Québécois] or none of these?

refi2: Did you vote in the last federal election in 1988?

refi3: Which party did you vote for?

POST-REFERENDUM WAVE

prb1: Did *you* vote in the referendum?

prb3: Did you vote *Yes*, or did you vote *No*?

prc3: Do you *agree* or *disagree* with the following proposals? Recognizing Quebec as a distinct society?

prc4: Did the agreement go *too far, just far enough* or *not far enough* in recognizing Quebec as a distinct society?

prc8: *Even though none* of the other parts of the agreement will be implemented, do you think we should recognize Aboriginal self government?

[Quebec Only]

prd5: If you had to choose between federalism *as it is now* and Quebec sovereignty, that is Quebec is no longer a part of Canada, which would you choose?

prf1: Would you say that you are *better* off or *worse* off financially than you were a year ago, or about the *same*?

ELECTION CAMPAIGN WAVE

cpsg8a,b: Which comes closest to your own view:

One: Aboriginal people should have the right to make their own laws.

OR

Two: Aboriginal people should abide by the same laws as other Canadians.
[Order of alternatives randomly varied]

POST-ELECTION WAVE

pesa2: Did *you* vote in the election?

pesa4: Which party did you vote for: the Conservative party, the Liberal party, the New Democratic Party, the [Reform Party/Bloc Québécois], or another party?

Notes

INTRODUCTION

1 A *referendum* is a legally binding vote, conducted at elected politicians' initiative (the matter is *referred* by them) but in conformity with a legal-constitutional requirement. A *plebiscite* is similar to a referendum in that initiative lies with the political elite but, unlike a referendum, is only advisory. The "advice," obviously, can carry great moral weight. An *initiative*, called by that name, is a measure originating outside the elite; depending on the rules, it can be binding or non-binding. Strictly speaking, the 1992 vote, like the two earlier ones, was a plebiscite. On the distinctions, see Butler and Ranney (1978; 1994). Butler and Ranney have also persuaded us that the plural of referendum is referendums, referenda means a plurality of things referred.

  In fact, two referendums were held, as Quebec conducted its own. For more detail, see chapter 2.
2 The expression originates with Popkin (1992).
3 For more detail on the study, see Appendix A and Northrup and Oram (1994).

CHAPTER ONE

1 Also in question is the less explicitly representative mode embodied in judicial decision-making.
2 Laycock (1994) analyses Reform's own populist claims in light of this earlier history, as well as in current context.

3 "As she saw the No vote building across the country, [No advocate Deborah Coyne] would be happy that her faith in the Canadian public was confirmed. 'If people had the courage to say this, despite all the pressures, and the fear-mongering, and so forth, there's hope for the future,' she said" (Delacourt, 1993), p. 24.

4 This also seems to be the view of Greenwood (1946[1976]). It is not universally held, however; see Sharman and Stuart (1981) and discussion below.

5 See, for instance, the fears expressed by Coyne: "I thought the people might go in and just be scared into voting Yes, or spoiling their ballot or something" (Delacourt, 1993), p. 23.

6 The argument about change in the United States was made at greatest length in Nie, Verba, and Petrocik (1976), but was controverted by Bishop, Oldendick, and Tuchfarber (1978) and by Smith (1989).

7 Strikingly, the Converse-Pierce study was carried out in what was, if anything a superheated ideological period, around the May 1968 events. Of course, claims that the French electorate is ideologically divided sit uneasily with claims that it is vulnerable to Bonapartist appeals. But for counterclaims in other studies, see the review by Dalton and Wattenberg (1993).

8 See also Kuklinski et al. (1982).

9 This last point was made forcefully by Luskin (1995).

10 The claim was made in the Canadian context by Johnston (1986) and was also made by Converse himself in 1990.

11 Note, though, the theorem works only if the jury uses majority rule. The common law rule of unanimity is not designed to maximize the probability of a correct answer, but to minimize the probability of a certain kind of wrong answer.

12 Similarly reassured are Grofman and Withers (1993).

13 In the "common sense" image of referendums, of course, the easy-hard distinction is as untenable for answers as for questions.

14 On education and orientations to outgroups and to civil liberties, see Stouffer (1955), Sullivan et al. (1982), and McClosky and Brill (1983).

15 Although the United States has never conducted a nationwide vote, at subnational levels it is one of the world's main laboratories for direct democracy. Switzerland has averaged about four national votes a year, with an upward trend in recent years, and has held over four hundred altogether (Kobach, 1994, Table 4–1). Australia has had more than forty (Hughes, 1994, Table 5–1).

16 Australia provides no within-country comparisons, as all votes originate by elite referral and virtually none are on non-constitutional questions.

17 Another recent example is the non-referral of Czech and Slovak mutual separation, despite a legal requirement and Vaclav Havel's repeated calls for referral. The agenda was controlled by political forces who did not want a contrary result. See Brady and Kaplan (1994), pp. 210–12.

18 For more detail on and a strategic appreciation of the British Columbia move, see chapter 10.

19 Although it also seems likely that private proposers are less strategically sure-footed than experienced party actors, they are more likely to make an unfeasible proposal or to get the timing wrong.

20 Almost all Australian references concern narrowly defined issues. Four omnibus references were made (the last in 1944) but none passed (Aitken, 1978, p. 132).

21 Given the availability of strategic referral and non-referral, the routine failure of Australian initiatives is a mystery. If politicians in general know so much, why do Australian ones in particular persist in futile initiatives? Part of the explanation must be that alternative routes to constitutional change are blocked. Another part is the very high threshold for passage: many Australian failures win a majority of popular votes but not of states or vice versa, where success requires both. And Australian politicians may not really care whether a measure passes or not; merely posing the question may suffice for what is essentially partisan symbolism.

22 Reinforcing this presumption is the fact that politicians, in contrast with, say, movie stars or hockey players, are experts on policy matters (Lupia, 1995).

23 The coalition does not always span the entire spectrum, but it always embraces the broad centre and always includes the parties that regularly form or participate in government.

24 The exact Yes share among francophones is a matter of dispute. For one side in the controversy and a review, see Pinard and Hamilton (1984).

25 Links between arguments and elements, on one hand, and vote, on the other, may also be reciprocal. The more specific elements a voter supports, or the more intensely the voter wants some particular element, the more likely he or she should be to vote Yes. The same relationship should hold for general arguments. This is so obvious as to be trite. But one may also resolve to vote Yes (or No) for one reason, express this commitment publicly, and then reorganize all other opinions to rationalize the behavioural commitment, a classic post-decision cognitive-dissonance reduction sequence (Festinger, 1957). At this point, though, the complexities defeat us, and so we represent the relationship as one-way.

26 For Canada, the relevant evidence is Johnston et al. (1992), chapters 7 and 8.

CHAPTER TWO

1 The government was not absolutely on its own, as the federal NDP and Conservative governments in Ontario and New Brunswick rallied to its initiative.

2 Trudeau himself felt sufficiently anxious on this front to offer cabinet positions to western MPs from the New Democratic Party (Trudeau, 1993),
p. 272.

3 Alberta committed itself to Senate reform only after Peter Lougheed retired as premier in 1985. His own view was that representation questions
were a distraction, that Alberta would never dominate a reformed Senate,
and that the province's real need was more power, especially over energy.
In the late 1970s and early 1980s, the province most beguiled by Senate
schemes was British Columbia. See Gibbins (1983), p. 121.

4 See Cairns (1992), and the exchange between Cairns (1993) and Brodie
and Nevitte (1993a,b).

5 Embodied as sections 35 (3) and (4) and section 35(1) of the Constitution
Act, 1982.

6 A useful summary is Hawkes (1989).

7 For a telling example of the reaction on the English-Canadian left, see
Resnick (1990).

8 The text describes elite rhetoric more than popular response. No shift in
mass opinion on the Meech Lake Accord was visible in late 1988 or early
1989. More critical to the collapse in support seems to have been spreading awareness of its distinct society clause (Blais and Crête, 1991).

9 On the clause in the Manitoba hearing, see Monahan (1991), pp. 177–8;
on its treatment by Charest, see p. 193; for the government's idea, see
pp. 202–3; and for Bourassa's veto, see p. 206ff.

10 This is the interpretation in Lisée (1994a), p. 400ff.

11 For an account of the Oka crisis, see Campbell and Pal (1991).

12 A fourth forum, the Royal Commission on Aboriginal Peoples, was also
empowered to comment on the constitutional process, but did not do so.

13 The forum for much of this argument was the John Deutsch Institute at
Queen's University, and the most pointed statements were Harris and
Purvis (1991a,b) and Boadway, Purvis, and Wen (1991).

14 "... too much flexibility may make it too easy to renege opportunistically
on specific aspects of the social contract. Society as a whole has an interest
in ensuring that the social contract does not start to unravel. Thus while
the rights of access to a minimum income must be general, they must
have some teeth" (Norrie, Boadway, and Osberg, 1991, p. 245).

15 This strategy seems to have been rejected by Bourassa himself, but was seriously discussed among his advisers and was foreshadowed in Ottawa's
strategic thinking by Norman Spector (Lisée, 1994b, pp. 289–91; on Spector's foreshadowing, p. 154).

16 "Un jour que l'Albertain Horsman évoque une conversation qu'il vient
tout juste d'avoir avec son copain Gil Rémillard, Clarke trouve l'anecdote
bien bonne, car lui aussi a parlé à Rémillard dans les jours précédents:
'Est-ce que Gil jouait avec toi la même partition qu'il jouait avec moi?

Étions-nous sur la même page?' " (Lisée, 1994b, p. 222). See also Delacourt
(1993), pp. 274–5. Avenues of access by Quebec seem to have been positively sinuous. At one point, Quebec inserted a weighted-vote Senate proposal (called for a time the Beauchamp plan) into the process by working
through Frank McKenna, although it appears that Roy Romanow of
Saskatchewan was the ultimate target of this plan, which for a time became associated with his name. The plan may have reached Quebec
through Ottawa, however. It was fronted by Jocelyne Bourgon, secretary
to the Cabinet for Federal-Provincial Relations, and was first proposed by
Peter Nicholson of the Bank of Nova Scotia. See Delacourt, p. 155ff.

17 Graham Fraser, "Fumbling on Both Fronts," *Globe and Mail* (Toronto),
8 June 1992.

18 Delacourt (1993), pp. 280–1; Lisée (1994b), p. 246ff.

19 It apparently did not help that Bourassa did not indicate clearly what was
unacceptable; this beguiled his allies into thinking he could live with a
Triple-E Senate. Lisée (1994b, p. 240ff) infers that Bourassa assumed Rae
would block the Triple-E and that he anticipated Mulroney's 15 July
move; accordingly, he saw no need to make himself the villain who killed
the Triple-E. Delacourt implies the same, at pp. 131, 164, and 167ff.

20 Quebec was not the only province opposed to the proportional formula.
Premiers Getty of Alberta and Cameron of Nova Scotia also opposed it
but yielded to the majority in the Pearson Accord. Direct election, on the
other hand, was unassailable in those provinces.

21 Where this left natural resources measures in the budget was unclear.

22 Another compensation for Quebec's reduced place in the Senate was a
proposal of several years' standing: a double-majority voting rule (a majority of francophone members together with a majority of the whole
chamber for passage) for matters touching language and culture. This
seemed to be a standard arrow in the Senate reform quiver and was incorporated in the government's September 1991 package. But it flew in the
face of public opinion in the rest of Canada (on which see Johnston, 1986,
pp. 33–41).

23 Lisée (1994b, p. 360ff) claims all three things were true.

24 Two other questions of substance might have become central issues but
seemed instead to lurk on the periphery of the debate, the Social Charter
(too little for the left to fight for, too much for the right to stomach?) and
the Economic Union proposals (too much for the left to stomach, too little
for the right to fight for?)

25 Our account of the referendum rules, in the three provinces (Quebec, Alberta, and British Columbia) precommitted to a referendum and in Canada, is heavily indebted to the Canada West Foundation (1992).

26 Lisée reports (p. 413) that Quebec made one last attempt to have the rest-
of-Canada vote precede the Quebec one, consistent with the Bélanger-

Campeau requirement that Quebec consider only binding offers and to
spare Quebec the possible embarrassment of being odd province out. This
conflicted with the federal government's long-standing objective of mini-
mizing Quebec's strategic room over the vote. In any case, by the time
the Accord was reached it was next to impossible to schedule a rest-of-
Canada vote for any earlier than 25 October.

27 One other major divergence between Quebec and the rest of Canada can
be noted only in passing. Quebec permits expatriate voting, where expa-
triates can live elsewhere in Canada. Thus some Canadians got to vote
twice, once under federal law in their place of residence and once *in absen-
tia* in Quebec. However troubling this may be philosophically, it seems to
have had a negligible effect on the 1992 vote.

28 The Alberta law requires the legislature to follow the dictates of the popular vote. Presumably this would be deemed to extend to a vote conducted
by Ottawa. It is not clear, however, that any Canadian parliament can legally bind itself in this way and none of the others tried. The controlling
case is the *Initiative and Referendum Reference* (1919), in which the Judicial
Committee of the Privy Council ruled that direct votes under Manitoba's
Initiative and Referendum Act (1916) could not be binding as they would
derogate from the powers of the lieutenant-governor, whose position is
controlled by the Constitution Act, 1867 and thus cannot be modified by
the provincial Parliament alone. The 1982 settlement subjected the powers
of the governor general to the unanimity rule and, by analogy, rendered
binding votes beyond the power of the federal Parliament to enact as
well. The issue is confused, however, by *Regina* v. *Nat Bell Liquors* (1922) in
which the Judicial Committee upheld a direct-vote component of the Alberta Liquor Act (1916). See Hogg (1985), pp. 290–2 (Manitoba) and
pp. 292–5 (Alberta).

29 For more detail on published polls in Quebec, see chapter 8.

30 The figure gives a daily tracking of vote intentions, in which daily sampling fluctuation is smoothed by a five-day (-2, ... +2) moving averaging.
Respondents with no vote intention, even in response to a follow-up
question, are excluded from consideration. The first day of interviewing
was Thursday, 24 September, four days after the beginning of the writ period outside Quebec. Because of averaging and the fact that a few days
had to pass before our daily completion profiles settled down (see
Appendix A), this book's presentations of tracking data tend to start no
earlier than the 25th. The basic vote question is **refc2**. The follow-up is
refc3. **Refc2** was asked in two ways as an experiment, to test whether or
not the wording of the referendum ballot made any difference to vote intentions: a random half of the sample was read the official text of referendum question and were then asked whether they thought they would
vote Yes or No; the other half was asked vote intention directly, without

hearing the wording of the referendum question. In Quebec only, the version with the text produced five points more support for the Yes, which suggests that the positive formulation of the question slightly increased the Yes vote. This could reflect the use of "Acceptez-vous ..." in the French version of the offical question. It may be easier merely to accept a proposal than to agree with it. The least informed were not more likely to be swayed by the official text. Finally, the two versions were equally good predictors of actual behaviour, as reported in the post-referendum survey.

31 Deborah Wilson and Milo Cernetig, "Anger grows in West over Senate reform," *Globe and Mail*, 22 August 1992, p. A6.

32 "Women's group says No," *Globe and Mail*, 14 September 1992, pp. A1–2.

33 See article by David Roberts, "Manning under attack at Reform convention," in *Globe and Mail*, 24 October 1992, p. A13, which suggested that Manning supported some parts of the Accord, worried about bucking a Yes tide in English Canada, and asked his key advisers to consider the Yes.

34 All direct quotations are from André Picard, "Trudeau denounces accord," *Globe and Mail*, 2 October 1992, pp. A1–2. The text has been reproduced, along with a transcript of the question and answer period which followed the speech, all in translation, as Trudeau (1992).

35 Bruce Little, "Canadian dollar gains strength," *Globe and Mail*, 14 October 1992, pp. A1–2. One analyst was quoted as saying: "There is a growing number ... who think No won't mean [Quebec's separation] ... and that ultimately Canada will be successful in keeping Quebec in" (p. A1).

36 The typical non-Quebec daily sample had about fifty observations (as compared with thirty in Quebec), implying a daily 95 percent confidence interval of ± 14 percentage points, much less than the overnight drop.

37 Our tracking is broadly consistent with Lisée's (1994b, p. 590) reporting of the Decima tracking for the Yes Committee. Certainly, both trackings indicate a sudden drop and a partial recovery.

CHAPTER THREE

1 See above, chapter 2. Numbering of elements in the clause refer to its intended place in the Constitution Act, 1982.

2 For most figures and tables in this chapter, opinion on elements is drawn from the referendum study's campaign wave and non-voters are excluded. For the distinct society measure, however, heroic efforts were required. The measure synthesizes response to **refe10** (campaign wave) and **prc3** (identical wording, post-referendum wave). A programming bug, missed in the pressure to get into the field, caused **refe10** to be skipped for about 39 percent of respondents. For respondents skipped in the first wave, we use the post-referendum item. We resisted using post-referendum information all round for two reasons: for campaign-period vote inten-

tion estimations we would lose all non-panel respondents; post-campaign response would have been more infused than campaign-period response with post-decision rationalization. This is a fear about estimated individual-level relationships; in the aggregate, no movement was discernible on any of these questions, neither during the campaign nor pre-/post vote.

3 All quotations are from the special Charlottetown Accord number of the *Reformer.*

4 Pro-Accord positions were first coded as 1, anti-Accord positions as 0, and "don't know" as 0.5. This coding is the nearly universal usage in the rest of this book, especially for estimation of equations, on which more below. For visual impact in Figure 3–2, the 0, 1 range is translated downward to -0.5, +0.5, so that an element on which the balance of opinion was negative also comes out as negative visually.

5 The futility of the rhetoric around the guarantee is revealed by an experiment, a two-way factorial design, around two potentially key arguments. One dimension involved random assignment of respondents to control or to a "compensation" treatment: roughly half the respondents heard no justification for the guarantee, the other half were told that the guarantee was compensation for loss of Senate seats. The other dimension involved a "population" treatment: half the sample heard nothing about the permanence of the guarantee, while for the other half that permanence was underlined by stating that the guarantee held regardless of Quebec's population. Hearing about permanence hurt, but hearing about compensation did not help.

6 All direct quotes on Reform's position are from the *Reformer,* 10 September 1992.

7 The general item is a synthesis of **refe3a,b**, and **c**, which randomize order of presentation for the three alternatives. As a point of information, each alternative received its greatest support when presented last. Going first or second made no difference relative to the other. The greatest boost from order accrued to the abolition alternative. The representation question was **refe4** and the power question was **refe5.**

8 The basic coding scheme was the same as for other items in Figure 3–2. Support either for the old Senate or for outright abolition were both coded as 0.

9 Only in Alberta did more respondents say "too little" than "too much." Even there the margin was small and the plurality choice was still "about right" and the volume of "don't know" large. Only in New Brunswick did more than 15 percent say "too little." In some provinces the "too little" percentage was under 10; among these was British Columbia.

10 Specifically, endorsement of both features would shift the likelihood up 0.15 (0.06 + 0.09), from 0.26 (intercept) to 0.41.

11 *Globe and Mail,* 5 September 1992.
12 Calgary *Herald*, 12 September 1992.
13 Ibid., 14 September 1992.
14 The margin was roughly the same for the full 1993 sample. The item is **cpsg8**, on which the order of alternatives was randomized.

CHAPTER FOUR

1 These two Quebec arguments are more complicated than just mirror images. A voter could conceivably accept both or reject both. One can fear secession even if one believes that Quebeckers do not *really* want to leave. This conclusion is dictated by reasoning back from the end of the game: threatening secession but not carrying through if the bluff is called would be the worst possible outcome for Quebec; Quebec would be unwise to allow a bluff to be called; the only insurance against this is resolve to carry the threat out. But if one senses that willingness to secede is an instrumental position, not something desired for itself, then ready acquiescence in the threat actually stiffens the instrumental resolve behind the threat. As well, by reinforcing Quebeckers' sense of distinctiveness and by strengthening the province's institutions, the concessions may actually facilitate Quebec's eventual secession. For an argument along these lines, see McCallum and Green (1991), pp. 4–7. On the other side, one could also reject both arguments: be sanguine about Quebec's continued adhesion, yet not see Quebec as always asking for more. .

2 Of the five general arguments considered in this chapter, four are based on single items from the campaign wave: "province winner" on **refd7**; "best compromise" on **refd3**; "move on" on **refd4**; and "Quebec never satisfied" on **refd1**. "Fear of separation" is a compound of three items: **refd5** and **reff7**, alternative renderings of a statement that defeat of the Accord will lead to Quebec's separation, and **reff12**, opinion on separation itself. To score 1 on "fear," a respondent must answer at least one of **refd5** or **reff7** affirmatively and indicate personal opposition to a secessionist outcome.

Few respondents outside Quebec desired that province's departure but few also saw a connection between that outcome and vote on the Accord. Specifically, 78 percent of voters disapproved the prospect of secession. On each measure, only 24 percent saw a connection between the Accord vote and the probability of secession. But the 24 percent on each measure were remarkably non-overlapping: cumulatively, 39 percent of voters saw a connection one way or the other, if not both ways. Some voters who saw the connection were happy about it, but generally, voters who approved secession also saw it is as very unlikely. This left 27 percent of voters, averaged over the campaign, fearful of secession and seeing its likelihood connected to the vote.

3 Because of averaging, Figure 4–1 understates the discontinuity around 2–3 October. For 24 September–1 October inclusive, the balance was positive four days in eight, including 1 October itself. After 1 October, the balance was positive only two, widely spaced days. The gap between 1 and 4 October was almost 0.25 (out of a maximum possible 1.0). After the 4th, the impulse decayed modestly; on only one other day (15 October) was judgment on the compromise as harsh as on the 4th.

4 Strictly speaking, the notion of a regional base was inconsistent with Joe Clark's unanimity rule for counting provinces' votes. Still, a base wide enough to carry several provinces (seven?) might have buttressed the Accord's moral presumption. In the campaign, evidence of support in key regions might have increased pressure on other regions. After the campaign, it might have signalled an avenue for legislative action.

5 Prairie data do not mask a peculiar alienation in Alberta. On each of these questions Albertans were modestly more accepting than either British Columbians or Ontarians and feeling was more bitter in Manitoba and Saskatchewan.

6 The technique we have just outlined is Two-Stage Least Squares (2SLS) regression. We were simply unable to identify instruments in the background which would enable us to disentangle causality in the foreground. The relevant data are in chapter 7.

7 As before, all statements about likelihoods and shares for general arguments are averaged over the campaign. Recall from figures 4–1 and 4–2 that acceptance of positive arguments dropped over the campaign.

8 Except to the extent that conceding self-government gets Aboriginal questions off the agenda, but this starts to send the argument in circles. See the discussion about reciprocal causation above.

9 Figures in the text are based on evaluation of equations in Table 4–5.

10 The sum of intercept and the coefficient on the "best compromise" term in Table 4–6 is exactly 0.50.

11 This reading must be qualified, however, by considering two mutually supportive, essentially artifactual explanations. First is time lag between measurements. All general arguments were posed to respondents in the campaign-wave questionnaire only – that is, within minutes of the vote-intention question. The vote question could only be asked after the event and the gap between interviews varied from a few days to more than a month. Other things being equal, the wider the interval, the weaker a relationship is likely to be, and the general argument–intention gap was always smaller than the general argument–actual vote gap. Second is the fact that response to each overall evaluation was a compound of cross-sectional and time-series variance. The position imputed to many early interviewees must be more positive than the one they actually held when

they cast their votes. This error may attenuate each argument's estimated impact.

12 It did pass the one-tailed test.

13 Table 4–7 contains two hints that loss of power by general arguments was real, at least relative to specific elements, not just a measurement artifact. One hint lies in opinion on specific elements. These measures were also taken before the vote; response to them was gathered as distantly in time from the vote as was response to general questions. (A partial and mildly worrisome exception is some response to the distinct society item; see chapter 3 for more detail.) If mere passage of time attenuated relationships, this did not stop specific-elements coefficients from growing. This does not address the other longitudinal factor, "time-series error": while four general arguments exhibited significant movement, specific elements exhibited none. But the table's other hint lies in "province winner," the one general argument with no longitudinal displacement (see Figure 4–1); this argument also lost power.

CHAPTER FIVE

1 Although this book supplies no further formalization, it suggests two avenues for elaboration on Lupia's initiative. First is the dimensionality of the ballot measure; Lupia's own analysis is unidimensional, but the Charlottetown Accord was clearly multidimensional, at least in negotiators' eyes. Possible slippage between negotiators' and voters' perceptions of dimensionality is an implicit theme in this chapter. Second is the continued viability of the status quo. Lupia assumes that the status quo is the reversion point, where the system stays if the ballot measure fails. For narrowly defined measures, California-style, this is a reasonable stylization. But in Canada in 1992 the reversion point was hotly disputed. Accord supporters argued that the status quo was not viable, that the failure of the Accord would lead, sooner or later, to an even greater displacement than the document itself envisaged. Accord opponents claimed either that the status quo was viable, certainly more self-replicating than the system embodied in the Accord (Manning), or that the status quo was more properly contested in a fundamentally different direction and that acceptance of the status quo did not prejudice future contestation (No side in Quebec).

2 Rating items are **refh2** to **refh9** for individuals and **refh31**, **refh32**, and **refh34** for groups. Respondents unable to rate an object were assigned a score of 50. Preston Manning and Peter Lougheed evoked the most nonresponse. In Manning's case, in particular, this made him seem modestly less unpopular than he was among respondents with active ratings.

3 In contrast to Lougheed, time had not rendered Trudeau obscure; almost as many respondents could place him as could place Brian Mulroney.

4 Two premiers, Bob Rae and Don Getty, received lower ratings than Manning's national one and Mike Harcourt received lower ratings than Manning in British Columbia.

5 As group ratings were even less differentiated than individual ones by region, they do not appear in the figure.

6 Rotation applies no further statistical leverage; the setup explains no more total variance than before; explained variance is just repartitioned among the four significant factors as these are rotated. For rotation, two choices must be confronted. First, should the rotation be orthogonal or oblique? When factors are first extracted, each is orthogonal to the others; this is what it means to let the second factor deal only with variance not explained by the first, and so on. But now, if we wish, we can let factors find more "natural" relationships among themselves: conceivably, one factor may overlap – may be correlated with – another. If such overlap occurs, factors are not orthogonal, for orthogonal means at right angles. Factors which overlap, and rotations which yield them, are called *oblique*. Such realism as one gains through oblique rotation carries a price in interpretive complexity. The Pythagorean world of right angles is much simpler to show visually, and visual representation of coalitions for and against the Accord is the goal. For this reason, we use an orthogonal rotation, forcing factors to be at right angles to each other *ex hypothesi*. Having decided on an orthogonal rotation, we then must choose which kind of differentiation to maximize: the factorial simplicity of individual evaluations or the interpretive clarity of individual factors. We opt for the latter, at the price of allowing individual persons or objects to reflect two or more factors; the rotation which does this is known as *varimax*.

We also performed an oblique rotation as a check and found that the four factors are effectively orthogonal anyway; assuming them to be orthogonal thus did minimal damage to the facts. Of the four factors, three were just not correlated with each other at all. Of these three, two were weakly correlated with the fourth, most powerful, factor but the maximum interfactor correlation in the whole setup was small: -0.19.

7 As hinted in the body of the text, the existence of an organization factor may reflect a measurement artifact. If so, we do not have a label for it. We performed an analysis with group ratings computed as deviations from the mean for all three groups and individual ratings cast as deviations from the mean for all seven individuals. This yields a factor solution dominated by left-right orientations, but with relations among other, non-organizational factors roughly as before. The overall pattern was less crisp, however, and we decided just to go with untransformed measures.

8 One arresting visual point is that all the actors in Figure 5–2, supporters and opponents alike, are oriented northwest/southeast, and that business values and conventional politics are at odds, even though the defining factors

are orthogonal. This does seem intuitively reasonable, as the union and women's movements and the NDP argue for a broad definition of the political, certainly resist the notion that markets are or should be outside politics.

9 There seemed to be no point in illustrating the "organizations as such" dimension, as all organizations cluster in one place and all persons cluster in another place, and the distinction may be artifactual. The person/organization distinction is of no consequence for our argument, in any case. It was important to get organizations into the factor analysis, however, so that we could locate them on other dimensions.

10 Awareness items are **refg1a** to **refg8b**. Two questions were asked about each intervenor: as far as the respondent knew, did the person or group take a position? If yes, was that for or against the Accord? Respondents were assigned to the unaware category if they either admitted unawareness straight up, or if they gave the wrong answer. For most intervenors an answer could just be wrong; for others, "wrong" meant the minority view. Obviously, we are not making evaluative judgments; disagreement over a position is a valuable indicator in its own right.

11 In awareness estimations, only vote intention appears as a dependent variable. Awareness has a strong longitudinal component (whose description was the objective of figures 5–2 and 5–3), even stronger than the longitudinal element in general arguments about the Accord, described in chapter 4. At the same time, awareness terms lost cross-sectional power in late campaign, as described below. Given all this there just seemed no point in including the vote in estimations.

12 Readers might worry that coefficients in Table 5–3 conflate two effects. Here, concern is with the impulse *transmitted* by the intervenor. But coefficients might also pick up differences among respondents in overall cognitive capacity, in ability to *receive* an impulse, any impulse. If cognitive capacity as such is related to the vote, as chapter 1 speculated it might be, then this general relationship could also, artifactually, create the appearance of a connection between awareness of a specific intervention and the vote. Cognitive capacity should enhance general awareness and, in turn, bias estimated awareness coefficients. If capacity promotes a Yes vote, coefficients will be biased upward, away from zero for supporters, toward zero for opponents. If capacity promotes a No vote, bias would be in the opposite direction. These relationships are the focus of chapter 9. Suffice it to say here that adding a measure of respondents' substantive knowledge of the Accord and dummy variables for educational attainment to Table 5–3's basic equation affects coefficients on awareness of specific intervenors hardly at all. The Trudeau coefficient changed not at all and the Manning coefficient shrank by 0.01.

13 Other facets of the early/late contrast confirm this interpretation: the overall power of the equation drops, and Peter Lougheed's coefficient

shifts from borderline positive (statistically significant by a one-tailed test) to weakly negative.

14 In these estimations, for instance, the intercept is 0.59 for non-members, 0.44 for members. See also, below, evidence about the relationship between liking for union leaders and the Yes share, and the discussion of the social structure of support in chapter 7.

15 Trudeau and Manning coefficients were both significantly different from zero for non-members, insignificant for members. No other coefficient was significant in either group.

16 Men were also more aware than women of the movement's position: 48 percent of men and 41 percent of women identified the women's movement as Accord opponents.

17 Party identification was measured by **refi1c**.

18 Disconnection did not mean lack of awareness, however. Among voters, nonpartisans were more likely than partisans to make the correct attribution for each intervenor. Partisans were just more likely to act on the awareness.

19 The other leaders rating is the average for the three.

20 It might make sense to include all potential confounding factors in the estimation. Doing so would be editorially disruptive, however, and would require us to detour through a description of each factor. For theoretical reasons, such description belongs in chapter 7. Suffice it to say here that including everything in the background reduces ratings coefficients by 0.10–0.20, on average, except for Trudeau, whose coefficients increase. This simply is further indication of Trudeau's role as evaluative pivot for the whole system, a point we expand on below. Notwithstanding the reduction of effect for all others and the increase for Trudeau, the rank order of coefficients remains as reported in this section, and no coefficient meeting a test of statistical significance here fails that test when background factors are included.

21 For further analysis of the gradient, see chapter 7.

22 Neither campaign-period coefficient, in fact, came close to statistical significance.

23 This positive Trudeau coefficient (0.39) was highly significant; it was nearly three times as large as its standard error, and almost as large as the coefficient for Mulroney feelings (0.47).

The demonstration described in this paragraph is the nub of an interpretive difference between ourselves and LeDuc and Pammett (1995), who argue that while Trudeau may have had a dynamic effect, he did not carry with him any of his own following. They base this claim on their finding of essentially zero coefficients between Trudeau ratings and the vote. Without conditioning on awareness, we too find that the relationship is weak, if not actually zero. The divergence of direction between the aware and the unaware illustrates just how pivotal Trudeau himself was. Apart from this divergence, made possible only by our having asked about awareness, the broad thrust of LeDuc and Pammett is generally consistent with our own arguments. They too wonder if Preston Manning hurt his cause as much as helped it, and their broad interpretation of Trudeau's positioning is consistent with ours. And both their arguments and ours give partial support to Lusztig's (1994) speculation that supporters of Trudeau's "macro-constitutional orientation" were not the most irreconcilable opponents of the Charlottetown Accord.

CHAPTER SIX

1 All claims in this paragraph are based on Johnston et al. (1992), chapter 7.

2 It testified to the power of the unanimity rule, though, that some campaign-period samples were extraordinarily large by commercial standards. The Angus Reid group's main pre-referendum poll had a sample of 3577, the Environics-CTV equivalent had 1849 respondents, and the *Globe and Mail* interviewed about 200 respondents *per day* from 1 October to the campaign's last weekend.

3 Expectations measures are **reff1** (province), **reff2** (Quebec), and **reff3** (Canada).

4 Obviously, not every provincial expectation should have been above the national one. For regional differences, see below.

5 In the 1988 seven-week campaign, Gallup alone published seven polls. Five of these were part of a regular Monday news feature in the Toronto *Star*. CTV, with fieldwork by Insight Canada, published six polls, tied to the Friday national news broadcast. Other sources were spottier. They tended to produce polls right after key events and the overall density of poll information went up toward the end.

6 Two each by Reid and Gallup, one by Environics. The lower-profile *Globe and Mail* poll reached a mass audience only through regular updating of polls by the CBC *National* news broadcast.

7 The headline for the Gallup release read: "Unity Deal Faces Defeat in Quebec and BC."

8 Especially striking were the confident projections by Angus Reid and Lorne Bozinoff (Gallup) on the CBC *Journal*, 9 September.

9 As all polls were newspaper polls in the first instance (the one television poll, the Environics poll of 17 October, was already in the pages of the Toronto *Star* well before prime time and was, in any case, reported on the CTV supper-hour newscast), they were updated on the day of publication.

10 The exception is the reading for the 20th, which seems very high. This reading is unlikely to be the product of the small apparent recovery in the Yes's standing noted by the new poll reading on the 20th: this poll result is

from a *Globe and Mail* story off the front page and was a hardly a dramatic departure from before. That standing may be a lagged reflection of the Thanksgiving weekend Yes recovery outside Quebec, noted in Figure 2–1, and is most probably the result of sampling error.

11 Ontario is the reference category, so that coefficients on the regional dummy variables represent the expectation difference between the indicated region and Ontario.

12 Although some of this was sampling error, reflecting smaller numbers of cases in the Atlantic provinces, sampling could not be the whole story, as visual inspection of expectations series (not reported in a figure or table) suggests that movement in Atlantic provinces' expectations was mainly secular.

13 As happened in 1988, before the leaders' debates for the Conservatives and after the debates for the NDP. Although the Conservatives lost a little ground in published polls before the debates, the cumulative message of those polls was that the Conservatives were far ahead, and Conservative expectations rose accordingly. After the debates the NDP experience was exactly the opposite – repeated confirmation that the party had been marginalized, which made expectations continue to drop well after the NDP share stablilized.

14 This projection resembles the re-evaluation of the Liberal party's chances right after the leaders' debates in the 1988 election – expectations gained even before the first post-debates polls were published.

15 Recall that shrinkage reported in chapter 4 for positive-argument coefficients came in the post-referendum wave, with estimations for actual vote.

16 A temptation we feel compelled to resist for now is to estimate by multivariate means the relative contribution of the Egg Roll speech and the late poll surge to the total drop in Yes share. We feel more comfortable proceeding allusively, by noting that Trudeau's impact was less than 20 points, probably about 10, and by inferring by default that the rest was attributable to polls. This is all gleaned from visual inspection of Figure 2–1 combined with the side evidence presented in this chapter. A time-series regression with dummy variables for two periods, pre- versus post-Egg Roll and pre- versus post-polls, assigns about 16 points of the total drop to the Egg Roll intervention and only 4 points to the polls. This simply reflects the fact that for some days after Egg Roll the Yes share was down around 40 and then took its time coming back. We trust our intuitive reading of Figure 2–1 more than such a regression estimate. Meanwhile, we do not have an alternative, more temporally realistic estimation model to propose. We tried a Koyck-lag setup but this stumbled over the awkward fact that in raw data consecutive daily readings are not smoothly distributed, but rather have the sawtoothed pattern typical of sampling variation with small Ns.

CHAPTER SEVEN

1 Based on estimations not presented. We used the term "immigrants" as it seemed to us to be code for ethnic and racial minorities, but some observers may demur at this identity. As a further test, we regressed the 1992 vote on "Quebec," "Aboriginal peoples," and "racial minorities" ratings from the 1993 post-election wave of the 1992–3 panel. This confirmed the strength of Quebec and the weakness of the others. The coefficient on Quebec feelings as measured in 1993 was slightly over half the values, presented below, estimated on 1992 measurements. This dropoff testifies to error in the measure (Achen, 1975), and the nullity of the other two coefficients may partly reflect similar operation of error. But the discontinuity between them and the Quebec measure is stark, and we are inclined at this point to refer back to the null coefficient on the 1992 immigrants measure. The original point just seems reinforced: ethnically speaking, the Charlottetown Accord was about Quebec in voters' minds. This said, non-French ethnicity itself – as opposed to *feelings* about non-French ethnicity – did constrain response to the Accord, a point we substantiate below.

2 Ratings are by "feeling thermometers" exactly like those in chapter 5. The items are **refh26** (Canada), **refh27** (Quebec), **refh27** (province), **refh29** (English Canadians), and **refh30** (immigrants).

3 About one voter in four rated Quebec below 50. On the low side of the mode (50, reflecting assignment of don't knows to this value), frequencies fell off monotonically. On the high side, however, there were clear pockets of affection: more voters in the 70s than in the 60s; nearly one in ten rated Quebec at 100.

4 On a kindred matter, voters' perceptions of their own province as winner or loser were unrelated to their perceptions of whether Quebec won or lost ($r = -0.04$).

5 A functionally similar claim is lodged for separate schools, where they exist. Guaranteeing denominational schooling rights was a price of Confederation and the deal, once made, should be kept, even if non-Catholics find it offensive, even if it represents unequal treatment of groups and thus offends against principles no less compelling but not constitutionally recognized until later.

6 All quotations in this paragraph are from the *Globe and Mail*, 14 September 1992, pp. A1–2.

7 Rebick was explicit on this, in her statement that the NAC supported strong language on distinct society recognition, Aboriginal self-government, and minority linguistic rights. The NAC was one of the few organizations to claim to prefer an asymmetric solution. See *Globe and Mail*, 17 September 1992, p. A19, and Rebick (1993).

8 Strikingly, the biggest anti-Accord billboard between Kingston and Brockville featured the expression, "Equal Rights for *All* Canadians."
9 The variable is a compound of response to two items, **refh16**, which refers
  to two groups by name, French and English, and **refh17**, which uses the
  number three and prompts additionally for Aboriginal peoples. When
  prompted for two groups only, a majority of respondents agreed with the
  founding-peoples characterization, but the ratio of agreement/disagree-
  ment was only about 60: 40. Of those disagreeing, over 60 percent clearly
  did so because Aboriginal peoples were not mentioned. Among those
  agreeing with the two-group version, about 20 percent rejected the three-
  group characterization when it was offered.
10 Ideas and feelings also played a role independently of group membership. Controlling sociodemographic background variables has only a mi-
  nuscule effect on coefficients: founders drops from 0.12 to 0.08; majority/
  minority drops from 0.07 to 0.06; and Quebec feeling from 0.45 to 0.44.
  This confirms Figure 1–1's demonstration of ideas and sentiments as further along the causal chain than background characteristics.
11 Our hunch is that in 1992 the words "founding people" had less resonance than "distinct society," which had been a matter of controversy at
  least since 1987 and which referred to Quebec, an easier object to dislike
  than the category of founding peoples, which, after all, includes a large
  fraction of English-speaking Canada.
12 This claim derives from evaluation of the function in the table:
  $$0.01 + 0.07 + 0.12 + (0.45)(0.50) = 0.43.$$
  This excludes all factors discussed in earlier chapters, of course, but all
  those factors are in the constant.
13 From solution of the following:
  $$0.50 = 0.01 + 0.07 + 0.12 + 0.45R.$$
  $$R = (0.50 - 0.01 - 0.07 - 0.12)/0.45 = 0.67,$$
  where R is the Quebec rating.
14 The 1988 election turned on the Canada-US Free Trade Agreement, but
  our sense is that the FTA was not absolutely fated to dominate the choice
  as completely as it did. Had one of the three core parties opposed the
  Meech Lake Accord, it might well have profited enormously, outside
  Quebec only, of course, and perhaps only for the short run. See Johnston
  et al. (1992), chapters 2, 3, and 8.
15 By 1980 the Liberal party won virtually every seat in the province and its
  share of the popular vote rivalled historic maximums.
16 So, in a way, did Trudeau. See, for instance, his post-Egg Roll answers to
  questions about divergences between himself and his erstwhile close allies,
  especially Jean Chrétien. He argued that his former allies had political positions to defend and thus spoke strategically whilst he himself no longer
  need do so, and therefore could speak sincerely. His statement of this case

was remarkably cool, analytical, and nonjudgmental, but the thrust was clear: he personally was now above politics. See Trudeau (1992), p. 41.

17 Strictly speaking, this is an exaggeration, for there was an anti-Quebec party in the field, Reform. But in 1992 Reform identifiers were few in number, swamped by non-partisans, as indicated in chapter 5. The handful of voters who did claim a Reform identification gave Quebec the most negative ratings of all.

18 Equations vary considerably in power. In the weakest, for fear of separation and for the new Senate, only 2 percent of the variance is explained; for the strongest, recognition of Quebec as a distinct society, the R^2 is 0.16. In every equation, standard errors are roughly as follows: Quebec rating, 0.05–0.06; minority rights, 0.03; founding peoples, 0.04.

19 When feelings about intervenors are controlled, party identification makes no difference to any opinion, general or specific. To the extent that the party system mediated opinion, then, it was through voters' judgments of leaders, not through mobilization of general partisan orientation.

20 Further proof of this is the response to a post-referendum question on whether or not we should go ahead with the Accord's self-government provisions anyway. The answer was one-sidedly positive.

21 Conventionally, the alternative to "ascription" has been styled "achievement." We do not mean to suggest that everything in Figure 7–4 is absolutely ascriptive; religion has some choice built into it, for example. Our concern was just to sort factors in a reasonably defensible way, mostly for graphical convenience.

22 In the 1992 survey Protestants were about twice as likely as Catholics to identify with the Conservative party (29 versus 15 percent), and just over half as likely as Catholics to identify with the Liberals (25 versus 41 percent).

23 Ethnic categories are inescapably crude, reflecting small numbers in more narrowly defined categories. As it is, non-Europeans make up a tiny fraction of the sample. It seemed important, however, to let them speak for themselves. Most, as a practical matter, are of Asian origin, from the Chinese culture area or the Indian subcontinent. Southern Europeans are mostly Italian. Eastern Europeans have origins in former Communist Bloc states. Northern Europeans are from the Low countries, Scandinavia, and countries with German as an official language. French is defined ethnically, rather than linguistically, as preliminary research indicated that that was indeed the critical divide, and outside Quebec ethnicity is a more inclusive definition than language use. Given the issues and the way votes were counted, it would have been interesting to track Aboriginal respondents, but only 8 turned up in the sample.

24 Strictly speaking, British ethnicity or no reported ethnicity. Respondents unable or unwilling to volunteer an origin are behaviourally and attitudi-

nally indistinguishable from British-origin respondents, and were most likely to have British ancestors, among others.

25 Among francophones outside Quebec, 45 percent gave priority to minority rights, 42 percent to majority rule, and 13 percent were undecided. The only other group in which more than 40 percent favoured minority rights was non-Europeans, but in this group no respondent failed to offer an opinion and so the balance still favoured majority rule. In every other group, over 55 percent favoured majority rule (over 60 percent for British and Eastern Europeans). Groups did not differ in recognition of founding peoples, so one-sided was the balance of three-group recognition.

26 Interpretation must be careful in this area, as the connection with Preston Manning almost certainly has a lot of spuriousness built into it. Many people would have been attracted by the Accord and repelled by Manning all at once, or attracted by Manning, with no direct causal connection between Manning's position and the voter's decision. This consideration also applies to voters on the other side, those repelled by the Accord but attracted by Manning. See the discussion of Northern Europeans and non-Europeans below.

27 As in the past, however, Liberal dominance in this group is more religious than ethnolinguistic. A multivariate estimation of factors in party identification confirms that in 1992 Catholics were about 15 points more Liberal, other things being equal, than all others. The specifically French component of Liberal orientation may have been worth another 7 points, but the French coefficient did not clear the traditional 5 percent significance threshold, even by a one-tailed test; it was only slightly larger than its standard error.

28 As with French Canadians, a big slice of Southern Europeans' Liberal connection reflects the group's nearly total Catholicism.

29 It would be tempting to attribute this effect to education or to encyclopaedic knowledge. More educated voters were more likely to know that the women's movement had come out against the Accord and, as the next section shows, the more educated were also more likely to endorse the Accord's key components. Even among the college-educated, however, women who knew that the women's movement was against the Accord were still more likely than women who did not to endorse the Aboriginal self-government and distinct society proposals.

30 *Maclean's*, 28 September 1992, p. 16.

31 Strictly speaking, if they attributed opposition to the "women's movement", as indicated by response to items **refg3a** and **refg3b**. The item on whether women were winners or losers in the Accord is **refd10**.

32 The reserved-seat items are **refe6** (some guaranteed for women), **refe7** (half guaranteed for women), and **refe8** (some guaranteed for Aboriginal peoples). These items were adminstered to random subsamples, to test

each alternative's rhetorical power. Supporters of the new Senate were less likely than opponents to support either variant of a female quota, but supporters and opponents were indistinguishable in approval of reserved seats for Aboriginal representatives.

33 Strictly speaking, the university coefficient contrasts university-educated respondents with high school graduates, as the other two groups were also represented in the equation. Figure 7–6 indicated that those groups were actually more distinct from the university group and so the university coefficient in Figure 7–7 slightly understates the true net effect.

34 The contrast is most striking with voters with post-secondary trade school or community college education, of whom only 18 percent affirmed minority rights, as compared with 27 percent for high school graduates and 34 percent for the university educated. Voters with less than high school education were as minority-oriented as university voters, but less willing to act on the orientation.

35 The group with truly distinctive attitudes outside Quebec were French Canadians.

CHAPTER EIGHT

1 Polls are entered in the figure by approximate date of fieldwork, not of publication. Where, as is typical, more than one day of fieldwork is reported, the entry is centred toward the beginning days, day two, as a rule, reflecting our own experience that over half the ultimate completions are recorded before the end of that clearance day. Poll data were furnished by Edouard Cloutier, of the Université de Montréal. A complete record can be found in Blais (1993).

2 Throughout the analysis, polls in Quebec (ours among them) tended to underestimate the Yes vote. See Blais (1993).

3 These two polls, by Environics and Angus Reid, were national polls with small Quebec subsamples, hence the diffident wording in the body of the text. We are inclined to take Environics-Reid numbers at face value, however, for three reasons. An early surge of support is typical for prospective ballot measures, the two polls essentially agree with each other, and later polls by both firms agreed with other results from Quebec.

4 Fieldwork houses differed in treatment of "leaners." Léger & Léger commonly did not assign them to sides, but rather left them with the undecided. As leaners broke disproportionately to the Yes side, the Léger & Léger strategy yielded low estimates of the Yes.

5 Recall that our vote question embodies an experiment. See chapter 2.

6 The same no-impact verdict is reached from comparing published polls before and after the debate (Blais, 1993). The Comquest-*Globe and Mail* tracking poll did indicate an increase in Yes support after the debate, but

that poll underestimated the Yes vote before the debate. In our own data, ratings of Bourassa increased 4 points in the week following the debate, but Parizeau ratings also increased, by 6 points.

7 As defined by language first spoken and still understood, in our file **refn16**.

8 The three-point difference made by taking citizenship into account is derived from Hamilton and Pinard (1984, p. 341).

9 The longest-term evidence is from Bernard (1976). Blais (1980) found this relationship for the 1980 referendum, as did Drouilly (1993) for the 1992 one. In each case the differential was produced by anglophones, not allophones.

10 The question is **reff11**.

11 This figure and all others in this chapter refers to respondents claiming to have voted in the referendum. Among non-voters, pro-sovereignty figures are lower.

12 The demographic modelling in Table 8–1 borrows directly from the setup for the rest of Canada in chapter 7. Characteristics not relevant to a homogeneous population sited in one province are omitted. For the record, sovereignty sentiment is also unrelated to region of residence (Montreal versus the rest of the province), occupation (manual versus non-manual), sector of employment (public versus private), and religiosity (importance of God in one's life).

13 The union coefficient had 6 chances in 100 of being generated by chance.

14 Nadeau indicates that the surge started before the ultimate failure of the Accord, either because the deal was expected to fail or in response to anti-Quebec manifestations, such as the Brockville flag-trampling incident.

15 As indicated by ratings on Canada and Quebec 100-point scales, **refh26** and **refh27** respectively.

16 The comparison must be made with care, given language differences between samples. Quebeckers rate Quebec lower than respondents outside Quebec rate Canada and their own provinces. This hints at a modest language artifact.

17 The threat question is **refe12**.

18 The question is **reff14**.

19 Support for sovereignty takes the value of 0 for those very opposed to sovereignty, .25 for those somewhat opposed, .75 for those somewhat favourable, 1 for those very favourable and .50 for those with no opinion. Threat is coded as 1 for perceiving a threat to the language, 0 for seeing none, and 0.50 for having no opinion. Concern over the economic impact of separation is coded as 1 for "much worse," 0.75 for "somewhat worse," 0.50 for "don't know" and "no difference," 0.25 for "somewhat better," and 0.00 for "much better."

20 The youngest voters, aged 18–24, are very pessimistic: 78 percent see French as threatened.

21 See also Nevitte and Gingras (1983). Perception of linguistic threat has some puzzling features. For instance, the gender gap is wide – 62 percent of women, compared to 37 percent of men, feel that the French language is threatened – but we can find no compelling explanation for any difference, much less one this huge. On the other hand, residence in the Montreal area, where the threat is objectively greatest, does not make one more concerned, nor does education.

22 The No side may have fared better in specific communities, Latin Americans for instance (see Drouilly, 1993).

23 This is one place where the induction seems backwards, where the Yes share is higher in treatment than in control. Presumably treatment "don't know's" include many who would have been "somewhat favourable" to sovereignty had they received the control (no definition) wording.

24 Only half of francophone sovereignists agreed that the Accord will reduce Quebec to the status of a province like the others (**refd2**), and there is little difference between sovereignists' and non-sovereignists' response to this question. Perhaps some respondents reasoned that the Accord simply did not alter Quebec's status. The question may have been too highly conceptualized, too attuned to the debate over asymmetry versus equality of the provinces, as it produced many "don't know" responses.

25 As well, the Yes share is underestimated for the whole sample. Adjusting for the global underestimation while preserving French/non-French differences would produce a non-francophone vote share over 80 percent.

26 The standard source on cross-level inference is now Achen and Shively (1995), who are generally sceptical of "contextualist" claims (p. 227n).

27 If many saw Quebec as a loser, who were seen as winners? Most commonly chosen was Aboriginal peoples. Also critical is the correlation between perceptions for Quebec and for other key players: does seeing Quebec as a loser entail seeing another as a winner? For no other group perception – Aboriginal peoples, the West, or the federal government – was the correlation with the Quebec perception significantly different from zero. Finally, inserting other group perceptions into estimations such as those in tables 8–2 and 8–3 adds no explanatory power. We show below that perceptions of Quebec's performance were important, but these perceptions were of Quebec alone. Quebeckers did not see negotiations as a zero-sum game and did not therefore express frustration with gains by other groups.

28 The coding of distinct society opinion differs subtly from that for the rest of Canada and for initial Quebec estimations in chapter 3. Here, voters believing that the clause did not go far enough – a very numerous group – were coded at 0.5, along with the "don't know" response. This allows the qualification to be represented directly in impact estimations below, and means that a score of 1 indicates, as it should, unqualified support for the

clause. Outside Quebec qualified support (where the qualification was almost always that the clause went too far) was the best that could be expected. This coding has the effect of reducing the apparent francophone/non-francophone difference. Almost all non-francophones who supported the clause supported it unqualifiedly or with the qualification that it went too far (the latter still were coded at 1). More francophones than non-francophones supported recognition, but a clear majority then went on to qualify their support by saying the clause did not go far enough. The difference in overall willingness to support recognition keeps the francophone balance more positive than the non-francophone one, but qualifications bring the measured balance back toward the neutral point.

29 In support for self-government, non-francophones were hardly distinguishable from sovereignists. Perhaps the latter recognized affinity in the principle of self-determination.

30 This factor was included here to test the possibility that Quebeckers, like voters elsewhere, punished the political class for the post-1990 recession. They did not. It did not make sense to include this factor in the sovereignty estimation, given that debate's ongoing character.

31 The "woman" coefficient in the leftmost column has one chance in eight of being generated by chance.

32 In this estimation education is represented by a single dummy variable, for university education. The education gradient extended further down the ladder than in the rest of Canada, such that with three levels represented, the university dummy understated the total education effect. As the dummies on the other side were unstable and not significant, it seemed best to average the university effect against all others; this gave a more robust reading than setting high school graduates as the reference category.

33 This is best seen by comparing sentimental extremes: 70 percent of francophone non-sovereignists more or equally attached to Canada voted Yes, compared to 37 percent of those more attached to Quebec.

34 The item is **refh1**, asked in each province. Generally speaking, division of powers questions perform rather like those for Senate reform: they evoke one-sided response, in this case against Ottawa. But probing about specific areas of jurisdiction tends to draw a mixture of blanks and reaffirmation of the status quo. As with Senate reform, survey items on the division of powers respond to an elite debate which has very little resonance on the street. An extended discussion is Johnston (1986).

35 The direction of causation is most likely as implied in this setup – that is, from group sentiment to leader evaluation, not the other way around. If it were the other away around, coefficients on group sentiments would not drop so much; that they drop indicates that leader ratings follow rather than lead group sentiment. Also, of course, adding leaders to the setup

does not just shuffle covariance; the setup's overall explanatory power surges.

36 Although Castonguay's support for the Yes may be factored into recognition of the business community's support.

37 In a more refined estimation, the quality of the compromise also emerged as significant. But the fact that it disappeared when specific elements entered estimation, combined with the fact that the only specific element that mattered was the distinct society clause, suggested a Quebec-centred judgment.

CHAPTER NINE

1 Delli Carpini and Keeter proposed five potential knowledge factors but found in a LISREL analysis that these were effectively one factor, that "individuals knowledgeable about one aspect of politics were apt to be knowledgeable about others" (p. 1185).

2 A case might be made for shortening the Quebec scale, but we could not really find a basis for doing so, and if we did we would lose a key point in Table 9–2. Later in the chapter, we dichotomize the measure separately for Quebec and the rest of Canada at their respective medians.

3 The linear fits in Figure 9–1 are based on individual-level regressions; parameters are as in equations (2) in Table 9–5. As numbers in the two highest-information cells in Quebec were small, estimates were pooled and, arbitrarily, placed in level four on the 0–6 scale.

The Quebec-All line might actually be curvilinear. There is a precedent in the literature for this, starting with Converse's classic 1966 statement that turnover in vote and other quantities was greatest at middling levels of information, a point which Zaller (1992) pursues at some length. The difficulty here is that we do not have a change measure. In the static case, we would expect the curve's concavity to reflect the strongest (not on its substance, just its sheer loudness) signal. If Yes forces made the loudest noise, the curve should be concave downwards. If the No forces made the loudest noise, then the curve should be concave upwards, as in fact is the case. The No side did win, so perhaps they made the loudest noise. Then again, Quebec rules seemed to level the playing field. Strikingly, resources were most one-sided in the rest of Canada and there no concavity was visible. For our purposes, in any case, this is a side issue. The critical thing about the all-Quebec relationship is that knowledge did not favour either side, in contrast with the rest of Canada.

4 As argued by Luskin and Ten Barge (1995).

5 Quebec respondents are excluded from the table for two reasons: we did not ask for provincial party identification and would have been forced to

use the 1989 vote as a proxy; but cross-party consensus was absent, of course, and partisanship as such was not at issue.

6 As the education coefficient is -0.23 and the intercept is 0.74, the estimated value for university-educated voters on the dependent variable is 0.51, a virtually exact balance between acceptance and rejection.

7 For Quebec we are not absolutely wedded to this particular interpretation of the information-feeling-vote relation, and two alternative interpretations are imaginable. With data and estimations in hand, we can rule out one alternative but not the other. To make the point, abstract from relationships in Figure 1–2 to focus on these three variables. Figure 1–2 and this chapter assume that the basic sequence is:

(1) Information $\longrightarrow$ Canada feeling $\longrightarrow$ Vote .

But the sequence could also be:

(2) Canada feeling $\longrightarrow$ Information $\longrightarrow$ Vote .

In this case, liking Canada makes one seek out information, rather than the reverse, and information is then itself a factor in the vote. This sequence is not borne out by the data, however. If information intervened between feeling and the vote, feeling coefficients would shrink as information is controlled; the information coefficient should not shrink as feeling is controlled. But we know from Table 9–9 that the information coefficient does shrink as feeling is controlled, and we assert without presenting tabular evidence that the feeling coefficient in the source estimations for Table 9–9 is as large as (actually slightly larger than) the coefficient reported in chapter 8. Clearly, the sequence in (2) is ruled out. But a third sequence is possible:

(3) Canada feeling $\longrightarrow$ Information
$\longrightarrow$ Vote.

In this case, feeling leads to learning but information has no intrinsic non-interactive relation to the vote. Unfortunately we have no critical test between this sequence and (1), for each predicts that the information-vote relation will disappear when feeling is controlled, as actually happens. The issue is thus left hanging. These doubts do not prejudice interaction-effect analyses in the next section.

8 In Quebec, the group structure was too weak to merit further exploration; in a sense, Quebec was the group in question, and the issue was how vulnerable its members felt themselves to be.

9 The logic of the setup is based on Bartels (1990; 1995), the most focused assault on the question to date. Bartels's own setup is more sophisticated, but nothing fundamental is lost by the crudity of our design. The cutpoint between low- and high-information is roughly at the median: between two and three correct attributions for the rest of Canada; between one and two correct for francophone non-sovereignists.

10 Are the relationships here somehow tautological or artifactual, produced by the fact that the information measure is built from awareness of the

very intervenors whose impact we now condition on that measure? Three points need to be made in reply. First, evaluation of intervenors is by a separate measure, the feeling thermometer. Second, the awareness-impact sequence is highly commonsensical. Third, and perhaps most telling, not all evaluative impact is from the intervenors whose visibility is at issue; most in fact is from agenda-setters, who do not figure in computation of the information index. In the Quebec setup, in fact, no outside intervenor appears directly; the story is entirely about Bourassa and Parizeau.

11 This is easy to see in the bivariate case. Where r is the correlation between X and Y, S_x and S_y are standard deviations for X and Y respectively, and b is the unstandardized regression coefficient of Y on X:
$$r = b \, (S_x/S_y) .$$
Thus r, and by implication r^2, increases as either b or S_x increases. The analogue holds true in the multivariate case, where R^2 corresponds to r^2.

12 Inside Quebec low-information voters did not connect group feeling – for Canada – all that efficiently to the choice.

13 Some of these must have been guessers, however, especially given the high level of attributions before he made his opposition official. In Trudeau's case, to be sure, guessing need not have been as random as for other potential intervenors.

CHAPTER TEN

1 A generally sour note on the idea of consociational democracy, and the observation that resort to referendums may signal the breakdown of consociationalism, is Barry (1978).

2 Argument along these lines can be found in Weaver (1992b), p. 74; Ajzenstat (1994); and Luzstig (1994). The most extended consideration of consociationalism as it applies to Canada is McRae (1974).

3 Pal and Seidle (1993) certainly saw the 1990–1 phases in both Quebec and the rest of Canada as cathartic (pp. 148–54). We argue that proper catharsis required the full sequence, including the vote.

4 See our own consultation of Canada's plebisicitory history, below, and various chapters in Butler and Ranney (1994a), especially those by Bogdanor, and Brady and Kaplan. See also the extraordinary dissection of French experience in Wright (1978).

5 As quoted in Butler and Kitzinger (1976), p. 12.

6 It does imply, though, that the party's potential electoral coalition is split on the issue.

7 Gallup evidence on Canadian attitudes to conscription can be found in *Public Opinion Quarterly* 6 (Spring 1942), pp. 158ff; and ibid. (Fall 1942), pp. 488–9.

8 Our 1942 account draws principally upon Granatstein and Hitsman (1977).

9 See Cloutier et al., (1992), pp. 66, 68.

10 See above, chapter 1.

11 Quotation taken from Bogdanor (1994), p. 35.

12 The law went on the books as the Referendum Act, Statutes of British Columbia 1990, c. 68.

13 Interestingly, Saskatchewan also adopted referendum legislation in this period (Referendum and Plebiscite Act, SS 1991, c. R-8.01, s.5) and voters in that province cast votes on three references in the 1991 provincial general election. One of the references was on a statutory requirement for referral of any constitutional amendment. The results were deemed to bind only the existing government, and that government, led by Grant Devine, fell with the election. The NDP government under Roy Romanow did not seem to feel bound by the requirement, although had the Canada-wide 1992 referendum not been organized, pressure on it might have mounted. The sequence in British Columbia was quite similar, but the NDP in that province was less confident in resisting pressure for referral. See Canada West Foundation (1992).

14 Cairns (1991), Schwartz (1987), and Jeffrey (1993) argue that the closed-door nature of the Meech Lake negotiations themselves contributed to its illegitimacy.

15 The 1988 "None" rows include Reform, Christian Heritage, and other party voters, but their numbers are swamped by outright non-voters and ineligibles.

16 Strictly speaking, the divide is between No voters and all others: 1988 Conservatives who sat 1992 out and who turned out in 1993 were one-sidedly Conservative, and virtually none of their defection was to Reform.

17 Of course, the same was even more true of the small 1988 NDP base in Quebec.

18 In the Quebec sample, only 10 percent were Conservative Yes voters, in contrast to the 16 percent who were Liberal Yes voters (calculations include non-voters).

19 It may have helped that Liberal leaders in British Columbia and Manitoba opposed the Accord, along with Trudeau.

20 These are arguments about the rest of Canada. Alternative scenarios are harder to imagine for Quebec, given the narrowness of the real battleground in that province: non-francophones could hardly more supportive than they actually were, while sovereignists would be unmoved by rest-of-Canada cues.

21 The questionnaire item is **prd5**.

22 Francophone non-sovereignists who voted Yes were overwhelmingly likely (85 percent) to choose "federalism as it now"; this suggests that their Yes vote was something of an act of desperation. Among non-sovereignists who voted No, the balance was closer – 52 percent "as

now," 30 percent a sovereign Quebec – but still leaning clearly to the status quo.

23 This depends on how well survey response on such matters predicts actual vote.

CHAPTER ELEVEN

1 The landmark contribution is Luskin (1987).

Bibliography

Achen, Christopher H. 1975. "Mass Political Attitudes and the Survey Response." *American Political Science Review* 69: 1218–37.
– and W. Phillips Shively. 1995. *Cross-Level Inference.* Chicago: University of Chicago Press.
Aitken, Don. 1978. "Australia," in Butler and Ranney (1978).
Ajzenstat, Janet. 1994. "Constitution-Making and the Myth of the People," in Cook (1994).
Apter, David E., ed. 1964. *Ideology and Discontent.* New York: Free Press.
Aubert, Jean-François. 1978. "Switzerland," in Butler and Ranney (1978).
Bakvis, Herman and Laura G. Macpherson. 1995. "Quebec Block Voting and the Canadian Electoral System." *Canadian Journal of Political Science* 28: 659–92.
Banting, Keith and Richard Simeon, eds. 1983. *And No One Cheered: Federalism, Democracy, and the Constitution Act.* Toronto: Methuen.
Barber, Benjamin R. 1984. *Strong Democracy: Participatory Politics for a New Age.* Berkeley: University of California Press.
Barker, Sir Ernest. 1942. *Reflections on Government.* London: Oxford University Press.
Barry, Brian M. 1978. *Sociologists, Economists, and Democracy.* Chicago: University of Chicago Press.
Bartels, Larry M. 1988. *Presidential Primaries and the Dynamics of Public Choice.* Princeton, NJ: Princeton University Press.
– 1990. "Public Opinion and Political Interests." Paper presented at the annual meeting of the Midwest Political Science Association, Chicago.
– 1995. "Uninformed Votes: Information Effects in Presidential Elections." Princeton University: unpublished manuscript.

Bennett, W. Lance and David L. Paletz, eds. 1994. *Taken by Storm: The Media, Public Opinion, and US Foreign Policy in the Gulf War.* Chicago: University of Chicago Press.

Bernard, André. 1976. "L'abstenionisme des électeurs de langue anglaise au Québec," in Daniel Latouche, Guy Lord, and Jean-Guy Vaillancourt, eds., *Le Processus Electorale au Québec: Les Elections Provinciales de 1970 et 1973.* Montréal: Hurtubise HMH.

Bishop, George F., Robert W. Oldendick, and A.J. Tuchfarber. 1978. "Effects of Question Wording and Format on Political Attitude Consistency." *Public Opinion Quarterly* 42: 81–92.

Blais, André. 1980. "Le vote: ce que l'on sait ... ce que l'on ne sait pas," in *Québec: Un Pays Incertain.* Montreal: Québec/Amérique.

– 1992. "Les québécois sont-ils confus?" *La Presse,* 31 March 1992, p. B1.

– 1993. "The Quebec Referendum: Quebeckers Say No," in McRoberts and Monahan (1993).

Blais, André and Martin Boyer. 1996. "Assessing the Impact of Televised Debates." *British Journal of Political Science* 26: 143–64.

Blais, André and Jean Crête. 1991. "Pourquoi l'opinion publique au Canada anglaise a-t-elle rejeté l'Accord du Lac Meech?" in Raymond Hudon and Réjean Pelletier, eds. *L'Engagement intellectuel: Mélange en l'honneur de Léon Dion.* Sainte-Foy: Les Presses de l'Université Laval.

Blais, André, Jean Crête, and Guy Lachapelle. 1986. "L'élection québécois de 1985: un bilan des sondages." *Canadian Journal of Political Science* 19: 325–37.

Blais, André and Richard Nadeau. 1984. "La clientèle du oui," in Crête (1984).

Boadway, Robin W., Thomas J. Courchene, and Douglas D. Purvis. 1991. *Economic Dimensions of Constitutional Change.* Kingston, Ont: Queen's University, John Deutsch Institute for the Study of Economic Policy.

Boadway, Robin W., Douglas D. Purvis, and Jean-François Wen. 1991. "Economic Dimensions of Constitutional Change: A Survey of the Issues," in Boadway et al. (1991), pp. 11–44.

Bochel, John, David Denver, and Allan Macartney, eds. 1981. *The Referendum Experience: Scotland 1979.* Aberdeen: Aberdeen University Press.

Bochel, John and David Denver. 1981. "The Outcome," in Bochel, Denver, and Macartney (1981).

Bogdanor, Vernon. 1994. "Western Europe," in Butler and Ranney (1994).

Brady, Henry E. and Richard Johnston. 1993. "The Electoral Consequences of Issue Cleavages in Recent Canadian Elections." Delivered at the Conference on Canada in Comparative Perspective, Stanford University.

Brady, Henry E. and Cynthia S. Kaplan. 1994. "Eastern Europe and the Former Soviet Union," in Butler and Ranney (1994).

Breton, Raymond. 1984. "The Production and Allocation of Symbolic Resources: An Analysis of the Linguistic and Ethnocultural Fields in Canada." *Canadian Review of Sociology and Anthropology* 21: 123–44.

Brodie, Ian and Neil Nevitte. 1993a. "Evaluating the Citizens' Constitution Theory." *Canadian Journal of Political Science* 26: 235–67.

– 1993b. "Clarifying Differences: A Rejoinder to Alan Cairns's Defence of the Citizen's Constitution Theory." *Canadian Journal of Political Science* 26: 269–72.

Brown, R. Craig and Ramsay Cook. 1974. *Canada, 1896–1921: A Nation Transformed.* Toronto: McClelland and Stewart.

Butler, David. 1981. "The World Experience," in Austin Ranney, ed. *The Referendum Device.* Washington, DC: American Enterprise Institute for Public Policy Research.

Butler, David and Uwe Kitzinger. 1976. *The 1975 Referendum.* London: Macmillan.

Butler, David and Austin Ranney. 1978. *Referendums: A Study in Practice and Theory.* Washington, DC: American Enterprise Institute for Public Policy Research.

–, eds. 1994. *Referendums around the World: The Growing Use of Direct Democracy.* Washington, DC: AEI Press.

Cairns, Alan C. 1991. "Citizens (Outsiders) and Governments (Insiders) in Constitution-Making: The Case of Meech Lake," in Cairns, *Disruptions.* Toronto: McClelland and Stewart.

– 1992. *Charter vs Federalism: The Dilemmas of Constitutional Reform.* Montreal: McGill-Queen's University Press.

– 1993. "A Defence of the Citizens' Constitution Theory Theory: A Response to Ian Brodie and Neil Nevitte." *Canadian Journal of Political Science* 26: 261–7.

Campbell, Angus, Philip E. Converse, Warren Miller, and Donald E. Stokes. 1966. *Elections and the Political Order.* New York: Wiley.

Campbell, Robert M. and Leslie A. Pal. 1991. *The Real Worlds of Canadian Politics: Cases in Process and Policy.* Peterborough, Ont: Broadview.

Canada West Foundation. 1992. *Letting the People Decide: A Canadian Constitutional Referendum.* Calgary: Canada West Foundation.

Cantril, Hadley. 1944. *Gauging Public Opinion.* Princeton, NJ: Princeton University Press.

Carmines, Edward G. and James A. Stimson. 1980 "The Two Faces of Issue Voting." *American Political Science Review* 74: 78–91.

Chong, Dennis, Herbert McClosky, and John R. Zaller. 1983. "Patterns of Support for Democratic and Capitalist Values." *British Journal of Political Science* 13: 401–40.

Christiansen, Niels Finn. 1992. "The Danish No to Maastricht." *New Left Review* 195: 97–101.

Cloutier, Édouard, Jean H. Guy, and Daniel Latouche. 1992. *Le Virage: L'évolution de l'Opinion publique au Québec depuis 1960.* Montréal: Québec/ Amérique.

Cohen, Andrew. 1990. *A Deal Undone: The Making and Breaking of the Meech Lake Accord.* Vancouver: Douglas and McIntyre.

Collas, Patrice. 1992. "Popular consultations and the latest French referendum." *Revue politique et parlementaire* (September-October): 29–43.

Converse, Philip E. 1964. "The Nature of Belief Systems in Mass Publics," in Apter (1964).

– 1966. "Information Flow and the Stability of Partisan Attitudes," in Campbell, Converse, Miller, and Stokes (1966).

– 1990. "Popular Representation and the Distribution of Information," in Ferejohn and Kuklinski (1990).

Converse, Philip E. and Roy Pierce. 1986. *Political Representation in France.* Cambridge, MA: Harvard University Press.

Cook, Curtis, ed. 1994. *Constitutional Predicament: Canada after the Referendum of 1992.* Montreal: McGill-Queen's University Press.

Crête, Jean, ed. 1984. *Le Comportement électorale au Québec.* Chicoutimi: Gaëtan Morin.

Cronin, Thomas E. 1989. *Direct Democracy: The Politics of Initiative, Referendum, and Recall.* Cambridge, MA: Harvard University Press.

Dalton, Russell J. 1988. *Citizen Politics in Western Democracies.* Chatham, NJ: Chatham House.

Dalton, Russell and Martin J. Wattenberg. 1993. "The Not So Simple Act of Voting," in Finifter (1993).

Daudt, H. 1961. *Floating Voters and the Floating Vote: A Critical Analysis of American and English Election Studies.* Leiden: H.E. Stenfert Kroese.

Davison, W.P. and L. Gordenker, eds. 1980. *Resolving Nationality Conflicts: The Role of Public Opinion Research.* New York: Praeger.

Delacourt, Susan. 1993. *United We Fall: The Crisis of Democracy in Canada.* Toronto: Viking.

Delli Carpini, Michael X. and Scott Keeter. 1993. "Measuring Political Knowledge: Putting First Things First." *American Journal of Political Science* 37: 1179–1206.

Dicey, Albert Venn. 1890. "Ought the Referendum Be Introduced into England?" *Contemporary Review.*

Dion, Stéphane. 1992. "Explaining Quebec Nationalism," in Weaver (1992a), pp. 77–121.

Downs, Anthony. 1957. *An Economic Theory of Democracy.* New York: Harper.

Drouilly, Pierre. 1993. "L'analyse des résultats référendaires," in Denis Monière, ed. *L'Année politique au Québec, 1992.* Montréal: Université de Montréal.

Elster, Jon. 1986. "The Market and the Forum: Three Varieties of Political Theory," in Elster and Hylland (1986).

Elster, Jon and Aanund Hylland. 1986. *Foundations of Social Choice Theory.* Cambridge: Cambridge University Press.

English, John. 1977. *The Decline of Party: The Conservatives and the Party System, 1901–21.* Toronto: University of Toronto Press.

Farquharson, Robin. 1969. *Theory of Voting.* New Haven: Yale University Press.

Ferejohn, John A. and James H. Kuklinski, eds., *Information and Democratic Processes.* Urbana and Chicago: University of Illinois Press, pp. 369–88.

Festinger, Leon. 1957. *Theory of Cognitive Dissonance.* Stanford: Stanford University Press.

Finifter, Ada W., ed. 1993. *Political Science: The State of the Dsicipline.* Washington, DC: American Political Science Association.

Fishkin, James. 1991. *Democracy and Deliberation: New Directions for Democratic Reform.* New Haven: Yale University Press.

Gamson, William A. and André Modigliani. 1966. "Knowledge and Foreign Policy Opinion: Some Models for Consideration." *Public Opinion Quarterly* 30: 187–99.

Gibbins, Roger. 1983. "Constitutional Politics and the West," in Banting and Simeon (1983).

Gibbins, Roger and J. Rick Ponting. 1978. *Canadians' Opinions and Attitudes Towards Indians and Indian Issues: Findings of a National Study.* Ottawa: Department of Indian Affairs and Northern Development.

Granatstein, J.L. and J.M. Hitsman. 1977. *Broken Promises: A History of Conscription in Canada.* Toronto: Oxford University Press.

Green. Donald P. 1988. "On the Dimensionality of Partisan and Ideological Affect." *American Journal of Political Science* 32: 758–80.

– 1992. "The Price Elasticity of Mass Preferences." *American Political Science Review* 86: 128–48.

Greenwood, Gordon. 1946 [1976]. *The Future of Australian Federalism.* St. Lucia: University of Queensland Press (2nd ed.).

Grofman, Bernard, ed. 1993. *Information, Participation, and Choice:* An Economic Theory of Democracy *in Perspective.* Ann Arbor: University of Michigan Press.

Grofman, Bernard and Guillermo Owen, eds. 1986. *Information Pooling and Group Decision Making.* Greenwich, Conn. and London, UK: JAI Press.

Grofman, Bernard and Julie Withers. 1993. "Information-pooling Models of Electoral Politics," in Grofman (1993).

Habert, Philippe. 1992–3. "Europe's choice and the French voter's decision." *Commentaire* (hiver): 871–80.

Hawkes, David. 1989. *Aboriginal Peoples and Constitutional Reform: What Have We Learned?* Kingston, Ont: Queen's University, Institute of Intergovernmental Relations.

Harris, Richard G. and Douglas D. Purvis. 1991a. "Constitutional Change and Canada's Economic Prospects." Kingston, Ont.: Queen's University, unpublished ms.

– 1991b. "Some Economic Aspects of Political Restructuring," in Boadway et al. (1991), pp. 189–211.

Hofstadter, Richard. 1955. *The Age of Reform*. New York: Vintage.

Hogg, Peter W. 1985. *Constitutional Law of Canada*. Toronto: Carswell (2nd ed.).

Hughes, Colin. 1994. "Australia and New Zealand," in Butler and Ranney (1994).

Iyengar, Shanto, Mark D. Peters, and Donald R. Kinder. 1982. "Experimental Demonstrations of the Not-So-Minimal Consequences of Television News Programs." *American Political Science Review* 76: 848–58.

Jeffrey, Brooke. 1993. *Strange Bedfellows, Trying Times*. Toronto: Key Porter Books.

Johnston, Richard. 1986. *Public Opinion and Public Policy in Canada: Questions of Confidence*. Toronto: University of Toronto Press.

Johnston, Richard, André Blais, Henry E. Brady, and Jean Crête. 1992. *Letting the People Decide: Dynamics of a Canadian Election*. Montreal: McGill-Queen's University Press and Stanford: Stanford University Press.

Johnston, Richard, André Blais, Henry E. Brady, Elisabeth Gidengil, and Neil Nevitte. 1994. "The Collapse of a Party System? The 1993 Canadian Election." Prepared for delivery at the 1994 annual meeting of the American Political Science Association, New York.

Katz, Elihu and Paul F. Lazarsfeld. 1955. *Personal Influence*. New York: Free Press.

Kiewiet, D. Roderick and Mathew McCubbins. 1991. *The Logic of Delegation*. Chicago: University of Chicago Press.

Knight, Kathleen. 1984. "The Dimensionality of Partisan and Ideological Affect." *American Politics Quarterly* 12: 305–34.

– 1985. "Ideology in the 1980 Election: Ideological Sophistication Does Matter." *Journal of Politics* 47: 828–53.

Kobach, Chris. 1994. "Switzerland," in Butler and Ranney (1994).

Krehbiel, Keith. 1991. *Information and Legislative Organization*. Ann Arbor: University of Michigan Press.

Kuklinski, James H., ed. 1995. *Political Psychology and Political Behavior*. New York: Cambridge University Press.

Laycock, David. 1990. *Populism and Democratic Thought in the Canadian Prairies*. Toronto: University of Toronto Press.

– 1994. "Reforming Canadian Democracy? Institutions and Ideology in the Reform Party Project." *Canadian Journal of Political Science* 27: 213–47.

LeDuc, Lawrence and Jon Pammett. 1995. "Referendum Voting: Attitudes and Behaviour in the 1992 Constitutional Referendum." *Canadian Journal of Political Science* 28: 3–33.

Lijphart, Arend. 1968. *The Politics of Accommodation: Pluralism and Democracy in the Netherlands*. Berkeley: University of California Press.

– 1977. *Democracy in Plural Societies: A Comparative Exploration*. New Haven: Yale University Press.

Lisée, Jean-François. 1994a. *Le Tricheur: Robert Bourassa et les Québécois 1990–1991*. Montréal: Boréal.

– 1994b. *Le Naufrageur: Robert Bourassa et les Québécois 1991–1992*. Montréal: Boréal.

Lupia, Arthur. 1992. "Busy Voters, Agenda Control, and the Power of Information." *American Political Science Review* 86: 390–404.

– 1994. "Shortcuts versus Encyclopedias: Information and Voting Behavior in California Insurance Reform Elections." *American Political Science Review* 88: 63–76.

– 1995. "Who Can Persuade? A Formal Theory, a Survey and Implications for Democracy." Prepared for presentation at the annual meeting of the Midwest Political Science Association, Chicago, 6–8 April.

Luskin, Robert C. 1987. "Measuring Political Sophistication." *American Journal of Political Science* 31: 856–99.

– 1990. "Explaining Political Sophistication." *Political Behavior* 22: 331–61.

– 1995. "Political Psychology, Political Behavior, and Politics: Questions of Aggregation, Causal Distance, and Taste," in Kuklinski (1995).

Luskin, Robert C. and Joseph C. Ten Barge. 1995. "Education, Intelligence, and Political Sophistication." Prepared for presentation at the annual meeting of the Midwest Political Science Association, Chicago, 6–8 April.

Lusztig, Michael. 1994. "Constitutional Paralysis: Why Canadian Constitutional Initiatives Are Doomed to Fail." *Canadian Journal of Political Science* 27: 747–71.

Luthardt, Wolfgang. 1991–92. "Direct Democracy in Western Europe: The Case of Switzerland." *Telos* (Winter): 101–2.

– 1993. "European Integration and Referendums: Analytical Considerations and Empirical Evidence," in Alan W Cafruny and Glenda G Rosenthal, eds. *The State of the European Community 2: The Maastricht Debates and Beyond*. Boulder, CO: Lynne Rienner, pp. 53–71.

Macartney, Allan. 1981. "The Protagonists," in Bochel, Denver, and Macartney (1981).

Magleby, David B. 1984. *Direct Legislation: Voting on Ballot Propositions in the United States*. Baltimore: Johns Hopkins University Press.

Manin, Bernard. 1987. "On Legitimacy and Political Deliberation." *Political Theory* 15: 338–68.

Mansbridge, Jane. 1980. *Beyond Adversary Democracy*. New York: Basic Books.

McCallum, John and Chris Green. 1991. *Parting as Friends: The Economic Consequences for Quebec*. Toronto: C.D. Howe Institute.

McClosky, Herbert and Alida Brill. 1983. *Dimensions of Tolerance: What Americans Believe about Civil Liberties*. New York: Russell Sage.

McKelvey, Richard D. and Peter C. Ordeshook. 1986. "Information, Electoral Equilibria and the Democratic Ideal." *Journal of Politics* 48: 909–37.

McLean, Iain. 1991 "Rational Choice and Politics." *Political Studies* 39: 496–512.

McRae, Kenneth D., ed. 1974. *Consociational Democracy: Political Accommodation in Segmented Societies.* Toronto: McClelland and Stewart.

McRoberts, Kenneth and Patrick J. Monahan, eds. 1993. *The Charlottetown Accord, the Referendum, and the Future of Canada.* Toronto: University of Toronto Press.

Meadwell, Hudson. 1993. "The Politics of Nationalism in Quebec." *World Politics* 45: 203–42.

Miller, Arthur H. and Warren E. Miller. 1976. "Ideology in the 1972 Election: Myth or Reality – a Rejoinder." *American Political Science Review* 70: 753–78.

Miller, J.R. 1979. *Equal Rights: The Jesuits' Estates Act Controversy.* Montreal: McGill-Queen's University Press.

Miller, Nicholas R. 1986. "Information, Electorates, and Democracy: Some Extensions and Interpretations of the Condorcet Jury Theorem," in Grofman and Owen (1986).

Monahan, Patrick J. 1991. *Meech Lake: The Inside Story.* Toronto: University of Toronto Press.

Nadeau, Richard. 1992. "Le virage souverainiste des Québécois." *Recherches Sociographiques* 33: 9–28.

Nevitte, Neil and François-Pierre Gingras. 1983. "La Révolution en plan et le paradigme en cause." *Canadian Journal of Political Science* 16: 691–716.

Nie, Norman H., Sidney Verba, and John R. Petrocik. 1976. *The Changing American Voter.* Cambridge, MA: Harvard University Press.

Noël, Alain. 1994. "Deliberating the Constitution: The Meaning of the Canadian Referendum of 1992," in Cook (1994).

Norrie, Kenneth, Robin Boadway, and Lars Osberg. 1991. "The Constitution and the Social Contract," in Boadway et al. (1991), pp. 225–53.

Northrup, David A. and Anne E. Oram. 1994. *The 1992 Referendum on the Charlottetown Constitutional Accord: Technical Documentation.* North York, Ont.: York University, Institute for Social Research.

Pammett, Jon H., Jane Jenson, Harold D. Clarke, and Lawrence LeDuc. 1984. "Soutien politique et comportement électorale lors du référendum québécois," in Crête (1984).

Page, Benjamin I. and Robert Y. Shapiro. 1992. *The Rational Public: Fifty Years of Trends in Americans' Policy Preferences.* Chicago: University of Chicago Press.

Pal, Leslie A. and F. Leslie Seidle. 1993. "Constitutional Politics, 1990–92: The Paradox of Participation," in Phillips (1993).

Pateman, Carole. 1980. *Participation and Democratic Theory.* Cambridge: Cambridge University Press.

Pettersen, Per Arnt, Anders Todal Jenssen, and Ola Listhaug. 1995. "The 1994 Referendum in Norway: Continuity and Change." Prepared for presentation at the annual meeting of the Midwest Political Science Association, Chicago, 6–8 April.

Phillips, Susan D., ed. 1993. *How Ottawa Spends: A More Democratic Canada ...?* Ottawa: Carleton University Press.

Pinard, Maurice. 1980. "Self-Determination in Quebec: Loyalties, Incentives, and Constitutional Options Among French-Speaking Quebeckers," in Davison and Gordenker (1980).

Pinard, Maurice and Richard Hamilton, 1984 "Les québécois votent NON: Le sens et la portée du vote," in Crête (1984).

Popkin, Samuel. 1992. *The Reasoning Voter.* Chicago: University of Chicago Press.

Rae, Douglas W. 1975. "The Limits of Consensual Decision." *American Political Science Review* 69: 1270–94.

Rebick, Judy. 1993. "The Charlottetown Accord: A Faulty Framework and a Wrong-Headed Compromise," in McRoberts and Monahan (1993), pp. 102–6.

Resnick, Philip. 1990. *Letters to a Québécois Friend.* Montreal: McGill-Queen's University Press.

Russell, Peter H. 1993. *Constitutional Odyssey: Can Canadians Become a Sovereign People?* Toronto: University of Toronto Press.

Riker, William H. 1982. *Liberalism Against Populism: A Confrontation Between the Theory of Democracy and the Theory of Social Choice.* San Francisco: W.H. Freeman.

Sachdev, Itesh and Richard Y. Bourhis. 1991. "Power and Status Differentials in Minority and Majority Group Relations." *European Journal of Social Psychology* 21: 1–24.

Särlvik, Bo, Ivor Crewe, James Alt, and Anthony Fox. 1976. "Britain's Membership of the EEC: A Profile of Electoral Opinions in the Spring of 1974 – with a Postscript on the Referendum." *European Journal of Political Research* 4: 83–113.

Schmitt, Carl. 1926; 1985. *The Crisis of Parliamentary Democracy.* Cambridge, MA: MIT Press. (Originally published as *Die geistesgeschichtliche Lage des heutigen Parlamentarismus*, translated by Ellen Kennedy).

Schwartz, Bryan. 1987. *Fathoming Meech Lake.* Winnipeg: University of Manitoba, Legal Research Institute.

Sharman, C. and J. Stuart. 1981. "Patterns of State Voting in National Referendums." *Politics* 16: 261–70

Smith, Eric R.A.N. 1989. *The Unchanging American Voter.* Berkeley: University of California Press.

Smith, Gordon. 1976. "The Functional Properties of the Referendum." *European Journal of Political Research* 4: 1–23.

Sniderman, Paul M., Richard A. Brody, and Philip E. Tetlock. 1991. *Reasoning and Choice: Explorations in Social Psychology.* Cambridge: Cambridge University Press.

Stouffer, Samuel. 1955. *Communism, Conformity, and Civil Liberties.* New York: Doubleday.

Sullivan, John L., James Piereson, and George E. Marcus. 1982. *Political Tolerance and American Democracy*. Chicago: University of Chicago Press.

Tiersky, Ronald. 1994. *France in the New Europe: Changing Yet Steadfast*. Belmont, CA: Wadsworth.

Trudeau, Pierre Elliott. 1992. *A Mess that Deserves a Big No*. Toronto: Robert Davies (translated by George Tombs).

– 1993. *Memoirs*. Toronto: McClelland and Stewart.

Vaillancourt, François. 1988. *Langue et disparités de statut économique au Québec, 1970 et 1980*. Québec: Conseil de la langue française.

Valen, Henry. 1976. "National Conflict Structure and Foreign Politics: The Impact of the EEC Issue on Perceived Cleavages in Norwegian Politics." *European Journal of Political Research* 4: 47–82.

Vipond, Robert C. 1991. *Liberty and Community: Canadian Federalism and the Failure of the Constitution*. Albany, NY: State University of New York Press.

Weaver, R. Kent, ed. 1992a. *The Collapse of Canada*. Washington, DC: Brookings.

– 1992b. "Political Institutions and Canada's Constitutional Crisis," in Weaver (1992a), pp. 7–75.

Whitaker, Reg. 1993. "The Dog that Never Barked: Who Killed Asymmetrical Federalism?" in McRoberts and Monahan (1993), pp. 107–14.

Wilcox, Clyde, Lee Sigelman, and Elizabeth Cook. 1989. "Some Like It Hot: Individual Differences in Responses to Group Feeling Thermometers." *Public Opinion Quarterly* 53: 246–57.

Wohlfeld, Monica and Neil Nevitte. 1990. "Postindustrial Value Change and Support for Native Issues." *Canadian Ethnic Studies* 22: 56–88.

Wood, John R. 1978. "East Indians and Canada's New Immigration Policy." *Canadian Public Policy* 4: 547–67.

Wright, Vincent. 1978. "France," in Butler and Ranney (1978).

Zaller, John. 1992. *The Nature and Origins of Mass Opinion*. New York: Cambridge University Press.

– 1994. "Elite Leadership of Mass Opinion: New Evidence from the Gulf War," in Bennett and Paletz (1994).

Index